The Devil and Sherlock Holmes

Also by David Grann

The Lost City of Z

Tales of Murder, Madness, and Obsession

—◆—

David Grann

The

Devil

and

Sherlock

Holmes

DOUBLEDAY   New York London Toronto Sydney Auckland

DD

DOUBLEDAY

www.doubleday.com

DOUBLEDAY and the DD colophon are registered trademarks of
Random House, Inc.

The pieces in this work originally appeared in slightly different form
in *The Atlantic Monthly*, *The New Republic*, and *The New Yorker*.

Book design by Maria Carella

Library of Congress Cataloging-in-Publication Data
Grann, David.
The devil and Sherlock Holmes : tales of murder, madness, and
obsession / by David Grann.—1st ed.
p.   cm.
Summary: Collection of the journalist's articles previously published
in various periodicals.
I. Title.
PN4874.G672A25 2010
081—dc22   2009042230

ISBN 978-0-385-51792-8

PRINTED IN THE UNITED STATES OF AMERICA

1   3   5   7   9   10   8   6   4   2

First Edition

FOR ZACHARY AND ELLA

Contents

PART ONE
"Any truth is better than indefinite doubt."

Contents

Contents

The Devil and Sherlock Holmes

Introduction

Reporting, like detective work, is a process of elimination. It requires that you gather and probe innumerable versions of a story until, to borrow a phrase from Sherlock Holmes, "the one which remains must be the truth."

Although Holmes is the subject of just one of the stories in this collection, about the curious death of the world's foremost Holmes expert, all twelve contain elements of intrigue. Many of the protagonists are sleuths: a Polish detective trying to determine whether an author planted clues to a real murder in his postmodern novel; scientists who are stalking a sea monster; a con man who suddenly suspects that he may be the one who is being conned. Even the stories that seem cut from a different cloth deal in mystery of a kind: the secret world of sandhogs digging water tunnels under New York City, or the riddle of an aging but ageless baseball star.

Unlike the adventures of Sherlock Holmes, these tales are all true. The protagonists are mortal: as with Dr. Watson, they can observe, but they don't necessarily see. Pieces of the puzzle often remain elusive. Their stories do not always end happily. Some of the characters are driven to deception and murder. Others go mad.

Part of Holmes's appeal is that he restores order to a bewildering universe. But it is the messiness of life, and the human struggle to make sense of it, that drew me to the subjects in this collection. As Holmes once conceded to Dr. Watson, "If we could fly out of that window hand in hand, hover over this great city, gently remove the roofs, and peep in at the queer things which are going on, the strange coincidences, the plannings, the cross-purposes, the wonderful chains of events, working through generations, and leading to the most *outré* results, it would make all fiction with its conventionalities and foreseen conclusions most stale and unprofitable."

When I began investigating these stories, I knew almost nothing about them. Many originated from little more than a tantalizing hint: a tip from a friend, a reference buried in a news brief. While I tried to unearth the facts and reveal the hidden narrative, I occasionally found myself baffled by a clue or a missing piece of evidence. Yet in the end these stories seemed to provide at least glimpses of the human condition, and why some people devote themselves to good and others to evil. As Holmes put it, "Life is infinitely stranger than anything which the mind of man could invent."

Part One

"*Any truth is better than indefinite doubt.*"

Sherlock Holmes, in "The Yellow Face"

Mysterious Circumstances

Richard Lancelyn Green, the world's foremost expert on Sherlock Holmes, believed that he had finally solved the case of the missing papers. Over the past two decades, he had been looking for a trove of letters, diary entries, and manuscripts written by Sir Arthur Conan Doyle, the creator of Holmes. The archive was estimated to be worth nearly four million dollars, and was said by some to carry a deadly curse, like the one in the most famous Holmes story, "The Hound of the Baskervilles."

The papers had disappeared after Conan Doyle died, in 1930, and without them no one had been able to write a definitive biography—a task that Green was determined to complete. Many scholars feared that the archive had been discarded or destroyed; as the London *Times* noted, its whereabouts had become "a mystery as tantalizing as any to unfold at 221B Baker Street," the fictional den of Holmes and his fellow-sleuth, Dr. Watson.

Not long after Green launched his investigation, he discovered that one of Conan Doyle's five children, Adrian, had, with the other heirs' agreement, stashed the papers in a locked room of a château that he owned in Switzerland. Green then learned that Adrian had spirited some of the papers out of the château without his siblings' knowledge, hoping to sell them to collectors. In the midst of this scheme, he died of a heart attack—giving rise to the legend of the curse. After Adrian's death, the papers apparently vanished. And whenever Green tried to probe further he found himself caught in an impenetrable web of heirs—including a self-styled Russian princess—who seemed to have deceived and double-crossed one another in their efforts to control the archive.

For years, Green continued to sort through evidence and interview relatives, until one day the muddled trail led to London—and the doorstep of Jean Conan Doyle, the youngest of the author's children. Tall and elegant, with silver hair, she was an imposing woman in her late sixties. ("Something very strong and forceful seems to be at the back of that wee body," her father had written of Jean when she was five. "Her will is tremendous.") Whereas her brother Adrian had been kicked out of the British Navy for insubordination, and her elder brother Denis was a playboy who had sat out the Second World War in America, she had become an officer in the Royal Air Force, and was honored, in 1963, as a Dame Commander of the Order of the British Empire.

She invited Green into her flat, where a portrait of her father, with his walrus mustache, hung near the fireplace. Green had almost as great an interest in her father as she did, and she began sharing her memories, as well as family photographs. She asked him to return, and one day, Green later told friends, she showed him some boxes that had been stored in a London solicitor's office. Peering inside them, he said, he had glimpsed part of the archive. Dame Jean informed him that, because of an ongoing family dispute, she couldn't yet allow him to read the papers, but she said that she intended to bequeath nearly all of them to the British Library, so that scholars could finally examine them. After she died, in 1997, Green eagerly awaited their transfer—but nothing happened.

Then, in March, 2004, Green opened the London Sunday *Times* and was shocked to read that the lost archive had "turned up" at Christie's auction house and was to be sold, in May, for millions of dollars by three of Conan Doyle's distant relatives; instead of going to the British Library, the contents would be scattered among private collectors around the world, who might keep them inaccessible to scholars. Green was sure that a mistake had been made, and hurried to Christie's to inspect the materials. Upon his return, he told friends that he was certain that many of the papers were the same as those he had uncovered. What's more, he alleged, they had been stolen—and he had proof.

Over the next few days, he approached members of the Sherlock Holmes Society of London, one of hundreds of fan clubs devoted to the detective. (Green had once been chairman.) He alerted other so-called Sherlockians, including various American members of the Baker Street Irregulars, an invitation-only group that was founded in 1934 and named after the street urchins Holmes regularly employed to ferret out information. Green also contacted the more orthodox scholars of Conan Doyle, or Doyleans, about the sale. (Unlike Green, who moved between the two camps, many Doyleans distanced themselves from the Sherlockians, who often treated Holmes as if he were a real detective and refused to mention Conan Doyle by name.)

Green shared with these scholars what he knew about the archive's provenance, revealing what he considered the most damning piece of evidence: a copy of Dame Jean's will, which stated, "I give to The British Library all . . . my late father's original papers, personal manuscripts, diaries, engagement books, and writings." Determined to block the auction, the makeshift group of amateur sleuths presented its case to Members of Parliament. Toward the end of the month, as the group's campaign intensified and its objections appeared in the press, Green hinted to his sister, Priscilla West, that someone was threatening him. Later, he sent her a cryptic note containing three phone numbers and the message "PLEASE KEEP THESE NUMBERS SAFE." He also called a reporter from the London *Times,* warning that "something" might happen to him.

On the night of Friday, March 26th, he had dinner with a longtime friend, Lawrence Keen, who later said that Green had confided in him that "an American was trying to bring him down." After the two men left the restaurant, Green told Keen that they were being followed, and pointed to a car behind them.

The same evening, Priscilla West phoned her brother, and got his answering machine. She called repeatedly the next morning, but he still didn't pick up. Alarmed, she went to his house and knocked on the door;

there was no response. After several more attempts, she called the police, who came and broke open the entrance. Downstairs, the police found the body of Green lying on his bed, surrounded by Sherlock Holmes books and posters, with a cord wrapped around his neck. He had been garroted.

"I will lay out the whole case for you," John Gibson, one of Green's closest friends, told me when I phoned him shortly after learning of Green's death. Gibson had written several books with Green, including "My Evening with Sherlock Holmes," a 1981 collection of parodies and pastiches of the detective stories. With a slight stammer, Gibson said of his friend's death, "It's a complete and utter mystery."

Not long after, I travelled to Great Bookham, a village thirty miles south of London, where Gibson lives. He was waiting for me when I stepped off the train. He was tall and rail-thin, and everything about him—narrow shoulders, long face, unruly gray hair—seemed to slouch forward, as if he were supported by an invisible cane. "I have a file for you," he said, as we drove off in his car. "As you'll see, there are plenty of clues and not a lot of answers."

He sped through town, past a twelfth-century stone church and a row of cottages, until he stopped at a red brick house surrounded by hedges. "You don't mind dogs, I hope," he said. "I've two cocker spaniels. I only wanted one but the person I got them from said that they were inseparable, and so I took them both and they've been fighting ever since."

When he opened the front door, both spaniels leaped on us, then at each other. They trailed us into the living room, which was filled with piles of antique books, some reaching to the ceiling. Among the stacks was a near-complete set of *The Strand Magazine*, in which the Holmes stories were serialized at the turn of the twentieth century; a single issue, which used to sell for half a shilling, is now worth as much as five hundred dollars. "Altogether, there must be about sixty thousand books," Gibson said.

We sat on a couch and he opened his case file, carefully spreading the pages around him. "All right, dogs. Don't disturb us," he said. He looked up at me. "Now I'll tell you the whole story."

Gibson said that he had attended the coroner's inquest and taken careful notes, and as he spoke he picked up a magnifying glass beside him and peered through it at several crumpled pieces of paper. "I write everything on scraps," he said. The police, he said, had found only a few unusual things at the scene. There was the cord around Green's neck—a black shoelace. There was a wooden spoon near his hand, and several stuffed animals on the bed. And there was a partially empty bottle of gin.

The police found no sign of forced entry and assumed that Green had committed suicide. Yet there was no note, and Sir Colin Berry, the president of the British Academy of Forensic Sciences, testified to the coroner that, in his thirty-year career, he had seen only one suicide by garroting. "One," Gibson repeated. Self-garroting is extremely difficult to do, he explained; people who attempt it typically pass out before they are asphyxiated. Moreover, in this instance, the cord was not a thick rope but a shoelace, making the feat even more unlikely.

Gibson reached into his file and handed me a sheet of paper with numbers on it. "Take a look," he said. "My phone records." The records showed that he and Green had spoken repeatedly during the week before his death; if the police had bothered to obtain Green's records, Gibson went on, they would no doubt show that Green had called him only hours before he died. "I was probably the last person to speak to him," he said. The police, however, had never questioned him.

During one of their last conversations about the auction, Gibson recalled, Green had said he was afraid of something.

"You've got nothing to worry about," Gibson told him.

"No, I'm *worried*," Green said.

"What? You fear for your life?"

"I do."

Gibson said that, at the time, he didn't take the threat seriously but advised Green not to answer his door unless he was sure who it was.

Gibson glanced at his notes. There was something else, he said, something critical. On the eve of his death, he reminded me, Green had spoken to his friend Keen about an "American" who was trying to ruin him. The following day, Gibson said, he had called Green's house and heard a strange greeting on the answering machine. "Instead of getting Richard's voice in this sort of Oxford accent, which had been on the machine for a decade," Gibson recalled, "I got an American voice that said, 'Sorry, not available.' I said, 'What the hell is going on?' I thought I must've dialled the wrong number. So I dialled really slowly again. I got the American voice. I said, 'Christ almighty.' "

Gibson said that Green's sister had heard the same recorded greeting, which was one reason that she had rushed to his house. Reaching into his file, Gibson handed me several more documents. "Make sure you keep them in chronological order," he said. There was a copy of Jean Conan Doyle's will, several newspaper clippings on the auction, an obituary, and a Christie's catalogue.

That was pretty much all he had. The police, Gibson said, had not conducted any forensic tests or looked for fingerprints. And the coroner—who had once attended a meeting of the Sherlock Holmes Society to conduct a mock inquest of the murder from a Conan Doyle story in which a corpse is discovered in a locked room—found himself stymied. Gibson said that the coroner had noted that there was not enough evidence to ascertain what had happened, and, as a result, the official verdict regarding whether Green had killed himself or been murdered was left open.

Within hours of Green's death, Sherlockians seized upon the mystery, as if it were another case in the canon. In a Web chat room, one person, who called himself "inspector," wrote, "As for self-garroting, it is like trying to choke oneself to death by your own hands." Others invoked the "curse," as if only the supernatural could explain it. Gibson handed me an article from a British tabloid that was headlined " 'CURSE OF CONAN DOYLE' STRIKES HOLMES EXPERT."

"So what do you think?" Gibson asked.

"I'm not sure," I said.

Later, we went through the evidence again. I asked Gibson if he knew whose phone numbers were on the note that Green had sent to his sister.

Gibson shook his head. "It hadn't come up at the inquest," he said.

"What about the American voice on the answering machine?" I asked. "Do we know who that is?"

"Unfortunately, not a clue. To me that's the strangest and most telling piece of evidence. Did Richard put that on his machine? What was he trying to tell us? Did the murderer put it there? And, if so, why would he do that?"

I asked if Green had ever displayed any irrational behavior. "No, never," he said. "He was the most levelheaded man I ever met."

He noted that Priscilla West had testified at the inquest that her brother had no history of depression. Indeed, Green's physician wrote to the court to say that he had not treated Green for any illnesses for a decade.

"One last question," I said. "Was anything taken out of the apartment?"

"Not that we know of. Richard had a valuable collection of Sherlock Holmes and Conan Doyle books, and nothing appears to be missing."

As Gibson drove me back to the train station, he said, "Please, you must stay on the case. The police seem to have let poor Richard down." Then he advised, "As Sherlock Holmes says, 'When you have eliminated the impossible, whatever remains, however improbable, must be the truth.'"

Some facts about Richard Green are easy to discern—those which illuminate the circumstances of his life, rather than the circumstances of his death. He was born on July 10, 1953; he was the youngest of three children; his father was Roger Lancelyn Green, a best-selling children's author who popularized the Homeric myths and the legend of King Arthur, and who was a close friend of C. S. Lewis and J. R. R. Tolkien; and Richard was raised near Liverpool, on land that had been given to his ancestors in 1093, and where his family had resided ever since.

Nathaniel Hawthorne, who was the American consul in Liverpool in the eighteen-fifties, visited the house one summer, and he later described it in his "English Notebooks":

> We passed through a considerable extent of private road, and finally drove through a lawn, shaded with trees, and closely shaven, and reached the door of Poulton Hall. Part of the mansion is three or four hundred years old. . . . There is [a] curious, old, stately staircase, with a twisted balustrade, much like that of the old Province House in Boston. The drawing-room looks like a very handsome modern room, being beautifully painted, gilded, and paper-hung, with a white-marble fireplace, and rich furniture; so that the impression is that of newness, not of age.

By the time Richard was born, however, the Green family was, as one relative told me, "very English—a big house and no money." The curtains were thin, the carpets were threadbare, and a cold draft often swirled through the corridors.

Green, who had a pale, pudgy face, was blind in one eye from a childhood accident, and wore spectacles with tinted lenses. (One friend told me that, even as an adult, Green resembled "the god of Pan," with "cherubic-like features, a mouth which curved in a smile which was sympathetic, ironic, and always seeming to suggest that there was just one little thing that he was not telling you.") Intensely shy, with a ferociously logical mind and a precise memory, he would spend hours roaming through his father's enormous library, reading dusty first editions of children's books. And by the time he was eleven he had fallen under the spell of Sherlock Holmes.

Holmes was not the first great literary detective—that honor belongs to Edgar Allan Poe's Inspector Auguste Dupin—but Conan Doyle's hero was the most vivid exemplar of the fledgling genre, which Poe dubbed "tales of ratiocination." Holmes is a cold, calculating machine, a man who is, as one critic put it, "a tracker, a hunter-down, a combination of bloodhound, pointer, and bull-dog." The gaunt Holmes has no wife or children; as he explains, "I am a brain, Watson. The rest of me is a mere appendix." Rigidly scientific, he offers no spiritual bromides to his bereaved clients. Conan Doyle reveals virtually nothing about his character's interior life; he is defined solely by his method. In short, he is the perfect detective, the superhero of the Victorian era, out of which he blasted with his deerstalker hat and Inverness cape.

Richard read the stories straight through, then read them again. His rigorous mind had found its match in Holmes and his "science of deduction," which could wrest an astonishing solution from a single, seemingly unremarkable clue. "All life is a great chain, the nature of which is known whenever we are shown a single link of it," Holmes explains in the first story, "A Study in Scarlet," which establishes a narrative formula that subsequent tales nearly always follow. A new client arrives at Holmes's Baker Street consulting room. The detective stuns the visitor by deducing some element of his life by the mere observation of his demeanor or dress. (In "A Case of Identity," he divines that his client is a shortsighted typist by no more than the worn "plush upon her sleeves" and "the dint of a pince-nez at either side of her nose.") After the client presents the inexplicable facts of the case, "the game is afoot," as Holmes likes to say. Amassing clues that invariably boggle Watson, the stories' more earthbound narrator, Holmes ultimately arrives at a dazzling conclusion—one that, to him and him only, seems "elementary." In "The Red-Headed League," Holmes reveals to Watson how he surmised that an assistant pawnbroker was trying to rob a bank by tunnelling underneath it. "I thought of the assistant's fondness for photography, and his trick of vanishing into the cellar," Holmes says, explaining that he then went to see the assistant. "I hardly looked at his face. His knees were what I wished to see. You must yourself have remarked how worn, wrinkled and stained they were. They spoke of those hours of burrowing. The only remaining point was what they were burrowing for. I walked round the corner, saw the City and Suburban Bank abutted on our friend's premises, and felt that I had solved my problem."

Following the advice that Holmes often gave to Watson, Green practiced how to "see" what others merely "observed." He memorized Holmes's rules, as if they were catechism: "It is a capital mistake to theorize before one has data"; "never trust to general impressions, my boy, but concentrate yourself upon details"; "there is nothing more deceptive than an obvious fact."

Not long after Green turned thirteen, he carried an assortment of artifacts from local junk sales into the dimly lit attic of Poulton Hall. Part of the attic was known as the Martyr's Chamber and was believed to be haunted, having once "been tenanted by a lady, who was imprisoned there and persecuted to death for her religion," according to Hawthorne. Nevertheless, up in the attic, Green assembled his objects to create a strange tableau. There was a rack of pipes and a Persian slipper stuffed with tobacco. There was a stack of unpaid bills, which he stabbed into a mantel with a knife, so that they were pinned in place. There was a box of pills labelled "Poison"; empty ammunition cartridges and trompe-l'œil bullet marks painted on the walls ("I didn't think the attic would stand up to real bullets," he later remarked); a preserved snake; a brass microscope; and an invitation to the Gasfitters' Ball. Finally, outside the door of the room, Green hung a sign: "Baker Street."

Relying on the stray details sprinkled throughout Conan Doyle's stories, Green had pieced together a replica of Holmes and Watson's apartment—one so precise that it occasionally drew Holmes aficionados from other parts of England. One local reporter described the uncanny sensation of climbing the seventeen stairs—the same number specified in the stories—as a tape recording played in the background with the sounds of Victorian London: the rumble of cab wheels, the clopping of horses' hooves on cobblestones. By then, Green had become the youngest person ever inducted into the Sherlock Holmes Society of London, where members sometimes dressed in period costumes—in high-waisted trousers and top hats.

Though Holmes had first appeared in print nearly a century earlier, he had spawned a literary cult unlike that of any other fictional character. Almost from his inception, readers latched onto him with a zeal that bordered on "the mystical," as one Conan Doyle biographer has noted. When Holmes made his début, in the 1887 *Beeton's Christmas Annual*, a magazine of somewhat lurid fiction, he was considered not just a character but a paragon of the Victorian faith in all things scientific. He entered public consciousness around the same time as the development of the modern police force, at a moment when medicine was finally threatening to eradicate common diseases and industrialization offered to curtail mass poverty. He was proof that, indeed, the forces of reason could triumph over the forces of madness.

By the time Green was born, however, the worship of scientific thinking had been shattered by other faiths, by Nazism and Communism and Fascism, which had often harnessed the power of technology to demonic ends. Yet, paradoxically, the more illogical the world seemed, the more intense the cult surrounding Holmes became. This symbol of a new creed had become a figure of nostalgia—a person in "a fairy tale," as Green once put it. The character's popularity even surpassed the level of fame he had attained in Conan Doyle's day, as the stories were reenacted in some two hundred and sixty movies, twenty-five television shows, a musical, a ballet, a burlesque, and six hundred radio plays. Holmes inspired the creation of journals, memorabilia shops, walking tours, postage stamps, hotels, themed ocean cruises.

Edgar W. Smith, a former vice-president of General Motors and the first editor of the *Baker Street Journal*, which publishes scholarship on

Conan Doyle's stories, wrote in a 1946 essay, "What Is It That We Love in Sherlock Holmes?":

> We see him as the fine expression of our urge to trample evil and to set aright the wrongs with which the world is plagued. He is Galahad and Socrates, bringing high adventure to our dull existences and calm, judicial logic to our biased minds. He is the success of all our failures; the bold escape from our imprisonment.

What has made this literary escape unlike any other, though, is that so many people conceive of Holmes as a real person. T. S. Eliot once observed, "Perhaps the greatest of the Sherlock Holmes mysteries is this: that when we talk of him we invariably fall into the fancy of his existence." Green himself wrote, "Sherlock Holmes is a real character . . . who lives beyond life's span and who is constantly rejuvenated."

At the Sherlock Holmes Society of London, Green was introduced to "the great game," which Sherlockians had played for decades. It was built around the conceit that the stories' true author was not Conan Doyle but Watson, who had faithfully recounted Holmes's exploits. Once, at a gathering of the élite Baker Street Irregulars (which Green also joined), a guest referred to Conan Doyle as the creator of Holmes, prompting one outraged member to exclaim, "Holmes is a man! Holmes is a great man!" If Green had to invoke Conan Doyle's name, he was told, he should refer to him as merely Watson's "literary agent." The challenge of the game was that Conan Doyle had often written the four Holmes novels and fifty-six short stories—"the Sacred Writings," as Sherlockians called them—in haste, and they were plagued with inconsistencies that made them difficult to pass off as nonfiction. How, for instance, is it possible that in one story Watson is described as having been wounded in Afghanistan in the shoulder by a Jezail bullet, while in another story he complains that the wound was in his leg? The goal was thus to resolve these paradoxes, using the same airtight logic that Holmes exhibits. Similar textual inquiries had already given birth to a related field, known as Sherlockiana—mock scholarship in which fans tried to deduce everything from how many wives Watson has (one to five) to which university Holmes attended (surely Cambridge or

Oxford). As Green once conceded, quoting the founder of the Baker Street Irregulars, "Never had so much been written by so many for so few."

After Green graduated from Oxford, in 1975, he turned his attention to more serious scholarship. Of all the puzzles surrounding the Sacred Writings, the greatest one, Green realized, centered on the man whom the stories had long since eclipsed—Conan Doyle himself. Green set out to compile the first comprehensive bibliography, hunting down every piece of material that Conan Doyle wrote: pamphlets, plays, poems, obituaries, songs, unpublished manuscripts, letters to the editor. Carrying a plastic bag in place of a briefcase, Green unearthed documents that had long been hidden behind the veil of history.

In the midst of this research, Green discovered that John Gibson was working on a similar project, and they agreed to collaborate. The resulting tome, published in 1983 by Oxford University Press, with a foreword by Graham Greene, is seven hundred and twelve pages long and contains notations on nearly every scrap of writing that Conan Doyle ever produced, down to the kind of paper in which a manuscript was bound ("cloth," "light blue diaper-grain"). When the bibliography was done, Gibson continued in his job as a government property assessor. Green, however, had inherited a sizable sum of money from his family, who had sold part of their estate, and he used the bibliography as a launching pad for a biography of Conan Doyle.

Writing a biography is akin to the process of detection, and Green started to retrace every step of Conan Doyle's life, as if it were an elaborate crime scene. During the nineteen-eighties, Green followed Conan Doyle's movements from the moment he was born, on May 22, 1859, in a squalid part of Edinburgh. Green visited the neighborhood where Conan Doyle was raised, by a devout Christian mother and a dreamy father. (He drew one of the first illustrations of Sherlock Holmes—a sketch of the detective discovering a corpse, which accompanied a paperback edition of "A Study in Scarlet.") Green also amassed an intricate paper record that showed his subject's intellectual evolution. He discovered, for instance, that after Conan Doyle studied medicine, at the University of Edinburgh, and fell under the influence of rationalist thinkers like Oliver Wendell Holmes— who undoubtedly inspired the surname of Conan Doyle's detective—he renounced Catholicism, vowing, "Never will I accept anything which cannot be proved to me."

In the early eighties, Green published the first of a series of introductions to Penguin Classics editions of Conan Doyle's previously uncollected works—many of which he had helped to uncover. The essays, written in a clinical style, began garnering him attention outside the insular subculture of Sherlockians. One essay, running to more than a hundred pages, was a small biography of Conan Doyle unto itself; in another, Green cast further light on the short story "The Case of the Man Who Was Wanted," which had been found in a chest more than a decade after Conan Doyle's death and was claimed by his widow and sons to be the last unpublished Holmes story. Some experts had wondered if the story was a fake and even if Conan Doyle's two sons, in search of money to sustain their lavish life styles, had forged it. Yet Green conclusively showed that the story was neither by Conan Doyle nor a forgery; instead, it was written by an architect named Arthur Whitaker, who had sent it to Conan Doyle in hopes of collaborating. Scholars described Green's essays variously as "dazzling," "unparalleled," and—the ultimate compliment—"Holmesian."

Still, Green was determined to dig deeper for his now highly anticipated biography. As the mystery writer Iain Pears has observed, Conan Doyle's hero acts in nearly the same fashion as a Freudian analyst, piecing together his clients' hidden narratives, which he alone can perceive. In a 1987 review of Conan Doyle's autobiography, "Memories and Adventures," which was published in 1924, Green noted, "It is as if Conan Doyle—whose character suggested kindliness and trust—had a fear of intimacy. When he describes his life, he omits the inner man."

To reveal this "inner man," Green examined facts that Conan Doyle rarely, if ever, spoke of himself—most notably, that his father, an epileptic and an incorrigible alcoholic, was eventually confined to an insane asylum. Yet the more Green tried to plumb his subject, the more he became aware of the holes in his knowledge of Conan Doyle. He didn't want just to sketch Conan Doyle's story with a series of anecdotes; he wanted to know everything about him. In the draft of an early mystery story, "The Surgeon of Gaster Fall," Conan Doyle writes of a son who has locked his raving father inside a cage—but this incident was excised from the published version. Had Conan Doyle been the one to commit his father to the asylum?

Was Holmes's mania for logic a reaction to his father's genuine mania? And what did Conan Doyle mean when he wrote, in his deeply personal poem "The Inner Room," that he "has thoughts he dare not say"?

Green wanted to create an immaculate biography, one in which each fact led inexorably to the next. He wanted to be both Watson and Holmes to Conan Doyle, to be his narrator and his detective. Yet he knew the words of Holmes: "Data! Data! Data! I can't make bricks without clay." And the only way to succeed, he realized, was to track down the lost archive.

"Murder," Owen Dudley Edwards, a highly regarded Conan Doyle scholar, said. "I fear that is what the preponderance of the evidence points to."

I had called him in Scotland, after Gibson informed me that Edwards was pursuing an informal investigation into Green's death. Edwards had worked with Green to stop the auction, which took place, in spite of the uproar, almost two months after Green's body was found. Edwards said of his friend, "I think he knew too much about the archive."

A few days later, I flew to Edinburgh, where Edwards promised to share with me his findings. We had arranged to meet at a hotel on the edge of the old city. It was on a hill studded with medieval castles and covered in a thin mist, not far from where Conan Doyle had studied medicine under Dr. Joseph Bell, one of the models for Sherlock Holmes. (Once, during a class, Bell held up a glass vial. "This, gentlemen, contains a most potent drug," he said. "It is *extremely* bitter to the taste." To the class's astonishment, he touched the amber liquid, lifted a finger to his mouth, and licked it. He then declared, "Not one of you has developed his power of perception . . . while I placed my *index* finger in the awful brew, it was my *middle* finger—aye—which somehow found its way into my mouth.")

Edwards greeted me in the hotel lobby. He is a short, pear-shaped man with wild gray sideburns and an even wilder gray beard. A history professor at the University of Edinburgh, he wore a rumpled tweed coat over a V-neck sweater, and carried a knapsack on his shoulder.

We sat down at the restaurant, and I waited as he rummaged through the books in his bag. Edwards, who has written numerous books, including "The Quest for Sherlock Holmes," an acclaimed account of Conan

Doyle's early life, began pulling out copies of Green's edited collections. Green, he said, was "the world's greatest Conan Doyle expert. I have the authority to say it. Richard ultimately became the greatest of us all. That is a firm and definite statement of someone who knows."

As he spoke, he tended to pull his chin in toward his chest, so that his beard fanned out. He told me that he had met Green in 1981, while researching his book on Conan Doyle. At the time, Green was still working on his bibliography with Gibson; even so, he had shared all his data with Edwards. "That was the kind of scholar he was," he said.

To Edwards, Green's death was even more baffling than the crimes in a Holmes story. He picked up one of the Conan Doyle collections and read aloud from "A Case of Identity," in the cool, ironical voice of Holmes:

> Life is infinitely stranger than anything which the mind of man could invent. We would not dare to conceive the things which are really mere commonplaces of existence. If we could fly out of that window hand in hand, hover over this great city, gently remove the roofs, and peep in at the queer things which are going on, the strange coincidences, the plannings, the cross-purposes, the wonderful chains of events, working through generations, and leading to the most *outré* results, it would make all fiction with its conventionalities and foreseen conclusions most stale and unprofitable.

After Edwards closed the book, he explained that he had spoken frequently with Green about the Christie's sale. "Our lives have been dominated by the fact that Conan Doyle had five children, three of whom became his literary heirs," Edwards said. "The two boys were playboys. One of them, Denis, was, I gather, utterly selfish. The other one, Adrian, was a repulsive crook. And then there was an absolutely wonderful daughter."

Green, he said, had become so close to the daughter, Dame Jean, that he came to be known as the son she never had, even though in the past Conan Doyle's children had typically had fractious relationships with their father's biographers. In the early nineteen-forties, for example, Adrian and Denis had cooperated with Hesketh Pearson on "Conan Doyle: His Life and Art," but when the book came out and portrayed Conan Doyle as "the man in the street," a phrase Conan Doyle himself had used, Adrian rushed into print his own biography, "The True Conan Doyle," and Denis allegedly challenged Pearson to a duel. Dame Jean had subsequently taken it upon herself to guard her father's legacy against scholars who might present him in too stark a light. Yet she confided in Green, who had tried to balance his veneration of his subject with a commitment to the truth.

Edwards said that Dame Jean not only gave Green a glimpse of the treasured archive; she also asked for his help in transferring various papers to her solicitor's office. "Richard told me that he had physically moved them," Edwards said. "So his knowledge was really quite dangerous."

He claimed that Green was "the biggest figure standing in the way" of the Christie's auction, since he had seen some of the papers and could testify that Dame Jean had intended to donate them to the British Library. Soon after the sale was announced, Edwards said, he and Green had learned that Charles Foley, Sir Arthur's great-nephew, and two of Foley's cousins were behind the sale. But neither he nor Green could understand how these distant heirs had legally obtained control of the archive. "All we were clear about was that there was a scam and that, clearly, someone was robbing stuff that should go to the British Library," Edwards said. He added, "This was *not* a hypothesis—it was quite certain in our own minds."

Edwards also had little doubt that somebody had murdered his friend. He noted the circumstantial details—Green's mention of threats to his life, his reference to the American who was "trying to bring him down." Some observers, he said, had speculated that Green's death might have been the result of autoerotic asphyxiation, but he told me that there were no signs that Green was engaged in sexual activity at the time. He added that garroting is typically a brutal method of execution—"a method of murder which a skilled professional would use." What's more, Green had no known history of depression. Edwards pointed out that Green, on the day before he died, had made plans with another friend for a holiday in Italy the following week. Moreover, he said, if Green had killed himself, there surely would have been a suicide note; it was inconceivable that a man who kept notes on everything would not have left one.

"There are other things," Edwards continued. "He was garroted with a bootlace, yet he always wore slip-on shoes." And Edwards found meaning in seemingly insignificant details, the kind that Holmes might note—

particularly, the partially empty bottle of gin by his bed. To Edwards, this was a clear sign of the presence of a stranger, since Green, an oenophile, had drunk wine at supper that evening, and would never have followed wine with gin.

"Whoever did this is still at large," Edwards said. He put a hand on my shoulder. "Please be careful. I don't want to see you garroted, like poor Richard." Before we parted, he told me one more thing—he knew who the American was.

The American, who asked that I not use his name, lives in Washington, D.C. After I tracked him down, he agreed to meet me at Timberlake's pub near Dupont Circle. I found him sitting at the bar, sipping red wine. Though he was slumped over, he looked strikingly tall, with a hawkish nose and a thinning ring of gray hair. He appeared to be in his fifties and wore bluejeans and a button-down white shirt, with a fountain pen sticking out of the front pocket, like a professor.

After pausing a moment to deduce who I was, he stood and led me to a table in the back of the room, which was filled with smoke and sounds from a jukebox. We ordered dinner, and he proceeded to tell me what Edwards had loosely sketched out: that he was a longtime member of the Baker Street Irregulars and had, for many years, helped to represent Conan Doyle's literary estate in America. It is his main job, though, that has given him a slightly menacing air—at least in the minds of Green's friends. He works for the Pentagon in a high-ranking post that deals with clandestine operations. ("One of Donald Rumsfeld's pals," as Edwards described him.)

The American said that after he received a Ph.D. in international relations, in 1970, and became an expert on the Cold War and nuclear doctrine, he was drawn into the Sherlockian games and their pursuit of immaculate logic. "I've always kept the two worlds separate," he told me at one point. "I don't think a lot of people at the Pentagon would understand my fascination with a literary character." He met Green through the Sherlockian community, he said. As members of the Baker Street Irregulars, both had been given official titles from the Holmes stories. The American was "Rodger Prescott of evil memory," after the American counterfeiter in "The Adventure of the Three Garridebs." Green was known as "The

Three Gables," after the villa in "The Adventure of the Three Gables," which is ransacked by burglars in search of a scandalous biographical manuscript.

In the mid-nineteen-eighties, the American said, he and Green had collaborated on several projects. As the editor of a collection of essays on Conan Doyle, he had asked Green, whom he considered "the single most knowledgeable living person on Conan Doyle," to write the crucial chapter on the author's 1924 memoir. "My relationship with Richard was always productive," he recalled. Then, in the early nineteen-nineties, he said, they had had a falling out—a result, he added, of a startling rupture in Green's relationship with Dame Jean.

"Richard had gotten very close to Dame Jean, and was getting all sorts of family photographs, having represented himself as a great admirer of Conan Doyle," he said. "And then she saw something in print by him and suddenly realized that he had been representing his views very differently, and that was kind of the end of it."

The American insisted that he couldn't remember what Green had written that upset her. But Edwards, and others in Holmesian circles, said that the reason nobody could recall a specific offense was that Green's essays had never been particularly inflammatory. According to R. Dixon Smith, a friend of Green's and a longtime Conan Doyle book dealer, the American played on Dame Jean's sensitivities about her father's reputation and seized upon some of Green's candid words, which had never upset her before, then "twisted" them like "a screw." Edwards said of the American, "I think he did everything he possibly could to injure Richard. He drove a wedge between Richard and Dame Jean Conan Doyle." After Dame Jean cast Green out, Edwards and others noted, the American grew closer to her. Edwards told me that Green never got over the quarrel with Dame Jean. "He used to look at me like his heart was breaking," he said.

When I pressed the American further about the incident, he said simply, "Because I was Jean's representative, I got caught in the middle of it." Soon after, he said, "the good feeling and cooperation by Green toward me ended." At Sherlockian events, he said, they continued to see each other, but Green, always reserved, would often avoid him.

Smith had told me that in Green's final months he often seemed "preoccupied" with the American. "He kept wondering, What's he gonna do next?" During the last week of his life, Green told several friends that the American was working to defeat his crusade against the auction, and he expressed fear that his rival might try to damage his scholarly reputation. On March 24th, two days before he died, Green learned that the American was in London and was planning to attend a meeting that evening of the Sherlock Holmes Society. A friend said that Green called him and exclaimed, "I don't want to see him! I don't want to go." Green backed out of the meeting at the last minute. The friend said of the American, "I think he scared Richard."

As I mentioned some of the allegations of Green's friends, the American unfolded his napkin and touched the corners of his mouth. He explained that during his visit to London he had offered counsel to Charles Foley—whom he now served as a literary representative, as he had for Dame Jean—and discussed the sale of the archive at Christie's. But the American emphasized that he had not seen or spoken to Green for more than a year. On the night that Green died, he revealed with some embarrassment, he was walking through London with his wife on a group tour of Jack the Ripper's crime scenes. He said that he had learned only recently that Green had become fixated on him before his death, and he noted that some Sherlockians blurred the line between fandom and fanaticism. "It was because of the way people felt about the character," he said. Holmes was a sort of "vampire-like creature," he said; he consumed some people.

The waiter had served our meals, and the American paused to take a bite of steak and onion rings. He then explained that Conan Doyle had felt oppressed by his creation. Though the stories had made him the highest-paid author of his day, Conan Doyle wearied of constantly "inventing problems and building up chains of inductive reason," as he once said bitterly. In the stories, Holmes himself seems overwhelmed by his task, going days without sleep, and, after solving a case, often shooting up cocaine ("a seven-percent solution") in order to spell the subsequent drain and boredom. But, for Conan Doyle, there seemed to be no similar release, and he confided to one friend that "Holmes is becoming such a burden to me that it makes my life unendurable."

The very qualities that had made Holmes invincible—"his character admits of no light or shade," as Conan Doyle put it—eventually made him intolerable. Moreover, Conan Doyle feared that the detective stories eclipsed what he called his "more serious literary work." He had spent years researching several historical novels, which, he was convinced, would earn him a place in the pantheon of writers. In 1891, after he finished "The White Company," which was set in the Middle Ages and based on tales of "gallant, pious knights," he proclaimed, "Well, I'll never beat that." The book was popular in its day, but it was soon obscured by the shadow of Holmes, as were his other novels, with their comparatively stilted, lifeless prose. After Conan Doyle completed the domestic novel "A Duet with an Occasional Chorus," in 1899, Andrew Lang, a well-known critic who had helped publish one of his previous books, summed up the sentiment of most readers: "It may be a vulgar taste, but we decidedly prefer the adventures of Dr. Watson with Sherlock Holmes."

Conan Doyle was increasingly dismayed by the great paradox of his success: the more real Holmes became in the minds of readers, the less the author seemed to exist. Finally, Conan Doyle felt that he had no choice. As the American put it, "He had to kill Sherlock Holmes." Conan Doyle knew that the death had to be spectacular. "A man like that mustn't die of a pin-prick or influenza," he told a close friend. "His end must be violent and intensely dramatic." For months, he tried to imagine the perfect murder. Then, in December, 1893, six years after he gave birth to Holmes, Conan Doyle published "The Final Problem." The story breaks from the established formula: there is no puzzle to be solved, no dazzling display of deductive genius. And this time Holmes is the one pursued. He is being chased by Professor Moriarty, "the Napoleon of crime," who is "the organizer of half that is evil and of nearly all that is undetected in this great city" of London. Moriarty is the first true counterpart to Holmes, a mathematician who is, as Holmes informs Watson, "a genius, a philosopher, an abstract thinker." Tall and ascetic-looking, he even physically resembles Holmes.

What is most striking about the story, though, is that the two great logicians have descended into illogic—they are paranoid, and consumed only with each other. At one point, Moriarty tells Holmes, "This is not danger. . . . It is inevitable destruction." Finally, the two converge on a cliff overlooking Reichenbach Falls, in Switzerland. As Watson later deduces from evidence at the scene, Holmes and Moriarty struggled by the edge of the precipice before plunging to their deaths. After finishing the story, Conan Doyle wrote in his diary, with apparent delight, "Killed Holmes."

As the American spoke of these details, he seemed stunned that Conan Doyle had gone through with such an extraordinary act. Still, he pointed out, Conan Doyle could not escape from his creation. In England, men reportedly wore black armbands in mourning. In America, clubs devoted to the cause "Let's Keep Holmes Alive" were formed. Though Conan Doyle insisted that Holmes's death was "justifiable homicide," readers denounced him as a brute and demanded that he resuscitate their hero; after all, no one had actually seen him go over the cliff. As Green wrote in a 1983 essay, "If ever a murderer was to be haunted by the man he had killed and to be forced to atone for his act, it was the creator, turned destroyer, of Sherlock Holmes." In 1901, under increasing pressure, Conan Doyle released "The Hound of the Baskervilles," about an ancient family curse, but the events in the story antedated Holmes's death. Then, two years later, Conan Doyle succumbed completely, and began writing new Holmes stories, explaining, less than convincingly, in "The Adventure of the Empty House," that Holmes had never plunged to his death but merely arranged it to look that way so he could escape from Moriarty's gang.

The American told me that even after Conan Doyle died Holmes continued to loom over his descendants. "Dame Jean thought that Sherlock Holmes was the family curse," he said. Like her father, he said, she had tried to draw attention to his other works but was constantly forced to tend to the detective's thousands of fans—many of whom sent letters addressed to Holmes, requesting his help in solving real crimes. In a 1935 essay entitled "Sherlock Holmes the God," G. K. Chesterton observed of Sherlockians, "It is getting beyond a joke. The hobby is hardening into a delusion."

Several actors who played Holmes were also haunted by him, the American said. In a 1956 autobiography, "In and Out of Character," Basil Rathbone, who played the detective in more than a dozen films, complained that because of his portrayal of Holmes his renown for other parts, including Oscar-nominated ones, was "sinking into oblivion." The public conflated him with his most famous character, which the studio and audience demanded he play again and again, until by the end he, too, lamented that he "could not kill Mr. Holmes." Another actor, Jeremy Brett, had a breakdown while playing the detective and was eventually admitted to a psychiatric ward, where he was said to have cried out, "Damn you, Holmes!"

At one point, the American showed me a thick book, which he had brought to the pub. It was part of a multivolume history that he was writing on the Baker Street Irregulars and Sherlockian scholarship. He had started the project in 1988. "I thought if I searched pretty assiduously I'd find enough material to do a single hundred-and-fifty-page volume," he said. "I've now done five volumes of more than fifteen hundred pages, and I've only gotten up to 1950." He added, "It's been a slippery slope into madness and obsession."

As he spoke of his fascination with Holmes, he recalled one of the last times he had seen Green, three years earlier, at a symposium at the University of Minnesota. Green had given a lecture on "The Hound of the Baskervilles." "It was a multimedia presentation about the origins of the novel, and it was just dazzling," the American said. He repeated the word "dazzling" several times ("It's the only word to describe it"), and as he sat up in his chair and his eyes brightened I realized that I was talking not to Green's Moriarty but to his soul mate. Then, catching himself, he reminded me that he had a full-time job and a family. "The danger is if you have nothing else in your life but Sherlock Holmes," he said.

In 1988, Richard Green made a pilgrimage to Reichenbach Falls to see where his childhood hero had nearly met his demise. Conan Doyle himself had visited the site in 1893, and Green wanted to repeat the author's journey. Standing at the edge of the falls, Green stared at the chasm below, where, as Watson noted after he called out, "My only answer was my own voice reverberating in a rolling echo from the cliffs around me."

By the mid-nineteen-nineties, Green knew that he would not have access to the Conan Doyle archive until Dame Jean died—presuming that she bequeathed the papers to the British Library. In the meantime, he continued researching his biography, which, he concluded, would require no less than three volumes: the first would cover Conan Doyle's childhood; the second, the arc of his literary career; the third, his descent into a kind of madness.

Relying on public documents, Green outlined this last stage, which began after Conan Doyle started using his powers of observation to solve real-world mysteries. In 1906, Conan Doyle took up the case of George Edalji, a half-Parsi Indian living near Birmingham, who faced seven years of hard labor for allegedly mutilating his neighbors' cattle during the night. Conan Doyle suspected that Edalji had been tagged as a criminal merely because of his ethnicity, and he assumed the role of detective. Upon meeting his client, he noticed that the young man was holding a newspaper inches from his face.

"Aren't you astigmatic?" Conan Doyle asked.

"Yes," Edalji admitted.

Conan Doyle called in an ophthalmologist, who confirmed that Edalji's malady was so severe that he was unable to see properly even with glasses. Conan Doyle then trekked to the scene of the crime, traversing a maze of railroad tracks and hedges. "I, a strong and active man, in broad daylight, found it a hard matter to pass," he later wrote. Indeed, he contended, it would have been impossible for a nearly blind person to make the journey and then slaughter an animal in the pitch black of night. A tribunal soon concurred, and the New York *Times* declared, "CONAN DOYLE SOLVES A NEW DREYFUS CASE."

Conan Doyle even helped in solving the case of a serial killer, after he spotted newspaper accounts in which two women had died in the same bizarre manner: the victims were recent brides, who had "accidentally" drowned in their bathtubs. Conan Doyle informed Scotland Yard of his theory, telling the inspector, in an echo of Holmes, "No time is to be lost"; the killer, dubbed "the Bluebeard of the Bath," was subsequently caught and convicted in a sensational trial.

Around 1914, Conan Doyle tried to apply his rational powers to the most important matter of his day—the logic of launching the First World War. He was convinced that the war was not simply about entangling alliances and a dead archduke; it was a sensible way to restore the codes of honor and moral purpose that he had celebrated in his historical novels. That year, he unleashed a spate of propaganda, declaring, "Fear not, for our sword will not be broken, nor shall it ever drop from our hands." In the Holmes story "His Last Bow," which is set in 1914, the detective tells Watson that after the "storm has cleared" a "cleaner, better, stronger land will lie in the sunshine."

Though Conan Doyle was too old to fight, many of his relatives heeded his call "to arms," including his son Kingsley. The glorious battle Conan Doyle envisioned, however, became a cataclysm. The products of scientific reason—machines and engineering and electronics—were transformed into agents of destruction. Conan Doyle visited the battlefield by the Somme, where tens of thousands of British soldiers died, and where he later reported seeing a soldier "drenched crimson from head to foot, with two great glazed eyes looking upwards through a mask of blood." In 1918, a chastened Conan Doyle realized that the conflict was "evidently preventable." By that time, ten million people had perished, including Kingsley, who died from battle wounds and influenza.

After the war, Conan Doyle wrote a handful of Holmes stories, yet the field of detective fiction was changing. The all-knowing detective gradually gave way to the hardboiled dick, who acted more on instinct and gin than on reason. In "The Simple Art of Murder," Raymond Chandler, while admiring Conan Doyle, dismissed the tradition of the "grim logician" and his "exhausting concatenation of insignificant clues," which now seemed like an absurdity.

Meanwhile, in his own life, Conan Doyle seemed to abandon reason altogether. As one of Green's colleagues in the Baker Street Irregulars, Daniel Stashower, relates in a 1999 book, "Teller of Tales: The Life of Arthur Conan Doyle," the creator of Holmes began to believe in ghosts. He attended séances and received messages from the dead through "the power of automatic writing," a method akin to that of the Ouija board. During one session, Conan Doyle, who had once considered the belief in life after death as "a delusion," claimed that his dead younger brother said, "It is so grand to be in touch like this."

One day, Conan Doyle heard a voice in the séance room. As he later described the scene in a letter to a friend:

> I said, "Is that you, boy?"
> He said in a very intense whisper and a tone all his own, "Father!" and then after a pause, "Forgive me!"
> I said, "There was never anything to forgive. You were the best son a man ever had." A strong hand descended on my head which was slowly pressed forward, and I felt a kiss just above my brow.

"Are you happy?" I cried.

There was a pause and then very gently, "I am so happy."

The creator of Sherlock Holmes had become the St. Paul of psychics. Conan Doyle claimed to see not only dead family members but fairies as well. He championed photographs taken in 1917 by two girls that purported to show such phantasmal creatures, even though, as one of the girls later admitted, "I could see the hatpins holding up the figures. I've always marvelled that anybody ever took it seriously." Conan Doyle, however, was convinced, and even published a book called "The Coming of Fairies." He opened the Psychic Bookshop, in London, and told friends that he had received messages that the world was coming to an end. "I suppose I am Sherlock Holmes, if anybody is, and I say that the case for spiritualism is absolutely proved," he declared. In 1918, a headline in the *Sunday Express* asked, "IS CONAN DOYLE MAD?"

For the first time, Green struggled to rationalize his subject's life. In one essay, he wrote, "It is hard to understand how a man who had stood for sound common sense and healthy attitudes could sit in darkened rooms watching for ectoplasm." Green reacted at times as if his hero had betrayed him. In one passage, he wrote angrily, "Conan Doyle was deluding himself."

"One thing Richard couldn't stand was Conan Doyle's being involved with spiritualism," Edwards said. "He thought it crazy." His friend Dixon Smith told me, "It was all Conan Doyle. He pursued him with all his mind and body." Green's house became filled with more and more objects from Conan Doyle's life: long-forgotten propaganda leaflets and speeches on spiritualism; an arcane study of the Boer War; previously unknown essays on photography. "I remember once, I discovered a copy of 'A Duet with an Occasional Chorus,' " Gibson said. "It had a great red cover on it. I showed it to Richard and he got really excited. He said, 'God, this must have been the salesman's copy.' " When Green found one of the few surviving copies of the 1887 *Beeton's Christmas Annual,* with "A Study in Scarlet," which was worth as much as a hundred and thirty thousand dollars, he sent a card to a friend with two words on it: "At last!"

Green also wanted to hold things that Conan Doyle himself had held: letter openers and pens and spectacles. "He would collect all day and all night, and I mean night," his brother, Scirard, told me. Green covered many of his walls with Conan Doyle's family photographs. He even had a piece of wallpaper from one of Conan Doyle's homes. " 'Obsession' is by no means too strong a word to describe what Richard had," his friend Nicholas Utechin, the editor of *The Sherlock Holmes Journal,* said.

"It's self-perpetuating and I don't know how to stop," Green confessed to an antiques magazine in 1999.

By 2000, his house resembled the attic at Poulton Hall, only now he seemed to be living in a museum dedicated to Conan Doyle rather than to Holmes. "I have around forty thousand books," Green told the magazine. "Then, of course, there are the photographs, the pictures, the papers, and all the other ephemera. I know it sounds a lot, but, you see, the more you have, the more you feel you need."

And what he longed for most remained out of reach: the archive. After Dame Jean died, in 1997, and no papers materialized at the British Library, he became increasingly frustrated. Where he had once judiciously built his conjectures about Conan Doyle's life, he now seemed reckless. In 2002, to the shock of Doyleans around the world, Green wrote a paper claiming that he had proof that Conan Doyle had had a tryst with Jean Leckie, his delicately beautiful second wife, before his first wife, Louisa, died of tuberculosis, in 1906. Though it was well known that Conan Doyle had formed a bond with Leckie during his wife's long illness, he had always insisted, "I fight the devil and I win." And, to maintain an air of Victorian rectitude, he often brought along chaperones when he and Leckie were together. Green based his allegation on the 1901 census, which reported that on the day the survey was taken Conan Doyle was staying at the Ashdown Forest Hotel, in East Sussex. So, too, was Leckie. "Conan Doyle could not have chosen a worse weekend on which to have a private tryst," Green wrote. Yet Green failed to note one crucial fact also contained in the census report—Conan Doyle's mother was staying in the hotel with him, apparently as a chaperone. Later, Green was forced to recant, in a letter to *The Sherlock Holmes Journal,* saying, "I was guilty of the capital mistake of theorising without data."

Still, he continued to lash out at Conan Doyle, as Conan Doyle once had at Sherlock Holmes. Edwards recalled that, in one conversation, Green decried Conan Doyle as "unoriginal" and "a plagiarist." He confessed to another friend, "I've wasted my whole life on a second-rate writer."

"I think he was frustrated because the family wasn't coming to any agreement," Smith said. "The archive wasn't made available, and he got angry not at the heirs but at Conan Doyle."

In March of 2004, when Green hurried to Christie's after the auction of the papers was announced, he discovered that the archive was as rich and as abundant as he'd imagined. Among the thousands of items were fragments of the first tale that Conan Doyle wrote, at the age of six; illustrated logs from when Conan Doyle was a surgeon on a Scottish whaling ship, in the eighteen-eighties; letters from Conan Doyle's father (whose drawings in the asylum resembled the fairies that his son later seized upon as real); a brown envelope with a cross and the name of his dead son inscribed upon it; the manuscript of Conan Doyle's first novel, which was never published; a missive from Conan Doyle to his brother, which seemed to confirm that Green's hunch had been right, and that Conan Doyle had in fact begun an affair with Leckie. Jane Flower, who helped to organize the papers for Christie's, told reporters, "The whereabouts of this material was previously unknown, and it is for this reason that no modern-day biography of the author exists."

Meanwhile, back at his home, Green tried to piece together why the archive was about to slip into private hands once more. According to Green's family, he typed notes in his computer, reexamining the trail of evidence, which he thought proved that the papers belonged to the British Library. He worked late into the night, frequently going without sleep. None of it, however, seemed to add up. At one point, he typed in bold letters, "STICK TO THE FACTS." After another sleepless night, he told his sister that the world seemed "Kafkaesque."

Several hours before Green died, he called his friend Utechin at home. Green had asked him to find a tape of an old BBC radio interview, which, Green recalled, quoted one of Conan Doyle's heirs saying that the archive should be given to the British Library. Utechin said that he had found the tape, but there was no such statement on the recording. Green became apoplectic, and accused his friend of conspiring against him, as if he were another Moriarty. Finally, Utechin said, "Richard, you've lost it!"

One afternoon while I was at my hotel in London, the phone rang. "I need to see you again," John Gibson said. "I'll take the next train in." Before he hung up, he added, "I have a theory."

I met him in my hotel room. He was carrying several scraps of paper, on which he had taken notes. He sat down by the window, his slender figure silhouetted in the fading light, and announced, "I think it was suicide."

He had sifted through the data, including details that I had shared with him from my own investigation. There was mounting evidence, he said, that his rationalist friend was betraying signs of irrationality in the last week of his life. There was the fact that there was no evidence of forced entry at Green's home. And there was the fact, perhaps most critically, of the wooden spoon by Green's hand.

"He had to have used it to tighten the cord" like a tourniquet, Gibson said. "If someone else had garroted him, why would he need the spoon? The killer could simply use his hands." He continued, "I think things in his life had not turned out the way he wanted. This Christie's sale simply brought everything to a head."

He glanced nervously at his notes, which he strained to see without his magnifying glass. "That's not all," he said. "I think he wanted it to look like murder."

He waited to assess my reaction, then went on, "That's why he didn't leave a note. That's why he took his voice off the answering machine. That's why he sent that message to his sister with the three phone numbers on it. That's why he spoke of the American who was after him. He must have been planning it for days, laying the foundation, giving us false clues."

I knew that, in detective fiction, the reverse scenario generally turns out to be true—a suicide is found to have been murder. As Holmes declares in "The Resident Patient," "This is no suicide. . . . It is a very deeply planned and cold-blooded murder." There is, however, one notable exception. It is, eerily enough, in one of the last Holmes mysteries, "The Problem of Thor Bridge," a story that Green once cited in an essay. A wife is found lying dead on a bridge, shot in the head at point-blank range. All the evidence points to one suspect: the governess, with whom the husband had been flirting. Yet Holmes shows that the wife had not been killed by anyone; rather, enraged by jealousy over her husband's illicit overtures to the governess, she had killed herself and framed the woman whom she blamed for her misery. Of all Conan Doyle's stories, it digs deepest into the human psyche and its criminal motivations. As the governess tells Holmes, "When I reached the bridge she was waiting for me. Never did I realize till that moment how this poor creature hated me. She was like a mad woman—indeed, I think she was a mad woman, subtly mad with the deep power of deception which insane people may have."

I wondered if Green could have been so enraged with the loss of the archive that he might have done something similar, and even tried to frame the American, whom he blamed for ruining his relationship with Dame Jean and for the sale of the archive. I wondered if he could have tried, in one last desperate attempt, to create order out of the chaos around him. I wondered if this theory, however improbable, was in fact the least "impossible."

I shared with Gibson some other clues I had uncovered: the call that Green had made to the reporter days before his death, saying that "something" might happen to him; a reference in a Holmes story to one of Moriarty's main henchmen as a "garroter by trade"; and a statement to the coroner by Green's sister, who said that the note with the three phone numbers had reminded her of "the beginning of a thriller."

After a while, Gibson looked up at me, his face ghastly white. "Don't you see?" he exclaimed. "He staged the whole thing. He created the perfect mystery."

Before I went back to America, I went to see Green's sister, Priscilla West. She lives near Oxford, in a three-story, eighteenth-century brick house with a walled garden. She had long, wavy brown hair, an attractive round face, and small oval glasses. She invited me inside with a reticent voice, saying, "Are you a drawing-room person or a kitchen person?"

I shrugged uncertainly, and she led me into the drawing room, which had antique furniture and her father's children's books on the shelves. As we sat down, I explained to her that I had been struggling to write her brother's story. The American had told me, "There is no such thing as a definitive biography," and Green seemed particularly resistant to explication.

"Richard compartmentalized his life," his sister said. "There are a lot of things we've only found out since he died." At the inquest, his family, and most of his friends, had been startled when Lawrence Keen, who was nearly half Green's age, announced that he had been Richard's lover years ago. "No one in the family knew" that Green was gay, his sister explained. "It wasn't something he ever talked about."

As West recalled other surprising fragments of Green's biography (travels to Tibet, a brief attempt at writing a novel), I tried to picture him as best I could with his glasses, his plastic bag in hand, and his wry smile. West had seen her brother's body lying on the bed, and several times she told me, "I just wish . . ." before falling silent. She handed me copies of the eulogies that Green's friends had delivered at the memorial service, which was held on May 22nd, the day Conan Doyle was born. On the back of the program from the service were several quotes from Sherlock Holmes stories:

> I caught a glimpse of a great heart as well as of a great brain.
> He appears to have a passion for definite and exact knowledge.
> His career has been an extraordinary one.

After a while, she got up to pour herself a cup of tea. When she sat down again, she said that her brother had willed his collection to a library in Portsmouth, near where Conan Doyle wrote the first two Holmes stories, so that other scholars could have access to it. The collection was so large that it had taken two weeks, and required twelve truckloads, to cart it all away. It was estimated to be worth several million dollars—far more, in all likelihood, than the treasured archive. "He really did not like the idea of scholarship being put second to greed," West said. "He lived and died by this."

She then told me something about the archive which had only recently come to light, and which her brother had never learned: Dame Jean Conan Doyle, while dying of cancer, had made a last-minute deed of apportionment, splitting the archive between herself and the three heirs of her former sister-in-law, Anna Conan Doyle. What was being auctioned off, therefore, belonged to the three heirs, and not to Dame Jean, and, though some people still questioned the morality of the sale, the British Library had reached the conclusion that it was legal.

Green also could not know that after the auction, on May 19th, the most important papers ended up at the British Library. Dame Jean had not allotted those documents to the other heirs, and had willed many of them to the library; at the same time, the library had purchased much of the remaining material at the auction. As Gibson later told me, "The tragedy is that Richard could have still written his biography. He would have had everything he needed."

Two questions, however, remained unclear. How, I asked West, did an American voice wind up on her brother's answering machine?

"I'm afraid it's not that complicated," she said. The machine, she continued, was made in the United States and had a built-in recorded message; when her brother took off his personal message, a prerecorded American voice appeared.

I then asked about the phone numbers in the note. She shook her head in dismay. They added up to nothing, she said. They were merely those of two reporters her brother had spoken to, and the number of someone at Christie's.

Finally, I asked what she thought had happened to her brother. At one point, Scirard Lancelyn Green had told the London *Observer* that he thought murder was "entirely possible"; and, for all my attempts to build a case that transcended doubt, there were still questions. Hadn't the police told the coroner that an intruder could have locked Green's apartment door while slipping out, thus giving the illusion that his victim had died alone? Wasn't it possible that Green had known the murderer and simply let him in? And how could someone, even in a fit of madness, garrote himself with merely a shoelace and the help of a spoon?

His sister glanced away, as if trying one last time to arrange all the pieces. Then she said, "I don't think we'll ever know for sure what really happened. Unlike in detective stories, we have to live without answers."

— *December, 2004*

Trial by Fire

DID TEXAS EXECUTE
AN INNOCENT MAN?

The fire moved quickly through the house, a one-story wood-frame structure in a working-class neighborhood of Corsicana, in northeast Texas. Flames spread along the walls, bursting through doorways, blistering paint and tiles and furniture. Smoke pressed against the ceiling, then banked downward, seeping into each room and through crevices in the windows, staining the morning sky.

Buffie Barbee, who was eleven years old and lived two houses down, was playing in her back yard when she smelled the smoke. She ran inside and told her mother, Diane, and they hurried up the street; that's when they saw the smoldering house and Cameron Todd Willingham standing on the front porch, wearing only a pair of jeans, his chest blackened with soot, his hair and eyelids singed. He was screaming, "My babies are burning up!" His children—Karmon and Kameron, who were one-year-old twin girls, and two-year-old Amber—were trapped inside.

Willingham told the Barbees to call the Fire Department, and while Diane raced down the street to get help he found a stick and broke the children's bedroom window. Fire lashed through the hole. He broke another window; flames burst through it, too, and he retreated into the yard, kneeling in front of the house. A neighbor later told police that Willingham intermittently cried, "My babies!" then fell silent, as if he had "blocked the fire out of his mind."

Diane Barbee, returning to the scene, could feel intense heat radiating off the house. Moments later, the five windows of the children's room exploded and flames "blew out," as Barbee put it. Within minutes, the first firemen had arrived, and Willingham approached them, shouting that his children were in their bedroom, where the flames were thickest. A fireman sent word over his radio for rescue teams to "step on it."

More men showed up, uncoiling hoses and aiming water at the blaze. One fireman, who had an air tank strapped to his back and a mask covering his face, slipped through a window but was hit by water from a hose and had to retreat. He then charged through the front door, into a swirl of smoke and fire. Heading down the main corridor, he reached the kitchen, where he saw a refrigerator blocking the back door.

Todd Willingham, looking on, appeared to grow more hysterical, and a police chaplain named George Monaghan led him to the back of a fire truck and tried to calm him down. Willingham explained that his wife, Stacy, had gone out earlier that morning, and that he had been jolted from sleep by Amber screaming, "Daddy! Daddy!"

"My little girl was trying to wake me up and tell me about the fire," he said, adding, "I couldn't get my babies out."

While he was talking, a fireman emerged from the house, cradling Amber. As she was given C.P.R., Willingham, who was twenty-three years old and powerfully built, ran to see her, then suddenly headed toward the babies' room. Monaghan and another man restrained him. "We had to wrestle with him and then handcuff him, for his and our protection," Monaghan later told police. "I received a black eye." One of the first firemen at the scene told investigators that, at an earlier point, he had also held Willingham back. "Based on what I saw on how the fire was burning, it would have been crazy for anyone to try and go into the house," he said.

Willingham was taken to a hospital, where he was told that Amber—who had actually been found in the master bedroom—had died of smoke inhalation. Kameron and Karmon had been lying on the floor of the children's bedroom, their bodies severely burned. According to the medical examiner, they, too, died from smoke inhalation.

News of the tragedy, which took place on December 23, 1991, spread through Corsicana. A small city fifty-five miles northeast of Waco, it had once been the center of Texas's first oil boom, but many of the wells had since dried up, and more than a quarter of the city's twenty thousand inhabitants had fallen into poverty. Several stores along the main street were shuttered, giving the place the feel of an abandoned outpost.

Willingham and his wife, who was twenty-two years old, had virtually no money. Stacy worked in her brother's bar, called Some Other Place, and Willingham, an unemployed auto mechanic, had been caring for the kids. The community took up a collection to help the Willinghams pay for funeral arrangements.

Fire investigators, meanwhile, tried to determine the cause of the blaze. (Willingham gave authorities permission to search the house: "I know we might not ever know all the answers, but I'd just like to know why my babies were taken from me.") Douglas Fogg, who was then the assistant fire chief in Corsicana, conducted the initial inspection. He was tall, with a crew cut, and his voice was raspy from years of inhaling smoke from fires and cigarettes. He had grown up in Corsicana and, after graduating from high school, in 1963, he had joined the Navy, serving as a medic in Vietnam, where he was wounded on four occasions. He was awarded a Purple Heart each time. After he returned from Vietnam, he became a firefighter, and by the time of the Willingham blaze he had been battling fire—or what he calls "the beast"—for more than twenty years, and had become a certified arson investigator. "You learn that fire talks to you," he told me.

He was soon joined on the case by one of the state's leading arson sleuths, a deputy fire marshal named Manuel Vasquez, who has since died. Short, with a paunch, Vasquez had investigated more than twelve hundred fires. Arson investigators have always been considered a special breed of detective. In the 1991 movie "Backdraft," a heroic arson investigator says of fire, "It breathes, it eats, and it hates. The only way to beat it is to think like it. To know that this flame will spread this way across the door and up across the ceiling." Vasquez, who had previously worked in Army intelligence, had several maxims of his own. One was "Fire does not destroy evidence—it creates it." Another was "The fire tells the story. I am just the interpreter." He cultivated a Sherlock Holmes–like aura of invincibility. Once, he was asked under oath whether he had ever been mistaken in a case. "If I have, sir, I don't know," he responded. "It's never been pointed out."

Vasquez and Fogg visited the Willinghams' house four days after the blaze. Following protocol, they moved from the least burned areas toward the most damaged ones. "It is a systematic method," Vasquez later testified, adding, "I'm just collecting information. . . . I have not made any determination. I don't have any preconceived idea."

The men slowly toured the perimeter of the house, taking notes and photographs, like archeologists mapping out a ruin. Upon opening the back door, Vasquez observed that there was just enough space to squeeze past the refrigerator blocking the exit. The air smelled of burned rubber and melted wires; a damp ash covered the ground, sticking to their boots. In the kitchen, Vasquez and Fogg discerned only smoke and heat damage—a sign that the fire had not originated there—and so they pushed deeper into the nine-hundred-and-seventy-five-square-foot building. A central corridor led past a utility room and the master bedroom, then past a small living room, on the left, and the children's bedroom, on the right, ending at the front door, which opened onto the porch. Vasquez tried to take in everything, a process that he compared to entering one's mother-in-law's house for the first time: "I have the same curiosity."

In the utility room, he noticed on the wall pictures of skulls and what he later described as an image of "the Grim Reaper." Then he turned into the master bedroom, where Amber's body had been found. Most of the damage there was also from smoke and heat, suggesting that the fire had started farther down the hallway, and he headed that way, stepping over debris and ducking under insulation and wiring that hung down from the exposed ceiling.

As he and Fogg removed some of the clutter, they noticed deep charring along the base of the walls. Because gases become buoyant when heated, flames ordinarily burn upward. But Vasquez and Fogg observed that the fire had burned extremely low down, and that there were peculiar char patterns on the floor, shaped like puddles.

Vasquez's mood darkened. He followed the "burn trailer"—the path etched by the fire—which led from the hallway into the children's bed-room. Sunlight filtering through the broken windows illuminated more of the irregularly shaped char patterns. A flammable or combustible liquid doused on a floor will cause a fire to concentrate in these kinds of pockets, which is why investigators refer to them as "pour patterns" or "puddle con-figurations."

The fire had burned through layers of carpeting and tile and plywood flooring. Moreover, the metal springs under the children's beds had turned white—a sign that intense heat had radiated beneath them. Seeing that the floor had some of the deepest burns, Vasquez deduced that it had been hotter than the ceiling, which, given that heat rises, was, in his words, "not normal."

Fogg examined a piece of glass from one of the broken windows. It contained a spiderweb-like pattern—what fire investigators call "crazed glass." Forensic textbooks had long described the effect as a key indicator that a fire had burned "fast and hot," meaning that it had been fuelled by a liquid accelerant, causing the glass to fracture.

The men looked again at what appeared to be a distinct burn trailer through the house: it went from the children's bedroom into the corridor, then turned sharply to the right and proceeded out the front door. To the investigators' surprise, even the wood under the door's aluminum thresh-old was charred. On the concrete floor of the porch, just outside the front door, Vasquez and Fogg noticed another unusual thing: brown stains, which, they reported, were consistent with the presence of an accelerant.

The men scanned the walls for soot marks that resembled a "V." When an object catches on fire, it creates such a pattern, as heat and smoke radi-ate outward; the bottom of the "V" can therefore point to where a fire began. In the Willingham house, there was a distinct "V" in the main cor-ridor. Examining it and other burn patterns, Vasquez identified three places where fire had originated: in the hallway, in the children's bedroom, and at the front door. Vasquez later testified that multiple origins pointed to one conclusion: the fire was "intentionally set by human hands."

By now, both investigators had a clear vision of what had happened. Someone had poured liquid accelerant throughout the children's room, even under their beds, then poured some more along the adjoining hallway and out the front door, creating a "fire barrier" that prevented anyone from escaping; similarly, a prosecutor later suggested, the refrigerator in the kitchen had been moved to block the back-door exit. The house, in short, had been deliberately transformed into a death trap.

The investigators collected samples of burned materials from the house and sent them to a laboratory that could detect the presence of a liquid accelerant. The lab's chemist reported that one of the samples contained evidence of "mineral spirits," a substance that is often found in charcoal-lighter fluid. The sample had been taken by the threshold of the front door.

The fire was now considered a triple homicide, and Todd Willingham—the only person, besides the victims, known to have been in the house at the time of the blaze—became the prime suspect.

Police and fire investigators canvassed the neighborhood, interviewing witnesses. Several, like Father Monaghan, initially portrayed Willingham as devastated by the fire. Yet, over time, an increasing number of witnesses offered damning statements. Diane Barbee said that she had not seen Willingham try to enter the house until after the authorities arrived, as if he were putting on a show. And when the children's room exploded with flames, she added, he seemed more preoccupied with his car, which he moved down the driveway. Another neighbor reported that when Willingham cried out for his babies he "did not appear to be excited or concerned." Even Father Monaghan wrote in a statement that, upon further reflection, "things were not as they seemed. I had the feeling that [Willingham] was in complete control."

The police began to piece together a disturbing profile of Willingham. Born in Ardmore, Oklahoma, in 1968, he had been abandoned by his mother when he was a baby. His father, Gene, who had divorced his mother, eventually raised him with his stepmother, Eugenia. Gene, a former U.S. Marine, worked in a salvage yard, and the family lived in a cramped house; at night, they could hear freight trains rattling past on a nearby track. Willingham, who had what the family called the "classic Willingham look"—a handsome face, thick black hair, and dark eyes—struggled in school, and as a teen-ager began to sniff paint. When he was seventeen, Oklahoma's Department of Human Services evaluated him, and reported, "He likes 'girls,' music, fast cars, sharp trucks, swimming, and hunting, in that order." Willingham dropped out of high school, and over time was arrested for, among other things, driving under the influence, stealing a bicycle, and shoplifting.

In 1988, he met Stacy, a senior in high school, who also came from a troubled background: when she was four years old, her stepfather had strangled her mother to death during a fight. Stacy and Willingham had a turbulent relationship. Willingham, who was unfaithful, drank too much Jack Daniel's and sometimes hit Stacy—even when she was pregnant. A neighbor said that he once heard Willingham yell at her, "Get up, bitch, and I'll hit you again."

On December 31st, the authorities brought Willingham in for questioning. Fogg and Vasquez were present for the interrogation, along with Jimmie Hensley, a police officer who was working his first arson case. Willingham said that Stacy had left the house around 9 A.M. to pick up a Christmas present for the kids, at the Salvation Army. "After she got out of the driveway, I heard the twins cry, so I got up and gave them a bottle," he said. The children's room had a safety gate across the doorway, which Amber could climb over but not the twins, and he and Stacy often let the twins nap on the floor after they drank their bottles. Amber was still in bed, Willingham said, so he went back into his room to sleep. "The next thing I remember is hearing 'Daddy, Daddy,'" he recalled. "The house was already full of smoke." He said that he got up, felt around the floor for a pair of pants, and put them on. He could no longer hear his daughter's voice ("I heard that last 'Daddy, Daddy' and never heard her again"), and he hollered, "Oh God—Amber, get out of the house! Get out of the house!"

He never sensed that Amber was in his room, he said. Perhaps she had already passed out by the time he stood up, or perhaps she came in after he left, through a second doorway, from the living room. He said that he went down the corridor and tried to reach the children's bedroom. In the hallway, he said, "you couldn't see nothing but black." The air smelled the way it had when their microwave had blown up, three weeks earlier—like "wire and stuff like that." He could hear sockets and light switches popping, and he crouched down, almost crawling. When he made it to the children's bedroom, he said, he stood and his hair caught on fire. "Oh God, I never felt anything that hot before," he said of the heat radiating out of the room.

After he patted out the fire on his hair, he said, he got down on the floor and groped in the dark. "I thought I found one of them once," he said, "but it was a doll." He couldn't bear the heat any longer. "I felt myself passing out," he said. Finally, he stumbled down the corridor and out the front door, trying to catch his breath. He saw Diane Barbee and yelled for her to call the Fire Department. After she left, he insisted, he tried without success to get back inside.

The investigators asked him if he had any idea how the fire had started. He said that he wasn't sure, though it must have originated in the children's room, since that was where he first saw flames; they were glowing like "bright lights." He and Stacy used three space heaters to keep the house warm, and one of them was in the children's room. "I taught Amber not to play with it," he said, adding that she got "whuppings every once in a while for messing with it." He said that he didn't know if the heater, which had an internal flame, was turned on. (Vasquez later testified that when he had checked the heater, four days after the fire, it was in the "Off" position.) Willingham speculated that the fire might have been started by something electrical: he had heard all that popping and crackling.

When pressed whether someone might have a motive to hurt his family, he said that he couldn't think of anyone that "cold-blooded." He said of his children, "I just don't understand why anybody would take them, you know? We had three of the most pretty babies anybody could have ever asked for." He went on, "Me and Stacy's been together for four years, but off and on we get into a fight and split up for a while and I think those babies is what brought us so close together . . . neither one of us . . . could live without them kids." Thinking of Amber, he said, "To tell you the honest-to-God's truth, I wish she hadn't woke me up."

During the interrogation, Vasquez let Fogg take the lead. Finally, Vasquez turned to Willingham and asked a seemingly random question: had he put on shoes before he fled the house?

"No, sir," Willingham replied.

A map of the house was on a table between the men, and Vasquez pointed to it. "You walked out this way?" he said.

Willingham said yes.

Vasquez was now convinced that Willingham had killed his children. If the floor had been soaked with a liquid accelerant and the fire had burned low, as the evidence suggested, Willingham could not have run out of the house the way he had described without badly burning his feet. A medical report indicated that his feet had been unscathed.

Willingham insisted that, when he left the house, the fire was still around the top of the walls and not on the floor. "I didn't have to jump through any flames," he said. Vasquez believed that this was impossible, and that Willingham had lit the fire as he was retreating—first, torching the children's room, then the hallway, and then, from the porch, the front door. Vasquez later said of Willingham, "He told me a story of pure fabrication. . . . He just talked and he talked and all he did was lie."

Still, there was no clear motive. The children had life-insurance policies, but they amounted to only fifteen thousand dollars, and Stacy's grandfather, who had paid for them, was listed as the primary beneficiary. Stacy told investigators that even though Willingham hit her he had never abused the children—"Our kids were spoiled rotten," she said—and she did not believe that Willingham could have killed them.

Ultimately, the authorities concluded that Willingham was a man without a conscience whose serial crimes had climaxed, almost inexorably, in murder. John Jackson, who was then the assistant district attorney in Corsicana, was assigned to prosecute Willingham's case. He later told the Dallas *Morning News* that he considered Willingham to be "an utterly sociopathic individual" who deemed his children "an impediment to his lifestyle." Or, as the local district attorney, Pat Batchelor, put it, "The children were interfering with his beer drinking and dart throwing."

On the night of January 8, 1992, two weeks after the fire, Willingham was riding in a car with Stacy when SWAT teams surrounded them, forcing them to the side of the road. "They pulled guns out like we had just robbed ten banks," Stacy later recalled. "All we heard was 'click, click.' . . . Then they arrested him."

Willingham was charged with murder. Because there were multiple victims, he was eligible for the death penalty, under Texas law. Unlike many other prosecutors in the state, Jackson, who had ambitions of becoming a judge, was personally opposed to capital punishment. "I don't think it's effective in deterring criminals," he told me. "I just don't think it works." He also considered it wasteful: because of the expense of litigation and the appeals process, it costs, on average, $2.3 million to execute a prisoner in Texas—about three times the cost of incarcerating someone for forty years. Plus, Jackson said, "What's the recourse if you make a mistake?" Yet his boss, Batchelor, believed that, as he once put it, "certain people who commit bad enough crimes give up the right to live," and Jackson came to agree that the heinous nature of the crime in the Willingham case—"one of the worst in terms of body count" that he had ever tried—mandated death.

Willingham couldn't afford to hire lawyers, and was assigned two by the state: David Martin, a former state trooper, and Robert Dunn, a local defense attorney who represented everyone from alleged murderers to spouses in divorce cases—a "Jack-of-all-trades," as he calls himself. ("In a small town, you can't say 'I'm a so-and-so lawyer,' because you'll starve to death," he told me.)

Not long after Willingham's arrest, authorities received a message from a prison inmate named Johnny Webb, who was in the same jail as Willingham. Webb alleged that Willingham had confessed to him that he took "some kind of lighter fluid, squirting [it] around the walls and the floor, and set a fire." The case against Willingham was considered airtight.

Even so, several of Stacy's relatives—who, unlike her, believed that Willingham was guilty—told Jackson that they preferred to avoid the anguish of a trial. And so, shortly before jury selection, Jackson approached Willingham's attorneys with an extraordinary offer: if their client pleaded guilty, the state would give him a life sentence. "I was really happy when I thought we might have a deal to avoid the death penalty," Jackson recalls.

Willingham's lawyers were equally pleased. They had little doubt that he had committed the murders and that, if the case went before a jury, he would be found guilty, and, subsequently, executed. "Everyone thinks defense lawyers must believe their clients are innocent, but that's seldom true," Martin told me. "Most of the time, they're guilty as sin." He added of Willingham, "All the evidence showed that he was one hundred per cent guilty. He poured accelerant all over the house and put lighter fluid under the kids' beds." It was, he said, "a classic arson case": there were "puddle patterns all over the place—no disputing those."

Martin and Dunn advised Willingham that he should accept the offer, but he refused. The lawyers asked his father and stepmother to speak to him. According to Eugenia, Martin showed them photographs of the burned children and said, "Look what your son did. You got to talk him into pleading, or he's going to be executed."

His parents went to see their son in jail. Though his father did not believe that he should plead guilty if he was innocent, his stepmother beseeched him to take the deal. "I just wanted to keep my boy alive," she told me.

Willingham was implacable. "I ain't gonna plead to something I didn't do, especially killing my own kids," he said. It was his final decision. Martin says, "I thought it was nuts at the time—and I think it's nuts now."

Willingham's refusal to accept the deal confirmed the view of the prosecution, and even that of his defense lawyers, that he was an unrepentant killer.

In August, 1992, the trial commenced in the old stone courthouse in downtown Corsicana. Jackson and a team of prosecutors summoned a procession of witnesses, including Johnny Webb and the Barbees. The crux of the state's case, though, remained the scientific evidence gathered by Vasquez and Fogg. On the stand, Vasquez detailed what he called more than "twenty indicators" of arson.

"Do you have an opinion as to who started the fire?" one of the prosecutors asked.

"Yes, sir," Vasquez said. "Mr. Willingham."

The prosecutor asked Vasquez what he thought Willingham's intent was in lighting the fire. "To kill the little girls," he said.

The defense had tried to find a fire expert to counter Vasquez and Fogg's testimony, but the one they contacted concurred with the prosecution. Ultimately, the defense presented only one witness to the jury: the Willinghams' babysitter, who said she could not believe that Willingham could have killed his children. (Dunn told me that Willingham had wanted to testify, but Martin and Dunn thought that he would make a bad witness.) The trial ended after two days.

During his closing arguments, Jackson said that the puddle configurations and pour patterns were Willingham's inadvertent "confession," burned into the floor. Showing a Bible that had been salvaged from the fire, Jackson paraphrased the words of Jesus from the Gospel of Matthew: "Whomsoever shall harm one of my children, it's better for a millstone to be hung around his neck and for him to be cast in the sea."

The jury was out for barely an hour before returning with a unanimous guilty verdict. As Vasquez put it, "The fire does not lie."

When Elizabeth Gilbert approached the prison guard, on a spring day in 1999, and said Cameron Todd Willingham's name, she was uncertain about what she was doing. A forty-seven-year-old French teacher and playwright from Houston, Gilbert was divorced with two children. She had never visited a prison before. Several weeks earlier, a friend, who worked at an organization that opposed the death penalty, had encouraged her to volunteer as a pen pal for an inmate on death row, and Gilbert had offered her name and address. Not long after, a short letter, written with unsteady penmanship, arrived from Willingham. "If you wish to write back, I would be honored to correspond with you," he said. He also asked if she might visit him. Perhaps out of a writer's curiosity, or perhaps because she didn't feel quite herself (she had just been upset by news that her ex-husband was dying of cancer), she agreed. Now she was standing in front of the decrepit penitentiary in Huntsville, Texas—a place that inmates referred to as "the death pit."

She filed past a razor-wire fence, a series of floodlights, and a checkpoint, where she was patted down, until she entered a small chamber. Only a few feet in front of her was a man convicted of multiple infanticide. He was wearing a white jumpsuit with "DR"—for death row—printed on the back, in large black letters. He had a tattoo of a serpent and a skull on his left biceps. He stood nearly six feet tall and was muscular, though his legs had atrophied after years of confinement.

A Plexiglas window separated Willingham from her; still, Gilbert, who had short brown hair and a bookish manner, stared at him uneasily. Willingham had once fought another prisoner who called him a "baby killer," and since he had been incarcerated, seven years earlier, he had committed a series of disciplinary infractions that had periodically landed him in the segregation unit, which was known as "the dungeon."

Willingham greeted her politely. He seemed grateful that she had come. After his conviction, Stacy had campaigned for his release. She wrote to Ann Richards, then the governor of Texas, saying, "I know him in ways that no one else does when it comes to our children. Therefore, I believe that there is no way he could have possibly committed this crime." But within a year Stacy had filed for divorce, and Willingham had few visitors except for his parents, who drove from Oklahoma to see him once a month. "I really have no one outside my parents to remind me that I am a human being, not the animal the state professes I am," he told Gilbert at one point.

He didn't want to talk about death row. "Hell, I live here," he later wrote her. "When I have a visit, I want to escape from here." He asked her questions about her teaching and art. He expressed fear that, as a playwright, she might find him a "one-dimensional character," and apologized for lacking social graces; he now had trouble separating the mores in prison from those of the outside world.

When Gilbert asked him if he wanted something to eat or drink from the vending machines, he declined. "I hope I did not offend you by not accepting any snacks," he later wrote her. "I didn't want you to feel I was there just for something like that."

She had been warned that prisoners often tried to con visitors. He appeared to realize this, subsequently telling her, "I am just a simple man. Nothing else. And to most other people a convicted killer looking for someone to manipulate."

Their visit lasted for two hours, and afterward they continued to correspond. She was struck by his letters, which seemed introspective, and were not at all what she had expected. "I am a very honest person with my feelings," he wrote her. "I will not bullshit you on how I feel or what I think." He said that he used to be stoic, like his father. But, he added, "losing my three daughters . . . my home, wife and my life, you tend to wake up a little. I have learned to open myself."

She agreed to visit him again, and when she returned, several weeks later, he was visibly moved. "Here I am this person who nobody on the outside is ever going to know as a human, who has lost so much, but still trying to hold on," he wrote her afterward. "But you came back! I don't think you will ever know of what importance that visit was in my existence."

They kept exchanging letters, and she began asking him about the fire. He insisted that he was innocent and that, if someone had poured accelerant through the house and lit it, then the killer remained free.

Gilbert wasn't naïve—she assumed that he was guilty. She did not mind giving him solace, but she was not there to absolve him.

Still, she had become curious about the case, and one day that fall she drove down to the courthouse in Corsicana to review the trial records. Many people in the community remembered the tragedy, and a clerk expressed bewilderment that anyone would be interested in a man who had burned his children alive.

Gilbert took the files and sat down at a small table. As she examined the eyewitness accounts, she noticed several contradictions. Diane Barbee had reported that, before the authorities arrived at the fire, Willingham never tried to get back into the house—yet she had been absent for some time while calling the Fire Department. Meanwhile, her daughter Buffie had reported witnessing Willingham on the porch breaking a window, in an apparent effort to reach his children. And the firemen and police on the scene had described Willingham frantically trying to get into the house.

The witnesses' testimony also grew more damning after authorities had concluded, in the beginning of January, 1992, that Willingham was likely guilty of murder. In Diane Barbee's initial statement to authorities, she had portrayed Willingham as "hysterical," and described the front of the house exploding. But on January 4th, after arson investigators began suspecting Willingham of murder, Barbee suggested that he could have gone back inside to rescue his children, for at the outset she had seen only "smoke coming from out of the front of the house"—smoke that was not "real thick."

An even starker shift occurred with Father Monaghan's testimony. In his first statement, he had depicted Willingham as a devastated father who had to be repeatedly restrained from risking his life. Yet, as investigators were preparing to arrest Willingham, he concluded that Willingham had been *too* emotional ("He seemed to have the type of distress that a woman who had given birth would have upon seeing her children die"); and he expressed a "gut feeling" that Willingham had "something to do with the setting of the fire."

Dozens of studies have shown that witnesses' memories of events often change when they are supplied with new contextual information. Itiel Dror, a cognitive psychologist who has done extensive research on eyewitness and expert testimony in criminal investigations, told me, "The mind is not a passive machine. Once you believe in something—once you expect something—it changes the way you perceive information and the way your memory recalls it."

After Gilbert's visit to the courthouse, she kept wondering about Willingham's motive, and she pressed him on the matter. In response, he wrote, of the death of his children, "I do not talk about it much anymore and it is still a very powerfully emotional pain inside my being." He admitted that he had been a "sorry-ass husband" who had hit Stacy—something he deeply regretted. But he said that he had loved his children and would never have hurt them. Fatherhood, he said, had changed him; he stopped being a hoodlum and "settled down" and "became a man." Nearly three months before the fire, he and Stacy, who had never married, wed at a small ceremony in his home town of Ardmore. He said that the prosecution had seized upon incidents from his past and from the day of the fire to create a portrait of a "demon," as Jackson, the prosecutor, referred to him. For instance, Willingham said, he had moved the car during the fire simply because he didn't want it to explode by the house, further threatening the children.

Gilbert was unsure what to make of his story, and she began to approach people who were involved in the case, asking them questions. "My friends thought I was crazy," Gilbert recalls. "I'd never done anything like this in my life."

One morning, when Willingham's parents came to visit him, Gilbert arranged to see them first, at a coffee shop near the prison. Gene, who was in his seventies, had the Willingham look, though his black hair had gray streaks and his dark eyes were magnified by glasses. Eugenia, who was in her fifties, with silvery hair, was as sweet and talkative as her husband was stern and reserved. The drive from Oklahoma to Texas took six hours, and they had woken at three in the morning; because they could not afford a motel, they would have to return home later that day. "I feel like a real burden to them," Willingham had written Gilbert.

As Gene and Eugenia sipped coffee, they told Gilbert how grateful they were that someone had finally taken an interest in Todd's case. Gene said that his son, though he had flaws, was no killer.

The evening before the fire, Eugenia said, she had spoken on the phone with Todd. She and Gene were planning to visit two days later, on

Christmas Eve, and Todd told her that he and Stacy and the kids had just picked up family photographs. "He said, 'We got your pictures for Christmas,'" she recalled. "He put Amber on the phone, and she was tattling on one of the twins. Todd didn't seem upset. If something was bothering him, I would have known."

Gene and Eugenia got up to go: they didn't want to miss any of the four hours that were allotted for the visit with their son. Before they left, Gene said, "You'll let us know if you find anything, won't you?"

Over the next few weeks, Gilbert continued to track down sources. Many of them, including the Barbees, remained convinced that Willingham was guilty, but several of his friends and relatives had doubts. So did some people in law enforcement. Willingham's former probation officer in Oklahoma, Polly Goodin, recently told me that Willingham had never demonstrated bizarre or sociopathic behavior. "He was probably one of my favorite kids," she said. Even a former judge named Bebe Bridges—who had often stood, as she put it, on the "opposite side" of Willingham in the legal system, and who had sent him to jail for stealing—told me that she could not imagine him killing his children. "He was polite, and he seemed to care," she said. "His convictions had been for dumb-kid stuff. Even the things stolen weren't significant." Several months before the fire, Willingham tracked Goodin down at her office, and proudly showed her photographs of Stacy and the kids. "He wanted Bebe and me to know he'd been doing good," Goodin recalled.

Eventually, Gilbert returned to Corsicana to interview Stacy, who had agreed to meet at the bed-and-breakfast where Gilbert was staying. Stacy was slightly plump, with pale, round cheeks and feathered dark-blond hair; her bangs were held in place by gel, and her face was heavily made up. According to a tape recording of the conversation, Stacy said that nothing unusual had happened in the days before the fire. She and Willingham had not fought, and were preparing for the holiday. Though Vasquez, the arson expert, had recalled finding the space heater off, Stacy was sure that, at least on the day of the incident—a cool winter morning—it had been on. "I remember turning it down," she recalled. "I always thought, Gosh, could Amber have put something in there?" Stacy added that, more than once, she had caught Amber "putting things too close to it."

Willingham had often not treated her well, she recalled, and after his incarceration she had left him for a man who did. But she didn't think that her former husband should be on death row. "I don't think he did it," she said, crying.

Though only the babysitter had appeared as a witness for the defense during the main trial, several family members, including Stacy, testified during the penalty phase, asking the jury to spare Willingham's life. When Stacy was on the stand, Jackson grilled her about the "significance" of Willingham's "very large tattoo of a skull, encircled by some kind of a serpent."

"It's just a tattoo," Stacy responded.

"He just likes skulls and snakes. Is that what you're saying?"

"No. He just had—he got a tattoo on him."

The prosecution cited such evidence in asserting that Willingham fit the profile of a sociopath, and brought forth two medical experts to confirm the theory. Neither had met Willingham. One of them was Tim Gregory, a psychologist with a master's degree in marriage and family issues, who had previously gone goose hunting with Jackson, and had not published any research in the field of sociopathic behavior. His practice was devoted to family counselling.

At one point, Jackson showed Gregory Exhibit No. 60—a photograph of an Iron Maiden poster that had hung in Willingham's house—and asked the psychologist to interpret it. "This one is a picture of a skull, with a fist being punched through the skull," Gregory said; the image displayed "violence" and "death." Gregory looked at photographs of other music posters owned by Willingham. "There's a hooded skull, with wings and a hatchet," Gregory continued. "And all of these are in fire, depicting—it reminds me of something like Hell. And there's a picture—a Led Zeppelin picture of a falling angel. . . . I see there's an association many times with cultive-type of activities. A focus on death, dying. Many times individuals that have a lot of this type of art have interest in satanic-type activities."

The other medical expert was James P. Grigson, a forensic psychiatrist. He testified so often for the prosecution in capital-punishment cases that he had become known as Dr. Death. (A Texas appellate judge once wrote that when Grigson appeared on the stand the defendant might as well "commence writing out his last will and testament.") Grigson suggested that Willingham was an "extremely severe sociopath," and that "no pill" or treatment could help him. Grigson had previously used nearly the same words in helping to secure a death sentence against Randall Dale Adams, who had been convicted of murdering a police officer, in 1977. After Adams, who had no prior criminal record, spent a dozen years in prison—and once came within seventy-two hours of being executed—new evidence emerged that absolved him, and he was released. In 1995, three years after Willingham's trial, Grigson was expelled from the American Psychiatric Association for violating ethics. The association stated that Grigson had repeatedly arrived at a "psychiatric diagnosis without first having examined the individuals in question, and for indicating, while testifying in court as an expert witness, that he could predict with 100-per-cent certainty that the individuals would engage in future violent acts."

After speaking to Stacy, Gilbert had one more person she wanted to interview: the jailhouse informant Johnny Webb, who was incarcerated in Iowa Park, Texas. She wrote to Webb, who said that she could see him, and they met in the prison visiting room. A man in his late twenties, he had pallid skin and a closely shaved head; his eyes were jumpy, and his entire body seemed to tremble. A reporter who once met him described him to me as "nervous as a cat around rocking chairs." Webb had begun taking drugs when he was nine years old, and had been convicted of, among other things, car theft, selling marijuana, forgery, and robbery.

As Gilbert chatted with him, she thought that he seemed paranoid. During Willingham's trial, Webb disclosed that he had been given a diagnosis of "post-traumatic stress disorder" after he was sexually assaulted in prison, in 1988, and that he often suffered from "mental impairment." Under cross-examination, Webb testified that he had no recollection of a robbery that he had pleaded guilty to only months earlier.

Webb repeated for her what he had said in court: he had passed by Willingham's cell, and as they spoke through a food slot Willingham broke down and told him that he intentionally set the house on fire. Gilbert was dubious. It was hard to believe that Willingham, who had otherwise insisted on his innocence, had suddenly confessed to an inmate he barely knew. The conversation had purportedly taken place by a speaker system that allowed any of the guards to listen—an unlikely spot for an inmate to reveal a secret. What's more, Webb alleged that Willingham had told him that Stacy had hurt one of the kids, and that the fire was set to cover up the crime. The autopsies, however, had revealed no bruises or signs of trauma on the children's bodies.

Jailhouse informants, many of whom are seeking reduced time or special privileges, are notoriously unreliable. According to a 2004 study by the Center on Wrongful Convictions, at Northwestern University Law School, lying police and jailhouse informants are the leading cause of wrongful convictions in capital cases in the United States. At the time that Webb came forward against Willingham, he was facing charges of robbery and forgery. During Willingham's trial, another inmate planned to testify that he had overheard Webb saying to another prisoner that he was hoping to "get time cut," but the testimony was ruled inadmissible, because it was hearsay. Webb, who pleaded guilty to the robbery and forgery charges, received a sentence of fifteen years. Jackson, the prosecutor, told me that he generally considered Webb "an unreliable kind of guy," but added, "I saw no real motive for him to make a statement like this if it wasn't true. We didn't cut him any slack." In 1997, five years after Willingham's trial, Jackson urged the Texas Board of Pardons and Paroles to grant Webb parole. "I asked them to cut him loose early," Jackson told me. The reason, Jackson said, was that Webb had been targeted by the Aryan Brotherhood. The board granted Webb parole, but within months of his release he was caught with cocaine and returned to prison.

In March, 2000, several months after Gilbert's visit, Webb unexpectedly sent Jackson a Motion to Recant Testimony, declaring, "Mr. Willingham is innocent of all charges." But Willingham's lawyer was not informed of this development, and soon afterward Webb, without explanation, recanted his recantation. When I recently asked Webb, who was released from prison in 2007, about the turnabout and why Willingham would have confessed to a virtual stranger, he said that he knew only what "the dude told me." After I pressed him, he said, "It's very possible I misunderstood what he said." Since the trial, Webb has been given an additional diagnosis, bipolar disorder. "Being locked up in that little cell makes you kind of crazy," he said. "My memory is in bits and pieces. I was on a lot of medication at the time. Everyone knew that." He paused, then said, "The statute of limitations has run out on perjury, hasn't it?"

Aside from the scientific evidence of arson, the case against Willing-ham did not stand up to scrutiny. Jackson, the prosecutor, said of Webb's testimony, "You can take it or leave it." Even the refrigerator's placement by the back door of the house turned out to be innocuous; there were two refrigerators in the cramped kitchen, and one of them was by the back door. Jimmie Hensley, the police detective, and Douglas Fogg, the assistant fire chief, both of whom investigated the fire, told me recently that they had never believed that the fridge was part of the arson plot. "It didn't have nothing to do with the fire," Fogg said.

After months of investigating the case, Gilbert found that her faith in the prosecution was shaken. As she told me, "What if Todd really was innocent?"

In the summer of 1660, an Englishman named William Harrison vanished on a walk, near the village of Charingworth, in Gloucestershire. His bloodstained hat was soon discovered on the side of a local road. Police interrogated Harrison's servant, John Perry, and eventually Perry gave a statement that his mother and his brother had killed Harrison for money. Perry, his mother, and his brother were hanged.

Two years later, Harrison reappeared. He insisted, fancifully, that he had been abducted by a band of criminals and sold into slavery. Whatever happened, one thing was indisputable: he had not been murdered by the Perrys.

The fear that an innocent person might be executed has long haunted jurors and lawyers and judges. During America's Colonial period, dozens of crimes were punishable by death, including horse thievery, blasphemy, "man-stealing," and highway robbery. After independence, the number of crimes eligible for the death penalty was gradually reduced, but doubts persisted over whether legal procedures were sufficient to prevent an inno-cent person from being executed. In 1868, John Stuart Mill made one of the most eloquent defenses of capital punishment, arguing that executing a murderer did not display a wanton disregard for life but, rather, proof of its value. "We show, on the contrary, most emphatically our regard for it by the adoption of a rule that he who violates that right in another forfeits it for himself," he said. For Mill, there was one counterargument that carried weight—"that if by an error of justice an innocent person is put to death, the mistake can never be corrected."

The modern legal system, with its lengthy appeals process and clemency boards, was widely assumed to protect the kind of "error of justice" that Mill feared. In 2000, while George W. Bush was governor of Texas, he said, "I know there are some in the country who don't care for the death penalty, but . . . we've adequately answered innocence or guilt." His top policy adviser on issues of criminal justice emphasized that there is "super due process to make sure that no innocent defendants are executed."

In recent years, though, questions have mounted over whether the system is fail-safe. Since 1976, more than a hundred and thirty people on death row have been exonerated. DNA testing, which was developed in the eighties, saved seventeen of them, but the technique can be used only in rare instances. Barry Scheck, a co-founder of the Innocence Project, which has used DNA testing to exonerate prisoners, estimates that about eighty per cent of felonies do not involve biological evidence.

In 2000, after thirteen people on death row in Illinois were exonerated, George Ryan, who was then governor of the state, suspended the death penalty. Though he had been a longtime advocate of capital punishment, he declared that he could no longer support a system that has "come so close to the ultimate nightmare—the state's taking of innocent life." Former Supreme Court Justice Sandra Day O'Connor has said that the "execution of a legally and factually innocent person would be a constitutionally intolerable event."

Such a case has become a kind of grisly Holy Grail among opponents of capital punishment. In his 2002 book "The Death Penalty," Stuart Banner observes, "The prospect of killing an innocent person seemed to be the one thing that could cause people to rethink their support for capital punishment. Some who were not troubled by statistical arguments against the death penalty—claims about deterrence or racial disparities—were deeply troubled that such an extreme injustice might occur in an individual case." Opponents of the death penalty have pointed to several questionable cases. In 1993, Ruben Cantu was executed in Texas for fatally shooting a man during a robbery. Years later, a second victim, who survived the shooting, told the Houston *Chronicle* that he had been pressured by police to identify

Cantu as the gunman, even though he believed Cantu to be innocent. Sam Millsap, the district attorney in the case, who had once supported capital punishment ("I'm no wild-eyed, pointy-headed liberal"), said that he was disturbed by the thought that he had made a mistake.

In 1995, Larry Griffin was put to death in Missouri, for the drive-by shooting of a drug dealer. The case rested largely on the eyewitness testimony of a career criminal named Robert Fitzgerald, who had been an informant for prosecutors before and was in the witness-protection program. Fitzgerald maintained that he happened to be at the scene because his car had broken down. After Griffin's execution, a probe sponsored by the N.A.A.C.P.'s Legal Defense and Educational Fund revealed that a man who had been wounded during the incident insisted that Griffin was not the shooter. Moreover, the first police officer at the scene disputed that Fitzgerald had witnessed the crime.

These cases, however, stopped short of offering irrefutable proof that a "legally and factually innocent person" was executed. In 2005, a St. Louis prosecutor, Jennifer Joyce, launched an investigation of the Griffin case, upon being presented with what she called "compelling" evidence of Griffin's potential innocence. After two years of reviewing the evidence, and interviewing a new eyewitness, Joyce said that she and her team were convinced that the "right person was convicted."

Supreme Court Justice Antonin Scalia, in 2006, voted with a majority to uphold the death penalty in a Kansas case. In his opinion, Scalia declared that, in the modern judicial system, there has not been "a single case—not one—in which it is clear that a person was executed for a crime he did not commit. If such an event had occurred in recent years, we would not have to hunt for it; the innocent's name would be shouted from the rooftops."

"My problems are simple," Willingham wrote Gilbert in September, 1999. "Try to keep them from killing me at all costs. End of story."

During his first years on death row, Willingham had pleaded with his lawyer, David Martin, to rescue him. "You can't imagine what it's like to be here, with people I have no business even being around," he wrote.

For a while, Willingham shared a cell with Ricky Lee Green, a serial killer, who castrated and fatally stabbed his victims, including a sixteen-year-old boy. (Green was executed in 1997.) Another of Willingham's cell-mates, who had an I.Q. below seventy and the emotional development of an eight-year-old, was raped by an inmate. "You remember me telling you I had a new celly?" Willingham wrote in a letter to his parents. "The little retarded boy. . . . There was this guy here on the wing who is a shit sorry coward (who is the same one I got into it with a little over a month ago). Well, he raped [my cellmate] in the 3 row shower week before last." Willingham said that he couldn't believe that someone would "rape a boy who cannot even defend himself. Pretty damn low."

Because Willingham was known as a "baby killer," he was a target of attacks. "Prison is a rough place, and with a case like mine they never give you the benefit of a doubt," he wrote his parents. After he tried to fight one prisoner who threatened him, Willingham told a friend that if he hadn't stood up for himself several inmates would have "beaten me up or raped or"—his thought trailed off.

Over the years, Willingham's letters home became increasingly despairing. "This is a hard place, and it makes a person hard inside," he wrote. "I told myself that was one thing I did not want and that was for this place to make me bitter, but it is hard." He went on, "They have [executed] at least one person every month I have been here. It is senseless and brutal. . . . You see, we are not living in here, we are only existing." In 1996, he wrote, "I just been trying to figure out why after having a wife and 3 beautiful children that I loved my life has to end like this. And sometimes it just seems like it is not worth it all. . . . In the 3½ years I been here I have never felt that my life was as worthless and desolate as it is now." Since the fire, he wrote, he had the sense that his life was slowly being erased. He obsessively looked at photographs of his children and Stacy, which he stored in his cell. "So long ago, so far away," he wrote in a poem. "Was everything truly there?"

Inmates on death row are housed in a prison within a prison, where there are no attempts at rehabilitation, and no educational or training programs. In 1999, after seven prisoners tried to escape from Huntsville, Willingham and four hundred and fifty-nine other inmates on death row were moved to a more secure facility, in Livingston, Texas. Willingham was held in isolation in a sixty-square-foot cell, twenty-three hours a day. He tried to distract himself by drawing—"amateur stuff," as he put it—and writing poems. In a poem about his children, he wrote, "There is nothing more beautiful than you on this earth." When Gilbert once suggested some possible revisions to his poems, he explained that he wrote them simply as expressions, however crude, of his feelings. "So to me to cut them up and try to improve on them just for creative-writing purposes would be to destroy what I was doing to start with," he said.

Despite his efforts to occupy his thoughts, he wrote in his diary that his mind "deteriorates each passing day." He stopped working out and gained weight. He questioned his faith: "No God who cared about his creation would abandon the innocent." He seemed not to care if another inmate attacked him. "A person who is already dead inside does not fear" death, he wrote.

One by one, the people he knew in prison were escorted into the execution chamber. There was Clifton Russell, Jr., who, at the age of eighteen, stabbed and beat a man to death, and who said, in his last statement, "I thank my Father, God in Heaven, for the grace he has granted me—I am ready." There was Jeffery Dean Motley, who kidnapped and fatally shot a woman, and who declared, in his final words, "I love you, Mom. Goodbye." And there was John Fearance, who murdered his neighbor, and who turned to God in his last moments and said, "I hope He will forgive me for what I done."

Willingham had grown close to some of his prison mates, even though he knew that they were guilty of brutal crimes. In March, 2000, Willingham's friend Ponchai Wilkerson—a twenty-eight-year-old who had shot and killed a clerk during a jewelry heist—was executed. Afterward, Willingham wrote in his diary that he felt "an emptiness that has not been touched since my children were taken from me." A year later, another friend who was about to be executed—"one of the few real people I have met here not caught up in the bravado of prison"—asked Willingham to make him a final drawing. "Man, I never thought drawing a simple Rose could be so emotionally hard," Willingham wrote. "The hard part is knowing that this will be the last thing I can do for him."

Another inmate, Ernest Ray Willis, had a case that was freakishly similar to Willingham's. In 1987, Willis had been convicted of setting a fire, in West Texas, that killed two women. Willis told investigators that he had been sleeping on a friend's living-room couch and woke up to a house full of smoke. He said that he tried to rouse one of the women, who was sleeping in another room, but the flames and smoke drove him back, and he ran out the front door before the house exploded with flames. Witnesses maintained that Willis had acted suspiciously; he moved his car out of the yard, and didn't show "any emotion," as one volunteer firefighter put it. Authorities also wondered how Willis could have escaped the house without burning his bare feet. Fire investigators found pour patterns, puddle configurations, and other signs of arson. The authorities could discern no motive for the crime, but concluded that Willis, who had no previous record of violence, was a sociopath—a "demon," as the prosecutor put it. Willis was charged with capital murder and sentenced to death.

Willis had eventually obtained what Willingham called, enviously, a "bad-ass lawyer." James Blank, a noted patent attorney in New York, was assigned Willis's case as part of his firm's pro-bono work. Convinced that Willis was innocent, Blank devoted more than a dozen years to the case, and his firm spent millions, on fire consultants, private investigators, forensic experts, and the like. Willingham, meanwhile, relied on David Martin, his court-appointed lawyer, and one of Martin's colleagues to handle his appeals. Willingham often told his parents, "You don't know what it's like to have lawyers who won't even believe you're innocent." Like many inmates on death row, Willingham eventually filed a claim of inadequate legal representation. (When I recently asked Martin about his representation of Willingham, he said, "There were no grounds for reversal, and the verdict was absolutely the right one." He said of the case, "Shit, it's incredible that anyone's even thinking about it.")

Willingham tried to study the law himself, reading books such as "Tact in Court, or How Lawyers Win: Containing Sketches of Cases Won by Skill, Wit, Art, Tact, Courage and Eloquence." Still, he confessed to a friend, "The law is so complicated it is hard for me to understand." In 1996, he obtained a new court-appointed lawyer, Walter Reaves, who told me that he was appalled by the quality of Willingham's defense at trial and on appeal. Reaves prepared for him a state writ of habeas corpus, known as a Great Writ. In the byzantine appeals process of death-penalty cases, which frequently takes more than ten years, the writ is the most critical stage: a prisoner can introduce new evidence detailing such things as perjured testimony, unreliable medical experts, and bogus scientific findings. Yet most indigent inmates, like Willingham, who constitute the bulk of those on death row, lack the resources to track down new witnesses or dig up fresh evidence. They must depend on court-appointed lawyers, many of whom are "unqualified, irresponsible, or overburdened," as a study by the Texas Defender Service, a nonprofit organization, put it. In 2000, a Dallas *Morning News* investigation revealed that roughly a quarter of the inmates condemned to death in Texas were represented by court-appointed attorneys who had, at some point in their careers, been "reprimanded, placed on probation, suspended or banned from practicing law by the State Bar." Although Reaves was more competent, he had few resources to reinvestigate the case, and his writ introduced no new exculpatory evidence: nothing further about Webb, or the reliability of the eyewitness testimony, or the credibility of the medical experts. It focussed primarily on procedural questions, such as whether the trial court erred in its instructions to the jury.

The Texas Court of Criminal Appeals was known for upholding convictions even when overwhelming exculpatory evidence came to light. In 1997, DNA testing proved that sperm collected from a rape victim did not match Roy Criner, who had been sentenced to ninety-nine years for the crime. Two lower courts recommended that the verdict be overturned, but the Court of Criminal Appeals upheld it, arguing that Criner might have worn a condom or might not have ejaculated. Sharon Keller, who is now the presiding judge on the court, stated in a majority opinion, "The new evidence does not establish innocence." In 2000, George W. Bush pardoned Criner. (Keller was recently charged with judicial misconduct, for refusing to keep open past five o'clock a clerk's office in order to allow a last-minute petition from a man who was executed later that night.)

On October 31, 1997, the Court of Criminal Appeals denied Willingham's writ. After Willingham filed another writ of habeas corpus, this time in federal court, he was granted a temporary stay. In a poem, Willingham wrote, "One more chance, one more strike / Another bullet dodged, another date escaped."

Willingham was entering his final stage of appeals. As his anxieties mounted, he increasingly relied upon Gilbert to investigate his case and for emotional support. "She may never know what a change she brought into my life," he wrote in his diary. "For the first time in many years she gave me a purpose, something to look forward to."

As their friendship deepened, he asked her to promise him that she would never disappear without explanation. "I already have that in my life," he told her.

Together, they pored over clues and testimony. Gilbert says that she would send Reaves leads to follow up, but although he was sympathetic, nothing seemed to come of them. In 2002, a federal court of appeals denied Willingham's writ without even a hearing. "Now I start the last leg of my journey," Willingham wrote to Gilbert. "Got to get things in order."

He appealed to the U.S. Supreme Court, but in December, 2003, he was notified that it had declined to hear his case. He soon received a court order announcing that "the Director of the Department of Criminal Justice at Huntsville, Texas, acting by and through the executioner designated by said Director . . . is hereby DIRECTED and COMMANDED, at some hour after 6:00 p.m. on the 17th day of February, 2004, at the Department of Criminal Justice in Huntsville, Texas, to carry out this sentence of death by intravenous injection of a substance or substances in a lethal quantity sufficient to cause the death of said Cameron Todd Willingham."

Willingham wrote a letter to his parents. "Are you sitting down?" he asked, before breaking the news. "I love you both so much," he said.

His only remaining recourse was to appeal to the governor of Texas, Rick Perry, a Republican, for clemency. The process, considered the last gatekeeper to the executioner, has been called by the U.S. Supreme Court "the 'fail safe' in our criminal justice system."

One day in January, 2004, Dr. Gerald Hurst, an acclaimed scientist and fire investigator, received a file describing all the evidence of arson gathered in Willingham's case. Gilbert had come across Hurst's name and, along with one of Willingham's relatives, had contacted him, seeking his help. After their pleas, Hurst had agreed to look at the case pro bono, and Reaves, Willingham's lawyer, had sent him the relevant documents, in the hope that there were grounds for clemency.

Hurst opened the file in the basement of his house in Austin, which served as a laboratory and an office, and was cluttered with microscopes and diagrams of half-finished experiments. Hurst was nearly six and a half feet tall, though his stooped shoulders made him seem considerably shorter, and he had a gaunt face that was partly shrouded by long gray hair. He was wearing his customary outfit: black shoes, black socks, a black T-shirt, and loose-fitting black pants supported by black suspenders. In his mouth was a wad of chewing tobacco.

A child prodigy who was raised by a sharecropper during the Great Depression, Hurst used to prowl junk yards, collecting magnets and copper wires in order to build radios and other contraptions. In the early sixties, he received a Ph.D. in chemistry from Cambridge University, where he started to experiment with fluorine and other explosive chemicals, and once detonated his lab. Later, he worked as the chief scientist on secret weapons programs for several American companies, designing rockets and deadly fire bombs—or what he calls "god-awful things." He helped patent what has been described, with only slight exaggeration, as "the world's most powerful nonnuclear explosive": an Astrolite bomb. He experimented with toxins so lethal that a fraction of a drop would rot human flesh, and in his laboratory he often had to wear a pressurized moon suit; despite such precautions, exposure to chemicals likely caused his liver to fail, and in 1994 he required a transplant. Working on what he calls "the dark side of arson," he retrofitted napalm bombs with Astrolite, and developed ways for covert operatives in Vietnam to create bombs from local materials, such as chicken manure and sugar. He also perfected a method for making an exploding T-shirt by nitrating its fibres.

His conscience eventually began pricking him. "One day, you wonder, What the hell am I doing?" he recalls. He left the defense industry, and went on to invent the Mylar balloon, an improved version of Liquid Paper, and Kinepak, a kind of explosive that reduces the risk of accidental detonation. Because of his extraordinary knowledge of fire and explosives, companies in civil litigation frequently sought his help in determining the cause of a blaze. By the nineties, Hurst had begun devoting significant time to criminal-arson cases, and, as he was exposed to the methods of local and state fire investigators, he was shocked by what he saw.

Many arson investigators, it turned out, had only a high-school education. In most states, in order to be certified, investigators had to take a forty-hour course on fire investigation, and pass a written exam. Often, the bulk of an investigator's training came on the job, learning from "old-timers" in the field, who passed down a body of wisdom about the telltale signs of arson, even though a study in 1977 warned that there was nothing in "the scientific literature to substantiate their validity."

In 1992, the National Fire Protection Association, which promotes fire prevention and safety, published its first scientifically based guidelines to arson investigation. Still, many arson investigators believed that what they did was more an art than a science—a blend of experience and intuition. In 1997, the International Association of Arson Investigators filed a legal brief arguing that arson sleuths should not be bound by a 1993 Supreme Court decision requiring experts who testified at trials to adhere to the scientific method. What arson sleuths did, the brief claimed, was "less scientific." By 2000, after the courts had rejected such claims, arson investigators increasingly recognized the scientific method, but there remained great variance in the field, with many practitioners still relying on the unverified techniques that had been used for generations. "People investigated fire largely with a flat-earth approach," Hurst told me. "It looks like arson—therefore, it's arson." He went on, "My view is you have to have a scientific basis. Otherwise, it's no different than witch-hunting."

In 1998, Hurst investigated the case of a woman from North Carolina named Terri Hinson, who was charged with setting a fire that killed her seventeen-month-old son, and faced the death penalty. Hurst ran a series of experiments re-creating the conditions of the fire, which suggested that it had not been arson, as the investigators had claimed; rather, it had started accidentally, from a faulty electrical wire in the attic. Because of this research, Hinson was freed. John Lentini, a fire expert and the author of a leading scientific textbook on arson, describes Hurst as "brilliant." A Texas prosecutor once told the Chicago *Tribune*, of Hurst, "If he says it was an arson fire, then it was. If he says it wasn't, then it wasn't."

Hurst's patents yielded considerable royalties, and he could afford to work pro bono on an arson case for months, even years. But he received the files on Willingham's case only a few weeks before Willingham was scheduled to be executed. As Hurst looked through the case records, a statement by Manuel Vasquez, the state deputy fire marshal, jumped out at him. Vasquez had testified that, of the roughly twelve hundred to fifteen hundred fires he had investigated, "most all of them" were arson. This was an oddly high estimate; the Texas State Fire Marshals Office typically found arson in only fifty per cent of its cases.

Hurst was also struck by Vasquez's claim that the Willingham blaze had "burned fast and hot" because of a liquid accelerant. The notion that a flammable or combustible liquid caused flames to reach higher temperatures had been repeated in court by arson sleuths for decades. Yet the theory was nonsense: experiments have proved that wood and gasoline-fuelled fires burn at essentially the same temperature.

Vasquez and Fogg had cited as proof of arson the fact that the front door's aluminum threshold had melted. "The only thing that can cause that to react is an accelerant," Vasquez said. Hurst was incredulous. A natural-wood fire can reach temperatures as high as two thousand degrees Fahrenheit—far hotter than the melting point for aluminum alloys, which ranges from a thousand to twelve hundred degrees. And, like many other investigators, Vasquez and Fogg mistakenly assumed that wood charring beneath the aluminum threshold was evidence that, as Vasquez put it, "a liquid accelerant flowed underneath and burned." Hurst had conducted myriad experiments showing that such charring was caused simply by the aluminum conducting so much heat. In fact, when liquid accelerant is poured under a threshold a fire will extinguish, because of a lack of oxygen. (Other scientists had reached the same conclusion.) "Liquid accelerants can no more burn under an aluminum threshold than can grease burn in a skillet even with a loose-fitting lid," Hurst declared in his report on the Willingham case.

Hurst then examined Fogg and Vasquez's claim that the "brown stains" on Willingham's front porch were evidence of "liquid accelerant," which had not had time to soak into the concrete. Hurst had previously performed a test in his garage, in which he poured charcoal-lighter fluid on the concrete floor, and lit it. When the fire went out, there were no brown stains, only smudges of soot. Hurst had run the same experiment many times, with different kinds of liquid accelerants, and the result was always the same. Brown stains were common in fires; they were usually composed of rust or gunk from charred debris that had mixed with water from fire hoses.

Another crucial piece of evidence implicating Willingham was the "crazed glass" that Vasquez had attributed to the rapid heating from a fire fuelled with liquid accelerant. Yet, in November of 1991, a team of fire investigators had inspected fifty houses in the hills of Oakland, California, which had been ravaged by brush fires. In a dozen houses, the investigators discovered crazed glass, even though a liquid accelerant had not been used. Most of these houses were on the outskirts of the blaze, where firefighters had shot streams of water; as the investigators later wrote in a published study, they theorized that the fracturing had been induced by rapid cooling, rather than by sudden heating—thermal shock had caused the glass to contract so quickly that it settled disjointedly. The investigators then tested this hypothesis in a laboratory. When they heated glass, nothing happened. But each time they applied water to the heated glass the intricate patterns appeared. Hurst had seen the same phenomenon when he had blowtorched and cooled glass during his research at Cambridge. In his report, Hurst wrote that Vasquez and Fogg's notion of crazed glass was no more than an "old wives' tale."

Hurst then confronted some of the most devastating arson evidence against Willingham: the burn trailer, the pour patterns and puddle configurations, the V-shape and other burn marks indicating that the fire had multiple points of origin, the burning underneath the children's beds. There was also the positive test for mineral spirits by the front door, and Willingham's seemingly implausible story that he had run out of the house without burning his bare feet.

As Hurst read through more of the files, he noticed that Willingham and his neighbors had described the windows in the front of the house suddenly exploding and flames roaring forth. It was then that Hurst thought of the legendary Lime Street Fire, one of the most pivotal in the history of arson investigation.

On the evening of October 15, 1990, a thirty-five-year-old man named Gerald Wayne Lewis was found standing in front of his house on Lime Street in Jacksonville, Florida, holding his three-year-old son. His two-story wood-frame home was engulfed in flames. By the time the fire had been extinguished, six people were dead, including Lewis's wife. Lewis said that he had rescued his son but was unable to get to the others, who were upstairs.

When fire investigators examined the scene, they found the classic signs of arson: low burns along the walls and floors, pour patterns and puddle configurations, and a burn trailer running from the living room into the hallway. Lewis claimed that the fire had started accidentally, on a couch in the living room—his son had been playing with matches. But a V-shaped pattern by one of the doors suggested that the fire had originated elsewhere. Some witnesses told authorities that Lewis seemed too calm during the fire and had never tried to get help. According to the Los Angeles *Times*, Lewis had previously been arrested for abusing his wife, who had taken out a restraining order against him. After a chemist said that he had detected the presence of gasoline on Lewis's clothing and shoes, a report by the sheriff's office concluded, "The fire was started as a result of a petroleum product being poured on the front porch, foyer, living room, stairwell and second floor bedroom." Lewis was arrested and charged with six counts of murder. He faced the death penalty.

Subsequent tests, however, revealed that the laboratory identification of gasoline was wrong. Moreover, a local news television camera had captured Lewis in a clearly agitated state at the scene of the fire, and investigators discovered that at one point he had jumped in front of a moving car, asking the driver to call the Fire Department.

Seeking to bolster their theory of the crime, prosecutors turned to John Lentini, the fire expert, and John DeHaan, another leading investigator and textbook author. Despite some of the weaknesses of the case, Lentini told me that, given the classic burn patterns and puddle configurations in the house, he was sure that Lewis had set the fire. "I was prepared to testify and send this guy to Old Sparky"—the electric chair.

To discover the truth, the investigators, with the backing of the prosecution, decided to conduct an elaborate experiment and re-create the fire scene. Local officials gave the investigators permission to use a condemned house next to Lewis's home, which was about to be torn down. The two houses were virtually identical, and the investigators refurbished the condemned one with the same kind of carpeting, curtains, and furniture that had been in Lewis's home. The scientists also wired the building with heat and gas sensors that could withstand fire. The cost of the experiment came to twenty thousand dollars. Without using liquid accelerant, Lentini and DeHaan set the couch in the living room on fire, expecting that the experiment would demonstrate that Lewis's version of events was implausible.

The investigators watched as the fire quickly consumed the couch, sending upward a plume of smoke that hit the ceiling and spread outward, creating a thick layer of hot gases overhead—an efficient radiator of heat. Within three minutes, this cloud, absorbing more gases from the fire below, was banking down the walls and filling the living room. As the cloud approached the floor, its temperature rose, in some areas, to more than eleven hundred degrees Fahrenheit. Suddenly, the entire room exploded in flames, as the radiant heat ignited every piece of furniture, every curtain, every possible fuel source, even the carpeting. The windows shattered.

The fire had reached what is called "flashover"—the point at which radiant heat causes a fire in a room to become a room on fire. Arson investigators knew about the concept of flashover, but it was widely believed to take much longer to occur, especially without a liquid accelerant. From a single fuel source—a couch—the room had reached flashover in four and a half minutes.

Because all the furniture in the living room had ignited, the blaze went from a fuel-controlled fire to a ventilation-controlled fire—or what scientists call "post-flashover." During post-flashover, the path of the fire depends on new sources of oxygen, from an open door or window. One of the fire investigators, who had been standing by an open door in the living room, escaped moments before the oxygen-starved fire roared out of the room into the hallway—a fireball that caused the corridor to go quickly into flashover as well, propelling the fire out the front door and onto the porch.

After the fire was extinguished, the investigators inspected the hallway and living room. On the floor were irregularly shaped burn patterns that perfectly resembled pour patterns and puddle configurations. It turned out that these classic signs of arson can also appear on their own, after flashover. With the naked eye, it is impossible to distinguish between the pour patterns and puddle configurations caused by an accelerant and those caused naturally by post-flashover. The only reliable way to tell the difference is to take samples from the burn patterns and test them in a laboratory for the presence of flammable or combustible liquids.

During the Lime Street experiment, other things happened that were supposed to occur only in a fire fuelled by liquid accelerant: charring along the base of the walls and doorways, and burning under furniture. There was also a V-shaped pattern by the living-room doorway, far from where the fire had started on the couch. In a small fire, a V-shaped burn mark may pinpoint where a fire began, but during post-flashover these patterns can occur repeatedly, when various objects ignite.

One of the investigators muttered that they had just helped prove the defense's case. Given the reasonable doubt raised by the experiment, the charges against Lewis were soon dropped. The Lime Street experiment had demolished prevailing notions about fire behavior. Subsequent tests by scientists showed that, during post-flashover, burning under beds and furniture was common, entire doors were consumed, and aluminum thresholds melted.

John Lentini says of the Lime Street Fire, "This was my epiphany. I almost sent a man to die based on theories that were a load of crap."

Hurst next examined a floor plan of Willingham's house that Vasquez had drawn, which delineated all the purported pour patterns and puddle configurations. Because the windows had blown out of the children's room, Hurst knew that the fire had reached flashover. With his finger, Hurst traced along Vasquez's diagram the burn trailer that had gone from the children's room, turned right in the hallway, and headed out the front door. John Jackson, the prosecutor, had told me that the path was so "bizarre" that it had to have been caused by a liquid accelerant. But Hurst concluded that it was a natural product of the dynamics of fire during post-flashover. Willingham had fled out the front door, and the fire simply followed the ventilation path, toward the opening. Similarly, when Willingham had broken the windows in the children's room, flames had shot outward.

Hurst recalled that Vasquez and Fogg had considered it impossible for Willingham to have run down the burning hallway without scorching his bare feet. But if the pour patterns and puddle configurations were a result of a flashover, Hurst reasoned, then they were consonant with Willingham's explanation of events. When Willingham exited his bedroom, the hallway was not yet on fire; the flames were contained within the children's bedroom, where, along the ceiling, he saw the "bright lights." Just as the investigator safely stood by the door in the Lime Street experiment seconds before flashover, Willingham could have stood close to the children's room without being harmed. (Prior to the Lime Street case, fire investigators had generally assumed that carbon monoxide diffuses quickly through a house during a fire. In fact, up until flashover, levels of carbon monoxide can be remarkably low beneath and outside the thermal cloud.) By the time the Corsicana fire achieved flashover, Willingham had already fled outside and was in the front yard.

Vasquez had made a videotape of the fire scene, and Hurst looked at the footage of the burn trailer. Even after repeated viewings, he could not detect three points of origin, as Vasquez had. (Fogg recently told me that he also saw a continuous trailer and disagreed with Vasquez, but added that nobody from the prosecution or the defense ever asked him on the stand about his opinion on the subject.)

After Hurst had reviewed Fogg and Vasquez's list of more than twenty arson indicators, he believed that only one had any potential validity: the positive test for mineral spirits by the threshold of the front door. But why had the fire investigators obtained a positive reading only in that location? According to Fogg and Vasquez's theory of the crime, Willingham had poured accelerant throughout the children's bedroom and down the hallway. Officials had tested extensively in these areas—including where all the pour patterns and puddle configurations were—and turned up nothing. Jackson told me that he "never did understand why they weren't able to recover" positive tests in these parts.

Hurst found it hard to imagine Willingham pouring accelerant on the front porch, where neighbors could have seen him. Scanning the files for clues, Hurst noticed a photograph of the porch taken before the fire, which had been entered into evidence. Sitting on the tiny porch was a charcoal grill. The porch was where the family barbecued. Court testimony from witnesses confirmed that there had been a grill, along with a container of lighter fluid, and that both had burned when the fire roared onto the porch during post-flashover. By the time Vasquez inspected the house, the grill had been removed from the porch, during cleanup. Though he cited the container of lighter fluid in his report, he made no mention of the grill. At the trial, he insisted that he had never been told of the grill's earlier placement. Other authorities were aware of the grill but did not see its relevance. Hurst, however, was convinced that he had solved the mystery: when firefighters had blasted the porch with water, they had likely spread charcoal-lighter fluid from the melted container.

Without having visited the fire scene, Hurst says, it was impossible to pinpoint the cause of the blaze. But, based on the evidence, he had little doubt that it was an accidental fire—one caused most likely by the space heater or faulty electrical wiring. It explained why there had never been a motive for the crime. Hurst concluded that there was no evidence of arson, and that a man who had already lost his three children and spent twelve years in jail was about to be executed based on "junk science." Hurst wrote his report in such a rush that he didn't pause to fix the typos.

"I am a realist and I will not live a fantasy," Willingham once told Gilbert about the prospect of proving his innocence. But in February, 2004, he began to have hope. Hurst's findings had helped to exonerate more than ten people. Hurst even reviewed the scientific evidence against Willingham's friend Ernest Willis, who had been on death row for a strikingly similar arson charge. Hurst says, "It was like I was looking at the same case. Just change the names." In his report on the Willis case, Hurst concluded that not "a single item of physical evidence . . . supports a finding of arson." A second fire expert hired by Ori White, the new district attorney in Willis's district, concurred. After seventeen years on death row, Willis was set free. "I don't turn killers loose," White said at the time. "If Willis was guilty, I'd be retrying him right now. And I'd use Hurst as my witness. He's a brilliant scientist." White noted how close the system had come to murdering an innocent man. "He did not get executed, and I thank God for that," he said.

On February 13th, four days before Willingham was scheduled to be executed, he got a call from Reaves, his attorney. Reaves told him that the fifteen members of the Board of Pardons and Paroles, which reviews an application for clemency and had been sent Hurst's report, had made their decision.

"What is it?" Willingham asked.

"I'm sorry," Reaves said. "They denied your petition."

The vote was unanimous. Reaves could not offer an explanation: the board deliberates in secret, and its members are not bound by any specific criteria. The board members did not even have to review Willingham's materials, and usually don't debate a case in person; rather, they cast their votes by fax—a process that has become known as "death by fax." Between 1976 and 2004, when Willingham filed his petition, the State of Texas had approved only one application for clemency from a prisoner on death row. A Texas appellate judge has called the clemency system "a legal fiction." Reaves said of the board members, "They never asked me to attend a hearing or answer any questions."

The Innocence Project obtained, through the Freedom of Information Act, all the records from the governor's office and the board pertaining to Hurst's report. "The documents show that they received the report, but neither office has any record of anyone acknowledging it, taking note of its significance, responding to it, or calling any attention to it within the government," Barry Scheck said. "The only reasonable conclusion is that the governor's office and the Board of Pardons and Paroles ignored scientific evidence."

LaFayette Collins, who was a member of the board at the time, told me of the process, "You don't vote guilt or innocence. You don't retry the trial. You just make sure everything is in order and there are no glaring errors." He noted that although the rules allowed for a hearing to consider important new evidence, "in my time there had never been one called." When I asked him why Hurst's report didn't constitute evidence of "glaring errors," he said, "We get all kinds of reports, but we don't have the mechanisms to vet them." Alvin Shaw, another board member at the time, said that the case didn't "ring a bell," adding, angrily, "Why would I want to talk about it?" Hurst calls the board's actions "unconscionable."

Though Reaves told Willingham that there was still a chance that Governor Perry might grant a thirty-day stay, Willingham began to prepare his last will and testament. He had earlier written Stacy a letter apologizing for not being a better husband and thanking her for everything she had given him, especially their three daughters. "I still know Amber's voice, her smile, her cool Dude saying and how she said: I wanna hold you! Still feel the touch of Karmon and Kameron's hands on my face." He said that he hoped that "some day, somehow the truth will be known and my name cleared."

He asked Stacy if his tombstone could be erected next to their children's graves. Stacy, who had for so long expressed belief in Willingham's innocence, had recently taken her first look at the original court records and arson findings. Unaware of Hurst's report, she had determined that Willingham was guilty. She denied him his wish, later telling a reporter, "He took my kids away from me."

Gilbert felt as if she had failed Willingham. Even before his pleas for clemency were denied, she told him that all she could give him was her friendship. He told her that it was enough "to be a part of your life in some small way so that in my passing I can know I was at last able to have felt the heart of another who might remember me when I'm gone." He added, "There is nothing to forgive you for." He told her that he would need her to be present at his execution, to help him cope with "my fears, thoughts, and feelings."

On February 17th, the day he was set to die, Willingham's parents and several relatives gathered in the prison visiting room. Plexiglas still separated Willingham from them. "I wish I could touch and hold both of you," Willingham had written to them earlier. "I always hugged Mom but I never hugged Pop much."

As Willingham looked at the group, he kept asking where Gilbert was. Gilbert had recently been driving home from a store when another car ran a red light and smashed into her. Willingham used to tell her to stay in her kitchen for a day, without leaving, to comprehend what it was like to be confined in prison, but she had always found an excuse not to do it. Now she was paralyzed from the neck down.

While she was in an intensive-care unit, she had tried to get a message to Willingham, but apparently failed. Gilbert's daughter later read her a letter that Willingham had sent her, telling her how much he had grown to love her. He had written a poem: "Do you want to see beauty—like you have never seen? / Then close your eyes, and open your mind, and come along with me."

Gilbert, who spent years in physical rehabilitation, gradually regaining motion in her arms and upper body, says, "All that time, I thought I was saving Willingham, and I realized then that he was saving me, giving me the strength to get through this. I know I will one day walk again, and I know it is because Willingham showed me the kind of courage it takes to survive."

Willingham had requested a final meal, and at 4 P.M. on the seventeenth he was served it: three barbecued pork ribs, two orders of onion rings, fried okra, three beef enchiladas with cheese, and two slices of lemon cream pie. He received word that Governor Perry had refused to grant him a stay. (A spokesperson for Perry says, "The Governor made his decision based on the facts of the case.") Willingham's mother and father began to cry. "Don't be sad, Momma," Willingham said. "In fifty-five minutes, I'm a free man. I'm going home to see my kids." Earlier, he had confessed to his parents that there was one thing about the day of the fire he had lied about. He said that he had never actually crawled into the children's room. "I just didn't want people to think I was a coward," he said. Hurst told me, "People who have never been in a fire don't understand why those who survive often can't rescue the victims. They have no concept of what a fire is like."

The warden told Willingham that it was time. Willingham, refusing to assist the process, lay down; he was carried into a chamber eight feet wide and ten feet long. The walls were painted green, and in the center of the room, where an electric chair used to be, was a sheeted gurney. Several guards strapped Willingham down with leather belts, snapping buckles across his arms and legs and chest. A medical team then inserted intravenous tubes into his arms. Each official had a separate role in the process, so that no one person felt responsible for taking a life.

Willingham had asked that his parents and family not be present in the gallery during this process, but as he looked out he could see Stacy watching; whatever calm he had obtained was lost, and with his last breaths he cursed her. The warden pushed a remote control, and sodium thiopental, a barbiturate, was pumped into Willingham's body. Then came a second drug, pancuronium bromide, which paralyzes the diaphragm, making it impossible to breathe. Finally, a third drug, potassium chloride, filled his veins until his heart stopped, at 6:20 P.M. On his death certificate, the cause was listed as "Homicide."

After his death, his parents were allowed to touch his face for the first time in more than a decade. Later, at Willingham's request, they cremated his body and secretly spread some of his ashes over his children's graves. He had told his parents, "Please don't ever stop fighting to vindicate me."

In December, 2004, questions about the scientific evidence in the Willingham case began to surface. Maurice Possley and Steve Mills, of the Chicago *Tribune*, had published an investigative series on flaws in forensic science; upon learning of Hurst's report, Possley and Mills asked three fire experts, including John Lentini, to examine the original investigation. The experts concurred with Hurst's report. Nearly two years later, the Innocence Project commissioned Lentini and three other top fire investigators to conduct an independent review of the arson evidence in the Willingham case. The panel concluded that "each and every one" of the indicators of arson had been "scientifically proven to be invalid."

In 2005, Texas established a government commission to investigate allegations of error and misconduct by forensic scientists. The first cases that are being reviewed by the commission are those of Willingham and Willis. In August, 2009, the noted fire scientist Craig Beyler, who was hired by the commission, completed his investigation. In a scathing report, he concluded that investigators in the Willingham case had no scientific basis for claiming that the fire was arson, ignored evidence that contradicted their theory, had no comprehension of flashover and fire dynamics, relied on discredited folklore, and failed to eliminate potential accidental or alternative causes of the fire. He said that Vasquez's approach seemed to deny "rational reasoning" and was more "characteristic of mystics or psychics." What's more, Beyler determined that the investigation violated, as he put it to me, "not only the standards of today but even of the time period." The commission is reviewing his conclusions, and plans to release its own report. The commission will likely narrowly assess the reliability of the scientific evidence. But some legal scholars believe that its findings could eventually lead to Texas becoming the first state to acknowledge that, since the advent of the modern judicial system, it had carried out the "execution of a legally and factually innocent person."

Just before Willingham received the lethal injection, he was asked if he had any last words. He said, "The only statement I want to make is that I am an innocent man convicted of a crime I did not commit. I have been persecuted for twelve years for something I did not do. From God's dust I came and to dust I will return, so the Earth shall become my throne."

— *September, 2009*

———✺———

Days before the government commission on forensic science was scheduled to hear testimony from Dr. Craig Beyler about his findings, Governor Rick Perry removed the body's long-standing chairman and two of its members. Perry insisted that the three commissioners' terms had expired and the changeover was "business as usual." But the chairman, Sam Bassett, who had previously been reappointed and had asked to remain, told the Houston Chronicle *that he had heard from Perry's staffers that they were "concerned about the investigations we were conducting." Another of the removed commissioners told the Associated Press that Perry's office had informed her that the Governor was "going in a different direction."*

The Chameleon

On May 3, 2005, in France, a man called an emergency hot line for missing and exploited children. He frantically explained that he was a tourist passing through Orthez, near the western Pyrenees, and that at the train station he had encountered a fifteen-year-old boy who was alone, and terrified. Another hot line received a similar call, and the boy eventually arrived, by himself, at a local government child-welfare office. Slender and short, with pale skin and trembling hands, he wore a muffler around much of his face and had a baseball cap pulled over his eyes. He had no money and carried little more than a cell phone and an I.D., which said that his name was Francisco Hernandez Fernandez and that he was born on December 13, 1989, in Cáceres, Spain. Initially, he barely spoke, but after some prodding he revealed that his parents and younger brother had been killed in a car accident. The crash left him in a coma for several weeks and, upon recovering, he was sent to live with an uncle, who abused him. Finally, he fled to France, where his mother had grown up.

French authorities placed Francisco at the St. Vincent de Paul shelter in the nearby city of Pau. A state-run institution that housed about thirty-five boys and girls, most of whom had been either removed from dysfunctional families or abandoned, the shelter was in an old stone building with peeling white wooden shutters; on the roof was a statue of St. Vincent protecting a child in the folds of his gown. Francisco was given a single room, and he seemed relieved to be able to wash and change in private: his head and body, he explained, were covered in burns and scars from the car accident. He was enrolled at the Collège Jean Monnet, a local secondary school that had four hundred or so students, mostly from tough neighborhoods, and that had a reputation for violence. Although students were forbidden to wear hats, the principal at the time, Claire Chadourne, made an exception for Francisco, who said that he feared being teased about his scars. Like many of the social workers and teachers who dealt with Francisco, Chadourne, who had been an educator for more than thirty years, felt protective toward him. With his baggy pants and his cell phone dangling from a cord around his neck, he looked like a typical teen-ager, but he seemed deeply traumatized. He never changed his clothes in front of the other students in gym class, and resisted being subjected to a medical exam. He spoke softly, with his head bowed, and recoiled if anyone tried to touch him.

Gradually, Francisco began hanging out with other kids at recess and participating in class. Since he had enrolled so late in the school year, his literature teacher asked another student, Rafael Pessoa De Almeida, to help him with his coursework. Before long, Francisco was helping Rafael. "This guy can learn like lightning," Rafael recalls thinking.

One day after school, Rafael asked Francisco if he wanted to go ice-skating, and the two became friends, playing video games and sharing school gossip. Rafael sometimes picked on his younger brother, and Francisco, recalling that he used to mistreat his own sibling, advised, "Make sure you love your brother and stay close."

At one point, Rafael borrowed Francisco's cell phone; to his surprise, its address book and call log were protected by security codes. When Rafael returned the phone, Francisco displayed a photograph on its screen of a young boy who looked just like Francisco. "That's my brother," he said.

Francisco was soon one of the most popular kids in school, dazzling classmates with his knowledge of music and arcane slang—he even knew American idioms—and moving effortlessly between rival cliques. "The students loved him," a teacher recalls. "He had this aura about him, this charisma."

During tryouts for a talent show, the music teacher asked Francisco if he was interested in performing. He handed her a CD to play, then walked to the end of the room and tilted his hat flamboyantly, waiting for the music to start. As Michael Jackson's song "Unbreakable" filled the room, Francisco started to dance like the pop star, twisting his limbs and lip-synching the words "You can't believe it, you can't conceive it / And you can't touch me, 'cause I'm untouchable." Everyone in the room watched in awe. "He didn't just look like Michael Jackson," the music teacher subsequently recalled. "He *was* Michael Jackson."

Later, in computer class, Francisco showed Rafael an Internet image of a small reptile with a slithery tongue.

"What is it?" Rafael asked.

"A chameleon," Francisco replied.

On June 8th, an administrator rushed into the principal's office. She said that she had been watching a television program the other night about one of the world's most infamous impostors: Frédéric Bourdin, a thirty-year-old Frenchman who serially impersonated children. "I swear to God, Bourdin looks exactly like Francisco Hernandez Fernandez," the administrator said.

Chadourne was incredulous: thirty would make Francisco older than some of her teachers. She did a quick Internet search for "Frédéric Bourdin." Hundreds of news items came up about the "king of impostors" and the "master of new identities," who, like Peter Pan, "didn't want to grow up." A photograph of Bourdin closely resembled Francisco— there was the same formidable chin, the same gap between the front teeth. Chadourne called the police.

"Are you sure it's him?" an officer asked.

"No, but I have this strange feeling."

When the police arrived, Chadourne sent the assistant principal to summon Francisco from class. As Francisco entered Chadourne's office, the police seized him and thrust him against the wall, causing her to panic: what if he really was an abused orphan? Then, while handcuffing Bourdin, the police removed his baseball cap. There were no scars on his head; rather, he was going bald. "I want a lawyer," he said, his voice suddenly dropping to that of a man.

At police headquarters, he admitted that he was Frédéric Bourdin, and that in the past decade and a half he had invented scores of identities, in more than fifteen countries and five languages. His aliases included Benjamin Kent, Jimmy Morins, Alex Dole, Sladjan Raskovic, Arnaud Orions, Giovanni Petrullo, and Michelangelo Martini. News reports claimed that he had even impersonated a tiger tamer and a priest, but, in truth, he had nearly always played a similar character: an abused or abandoned child. He was unusually adept at transforming his appearance—his facial hair, his weight, his walk, his mannerisms. "I can become whatever I want," he liked to say. In 2004, when he pretended to be a fourteen-year-old French boy in the town of Grenoble, a doctor who examined him at the request of authorities concluded that he was, indeed, a teen-ager. A police captain in Pau noted, "When he talked in Spanish, he became a Spaniard. When he talked in English, he was an Englishman." Chadourne said of him, "Of course, he lied, but what an actor!"

Over the years, Bourdin had insinuated himself into youth shelters, orphanages, foster homes, junior high schools, and children's hospitals. His trail of cons extended to, among other places, Spain, Germany, Belgium, England, Ireland, Italy, Luxembourg, Switzerland, Bosnia, Portugal, Austria, Slovakia, France, Sweden, Denmark, and America. The U.S. State Department warned that he was an "exceedingly clever" man who posed as a desperate child in order to "win sympathy," and a French prosecutor called him "an incredible illusionist whose perversity is matched only by his intelligence." Bourdin himself has said, "I am a manipulator. . . . My job is to manipulate."

In Pau, the authorities launched an investigation to determine why a thirty-year-old man would pose as a teen-age orphan. They found no evidence of sexual deviance or pedophilia; they did not uncover any financial motive, either. "In my twenty-two years on the job, I've never seen a case like it," Eric Maurel, the prosecutor, told me. "Usually people con for money. His profit seems to have been purely emotional."

On his right forearm, police discovered a tattoo. It said *"caméléon nantais"*—"Chameleon from Nantes."

"Mr. Grann," Bourdin said, politely extending his hand to me. We were on a street in the center of Pau, where he had agreed to meet me one morning in the fall of 2007. For once, he seemed unmistakably an adult, with a faint five-o'clock shadow. He was dressed theatrically, in white pants, a white shirt, a checkered vest, white shoes, a blue satin bow tie, and a foppish hat. Only the gap between his teeth evoked the memory of Francisco Hernandez Fernandez.

After his ruse in Pau had been exposed, Bourdin moved to a village in the Pyrenees, twenty-five miles away. "I wanted to escape from all the glare," he said. As had often been the case with Bourdin's deceptions, the authorities were not sure how to punish him. Psychiatrists determined that he was sane. ("Is he a psychopath?" one doctor testified. "Absolutely not.") No statute seemed to fit his crime. Ultimately, he was charged with obtaining and using a fake I.D., and received a six-month suspended sentence.

A local reporter, Xavier Sota, told me that since then Bourdin had periodically appeared in Pau, always in a different guise. Sometimes he had a mustache or a beard. Sometimes his hair was tightly cropped; at other times, it was straggly. Sometimes he dressed like a rapper, and on other occasions like a businessman. "It was as if he were trying to find a new character to inhabit," Sota said.

Bourdin and I sat down on a bench near the train station, as a light rain began to fall. A car paused by the curb in front of us, with a couple inside. They rolled down the window, peered out, and said to each other, "Le Caméléon."

"I am quite famous in France these days," Bourdin said. "Too famous."

As we spoke, his large brown eyes flitted across me, seemingly taking me in. One of his police interrogators called him a "human recorder." To my surprise, Bourdin knew where I had worked, where I was born, the name of my wife, even what my sister and brother did for a living. "I like to know whom I'm meeting," he said.

Aware of how easy it is to deceive others, he was paranoid of being a mark. "I don't trust anybody," he said. For a person who described himself as a "professional liar," he seemed oddly fastidious about the facts of his own life. "I don't want you to make me into somebody I'm not," he said. "The story is good enough without embellishment."

I knew that Bourdin had grown up in and around Nantes, and I asked him about his tattoo. Why would someone who tried to erase his identity leave a trace of one? He rubbed his arm where the words were imprinted on his skin. Then he said, "I will tell you the truth behind all my lies."

Before he was Benjamin Kent or Michelangelo Martini—before he was the child of an English judge or an Italian diplomat—he was Frédéric Pierre Bourdin, the illegitimate son of Ghislaine Bourdin, who was eighteen and poor when she gave birth to him, in a suburb of Paris, on June 13, 1974. On government forms, Frédéric's father is often listed as "X," meaning that his identity was unknown. But Ghislaine, during an interview at her small house in a rural area in western France, told me that "X" was a twenty-five-year-old Algerian immigrant named Kaci, whom she had met at a margarine factory where they both worked. (She says that she can no longer remember his last name.) After she became pregnant, she discovered that Kaci was already married, and so she left her job and did not tell him that she was carrying his child.

Ghislaine raised Frédéric until he was two and a half—"He was like any other child, totally normal," she says—at which time child services intervened at the behest of her parents. A relative says of Ghislaine, "She liked to drink and dance and stay out at night. She didn't want anything to do with that child." Ghislaine insists that she had obtained another factory job and was perfectly competent, but the judge placed Frédéric in her parents' custody. Years later, Ghislaine wrote Frédéric a letter, telling him, "You are my son and they stole you from me at the age of two. They did everything to separate us from each other and we have become two strangers."

Frédéric says that his mother had a dire need for attention and, on the rare occasions that he saw her, she would feign being deathly ill and make him run to get help. "To see me frightened gave her pleasure," he says. Though Ghislaine denies this, she acknowledges that she once attempted suicide and her son had to rush to find assistance.

When Frédéric was five, he moved with his grandparents to Mouchamps, a hamlet southeast of Nantes. Frédéric—part Algerian and fatherless, and dressed in secondhand clothes from Catholic charities—was a village outcast, and in school he began to tell fabulous stories about himself. He said that his father was never around because he was a "British secret agent." One of his elementary-school teachers, Yvon Bourgueil, describes Bourdin as a precocious and captivating child, who had an extraordinary imagination and visual sense, drawing wild, beautiful comic strips. "He had this way of making you connect to him," Bourgueil recalls. He also noticed signs of mental distress. At one point, Frédéric told his grandparents that he had been molested by a neighbor, though nobody in the tightly knit village investigated the allegation. In one of his comic strips, Frédéric depicted himself drowning in a river. He increasingly misbehaved, acting out in class and stealing from neighbors. At twelve, he was sent to live at Les Grézillières, a private facility for juveniles, in Nantes.

There, his "little dramas," as one of his teachers called them, became more fanciful. Bourdin often pretended to be an amnesiac, intentionally getting lost in the streets. In 1990, after he turned sixteen, Frédéric was forced to move to another youth home, and he soon ran away. He hitchhiked to Paris, where, scared and hungry, he invented his first fake character: he approached a police officer and told him that he was a lost British teen named Jimmy Sale. "I dreamed they would send me to England, where I always imagined life was more beautiful," he recalls. When the police discovered that he spoke almost no English, he admitted his deceit and was returned to the youth home. But he had devised what he calls his "technique," and in this fashion he began to wander across Europe, moving in and out of orphanages and foster homes, searching for the "perfect shelter." In 1991, he was found in a train station in Langres, France, pretending to be sick, and was placed in a children's hospital in Saint-Dizier. According to his medical report, no one knew "who he was or where he came from." Answering questions only in writing, he indicated that his name was Frédéric Cassis—a play on his real father's first name, Kaci. Frédéric's doctor, Jean-Paul Milanese, wrote in a letter to a child-welfare judge, "We find ourselves confronted with a young runaway teen, mute, having broken with his former life."

On a piece of paper, Bourdin scribbled what he wanted most: "A home and a school. That's all."

When doctors started to unravel his past, a few months later, Bourdin confessed his real identity and moved on. "I would rather leave on my own than be taken away," he told me. During his career as an impostor, Bourdin often voluntarily disclosed the truth, as if the attention that came from exposure were as thrilling as the con itself.

On June 13, 1992, after he had posed as more than a dozen fictional children, Bourdin turned eighteen, becoming a legal adult. "I'd been in shelters and foster homes most of my life, and suddenly I was told, 'That's it. You're free to go,' " he recalls. "How could I become something I could not imagine?" In November, 1993, posing as a mute child, he lay down in the middle of a street in the French town of Auch and was taken by firemen to a hospital. *La Dépêche du Midi*, a local newspaper, ran a story about him, asking, "Where does this mute adolescent . . . come from?" The next day, the paper published another article, under the headline "THE MUTE ADOLESCENT WHO APPEARED OUT OF NOWHERE HAS STILL NOT REVEALED HIS SECRET." After fleeing, he was caught attempting a similar ruse nearby and admitted that he was Frédéric Bourdin. "THE MUTE OF AUCH SPEAKS FOUR LANGUAGES," *La Dépêche du Midi* proclaimed.

As Bourdin assumed more and more identities, he attempted to kill off his real one. One day, the mayor of Mouchamps received a call from the "German police" notifying him that Bourdin's body had been found in Munich. When Bourdin's mother was told the news, she recalls, "My heart stopped." Members of Bourdin's family waited for a coffin to arrive, but it never did. "It was Frédéric playing one of his cruel games," his mother says.

By the mid-nineties, Bourdin had accumulated a criminal record for lying to police and magistrates, and Interpol and other authorities were increasingly on the lookout for him. His activities were also garnering media attention. In 1995, the producers of a popular French television show called "Everything Is Possible" invited him on the program. As Bourdin appeared onstage, looking pale and prepubescent, the host teasingly asked the audience, "What's this boy's name? Michael, Jürgen, Kevin, or Pedro? What's his real age—thirteen, fourteen, fifteen?" Pressed about his motivations, Bourdin again insisted that all he wanted was love and a family. It was the same rationale he always gave, and, as a result, he was the rare impostor who elicited sympathy as well as anger from those he had duped. (His mother has a less charitable interpretation of her son's stated motive: "He wants to justify what he has become.")

The producers of "Everything Is Possible" were so affected by his story that they offered him a job in the station's newsroom, but he soon ran off to create more "interior fictions," as one of the producers later told a reporter. At times, Bourdin's deceptions were viewed in existential terms. One of his devotees in France created a Web site that celebrated his shape-shifting, hailing him as an "actor of life and an apostle of a new philosophy of human identity."

One day when I was visiting Bourdin, he described how he transformed himself into a child. Like the impostors he had seen in films such as "Catch Me If You Can," he tried to elevate his criminality into an "art." First, he said, he conceived of a child whom he wanted to play. Then he gradually mapped out the character's biography, from his heritage to his family to his tics. "The key is actually not lying about everything," Bourdin said. "Otherwise, you'll just mix things up." He said that he adhered to maxims such as "Keep it simple" and "A good liar uses the truth." In choosing a name, he preferred one that carried a deep association in his memory, like Cassis. "The one thing you better not forget is your name," he said.

He compared what he did to being a spy: you changed superficial details while keeping your core intact. This approach not only made it easier to convince people; it allowed him to protect a part of his self, to hold on to some moral center. "I know I can be cruel, but I don't want to become a monster," he said.

Once he had imagined a character, he fashioned a commensurate appearance—meticulously shaving his face, plucking his eyebrows, using hair-removal creams. He often put on baggy pants and a shirt with long sleeves that swallowed his wrists, emphasizing his smallness. Peering in a mirror, he asked himself if others would see what he wanted them to see. "The worst thing you can do is deceive yourself," he said.

When he honed an identity, it was crucial to find some element of the character that he shared—a technique employed by many actors. "People always say to me, 'Why don't you become an actor?' " he told me. "I think I would be a very good actor, like Arnold Schwarzenegger or Sylvester Stallone. But I don't want to play somebody. I want to be somebody."

In order to help ease his character into the real world, he fostered the illusion among local authorities that his character actually existed. As he had done in Orthez, he would call a hot line and claim to have seen the character in a perilous situation. The authorities were less likely to grill a child who appeared to be in distress. If someone noticed that Bourdin looked oddly mature, however, he did not object. "A teen-ager wants to look older," he said. "I treat it like a compliment."

Though he emphasized his cunning, he acknowledged what any con man knows but rarely admits: it is not that hard to fool people. People have basic expectations of others' behavior and are rarely on guard for someone to subvert them. By playing on some primal need—vanity, greed, loneliness—men like Bourdin make their mark further suspend disbelief. As a result, most cons are filled with logical inconsistencies, even absurdities, which seem humiliatingly obvious after the fact. Bourdin, who generally tapped into a mark's sense of goodness rather than into some darker urge, says, "Nobody expects a seemingly vulnerable child to be lying."

In October, 1997, Bourdin told me, he was at a youth home in Linares, Spain. A child-welfare judge who was handling his case had given him twenty-four hours to prove that he was a teen-ager; otherwise, she would take his fingerprints, which were on file with Interpol. Bourdin knew that, as an adult with a criminal record, he would likely face prison. He had already tried to run away once and was caught, and the staff was keeping an eye on his whereabouts. And so he did something that both stretched the bounds of credulity and threatened to transform him into the kind of "monster" that he had insisted he never wanted to become. Rather than invent an identity, he stole one. He assumed the persona of a missing sixteen-year-old boy from Texas. Bourdin, now twenty-three, not only had to convince the authorities that he was an American child; he had to convince the missing boy's family.

According to Bourdin, the plan came to him in the middle of the night: if he could fool the judge into thinking that he was an American, he might be let go. He asked permission to use the telephone in the shelter's office and called the National Center for Missing and Exploited Children, in Alexandria, Virginia, trolling for a real identity. Speaking in English, which he had picked up during his travels, he claimed that his name was Jonathan Durean and that he was a director of the Linares shelter. He said that a frightened child had turned up who would not disclose his identity but who spoke English with an American accent. Bourdin offered a description of the boy that matched himself—short, slight, prominent chin, brown hair, a gap between his teeth—and asked if the center had anyone similar in its database. After searching, Bourdin recalls, a woman at the center said that the boy might be Nicholas Barclay, who had been reported missing in San Antonio on June 13, 1994, at the age of thirteen. Barclay was last seen, according to his file, wearing "a white T-shirt, purple pants, black tennis shoes and carrying a pink backpack."

Adopting a skeptical tone, Bourdin says, he asked if the center could send any more information that it had regarding Barclay. The woman said that she would mail overnight Barclay's missing-person flyer and immediately fax a copy as well. After giving her the fax number in the office he was borrowing, Bourdin says, he hung up and waited. Peeking out the door, he looked to see if anyone was coming. The hallway was dark and quiet, but he could hear footsteps. At last, a copy of the flyer emerged from the fax machine. The printout was so faint that most of it was illegible. Still, the photograph's resemblance to him did not seem that far off. "I can do this," Bourdin recalls thinking. He quickly called back the center, he says, and told the woman, "I have some good news. Nicholas Barclay is standing right beside me."

Elated, she gave him the number of the officer in the San Antonio Police Department who was in charge of the investigation. This time pretending to be a Spanish policeman, Bourdin says, he phoned the officer and, mentioning details about Nicholas that he had learned from the woman at the center—such as the pink backpack—declared that the missing child had been found. The officer said that he would contact the F.B.I. and the U.S. Embassy in Madrid. Bourdin had not fully contemplated what he was about to unleash.

The next day at the Linares shelter, Bourdin intercepted a package from the National Center for Missing and Exploited Children addressed to Jonathan Durean. He ripped open the envelope. Inside was a clean copy of Nicholas Barclay's missing-person flyer. It showed a color photograph of a small, fair-skinned boy with blue eyes and brown hair so light that it appeared almost blond. The flyer listed several identifying features, including a cross tattooed between Barclay's right index finger and thumb. Bourdin stared at the picture and said to himself, "I'm dead." Not only did Bourdin not have the same tattoo; his eyes and hair were dark brown. In haste, he burned the flyer in the shelter's courtyard, then went into the bathroom and bleached his hair. Finally, he had a friend, using a needle and ink from a pen, give him a makeshift tattoo resembling Barclay's.

Still, there was the matter of Bourdin's eyes. He tried to conceive of a story that would explain his appearance. What if he had been abducted by a child sex ring and flown to Europe, where he had been tortured and abused, even experimented on? Yes, that could explain the eyes. His kidnappers had injected his pupils with chemicals. He had lost his Texas accent because, for more than three years of captivity, he had been forbidden to speak English. He had escaped from a locked room in a house in Spain when a guard carelessly left the door open. It was a crazy tale, one that violated his maxim to "keep it simple," but it would have to do.

Soon after, the phone in the office rang. Bourdin took the call. It was Nicholas Barclay's thirty-one-year-old half sister, Carey Gibson. "My God, Nicky, is that you?" she asked.

Bourdin didn't know how to respond. He adopted a muffled voice, then said, "Yes, it's me."

Nicholas's mother, Beverly, got on the phone. A tough, heavyset woman with a broad face and dyed-brown hair, she worked the graveyard shift at a Dunkin' Donuts in San Antonio seven nights a week. She had never married Nicholas's father and had raised Nicholas with her two older children, Carey and Jason. (She was divorced from Carey and Jason's father, though she still used her married name, Dollarhide.) A heroin addict, she had struggled during Nicholas's youth to get off drugs. After he disappeared, she had begun to use heroin again and was now addicted to methadone. Despite these difficulties, Carey says, Beverly was not a bad mother: "She was maybe the most functioning drug addict. We had nice things, a nice place, never went without food." Perhaps compensating for the instability in her life, Beverly fanatically followed a routine: working at the doughnut shop from 10 P.M. to 5 A.M., then stopping at the Make My Day Lounge to shoot pool and have a few beers, before going home to sleep. She had a hardness about her, with a cigarette-roughened voice, but people who know her also spoke to me of her kindness. After her night shift, she delivered any leftover doughnuts to a homeless shelter.

Beverly pulled the phone close to her ear. After the childlike voice on the other end said that he wanted to come home, she told me, "I was dumbfounded and blown away."

Carey, who was married and had two children of her own, had often held the family together during Beverly's struggles with drug addiction. Since Nicholas's disappearance, her mother and brother had never seemed the same, and all Carey wanted was to make the family whole again. She volunteered to go to Spain to bring Nicholas home, and the packing-and-shipping company where she worked in sales support offered to pay her fare.

When she arrived at the shelter, a few days later, accompanied by an official from the U.S. Embassy, Bourdin had secluded himself in a room. What he had done, he concedes, was evil. But if he had any moral reservations they did not stop him, and after wrapping his face in a scarf and putting on a hat and sunglasses he came out of the room. He was sure that Carey would instantly realize that he wasn't her brother. Instead, she rushed toward him and hugged him.

Carey was, in many ways, an ideal mark. "My daughter has the best heart and is so easy to manipulate," Beverly says. Carey had never travelled outside the United States, except for partying in Tijuana, and was unfamiliar with European accents and with Spain. After Nicholas disappeared, she had often watched television news programs about lurid child abductions. In addition to feeling the pressure of having received money from her company to make the trip, she had the burden of deciding, as her family's representative, whether this was her long-lost brother.

Though Bourdin referred to her as "Carey" rather than "sis," as Nicholas always had, and though he had a trace of a French accent, Carey says that she had little doubt that it was Nicholas. Not when he could attribute any inconsistencies to his unspeakable ordeal. Not when his nose now looked so much like her uncle Pat's. Not when he had the same tattoo as Nicholas and seemed to know so many details about her family, asking about relatives by name. "Your heart takes over and you want to believe," Carey says.

She showed Bourdin photographs of the family and he studied each one: this is my mother; this is my half brother; this is my grandfather.

Neither American nor Spanish officials raised any questions once Carey had vouched for him. Nicholas had been gone for only three years, and the F.B.I. was not primed to be suspicious of someone claiming to be a missing child. (The agency told me that, to its knowledge, it had never worked on a case like Bourdin's before.) According to authorities in Madrid, Carey swore under oath that Bourdin was her brother and an American citizen. He was granted a U.S. passport and, the next day, he was on a flight to San Antonio.

For a moment, Bourdin fantasized that he was about to become part of a real family, but halfway to America he began to "freak out," as Carey puts it, trembling and sweating. As she tried to comfort him, he told her that he thought the plane was going to crash, which, he later said, is what he wanted: how else could he escape from what he had done?

When the plane landed, on October 18, 1997, members of Nicholas's family were waiting for him at the airport. Bourdin recognized them from Carey's photographs: Beverly, Nicholas's mother; Carey's then husband, Bryan Gibson; Bryan and Carey's fourteen-year-old son, Codey, and their ten-year-old daughter, Chantel. Only Nicholas's brother, Jason, who was a recovering drug addict and living in San Antonio, was absent. A friend of the family videotaped the reunion, and Bourdin can be seen bundled up, his hat pulled down, his brown eyes shielded by sunglasses, his already fading tattoo covered by gloves. Though Bourdin had thought that Nicholas's relatives were going to "hang" him, they rushed to embrace him, saying how much they had missed him. "We were all just emotionally crazy," Codey recalls. Nicholas's mother, however, hung back. "She just didn't seem excited" the way you'd expect from someone "seeing her son," Chantel told me.

Bourdin wondered if Beverly doubted that he was Nicholas, but eventually she, too, greeted him. They all got in Carey's Lincoln Town Car and stopped at McDonald's for cheeseburgers and fries. As Carey recalls it, "He was just sitting by my mom, talking to my son," saying how much "he missed school and asking when he'd see Jason."

Bourdin went to stay with Carey and Bryan rather than live with Beverly. "I work nights and didn't think it was good to leave him alone," Beverly said. Carey and Bryan owned a trailer home in a desolate wooded area in Spring Branch, thirty-five miles north of San Antonio, and Bourdin stared out the window as the car wound along a dirt road, past rusted trucks on cinder blocks and dogs barking at the sound of the engine. As Codey puts it, "We didn't have no Internet, or stuff like that. You can walk all the way to San Antonio before you get any kind of communication."

Their cramped trailer home was not exactly the vision of America that Bourdin had imagined from movies. He shared a room with Codey, and slept on a foam mattress on the floor. Bourdin knew that, if he were to become Nicholas and to continue to fool even his family, he had to learn everything about him, and he began to mine information, secretly rummaging through drawers and picture albums, and watching home videos. When Bourdin discovered a detail about Nicholas's past from one family member, he would repeat it to another. He pointed out, for example, that Bryan once got mad at Nicholas for knocking Codey out of a tree. "He knew that story," Codey recalls, still amazed by the amount of intelligence that Bourdin acquired about the family. Beverly noticed that Bourdin knelt in front of the television, just as Nicholas had. Various members of the family told me that when Bourdin seemed more standoffish than Nicholas or spoke with a strange accent they assumed that it was because of the terrible treatment that he said he had suffered.

As Bourdin came to inhabit the life of Nicholas, he was struck by what he considered to be uncanny similarities between them. Nicholas had been reported missing on Bourdin's birthday. Both came from poor, broken families; Nicholas had almost no relationship with his father, who for a long time didn't know that Nicholas was his son. Nicholas was a sweet, lonely, combustible kid who craved attention and was often in trouble at school. He had been caught stealing a pair of tennis shoes, and his mother had planned to put him in a youth home. ("I couldn't handle him," Beverly recalls. "I couldn't control him.") When Nicholas was young, he was a diehard Michael Jackson fan who had collected all the singer's records and even owned a red leather jacket like the one Jackson wears in his "Thriller" video.

According to Beverly, Bourdin quickly "blended in." He was enrolled in high school and did his homework each night, chastising Codey when he failed to study. He played Nintendo with Codey and watched movies with the family on satellite TV. When he saw Beverly, he hugged her and said, "Hi, Mom." Occasionally on Sundays, he attended church with other members of the family. "He was really nice," Chantel recalls. "Really friendly." Once, when Carey was shooting a home movie of Bourdin, she asked him what he was thinking. "It's really good to have my family and be home again," he replied.

On November 1st, not long after Bourdin had settled into his new home, Charlie Parker, a private investigator, was sitting in his office in San Antonio. The room was crammed with hidden cameras that he deployed in the field: one was attached to a pair of eyeglasses, another was lodged inside a fountain pen, and a third was concealed on the handlebars of a ten-speed bicycle. On a wall hung a photograph that Parker had taken during a stakeout: it showed a married woman with her lover, peeking out of an apartment window. Parker, who had been hired by the woman's husband, called it the "money shot."

Parker's phone rang. It was a television producer from the tabloid show "Hard Copy," who had heard about the extraordinary return of sixteen-year-old Nicholas Barclay and wanted to hire Parker to help investigate the kidnapping. He agreed to take the job.

With silver hair and a raspy voice, Parker, who was then in his late fifties, appeared to have stepped out of a dime novel. When he bought himself a bright-red Toyota convertible, he said to friends, "How ya like that for an old man?" Though Parker had always dreamed about being a P.I., he had only recently become one, having spent thirty years selling lumber and building materials. In 1994, Parker met a San Antonio couple whose twenty-nine-year-old daughter had been raped and fatally stabbed. The case was unsolved, and he began investigating the crime each night after coming home from work. When he discovered that a recently paroled murderer had lived next door to the victim, Parker staked out the man's house, peering out from a white van through infrared goggles. The suspect was soon arrested and ultimately convicted of the murder. Captivated by the experience, Parker formed a "murders club," dedicated to solving cold cases. (Its members included a college psychology professor, a lawyer, and a fry cook.) Within months, the club had uncovered evidence that helped to convict a member of the Air Force who had strangled a fourteen-year-old girl. In 1995, Parker received his license as a private investigator, and he left his life in the lumber business behind.

After Parker spoke with the "Hard Copy" producer, he easily traced Nicholas Barclay to Carey and Bryan's trailer. On November 6th, Parker arrived there with a producer and a camera crew. The family didn't want

Bourdin to speak to reporters. "I'm a very private person," Carey says. But Bourdin, who had been in the country for nearly three weeks, agreed to talk. "I wanted the attention at the time," he says. "It was a psychological need. Today, I wouldn't do it."

Parker stood off to one side, listening intently as the young man relayed his harrowing story. "He was calm as a cucumber," Parker told me. "No looking down, no body language. None." But Parker was puzzled by his curious accent.

Parker spied a photograph on a shelf of Nicholas Barclay as a young boy, and kept looking at it and at the person in front of him, thinking that something was amiss. Having once read that ears are distinct, like fingerprints, he went up to the cameraman and whispered, "Zoom in on his ears. Get 'em as close as you can."

Parker slipped the photograph of Nicholas Barclay into his pocket, and after the interview he hurried back to his office and used a scanner to transfer the photo to his computer; he then studied video from the "Hard Copy" interview. Parker zeroed in on the ears in both pictures. "The ears were close, but they didn't match," he says.

Parker called several ophthalmologists and asked if eyes could be changed from blue to brown by injecting chemicals. The doctors said no. Parker also phoned a dialect expert at Trinity University, in San Antonio, who told him that, even if someone had been held in captivity for three years, he would quickly regain his native accent.

Parker passed his suspicions on to the authorities, even though the San Antonio police had declared that "the boy who came back claiming to be Nicholas Barclay is Nicholas Barclay." Fearing that a dangerous stranger was living with Nicholas's family, Parker phoned Beverly and told her what he had discovered. As he recalls the conversation, he said, "It's not him, ma'am. It's not him."

"What do you mean, it's not him?" she asked.

Parker explained about the ears and the eyes and the accent. In his files, Parker wrote, "Family is upset but maintains that they believe it is their son."

Parker says that a few days later he received an angry call from Bourdin. Although Bourdin denies that he made the call, Parker noted in his file at the time that Bourdin said, "Who do you think you are?" When

Parker replied that he didn't believe he was Nicholas, Bourdin shot back, "Immigration thinks it's me. The family thinks it's me."

Parker wondered if he should let the matter go. He had tipped off the authorities and was no longer under contract to investigate the matter. He had other cases piling up. And he figured that a mother would know her own son. Still, the boy's accent sounded French, maybe French Moroccan. If so, what was a foreigner doing infiltrating a trailer home in the back-woods of Texas? "I thought he was a terrorist, I swear to God," Parker says.

Beverly rented a small room in a run-down apartment complex in San Antonio, and Parker started to follow Bourdin when he visited her. "I'd set up on the apartment, and watch him come out," Parker says. "He would walk all the way to the bus stop, wearing his Walkman and doing his Michael Jackson moves."

Bourdin was struggling to stay in character. He found living with Carey and Beverly "claustrophobic," and was happiest when he was out-side, wandering the streets. "I was not used to being in someone else's fam-ily, to live with them like I'm one of theirs," he says. "I wasn't ready for it." One day, Carey and the family presented him with a cardboard box. Inside were Nicholas's baseball cards, records, and various mementos. He picked up each item, gingerly. There was a letter from one of Nicholas's girl-friends. As he read it, he said to himself, "I'm not this boy."

After two months in the United States, Bourdin started to come apart. He was moody and aloof—"weirding out," as Codey put it. He stopped attending classes (one student tauntingly said that he sounded "like a Nor-wegian") and was consequently suspended. In December, he took off in Bryan and Carey's car and drove to Oklahoma, with the windows down, listening to Michael Jackson's song "Scream": "Tired of the schemes / The lies are disgusting . . . / Somebody please have mercy / 'Cause I just can't take it." The police pulled him over for speeding, and he was arrested. Bev-erly, Carey, and Bryan picked him up at the police station and brought him home.

According to his real mother, Ghislaine, Bourdin called her in Europe. For all his disagreements with his mother, Bourdin still seemed to long for her. (He once wrote her a letter, saying, "I don't want to lose you. . . . If you disappear then I disappear.") Ghislaine says Bourdin confided that he was living with a woman in Texas who believed that he was her son. She became so upset that she hung up.

Shortly before Christmas, Bourdin went into the bathroom and looked at himself in the mirror—at his brown eyes, his dyed hair. He grabbed a razor and began to mutilate his face. He was put in the psychiatric ward of a local hospital for several days of observation. Later, Bourdin, paraphrasing Nietzsche, wrote in a notebook, "When you fight monsters, be careful that in the process you do not become one." He also jotted down a poem: "My days are phantom days, each one the shadow of a hope; / My real life never was begun, / Nor any of my real deeds done."

Doctors judged Bourdin to be stable enough to return to Carey's trailer. But he remained disquieted, and increasingly wondered what had happened to the real Nicholas Barclay. So did Parker, who, while trying to identify Bourdin, had started to gather information and interview Nicholas's neighbors. At the time that Nicholas disappeared, he was living with Beverly in a small one-story house in San Antonio. Nicholas's half brother, Jason, who was then twenty-four, had recently moved in with them after living for a period with his cousin, in Utah. Jason was wiry and strong, with long brown curly hair and a comb often tucked in the back pocket of his jeans. He had burn marks on his body and face: at thirteen, he had lit a cigarette after filling a lawn mower with gasoline and accidentally set himself on fire. Because of his scars, Carey says, "Jason worried that he would never meet somebody and he would always be alone." He strummed Lynyrd Skynyrd songs on his guitar and was a capable artist who sketched portraits of friends. Though he had only completed high school, he was bright and articulate. He also had an addictive personality, like his mother, often drinking heavily and using cocaine. He had his "demons," as Carey put it.

On June 13, 1994, Beverly and Jason told police that Nicholas had been playing basketball three days earlier and called his house from a pay phone, wanting a ride home. Beverly was sleeping, so Jason answered the phone. He told Nicholas to walk home. Nicholas never made it. Because Nicholas had recently fought with his mother over the tennis shoes he had stolen, and over the possibility of being sent to a home for juveniles, the police initially thought that he had run away—even though he hadn't taken any money or possessions.

Parker was surprised by police reports showing that after Nicholas's disappearance there were several disturbances at Beverly's house. On July 12th, she called the police, though when an officer arrived she insisted that she was all right. Jason told the officer that his mother was "drinking and scream[ing] at him because her other son ran away." A few weeks later, Beverly called the police again, about what authorities described as "family violence." The officer on the scene reported that Beverly and Jason were "exchanging words"; Jason was asked to leave the house for the day, and he complied. On September 25th, police received another call, this time from Jason. He claimed that his younger brother had returned and tried to break into the garage, fleeing when Jason spotted him. In his report, the officer on duty said that he had "checked the area" for Nicholas but was "unable to locate him."

Jason's behavior grew even more erratic. He was arrested for "using force" against a police officer, and Beverly kicked him out of the house. Nicholas's disappearance, Codey told me, had "messed Jason up pretty bad. He went on a bad drug binge and was shooting cocaine for a long time." Because he had refused to help Nicholas get a ride home on the day he vanished, Chantel says, Jason had "a lot of guilt."

In late 1996, Jason checked into a rehabilitation center and weaned himself from drugs. After he finished the program, he remained at the facility for more than a year, serving as a counsellor and working for a landscaping business that the center operated. He was still there when Bourdin turned up, claiming to be his missing brother.

Bourdin wondered why Jason had not met him at the airport and had initially made no effort to see him at Carey's. After a month and a half, Bourdin and family members say, Jason finally came for a visit. Even then, Codey says, "Jason was standoffish." Though Jason gave him a hug in front of the others, Bourdin says, he seemed to eye him warily. After a few minutes, Jason told him to come outside, and held out his hand to Bourdin. A necklace with a gold cross glittered in his palm. Jason said that it was for him. "It was like he had to give it to me," Bourdin says. Jason put it around his neck. Then he said goodbye, and never returned.

Bourdin told me, "It was clear that Jason knew what had happened to Nicholas." For the first time, Bourdin began to wonder who was conning whom.

The authorities, meanwhile, had started to doubt Bourdin's story. Nancy Fisher, who at the time was a veteran F.B.I. agent, had interviewed Bourdin several weeks after he arrived in the United States, in order to document his allegations of being kidnapped on American soil. Immediately, she told me, she "smelled a rat": "His hair was dark but bleached blond and the roots were quite obvious."

Parker knew Fisher and had shared with her his own suspicions. Fisher warned Parker not to interfere with a federal probe, but as they conducted parallel investigations they developed a sense of trust, and Parker passed on any information he obtained. When Fisher made inquiries into who may have abducted Nicholas and sexually abused him, she says, she found Beverly oddly "surly and uncooperative."

Fisher wondered whether Beverly and her family simply wanted to believe that Bourdin was their loved one. Whatever the family's motivations, Fisher's main concern was the mysterious figure who had entered the United States. She knew that it was impossible for him to have altered his eye color. In November, under the pretext of getting Bourdin treatment for his alleged abuse, Fisher took him to see a forensic psychiatrist in Houston, who concluded from his syntax and grammar that he could not be American, and was most likely French or Spanish. The F.B.I. shared the results with Beverly and Carey, Fisher says, but they insisted that he was Nicholas.

Believing that Bourdin was a spy, Fisher says, she contacted the Central Intelligence Agency, explaining the potential threat and asking for help in identifying him. "The C.I.A. wouldn't assist me," she says. "I was told by a C.I.A. agent that until you can prove he's European we can't help you."

Fisher tried to persuade Beverly and Bourdin to give blood samples for a DNA test. Both refused. "Beverly said, 'How dare you say he's not my son,'" Fisher recalls. In the middle of February, four months after Bourdin arrived in the United States, Fisher obtained warrants to force them to cooperate. "I go to her house to get a blood sample, and she lies on the floor and says she's not going to get up," Fisher says. "I said, 'Yes, you are.' "

"Beverly defended me," Bourdin says. "She did her best to stop them."

Along with their blood, Fisher obtained Bourdin's fingerprints, which she sent to the State Department to see if there was a match with Interpol.

Carey, worried about her supposed brother's self-mutilation and instability, was no longer willing to let him stay with her, and he went to live with Beverly in her apartment. By then, Bourdin claims, he had begun to look at the family differently. His mind retraced a series of curious interactions: Beverly's cool greeting at the airport, Jason's delay in visiting him. He says that, although Carey and Bryan had seemed intent on believing that he was Nicholas—ignoring the obvious evidence—Beverly had treated him less like a son than like a "ghost." One time when he was staying with her, Bourdin alleges, she got drunk and screamed, "I know that God punished me by sending you to me. I don't know who the hell you are. Why the fuck are you doing this?" (Beverly does not remember such an incident but says, "He must have got me pissed off.")

On March 5, 1998, with the authorities closing in on Bourdin, Beverly called Parker and said she believed that Bourdin was an impostor. The next morning, Parker took him to a diner. "I raise my pants so he can see I'm not wearing a gun" in his ankle holster, Parker says. "I want him to relax."

They ordered hotcakes. After nearly five months of pretending to be Nicholas Barclay, Bourdin says, he was psychically frayed. According to Parker, when he told "Nicholas" that he had upset his "mother," the young man blurted out, "She's not my mother, and you know it."

"You gonna tell me who you are?"

"I'm Frédéric Bourdin and I'm wanted by Interpol."

After a few minutes, Parker went to the men's room and called Nancy Fisher with the news. She had just received the same information from Interpol. "We're trying to get a warrant right now," she told Parker. "Stall him."

Parker went back to the table and continued to talk to Bourdin. As Bourdin spoke about his itinerant life in Europe, Parker says, he felt some guilt for turning him in. Bourdin, who despises Parker and disputes the details of their conversation, accuses the detective of "pretending" to have solved the case; it was as if Parker had intruded into Bourdin's interior fiction and given himself a starring role. After about an hour, Parker drove Bourdin back to Beverly's apartment. As Parker was pulling away, Fisher and the authorities were already descending on him. He surrendered quietly. "I knew I was Frédéric Bourdin again," he says. Beverly reacted less calmly. She turned and yelled at Fisher, "What took you so long?"

In custody, Bourdin told a story that seemed as fanciful as his tale of being Nicholas Barclay. He alleged that Beverly and Jason may have been complicit in Nicholas's disappearance, and that they had known from the outset that Bourdin was lying. "I'm a good impostor, but I'm not that good," Bourdin told me.

Of course, the authorities could not rely on the account of a known pathological liar. "He tells ninety-nine lies and maybe the one hundredth is the truth, but you don't know," Fisher says. Yet the authorities had their own suspicions. Jack Stick, who was a federal prosecutor at the time and who later served a term in the Texas House of Representatives, was assigned Bourdin's case. He and Fisher wondered why Beverly had resisted attempts by the F.B.I. to investigate Bourdin's purported kidnapping and, later, to uncover his deception. They also questioned why she had not taken Bourdin back to live with her. According to Fisher, Carey told her that it was because it was "too upsetting" for Beverly, which, at least to Fisher and Stick, seemed strange. "You'd be so happy to have your child back," Fisher says. It was "another red flag."

Fisher and Stick took note of the disturbances in Beverly's house after Nicholas had vanished, and the police report stating that Beverly was screaming at Jason over Nicholas's disappearance. Then there was Jason's claim that he had witnessed Nicholas breaking into the house. No evidence could be found to back up this startling story, and Jason had made the claim at the time that the police had started "sniffing around," as Stick put it. He and Fisher suspected that the story was a ruse meant to reinforce the idea that Nicholas was a runaway.

Stick and Fisher began to edge toward a homicide investigation. "I wanted to know what had happened to that little kid," Stick recalls.

Stick and Fisher gathered more evidence suggesting that Beverly's home was prone to violence. They say that officials at Nicholas's school had expressed concern that Nicholas might be an abused child, owing to bruises on his body, and that just before he disappeared the officials had alerted child-protective services. And neighbors noted that Nicholas had sometimes hit Beverly.

One day, Fisher asked Beverly to take a polygraph. Carey recalls, "I said, 'Mom, do whatever they ask you to do. Go take the lie-detector test. You didn't kill Nicholas.' So she did."

While Beverly was taking the polygraph, Fisher watched the proceedings on a video monitor in a nearby room. The most important question was whether Beverly currently knew the whereabouts of Nicholas. She said no, twice. The polygraph examiner told Fisher that Beverly had seemingly answered truthfully. When Fisher expressed disbelief, the examiner said that if Beverly was lying, she had to be on drugs. After a while, the examiner administered the test again, at which point the effects of any possible narcotics, including methadone, might have worn off. This time, when the examiner asked if Beverly knew Nicholas's whereabouts, Fisher says, the machine went wild, indicating a lie. "She blew the instruments practically off the table," Fisher says. (False positives are not uncommon in polygraphs, and scientists dispute their basic reliability.)

According to Fisher, when the examiner told Beverly that she had failed the exam, and began pressing her with more questions, Beverly yelled, "I don't have to put up with this," then got up and ran out the door. "I catch her," Fisher recalls. "I say, 'Why are you running?' She is furious. She says, 'This is so typical of Nicholas. Look at the hell he's putting me through.' "

Fisher next wanted to interview Jason, but he resisted. When he finally agreed to meet her, several weeks after Bourdin had been arrested, Fisher says, she had to "pull words out of him." They spoke about the fact that he had not gone to see his alleged brother for nearly two months: "I said, 'Here's your brother, long gone, kidnapped, and aren't you eager to see him?' He said, 'Well, no.' I said, 'Did he look like your brother to you?' 'Well, I guess.' " Fisher found his responses grudging, and developed a "very strong suspicion that Jason had participated in the disappearance of his brother." Stick, too, believed that Jason either had been "involved in Nicholas's disappearance or had information that could tell us what had happened." Fisher even suspected that Beverly knew what had happened to Nicholas, and may have helped cover up the crime in order to protect Jason.

After the interview, Stick and Fisher say, Jason refused to speak to the authorities again without a lawyer or unless he was under arrest. But Parker, who as a private investigator was not bound by the same legal restrictions as Stick and Fisher, continued to press Jason. On one occasion, he accused him of murder. "I think you did it," Parker says he told him. "I don't think you meant to do it, but you did." In response, Parker says, "He just looked at me."

Several weeks after Fisher and Parker questioned Jason, Parker was driving through downtown San Antonio and saw Beverly on the sidewalk. He asked her if she wanted a ride. When she got in, she told him that Jason had died of an overdose of cocaine. Parker, who knew that Jason had been off drugs for more than a year, says that he asked if she thought he had taken his life on purpose. She said, "I don't know." Stick, Fisher, and Parker suspect that it was a suicide.

Since the loss of her sons, Beverly has stopped using drugs and moved out to Spring Branch, where she lives in a trailer, helping a woman care for her severely handicapped daughter. She agreed to talk with me about the authorities' suspicions. At first, Beverly said that I could drive out to meet her, but later she told me that the woman she worked for did not want visitors, so we spoke by phone. One of her vocal cords had recently become paralyzed, deepening her already low and gravelly voice. Parker, who had frequently chatted with her at the doughnut shop, had told me, "I don't know why I liked her, but I did. She had this thousand yard stare. She looked like someone whose life had taken everything out of her."

Beverly answered my questions forthrightly. At the airport, she said, she had hung back because Bourdin "looked odd." She added, "If I went with my gut, I would have known right away." She admitted that she had taken drugs—"probably" heroin, methadone, and alcohol—before the polygraph exam. "When they accused me, I freaked out," she said. "I worked my ass off to raise my kids. Why would I do something to my kids?" She continued, "I'm not a violent person. They didn't talk to any of my friends or associates. . . . It was just a shot in the dark, to see if I'd admit something." She also said of herself, "I'm the world's worst liar. I can't lie worth crap."

I asked her if Jason had hurt Nicholas. She paused for a moment, then said that she didn't think so. She acknowledged that when Jason did cocaine he became "totally wacko—a completely different person—and it was scary." He even beat up his father once, she said. But she noted that Jason had not been a serious addict until after Nicholas disappeared. She agreed with the authorities on one point: she placed little credence in Jason's reported sighting of Nicholas after he disappeared. "Jason was having problems at that time," she said. "I just don't believe Nicholas came there."

As we spoke, I asked several times how she could have believed for nearly five months that a twenty-three-year-old Frenchman with dyed hair, brown eyes, and a European accent was her son. "We just kept making excuses—that he's different because of all this ugly stuff that had happened," she said. She and Carey wanted it to be him so badly. It was only after he came to live with her that she had doubts. "He just didn't act like my son," Beverly said. "I couldn't bond with him. I just didn't have that feeling. My heart went out for him, but not like a mother's would. The kid's a mess and it's sad, and I wouldn't wish that on anybody."

Beverly's experience, as incredible as it is, does have a precursor—an incident that has been described as one of "the strangest cases in the annals of police history." (It is the basis of a Clint Eastwood movie, "Changeling.") On March 10, 1928, a nine-year-old boy named Walter Collins disappeared in Los Angeles. Six months later, after a nationwide manhunt, a boy showed up claiming that he was Walter and insisting that he had been kidnapped. The police were certain that he was Walter, and a family friend testified that "things the boy said and did would convince anybody" that he was the missing child. When Walter's mother, Christine, went to retrieve her son, however, she did not think it was him. Although the authorities and friends persuaded her to take him home, she brought the boy back to a police station after a few days, insisting, "This is not my son." She later testified, "His teeth were different, his voice was different. . . . His ears were smaller." The authorities thought that she must be suffering emotional distress from her son's disappearance, and had her institutionalized in a psychiatric ward. Even then, she refused to budge. As she told a police captain,

"One thing a mother ought to know was the identity of her child." Eight days later, she was released. Evidence soon emerged that her son was likely murdered by a serial killer, and the boy claiming to be her son confessed that he was an eleven-year-old runaway from Iowa who, in his words, thought that it was "fun to be somebody you aren't."

Speaking of the Bourdin case, Fisher said that one thing was certain: "Beverly had to know that wasn't her son."

After several months of investigation, Stick determined that there was no evidence to charge anyone with Nicholas's disappearance. There were no witnesses, no DNA. The authorities could not even say whether Nicholas was dead. Stick concluded that Jason's overdose had all but "precluded the possibility" that the authorities could determine what had happened to Nicholas.

On September 9, 1998, Frédéric Bourdin stood in a San Antonio courtroom and pleaded guilty to perjury, and to obtaining and possessing false documents. This time, his claim that he was merely seeking love elicited outrage. Carey, who had a nervous breakdown after Bourdin was arrested, testified before his sentencing, saying, "He has lied, and lied, and lied again. And to this day he continues to lie. He bears no remorse." Stick denounced Bourdin as a "flesh-eating bacteria," and the judge compared what Bourdin had done—giving a family the hope that their lost child was alive and then shattering it—to murder.

The only person who seemed to have any sympathy for Bourdin was Beverly. She said at the time, "I feel sorry for him. You know, we got to know him, and this kid has been through hell. He has a lot of nervous habits." She told me, "He did a lot of things that took a lot of guts, if you think about it."

The judge sentenced Bourdin to six years—more than three times what was recommended under the sentencing guidelines. Bourdin told the courtroom, "I apologize to all the people in my past, for what I have done. I wish, I wish that you believe me, but I know it's impossible." Whether he was in jail or not, he added, "I am a prisoner of myself."

When I last saw Bourdin, in the spring of 2008, his life had undergone perhaps its most dramatic transformation. He had married a Frenchwoman, Isabelle, whom he had met two years earlier. In her late twenties, Isabelle was slim and pretty and soft-spoken. She was studying to be a lawyer. A victim of family abuse, she had seen Bourdin on television, describing his own abuse and his quest for love, and she had been so moved that she eventually tracked him down. "I told him what interests me in his life wasn't the way he bent the truth but why he did that and the things that he looked for," she said.

Bourdin says that when Isabelle first approached him he thought it must be a joke, but they met in Paris and gradually fell in love. He said that he had never been in a relationship before. "I've always been a wall," he said. "A cold wall." On August 8, 2007, after a year of courtship, they got married at the town hall of a village outside Pau.

Bourdin's mother says that Frédéric invited her and his grandfather to the ceremony, but they didn't go. "No one believed him," she says.

When I saw Isabelle, she was nearly eight months pregnant. Hoping to avoid public attention, she and Frédéric had relocated to Le Mans, and they had moved into a small one-bedroom apartment in an old stone building with wood floors and a window that overlooked a prison. "It reminds me of where I've been," Bourdin said. A box containing the pieces of a crib lay on the floor of the sparsely decorated living room. Bourdin's hair was now cropped, and he was dressed without flamboyance, in jeans and a sweatshirt. He told me that he had got a job in telemarketing. Given his skills at persuasion, he was unusually good at it. "Let's just say I'm a natural," he said.

Most of his family believes that all these changes are merely part of another role, one that will end disastrously for his wife and baby. "You can't just invent yourself as a father," his uncle Jean-Luc Drouart said. "You're not a dad for six days or six months. It is not a character—it is a reality." He added, "I fear for that child."

Bourdin's mother, Ghislaine, says that her son is a "liar and will never change."

After so many years of playing an impostor, Bourdin has left his family and many authorities with the conviction that this is who Frédéric Pierre Bourdin really is: he *is* a chameleon. Within months of being released from prison in the United States and deported to France, in October, 2003, Bourdin resumed playing a child. He even stole the identity of a fourteen-year-old missing French boy named Léo Balley, who had vanished almost eight years earlier, on a camping trip. This time, police did a DNA test that quickly revealed that Bourdin was lying. A psychiatrist who evaluated him concluded, "The prognosis seems more than worrying. . . . We are very pessimistic about modifying these personality traits." (Bourdin, while in prison in America, began reading psychology texts, and jotted down in his journal the following passage: "When confronted with his misconduct the psychopath has enough false sincerity and apparent remorse that he renews hope and trust among his accusers. However, after several repetitions, his convincing show is finally recognized for what it is—a show.")

Isabelle is sure that Bourdin "can change." She said, "I've seen him now for two years, and he is not that person."

At one point, Bourdin touched Isabelle's stomach. "My baby can have three arms and three legs," he said. "It doesn't matter. I don't need my child to be perfect. All I want is that this child feels love." He did not care what his family thought. "They are my shelter," he said of his wife and soon-to-be child. "No one can take that from me."

A month later, Bourdin called and told me that his wife had given birth. "It's a girl," he said. He and Isabelle had named her Athena, for the Greek goddess. "I'm really a father," he said.

I asked if he had become a new person. For a moment, he fell silent. Then he said, "No, this is who I am."

—August, 2008

True Crime

**A POSTMODERN
MURDER MYSTERY**

In the southwest corner of Poland, far from any town or city, the Oder River curls sharply, creating a tiny inlet. The banks are matted with wild grass and shrouded by towering pine and oak trees. The only people who regularly trek to the area are fishermen—the inlet teems with perch and pike and sun bass. On a cold December day in 2000, three friends were casting there when one of them noticed something floating by the shore. At first, he thought it was a log, but as he drew closer he saw what looked like hair. The fisherman shouted to one of his friends, who poked the object with his rod. It was a dead body.

The fishermen called the police, who carefully removed the corpse of a man from the water. A noose was around his neck, and his hands were bound behind his back. Part of the rope, which appeared to have been cut with a knife, had once connected his hands to his neck, binding the man in a backward cradle, an excruciating position—the slightest wiggle would have caused the noose to tighten further. There was no doubt that the man had been murdered. His body was clothed in only a sweatshirt and underwear, and it bore marks of torture. A pathologist determined that the victim had virtually no food in his intestines, which indicated that he had been starved for several days before he was killed. Initially, the police thought that he had been strangled and then dumped in the river, but an examination of fluids in his lungs revealed signs of drowning, which meant that he was probably still alive when he was dropped into the water.

The victim—tall, with long dark hair and blue eyes—seemed to match the description of a thirty-five-year-old businessman named Dariusz Janiszewski, who had lived in the city of Wroclaw, sixty miles away, and who had been reported missing by his wife nearly four weeks earlier; he had last been seen on November 13th, leaving the small advertising firm that he owned, in downtown Wroclaw. When the police summoned Janiszewski's wife to see if she could identify the body, she was too distraught to look, and so Janiszewski's mother did instead. She immediately recognized her son's flowing hair and the birthmark on his chest.

The police launched a major investigation. Scuba divers plunged into the frigid river, looking for evidence. Forensic specialists combed the forest. Dozens of associates were questioned, and Janiszewski's business records were examined. Nothing of note was found. Although Janiszewski and his wife, who had wed eight years earlier, had a brief period of trouble in their marriage, they had since reconciled and were about to adopt a child. He had no apparent debts or enemies, and no criminal record. Witnesses described him as a gentle man, an amateur guitarist who composed music for his rock band. "He was not the kind of person who would provoke fights," his wife said. "He wouldn't harm anybody."

After six months, the investigation was dropped, because of "an inability to find the perpetrator or perpetrators," as the prosecutor put it in his report. Janiszewski's family hung a cross on an oak tree near where the body was found—one of the few reminders of what the Polish press dubbed "the perfect crime."

One afternoon in the fall of 2003, Jacek Wroblewski, a thirty-eight-year-old detective in the Wroclaw police department, unlocked the safe in his office, where he stored his files, and removed a folder marked "Janiszewski." It was getting late, and most members of the department would soon be heading home, their thick wooden doors clapping shut, one after the other, in the long stone corridor of the fortresslike building, which the Germans had built in the early twentieth century, when Wroclaw was still part of Germany. (The building has underground tunnels leading to the jail and the courthouse, across the street.) Wroblewski, who preferred to work late at night, kept by his desk a coffeepot and a small refrigerator; that was about all he could squeeze into the cell-like room, which was decorated with wall-sized maps of Poland and with calendars of scantily clad women, which he took down when he had official visitors.

The Janiszewski case was three years old, and had been handed over to Wroblewski's unit by the local police who had conducted the original investigation. The unsolved murder was the coldest of cold cases, and Wroblewski was drawn to it. He was a tall, lumbering man with a pink, fleshy face and a burgeoning paunch. He wore ordinary slacks and a shirt to work, instead of a uniform, and there was a simplicity to his appearance, which he used to his advantage: people trusted him because they thought that they had no reason to fear him. Even his superiors joked that his cases must somehow solve themselves. "Jacek" is "Jack" in English, and *wróbel* means "sparrow," and so his colleagues called him Jack Sparrow—the name of the Johnny Depp character in "Pirates of the Caribbean." Wroblewski liked to say in response, "I'm more of an eagle."

After Wroblewski graduated from high school, in 1984, he began searching for his "purpose in life," as he put it, working variously as a municipal clerk, a locksmith, a soldier, an aircraft mechanic, and, in defiance of the Communist government, a union organizer allied with Solidarity. In 1994, five years after the Communist regime collapsed, he joined the newly refashioned police force. Salaries for police officers in Poland were, and remain, dismal—a rookie earns only a few thousand dollars a year—and Wroblewski had a wife and two children to support. Still, he had finally found a position that suited him. A man with a stark Catholic vision of good and evil, he relished chasing criminals, and after putting away his first murderer he hung a pair of goat horns on his office wall, to symbolize the capture of his prey. During his few free hours, he studied psychology at a local university: he wanted to understand the criminal mind.

Wroblewski had heard about the murder of Janiszewski, but he was unfamiliar with the details, and he sat down at his desk to review the file.

He knew that, in cold cases, the key to solving the crime is often an overlooked clue buried in the original file. He studied the pathologist's report and the photographs of the crime scene. The level of brutality, Wroblewski thought, suggested that the perpetrator, or perpetrators, had a deep grievance against Janiszewski. Moreover, the virtual absence of clothing on Janiszewski's battered body indicated that he had been stripped, in an attempt to humiliate him. (There was no evidence of sexual abuse.) According to Janiszewski's wife, her husband always carried credit cards, but they had not been used after the crime—another indication that this was no mere robbery.

Wroblewski read the various statements that had been given to the local police. The most revealing was from Janiszewski's mother, who had worked as a bookkeeper in his advertising firm. On the day that her son disappeared, she stated, a man had called the office at around 9:30 A.M., looking for him. The caller made an urgent request. "Could you make three signs, quite big ones, and the third one as big as a billboard?" he asked. When she inquired further, he said, "I will not talk to you about this," demanding again to speak to her son. She explained that he was out of the office, but she gave the caller Janiszewski's cell-phone number. The man hung up. He had not identified himself, and Janiszewski's mother had not recognized his voice, though she thought that he sounded "professional." During the conversation, she had heard noise in the background, a dull roar. Later, when her son showed up at the office, she asked him if the customer had called, and Janiszewski replied that they had arranged to meet that afternoon. According to a receptionist in the building, who was the last known person to see Janiszewski alive, he departed the office at around four o'clock. He left his car, a Peugeot, in the parking lot, which his family said was very unusual: although he often met with customers away from the office, he habitually took his car.

Investigators, upon checking phone records, discovered that the call to Janiszewski's office had come from a phone booth down the street—this explained the background noise, Wroblewski thought. Records also indicated that, less than a minute after the call ended, someone at the same public phone had rung Janiszewski's cell phone. Though the calls were suspicious, Wroblewski could not be certain that the caller was a perpetrator, just as he could not yet say how many assailants were involved in the crime.

Janiszewski was more than six feet tall and weighed some two hundred pounds, and tying him up and disposing of his body may have required accomplices. The receptionist reported that when Janiszewski left the office she had seen two men seemingly trailing him, though she could not describe them in any detail. Whoever was behind the abduction, Wroblewski thought, had been extremely organized and shrewd. The mastermind—Wroblewski assumed it was a man, based on the caller's voice—must have studied Janiszewski's business routine and known how to lure him out of his office and, possibly, into a car.

Wroblewski pored over the materials, trying to find something more, yet he remained stymied. After several hours, he locked the file in his safe, but over the next several days and nights he took it out again and again. At one point, he realized that Janiszewski's cell phone had never been found. Wroblewski decided to see if the phone could be traced—an unlikely possibility. Poland lagged behind other European countries in technological development, and its financially strapped police force was only beginning to adopt more sophisticated methods of tracking cellular and computer communications. Nevertheless, Wroblewski had taken a keen interest in these new techniques, and he began an elaborate search, with the help of the department's recently hired telecommunications specialist. Although Janiszewski's telephone number had not been used since his disappearance, Wroblewski knew that cell phones often bear a serial number from the manufacturer, and his men contacted Janiszewski's wife, who provided a receipt containing this information. To Wroblewski's astonishment, he and his colleague soon found a match: a cell phone with the same serial number had been sold on Allegro, an Internet auction site, four days after Janiszewski disappeared. The seller had logged in as ChrisB[7], who, investigators learned, was a thirty-year-old Polish intellectual named Krystian Bala.

It seemed inconceivable that a murderer who had orchestrated such a well-planned crime would have sold the victim's cell phone on an Internet auction site. Bala, Wroblewski realized, could have obtained it from someone else, or purchased it at a pawnshop, or even found it on the street. Bala had since moved abroad, and could not be easily reached, but as Wroblewski checked into his background he discovered that he had recently published a novel called "Amok." Wroblewski obtained a copy, which had on the cover a surreal image of a goat—an ancient symbol of the Devil. Like the works of the French novelist Michel Houellebecq, the book is sadistic, pornographic, and creepy. The main character, who narrates the story, is a bored Polish intellectual who, when not musing about philosophy, is drinking and having sex with women.

Wroblewski, who read mostly history books, was shocked by the novel's contents, which were not only decadent but vehemently anti-Church. He made note of the fact that the narrator murders a female lover for no reason ("What had come over me? What the hell did I do?") and conceals the act so well that he is never caught. Wroblewski was struck, in particular, by the killer's method: "I tightened the noose around her neck." Wroblewski then noticed something else: the killer's name is Chris, the English version of the author's first name. It was also the name that Krystian Bala had posted on the Internet auction site. Wroblewski began to read the book more closely—a hardened cop turned literary detective.

Four years earlier, in the spring of 1999, Krystian Bala sat in a café in Wroclaw, wearing a three-piece suit. He was going to be filmed for a documentary called "Young Money," about the new generation of businessmen in the suddenly freewheeling Polish capitalist system. Bala, who was then twenty-six, had been chosen for the documentary because he had started an industrial cleaning business that used advanced machinery from the United States. Though Bala had dressed up for the occasion, he looked more like a brooding poet than like a businessman. He had dark, ruminative eyes and thick curly brown hair. Slender and sensitive-looking, he was so handsome that his friends had nicknamed him Amour. He chain-smoked and spoke like a professor of philosophy, which is what he had trained, and still hoped, to become. "I don't feel like a businessman," Bala later told the interviewer, adding that he had always "dreamed of an academic career."

He had been the equivalent of high-school valedictorian and, as an undergraduate at the University of Wroclaw, which he attended from 1992 to 1997, he was considered one of the brightest philosophy students. The night before an exam, while other students were cramming, he often stayed out drinking and carousing, only to show up the next morning, dishevelled and hung over, and score the highest marks. "One time, I went out with him and nearly died taking the exam," his close friend and former classmate Lotar Rasinski, who now teaches philosophy at another university in Wroclaw, recalls. Beata Sierocka, who was one of Bala's philosophy professors, says that he had a voracious appetite for learning and an "inquisitive, rebellious mind."

Bala, who often stayed with his parents in Chojnow, a provincial town outside Wroclaw, began bringing home stacks of philosophy books, lining the hallways and filling the basement. Poland's philosophy departments had long been dominated by Marxism, which, like liberalism, is rooted in Enlightenment notions of reason and in the pursuit of universal truths. Bala, however, was drawn to the radical arguments of Ludwig Wittgenstein, who maintained that language, like a game of chess, is essentially a social activity. Bala often referred to Wittgenstein as "my master." He also seized on Friedrich Nietzsche's notorious contention that "there are no facts, only interpretations" and that "truths are illusions which we have forgotten are illusions."

For Bala, such subversive ideas made particular sense after the collapse of the Soviet Empire, where language and facts had been wildly manipulated to create a false sense of history. "The end of Communism marked the death of one of the great meta-narratives," Bala later told me, paraphrasing the postmodernist Jean-François Lyotard. Bala once wrote in an e-mail to a friend, "Read Wittgenstein and Nietzsche! Twenty times each!"

Bala's father, Stanislaw, who was a construction worker and a taxi-driver ("I'm a simple, uneducated man," he says), was proud of his son's academic accomplishments. Still, he occasionally wanted to throw away Krystian's books and force him to "plant with me in the garden." Stanislaw sometimes worked in France, and during the summer Krystian frequently went with him to earn extra money for his studies. "He would bring suitcases stuffed with books," Stanislaw recalls. "He would work all day and study through the night. I used to joke that he knew more about France from books than from seeing it."

By then, Bala had become entranced by French postmodernists such as Jacques Derrida and Michel Foucault. He was particularly interested in Derrida's notion that not only is language too unstable to pinpoint any absolute truth; human identity itself is the malleable product of language.

Bala wrote a thesis about Richard Rorty, the American philosopher, who famously declared, "The guise of convincing your peers is the very face of truth itself."

Bala interpreted these thinkers idiosyncratically, pulling threads here and there, and often twisting and turning and distorting them, until he had braided them into his own radical philosophy. To amuse himself, he began constructing myths about himself—an adventure in Paris, a romance with a schoolmate—and tried to convince friends that they were true. "He would tell these tall stories about himself," Rasinski says. "If he told one person, and that person then told someone else, who told someone else, it became true. It existed in the language." Rasinski adds, "Krystian even had a term for it. He called it 'mytho-creativity.' " Before long, friends had trouble distinguishing his real character from the one he had invented. In an e-mail to a friend, Bala said, "If I ever write an autobiography, it will be full of myths!"

Bala cast himself as an enfant terrible who sought out what Foucault had called a "limit-experience": he wanted to push the boundaries of language and human existence, to break free of what he deemed to be the hypocritical and oppressive "truths" of Western society, including taboos on sex and drugs. Foucault himself was drawn to homosexual sado-masochism. Bala devoured the works of Georges Bataille, who vowed to "brutally oppose all systems," and once contemplated carrying out human sacrifices; and William Burroughs, who swore to use language to "rub out the word"; and the Marquis de Sade, who demanded, "O man! Is it for you to say what is good or what is evil?" Bala boasted about his drunken visits to brothels and his submission to temptations of the flesh. He told friends that he hated "conventions" and was "capable of anything," and he insisted, "I will not live long but I will live furiously!"

Some people found such proclamations juvenile, even ridiculous; others were mesmerized by them. "There were legends that no woman could resist him," one friend recalled. Those closest to him regarded his tales simply as playful confabulations. Sierocka, his former professor, says that Bala, in reality, was always "kind, energetic, hardworking, and principled." His friend Rasinski says, "Krystian liked the idea of being this Nietzschean superman, but anyone who knew him well realized that, as with his language games, he was just playing around."

In 1995, Bala, belying his libertine posture, married his high-school sweetheart, Stanislawa—or Stasia, as he called her. Stasia, who had dropped out of high school and worked as a secretary, showed little interest in language or philosophy. Bala's mother opposed the marriage, believing Stasia was ill-suited for her son. "I thought he should at least wait until he had finished his studies," she says. But Bala insisted that he wanted to take care of Stasia, who had always loved him, and in 1997 their son Kacper was born. That year, Bala graduated from the university with the highest possible marks, and enrolled in its Ph.D. program in philosophy. Although he received a full academic scholarship, he struggled to support his family, and soon left school to open his cleaning business. In the documentary on Poland's new generation of businessmen, Bala says, "Reality came and kicked me in the ass." With an air of resignation, he continues, "Once, I planned to paint graffiti on walls. Now I'm trying to wash it off."

He was not a good businessman. Whenever money came in, colleagues say, instead of investing it in his company he spent it. By 2000, he had filed for bankruptcy. His marriage also collapsed. "The basic problem was women," his wife later said. "I knew that he was having an affair." After Stasia separated from him, he seemed despondent and left Poland, travelling to the United States, and later to Asia, where he taught English and scuba diving.

He began to work intensively on "Amok," which encapsulated all his philosophical obsessions. The story mirrors "Crime and Punishment," in which Raskolnikov, convinced that he is a superior being who can deliver his own form of justice, murders a wretched pawnbroker. "Wouldn't thousands of good deeds make up for one tiny little crime?" Raskolnikov asks. If Raskolnikov is a Frankenstein's monster of modernity, then Chris, the protagonist of "Amok," is a monster of postmodernity. In his view, not only is there no sacred being ("God, if you only existed, you'd see how sperm looks on blood"); there is also no truth ("Truth is being displaced by narrative"). One character admits that he doesn't know which of his constructed personalities is real, and Chris says, "I'm a good liar, because I believe in the lies myself."

Unbound by any sense of truth—moral, scientific, historical, biographical, legal—Chris embarks on a grisly rampage. After his wife catches him having sex with her best friend and leaves him (Chris says that he has, at least, "stripped her of her illusions"), he sleeps with one woman after another, the sex ranging from numbing to sadomasochistic. Inverting convention, he lusts after ugly women, insisting that they are "more real, more touchable, more alive." He drinks too much. He spews vulgarities, determined, as one character puts it, to pulverize the language, to "screw it like no one else has ever screwed it." He mocks traditional philosophers and blasphemes the Catholic Church. In one scene, he gets drunk with a friend and steals from a church a statue of St. Anthony—the Egyptian saint who lived secluded in the desert, battling the temptations of the Devil, and who fascinated Foucault. (Foucault, describing how St. Anthony had turned to the Bible to ward off the Devil, only to encounter a bloody description of Jews slaughtering their enemies, writes that "evil is not embodied in individuals" but "incorporated in words" and that even a book of salvation can open "the gates to Hell.")

Finally, Chris, repudiating what is considered the ultimate moral truth, kills his girlfriend Mary. "I tightened the noose around her neck, holding her down with one hand," he says. "With my other hand, I stabbed the knife below her left breast. . . . Everything was covered in blood." He then ejaculates on her. In a perverse echo of Wittgenstein's notion that some actions defy language, Chris says of the killing, "There was no noise, no words, no movement. Complete silence."

In "Crime and Punishment," Raskolnikov confesses his sins and is punished for them, while being redeemed by the love of a woman named Sonya, who helps to guide him back toward a pre-modern Christian order. But Chris never removes what he calls his "white gloves of silence," and he is never punished. ("Murder leaves no stain," he declares.) And his wife— who, not coincidentally, is also named Sonya—never returns to him.

The style and structure of "Amok," which is derivative of many post-modern novels, reinforces the idea that truth is illusory—what is a novel, anyway, but a lie, a mytho-creation? Bala's narrator often addresses the reader, reminding him that he is being seduced by a work of fiction. "I am starting my story," Chris says. "I must avoid boring you." In another typical flourish, Chris reveals that he is reading a book about the violent rebellion of a young author with a "guilty conscience"—in other words, the same story as "Amok."

Throughout the book, Bala plays with words in order to emphasize their slipperiness. The title of one chapter, "Screwdriver," refers simultaneously to the tool, the cocktail, and Chris's sexual behavior. Even when Chris slaughters Mary, it feels like a language game. "I pulled the knife and rope from underneath the bed, as if I were about to begin a children's fairy tale," Chris says. "Then I started unwinding this fable of rope, and to make it more interesting I started to make a noose. It took me two million years."

Bala finished the book toward the end of 2002. He had given Chris a biography similar to his own, blurring the boundary between author and narrator. He even posted sections of the book on a blog called Amok, and during discussions with readers he wrote comments under the name Chris, as if he were the character. After the book came out, in 2003, an interviewer asked him, "Some authors write only to release their . . . Mr. Hyde, the dark side of their psyche—do you agree?" Bala joked in response, "I know what you are driving at, but I won't comment. It might turn out that Krystian Bala is the creation of Chris . . . not the other way around."

Few bookstores in Poland carried "Amok," in part because of the novel's shocking content, and those which did placed it on the highest shelves, out of the reach of children. (The book has not been translated into English.) On the Internet, a couple of reviewers praised "Amok." "We haven't had this kind of book in Polish literature," one wrote, adding that it was "paralyzingly realistic, totally vulgar, full of paranoid and delirious images." Another called it a "masterpiece of illusion." Yet most readers considered the book, as one major Polish newspaper put it, to be "without literary merit." Even one of Bala's friends dismissed it as "rubbish." When Sierocka, the philosophy professor, opened it, she was stunned by its crude language, which was the antithesis of the straightforward, intelligent style of the papers that Bala had written at the university. "Frankly, I found the book hard to read," she says. An ex-girlfriend of Bala's later said, "I was shocked by the book, because he never used those words. He never acted obscenely or vulgar toward me. Our sex life was normal."

Many of Bala's friends believed that he wanted to do in his fiction what he never did in life: shatter every taboo. In the interview that Bala gave after "Amok" was published, he said, "I wrote the book not caring about any convention. . . . A simple reader will find interesting only a few violent scenes with a graphic description of people having sex. But if someone really looks, he will see that these scenes are intended to awaken the reader and . . . show how fucked up and impoverished and hypocritical this world is."

By Bala's own estimate, "Amok" sold only a couple of thousand copies. But he was confident that it would eventually find its place among the great works of literature. "I'm truly convinced that one day my book will be appreciated," he said. "History teaches that some works of art have to wait ages before they are recognized."

In at least one respect, the book succeeded. Chris was so authentically creepy that it was hard not to believe that he was the product of a genuinely disturbed mind, and that he and the author were indeed indistinguishable. On Bala's Web site, readers described him and his work as "grotesque," "sexist," and "psychopathic." During an Internet conversation, in June of 2003, a friend told Bala that his book did not give the reader a good impression of him. When Bala assured her that the book was fiction, she insisted that Chris's musings had to be "your thoughts." Bala became irritated. Only a fool, he said, would believe that.

Detective Wroblewski underlined various passages as he studied "Amok." At first glance, few details of Mary's murder resembled the killing of Janiszewski. Most conspicuously, the victim in the novel is a woman, and the killer's longtime friend. Moreover, although Mary has a noose around her neck, she gets stabbed, with a Japanese knife, and Janiszewski wasn't. One detail in the book, however, chilled Wroblewski: after the murder, Chris says, "I sell the Japanese knife on an Internet auction." The similarity to the selling of Janiszewski's cell phone on the Internet— a detail that the police had never released to the public—seemed too extraordinary to be a coincidence.

At one point in "Amok," Chris intimates that he has also killed a man. When one of his girlfriends doubts his endless mytho-creations, he says, "Which story didn't you believe—that my radio station went bankrupt or that I killed a man who behaved inappropriately toward me ten years ago?" He adds of the murder, "Everyone considers it a fable. Maybe it's better that way. Fuck. Sometimes I don't believe it myself."

Wroblewski had never read about postmodernism or language games. For him, facts were as indissoluble as bullets. You either killed someone or you didn't. His job was to piece together a logical chain of evidence that revealed the irrefutable truth. But Wroblewski also believed that, in order to catch a killer, you had to understand the social and psychological forces that had formed him. And so, if Bala had murdered Janiszewski or participated in the crime—as Wroblewski now fully suspected—then Wroblewski, the empiricist, would have to become a postmodernist.

To the surprise of members of his detective squad, Wroblewski made copies of the novel and handed them out. Everyone was assigned a chapter to "interpret": to try to find any clues, any coded messages, any parallels with reality. Because Bala was living outside the country, Wroblewski warned his colleagues not to do anything that might alarm the author. Wroblewski knew that if Bala did not voluntarily return home to see his family, as he periodically did, it would be virtually impossible for the Polish police to apprehend him. At least for the moment, the police had to refrain from questioning Bala's family and friends. Instead, Wroblewski and his team combed public records and interrogated Bala's more distant associates, constructing a profile of the suspect, which they then compared with the profile of Chris in the novel. Wroblewski kept an unofficial scorecard: both Bala and his literary creation were consumed by philosophy, had been abandoned by their wives, had a company go bankrupt, travelled around the world, and drank too much. Wroblewski discovered that Bala had once been detained by the police, and when he obtained the official report it was as if he had already read it. As Bala's friend Pawel, who was detained with him, later testified in court, "Krystian came to me in the evening and had a bottle with him. We started drinking. Actually, we drank till dawn." Pawel went on, "The alcohol ran out, so we went to a store to buy another bottle. As we were returning from the shop we passed by a church, and this is when we had a very stupid idea."

"What idea did you have?" the judge asked him.

"We went into the church and we saw St. Anthony's figure, and we took it."

"What for?" the judge inquired.

"Well, we wanted a third person to drink with. Krystian said afterward that we were crazy."

In the novel, when the police catch Chris and his friend drinking beside the statue of St. Anthony, Chris says, "We were threatened by prison! I was speechless. . . . I do not feel like a criminal, but I became one. I had done much worse things in my life, and never suffered any consequences."

Wroblewski began to describe "Amok" as a "road map" to a crime, but some authorities objected that he was pushing the investigation in a highly suspect direction. The police asked a criminal psychologist to analyze the character of Chris, in order to gain insight into Bala. The psychologist wrote in her report, "The character of Chris is an egocentric man with great intellectual ambitions. He perceives himself as an intellectual with his own philosophy, based on his education and high I.Q. His way of functioning shows features of psychopathic behavior. He is testing the limits to see if he can actually carry out his . . . sadistic fantasies. He treats people with disrespect, considers them to be intellectually inferior to himself, uses manipulation to fulfill his own needs, and is determined to satiate his sexual desires in a hedonistic way. If such a character were real—a true living person—his personality could have been shaped by a highly unrealistic sense of his own worth. It could also be . . . a result of psychological wounds and his insecurities as a man . . . pathological relationships with his parents or unacceptable homosexual tendencies." The psychologist acknowledged the links between Bala and Chris, such as divorce and philosophical interests, but cautioned that such overlaps were "common with novelists." And she warned, "Basing an analysis of the author on his fictional character would be a gross violation."

Wroblewski knew that details in the novel did not qualify as evidence—they had to be corroborated independently. So far, though, he had only one piece of concrete evidence linking Bala to the victim: the cell phone. In February, 2002, the Polish television program "997," which, like "America's Most Wanted," solicits the public's help in solving crimes (997 is the emergency telephone number in Poland), aired a segment devoted to Janiszewski's murder. Afterward, the show posted on its Web site the latest news about the progress of the investigation, and asked for tips. Wroblewski and his men carefully analyzed the responses. Over the years, hundreds of people had visited the Web site, from places as far away as Japan, South Korea, and the United States. Yet the police didn't turn up a single fruitful lead.

When Wroblewski and the telecommunications expert checked to see if Bala had purchased or sold any other items on the Internet while logged on as ChrisB[7], they made a curious discovery. On October 17, 2000, a month before Janiszewski was kidnapped, Bala had clicked on the Allegro auction site for a police manual called "Accidental, Suicidal, or Criminal Hanging." "Hanging a mature, conscious, healthy, and physically fit person is very difficult even for several people," the manual stated, and described various ways that a noose might be tied. Bala did not purchase the book on Allegro, and it was unclear if he obtained it elsewhere, but the fact that he was seeking such information was, at least to Wroblewski, a sign of premeditation. Still, Wroblewski knew that if he wanted to convict Bala of murder he would need more than the circumstantial evidence he had gathered: he would need a confession.

Bala remained abroad, supporting himself by publishing articles in travel magazines, and by teaching English and scuba diving. In January of 2005, while visiting Micronesia, he sent an e-mail to a friend, saying, "I'm writing this letter from paradise."

Finally, that fall, Wroblewski learned that Bala was coming home.

"At approximately 2:30 P.M., after leaving a drugstore at Legnicka Street, in Chojnow, I was attacked by three men," Bala later wrote in a statement, describing what happened to him on September 5, 2005, shortly after he returned to his home town. "One of them twisted my arms behind my back; another squeezed my throat so that I could not speak, and could barely breathe. Meanwhile, the third one handcuffed me."

Bala said that his attackers were tall and muscular, with close-cropped hair, like skinheads. Without telling Bala who they were or what they wanted, they forced him into a dark-green vehicle and slipped a black plastic bag over his head. "I couldn't see anything," Bala said. "They ordered me to lie face down on the floor."

Bala said that his assailants continued to beat him, shouting, "You fucking prick! You motherfucker!" He pleaded with them to leave him alone and not hurt him. Then he heard one of the men say on a cell phone, "Hi, boss! We got the shithead! Yes, he's still alive. So now what? At the meeting point?" The man continued, "And what about the money? Will we get it today?"

Bala said he thought that, because he lived abroad and was known to be a writer, the men assumed that he was wealthy and were seeking a ransom. "I tried to explain to them that I didn't have money," Bala stated. The more he spoke, though, the more brutally they attacked him.

Eventually, the car came to a stop, apparently in a wooded area. "We can dig a hole for this shit here and bury him," one of the men said. Bala struggled to breathe through the plastic bag. "I thought that this was going to be the last moment of my life, but suddenly they got back into the car and began driving again," he said.

After a long time, the car came to another stop, and the men shoved him out of the car and into a building. "I didn't hear a door, but because there was no wind or sun I assumed that we had entered," Bala said. The men threatened to kill him if he didn't cooperate, then led him upstairs into a small room, where they stripped him, deprived him of food, beat him, and began to interrogate him. Only then, Bala said, did he realize that he was in police custody and had been brought in for questioning by a man called Jack Sparrow.

"None of it happened," Wroblewski later told me. "We used standard procedures and followed the letter of the law."

According to Wroblewski and other officers, they apprehended Bala by the drugstore without violence and drove him to police headquarters in Wroclaw. Wroblewski and Bala sat facing each other in the detective's cramped office; a light bulb overhead cast a faint glow, and Bala could see on the wall the goat horns that eerily resembled the image on the cover of his book. Bala appeared gentle and scholarly, yet Wroblewski recalled how, in "Amok," Chris says, "It's easier for people to imagine that Christ can turn urine into beer than that someone like me can send to Hell some asshole smashed into a lump of ground meat."

Wroblewski initially circled around the subject of the murder, trying to elicit offhand information about Bala's business and his relationships, and concealing what the police already knew about the crime—an interrogator's chief advantage. When Wroblewski did confront him about the killing, Bala looked dumbfounded. "I didn't know Dariusz Janiszewski," he said. "I know nothing about the murder."

Wroblewski pressed him about the curious details in "Amok." Bala later told me, "It was insane. He treated the book as if it were my literal autobiography. He must have read the book a hundred times. He knew it by heart." When Wroblewski mentioned several "facts" in the novel, such as the theft of the statue of St. Anthony, Bala acknowledged that he had drawn certain elements from his life. As Bala put it to me, "Sure, I'm guilty of that. Show me an author who *doesn't* do that."

.Wroblewski then played his trump card: the cell phone. How did Bala get hold of it? Bala said that he couldn't remember—it was five years ago. Then he said that he must have bought the phone at a pawnshop, as he had done several times in the past. He agreed to take a polygraph test.

Wroblewski helped to prepare the questions for the examiner, who asked:

Just before Dariusz Janiszewski lost his life, did you know this would happen?
Were you the one who killed him?
Do you know who actually murdered him?
Did you know Janiszewski?
Were you in the place where Janiszewski was held hostage?

Bala replied no to each question. Periodically, he seemed to slow his breathing, in the manner of a scuba diver. The examiner wondered if he was trying to manipulate the test. On some questions, the examiner suspected Bala of lying, but, overall, the results were inconclusive.

In Poland, after a suspect is detained for forty-eight hours, the prosecutor in the case is required to present his evidence before a judge and charge the suspect; otherwise, the police must release him. The case against Bala remained weak. All Wroblewski and the police had was the cell phone, which Bala could have obtained, as he claimed, from a pawnshop; the sketchy results of a polygraph, a notoriously unreliable test; a book on hanging that Bala might not even have purchased; and clues possibly embedded in a novel. Wroblewski had no motive or confession. As a result, the authorities charged Bala only with selling stolen property—Janiszewski's phone—and with paying a bribe in an unrelated business matter, which Wroblewski had uncovered during the course of his investigation. Wroblewski knew that neither charge would likely carry any jail time, and although Bala had to remain in the country and relinquish his passport, he was otherwise a free man. "I had spent two years trying to build a case, and I was watching it all collapse," Wroblewski recalled.

Later, as he was flipping through Bala's passport, Wroblewski noticed stamps from Japan, South Korea, and the United States. He remembered that the Web site of the television show "997" had recorded page views from all of those countries—a fact that had baffled investigators. Why would anyone so far away be interested in a local Polish murder? Wroblewski compared the periods when Bala was in each country with the timing of the page views. The dates matched.

Bala, meanwhile, was becoming a cause célèbre. As Wroblewski continued to investigate him for murder, Bala filed a formal grievance with the authorities, claiming that he had been kidnapped and tortured. When Bala told his friend Rasinski that he was being persecuted for his art, Rasinski was incredulous. "I figured that he was testing out some crazy idea for his next novel," he recalls. Soon after, Wroblewski questioned Rasinski about his friend. "That's when I realized that Krystian was telling the truth," Rasinski says.

Rasinski was shocked when Wroblewski began to grill him about "Amok." "I told him that I recognized some details from real life, but that, to me, the book was a work of fiction," Rasinski says. "This was crazy. You cannot prosecute a man based on the novel he wrote." Beata Sierocka, Bala's former professor, who was also called in for questioning, says that she felt as if she were being interrogated by "literary theorists."

As outrage over the investigation mounted, one of Bala's girlfriends, Denise Rinehart, set up a defense committee on his behalf. Rinehart, an American theatre director, met Bala while she was studying in Poland, in 2001, and they had subsequently travelled together to the United States and South Korea. Rinehart solicited support over the Internet, writing, "Krystian is the author of a fictional philosophical book called 'Amok.' A lot of the language and content is strong and there are several metaphors that might be considered against the Catholic Church and Polish tradition. During his brutal interrogation they referenced his book numerous times, citing it as proof of his guilt."

Dubbing the case the Sprawa Absurd—the Absurd Matter—the committee contacted human-rights organizations and International PEN. Before long, the Polish Justice Ministry was deluged with letters on Bala's behalf from around the world. One said, "Mr. Bala deserves his rights in accordance with Article 19 of the U.N. Declaration of Human Rights that guarantees the right to freedom of expression. . . . We urge you to insure there is an immediate and thorough investigation into his kidnapping and imprisonment and that all of those found responsible are brought to justice."

Bala, writing in imperfect English, sent out frantic bulletins to the defense committee, which published them in a newsletter. In a bulletin on September 13, 2005, Bala warned that he was being "spied" on and said, "I want you to know that I will fight until the end." The next day, he said of Wroblewski and the police, "They have ruined my family life. We will never talk loud at home again. We will never use internet freely again. We will never make any phone calls not thinking about who is listening. My mother takes some pills to stay calm. Otherwise she would get insane, because of this absurd accusation. My old father smokes 50 cigs a day and I smoke three packs. We all sleep 3–4 hours daily and we are afraid of leaving a house. Every single bark of our little dog alerts us and we don't know what or who to expect. It's a terror! Quiet Terror!"

The Polish authorities, meanwhile, had launched an internal investigation into Bala's allegations of mistreatment. In early 2006, after months of probing, the investigators declared that they had found no corroborating evidence. In this instance, they insisted, Bala's tale was indeed a mythocreation.

"I have infected you," Chris warns the reader at the beginning of "Amok." "You will not be able to get free of me." Wroblewski remained haunted by one riddle in the novel, which, he believed, was crucial to solving the case. A character asks Chris, "Who was the one-eyed man among the blind?" The phrase derives from Erasmus (1469–1536), the Dutch theologian and classical scholar, who said, "In the kingdom of the blind, the one-eyed man is king." Who in "Amok," Wroblewski wondered, was the one-eyed man? And who were the blind men? In the novel's last line, Chris suddenly claims that he has solved the riddle, explaining, "This was the one killed by blind jealousy." But the sentence, with its strange lack of context, made little sense.

One hypothesis based on "Amok" was that Bala had murdered Janiszewski after beginning a homosexual affair with him. In the novel, after Chris's closest friend confesses that he is gay, Chris says that part of him wanted to "strangle him with a rope" and "chop a hole in a frozen river and dump him there." Still, the theory seemed dubious. Wroblewski had thoroughly investigated Janiszewski's background and there was no indication that he was gay.

Another theory was that the murder was the culmination of Bala's twisted philosophy—that he was a postmodern version of Nathan Leopold and Richard Loeb, the two brilliant Chicago students who, in the nineteen-twenties, were so entranced by Nietzsche's ideas that they killed a fourteen-year-old boy to see if they could execute the perfect murder and become supermen. At their trial, in which they received life sentences, Clarence Darrow, the legendary defense attorney who represented them, said of Leopold, "Here is a boy at sixteen or seventeen becoming obsessed with these doctrines. It was not a casual bit of philosophy with him; it was his life." Darrow, trying to save the boys from the death penalty, concluded, "Is there any blame attached because somebody took Nietzsche's philosophy seriously and fashioned his life upon it? . . . It is hardly fair to hang a nineteen-year-old boy for the philosophy that was taught him at the university."

In "Amok," Chris clearly aspires to be a postmodern *Übermensch*, speaking of his "will to power" and insisting that anyone who is "unable to kill should not stay alive." Yet these sentiments did not fully explain the murder of the unknown man in the novel, who, Chris says, had "behaved inappropriately" toward him. Chris, alluding to what happened between them, says teasingly, "Maybe he didn't do anything significant, but the most vicious Devil is in the details." If Bala's philosophy had justified, in his mind, a break from moral constraints, including the prohibition on murder, these passages suggested that there was still another motive, a deep personal connection to the victim—something that the brutality of the crime also indicated. With Bala unable to leave Poland, Wroblewski and his team began to question the suspect's closest friends and family.

Many of those interrogated saw Bala positively—"a bright, interesting man," one of his former girlfriends said of him. Bala had recently received a reference from a past employer at an English-instruction school in Poland, which described him as "intelligent," "inquisitive," and "easy to get along with," and praised his "keen sense of humor." The reference concluded, "With no reservation, I highly recommend Krystian Bala for any teaching position with children."

Yet, as Wroblewski and his men deepened their search for the "Devil in the details," a darker picture of Bala's life began to emerge. The years 1999 and 2000, during which time his business and his marriage collapsed—and Janiszewski was murdered—had been especially troubled. A friend recalled that Bala once "started to behave vulgarly and wanted to take his clothes off and show his manliness." The family babysitter described him as increasingly drunk and out of control. She said he constantly berated his wife, Stasia, shouting at her that "she slept around and cheated on him."

According to several people, after Bala and his wife separated, in 2000, he remained possessive of her. A friend, who called Bala an "authoritarian type," said of him, "He continuously controlled Stasia, and checked her phones." At a New Year's Eve party in 2000, just weeks after Janiszewski's body was found, Bala thought a bartender was making advances toward his wife and, as one witness put it, "went crazy." Bala screamed that he would take care of the bartender and that he had "already dealt with such a guy." At the time, Stasia and her friends had dismissed his drunken outburst. Even so, it took five people to restrain Bala; as one of them told police, "He was running amok."

As Wroblewski and his men were trying to fix on a motive, other members of the squad stepped up their efforts to trace the two suspicious telephone calls that had been made to Janiszewski's office and to his cell phone on the day he disappeared. The public telephone from which both calls were made was operated with a card. Each card was embedded with a unique number that registered with the phone company whenever it was used. Not long after Bala was released, the telecommunications expert on the Janiszewski case was able to determine the number on the caller's card. Once the police had that information, officials could trace all the telephone numbers dialled with that same card. Over a three-month period, thirty-two calls had been made. They included calls to Bala's parents, his girlfriend, his friends, and a business associate. "The truth was becoming clearer and clearer," Wroblewski said.

Wroblewski and his team soon uncovered another connection between the victim and the suspect. Malgorzata Drozdzal, a friend of Stasia's, told the police that in the summer of 2000 she had gone with Stasia to a night club called Crazy Horse, in Wroclaw. While Drozdzal was dancing, she saw Stasia talking to a man with long hair and bright-blue eyes. She recognized him from around town. His name was Dariusz Janiszewski.

Wroblewski had one last person to question: Stasia. But she had steadfastly refused to cooperate. Perhaps she was afraid of her ex-husband. Perhaps she believed Bala's claim that he was being persecuted by the police. Or perhaps she dreaded the idea of one day telling her son that she had betrayed his father.

Wroblewski and his men approached Stasia again, this time showing her sections of "Amok," which was published after she and Bala had split up, and which she had never looked at closely. According to Polish authorities, Stasia examined passages involving Chris's wife, Sonya, and was so disturbed by the character's similarities to her that she finally agreed to talk.

She confirmed that she had met Janiszewski at Crazy Horse. "I had ordered French fries, and I asked a man next to the bar whether the French fries were ready," Stasia recalled. "That man was Dariusz." They spent the entire night talking, she said, and Janiszewski gave her his phone number. Later, they went on a date and checked into a motel. But before anything happened, she said, Janiszewski admitted that he was married, and she left. "Since I know what it's like to be a wife whose husband betrays her, I didn't want to do that to another woman," Stasia said. The difficulties in Janiszewski's marriage soon ended, and he and Stasia never went out together again.

Several weeks after her date with Janiszewski, Stasia said, Bala showed up at her place in a drunken fury, demanding that she admit to having an affair with Janiszewski. He broke down the front door and struck her. He shouted that he had hired a private detective and knew everything. "He also mentioned that he had visited Dariusz's office, and described it to me," Stasia recalled. "Then he said he knew which hotel we went to and what room we were in."

Later, when she learned that Janiszewski had disappeared, Stasia said, she asked Bala if he had anything to do with it, and he said no. She did not pursue the matter, believing that Bala, for all his tumultuous behavior, was incapable of murder.

For the first time, Wroblewski thought he understood the last line of "Amok": "This was the one killed by blind jealousy."

Spectators flooded into the courtroom in Wroclaw on February 22, 2007, the first day of Bala's trial. There were philosophers, who argued with each other over the consequences of postmodernism; young lawyers, who wanted to learn about the police department's new investigative techniques; and reporters, who chronicled every tantalizing detail. "Killing doesn't make much of an impression in the twenty-first century, but allegedly killing and then writing about it in a novel is front-page news," a front-page article in *Angora*, a weekly based in Lodz, declared.

The judge, Lydia Hojenska, sat at the head of the courtroom, beneath an emblem of the white Polish eagle. In accordance with Polish law, the presiding judge, along with another judge and three citizens, acted as the jury. The defense and the prosecution sat at two unadorned wooden tables; next to the prosecutors were Janiszewski's widow and his parents, his mother holding a picture of her son. The public congregated in the back of the room, and in the last row was a stout, nervous woman with short red hair, who looked as if her own life were at stake. It was Bala's mother, Teresa; his father was too distraught to attend.

Everyone's attention, it seemed, was directed toward a zoolike cage near the center of the courtroom. It was almost nine feet high and twenty feet long, and had thick metal bars. Standing in the middle of it, wearing a suit and peering out calmly through his spectacles, was Krystian Bala. He faced up to twenty-five years in prison.

A trial is predicated on the idea that truth is obtainable. Yet it is also, as the writer Janet Malcolm has noted, a struggle between "two competing narratives," and "the story that can best withstand the attrition of the rules of evidence is the story that wins." In this case, the prosecution's narrative resembled that of "Amok": Bala, like his alter ego Chris, was a depraved hedonist, who, unbound by any sense of moral compunction, had murdered someone in a fit of jealous rage. The prosecution introduced files from Bala's computer, which Wroblewski and the police had seized during a raid of his parents' house. In one file, which had to be accessed with the password "amok," Bala catalogued, in graphic detail, sexual encounters with more than seventy women. The list included his wife, Stasia; a divorced cousin, who was "older" and "plump"; the mother of a friend, described as "old ass, hard-core action"; and a Russian "whore in an old car." The prosecution also presented e-mails in which Bala sounded unmistakably like Chris, using the same vulgar or arcane words, such as "joy juices" and "Madame Melancholy." In an angry e-mail to Stasia, Bala wrote, "Life is not only screwing, darling"—which echoed Chris's exclamation "Fucking is not the end of the world, Mary." A psychologist testified that "every author puts some part of his personality into his artistic creation," and that Chris and the defendant shared "sadistic" qualities.

During all this, Bala sat in the cage, taking notes on the proceedings or looking curiously out at the crowd. At times, he seemed to call into question the premise that the truth can be discerned. Under Polish law, the defendant can ask questions directly of the witnesses, and Bala eagerly did so, his professorial inquiries often phrased to reveal the Derridean instability of their testimony. When a former girlfriend testified that Bala once went out on her balcony drunk and acted as if he were on the verge of committing suicide, he asked her if her words might have multiple interpretations. "Could we just say that this is a matter of semantics—a misuse of the word 'suicide'?" he said.

But, as the trial wore on and the evidence mounted against him, the postmodernist sounded increasingly like an empiricist, a man desperately looking to show gaps in the prosecution's chain of evidence. Bala noted that no one had seen him kidnap Janiszewski, or kill him, or dump his body. "I'd like to say that I never met Dariusz, and there is not a single witness who would confirm that I did so," Bala said. He complained that the prosecution was taking random incidents in his personal life and weaving them into a story that no longer resembled reality. The prosecutors were constructing a mytho-creation—or, as Bala's defense attorney put it to me, "the plot of a novel." According to the defense, the police and the media had been seduced by the most alluring story rather than by the truth. (Stories about the case had appeared under headlines such as "TRUTH STRANGER THAN FICTION" and "MURDER, HE WROTE.")

Bala had long subscribed to the postmodernist notion of "the death of the author"—that an author has no more access to the meaning of his literary work than anyone else. Yet, as the prosecution presented to the jury potentially incriminating details from "Amok," Bala complained that his novel was being misinterpreted. He insisted that the murder of Mary was simply a symbol of the "destruction of philosophy," and he made one last attempt to assert authorial control. As he later put it to me, "I'm the fucking author! I know what I meant."

In early September, the case went to the jury. Bala never took the stand, but in a statement he said, "I do believe the court will make the right decision and absolve me of all the charges." Wroblewski, who had been promoted to inspector, showed up in court, hoping to hear the verdict. "Even when you're sure of the facts, you wonder if someone else will see them the same way you do," he told me.

At last, the judges and jurors filed back into the courtroom. Bala's mother waited anxiously. She had never read "Amok," which contains a scene of Chris fantasizing about raping his mother. "I started to read the book, but it was too hard," she told me. "If someone else had written the book, maybe I would have read it, but I'm his mother." Bala's father appeared in the courtroom for the first time. He had read the novel, and though he had trouble understanding parts of it, he thought it was an important work of literature. "You can read it ten, twenty times, and each time discover something new in it," he said. On his copy, Bala had written an inscription to both his parents. It said, "Thank you for your . . . forgiveness of all my sins."

As Judge Hojenska read the verdict, Bala stood perfectly straight and still. Then came the one unmistakable word: "Guilty."

The gray cinder-block prison in Wroclaw looks like a relic of the Soviet era. After I slipped my visitor's pass through a tiny hole in the wall, a disembodied voice ordered me to the front of the building, where a solid gate swung open and a guard emerged, blinking in the sunlight. The guard waved me inside as the gate slammed shut behind us. After being searched, I was led through several dank interlocking chambers and into a small visitors' room with dingy wooden tables and chairs. Conditions in Polish prisons are notorious. Because of overcrowding, as many as seven people are often kept in a single cell. In 2004, prison inmates in Wroclaw staged a three-day hunger strike to protest overcrowding, poor food, and insufficient medical care. Violence is also a problem: only a few days before I arrived, I was told, a visitor had been stabbed to death by an inmate.

In the corner of the visitors' room was a slender, handsome man with wire-rimmed glasses and a navy-blue artist's smock over a T-shirt that said "University of Wisconsin." He was holding a book and looked like an American student abroad, and it took me a moment to realize that I was staring at Krystian Bala. "I'm glad you could come," he said as he shook my hand, leading me to one of the tables. "This whole thing is farce, like something out of Kafka." He spoke clear English but with a heavy accent, so that his "s"es sounded like "z"s.

Sitting down, he leaned across the table, and I could see that his cheeks were drawn, he had dark circles around his eyes, and his curly hair was standing up in front, as if he had been anxiously running his fingers through it. "I am being sentenced to prison for twenty-five years for writing a book—a book!" he said. "It is ridiculous. It is bullshit. Excuse my language, but that is what it is. Look, I wrote a novel, a crazy novel. Is the book vulgar? Yes. Is it obscene? Yes. Is it bawdy? Yes. Is it offensive? Yes. I intended it to be. This was a work of provocation." He paused, searching for an example, then added, "I wrote, for instance, that it would be easier for Christ to come out of a woman's womb than for me—" He stopped, catching himself. "I mean, for the narrator to fuck her. You see, this is *supposed* to offend." He went on, "What is happening to me is like what happened to Salman Rushdie."

As he spoke, he placed the book that he was carrying on the table. It was a worn, battered copy of "Amok." When I asked Bala about the evidence against him, such as the cell phone and the calling card, he sounded evasive and, at times, conspiratorial. "The calling card is not mine," he said. "Someone is trying to set me up. I don't know who yet, but someone is out to destroy me." His hand touched mine. "Don't you see what they are doing? They are constructing this reality and forcing me to live inside it."

He said that he had filed an appeal, which cited logical and factual inconsistencies in the trial. For instance, one medical examiner said that Janiszewski had drowned, whereas another insisted that he had died of strangulation. The judge herself had admitted that she was not sure if Bala had carried out the crime alone or with an accomplice.

When I asked him about "Amok," Bala became animated and gave direct and detailed answers. "The thesis of the book is not my personal thesis," he said. "I'm not an anti-feminist. I'm not a chauvinist. I'm not heartless. Chris, in many places, is my antihero." Several times, he pointed to my pad and said, "Put this down" or "This is important." As he watched me taking notes, he said, with a hint of awe, "You see how crazy this is? You are here writing a story about a story I made up about a murder that never happened." On virtually every page of his copy of "Amok," he had underlined passages and scribbled notations in the margins. Later, he showed me several scraps of paper on which he had drawn elaborate diagrams revealing his literary influences. It was clear that, in prison, he had become even more consumed by the book. "I sometimes read pages aloud to my cellmates," he said.

One question that was never answered at the trial still hovered over the case: Why would someone commit a murder and then write about it in a novel that would help to get him caught? In "Crime and Punishment," Raskolnikov speculates that even the smartest criminal makes mistakes, because he "experiences at the moment of the crime a sort of failure of will and reason, which . . . are replaced by a phenomenal, childish thoughtlessness, just at the moment when reason and prudence are most necessary." "Amok," however, had been published three years after the murder. If Bala was guilty of murder, the cause was not a "failure of will and reason" but, rather, an excess of both.

Some observers wondered if Bala had wanted to get caught, or, at least, to unburden himself. In "Amok," Chris speaks of having a "guilty conscience" and of his desire to remove his "white gloves of silence." Though Bala maintained his innocence, it was possible to read the novel as a kind of confession. Wroblewski and the authorities, who believed that Bala's greatest desire was to attain literary immortality, saw his crime and his writing as indivisible. At the trial, Janiszewski's widow pleaded with the press to stop making Bala out to be an artist rather than a murderer. Since his arrest, "Amok" had become a sensation in Poland, selling out at virtually every bookstore.

"There's going to be a new edition coming out with an afterword about the trial and all the events that have happened," Bala told me excitedly. "Other countries are interested in publishing it as well." Flipping through the pages of his own copy, he added, "There's never been a book quite like this."

As we spoke, he seemed far less interested in the idea of the "perfect crime" than he was in the "perfect story," which, in his definition, pushed past the boundaries of aesthetics and reality and morality charted by his literary forebears. "You know, I'm working on a sequel to 'Amok,'" he said, his eyes lighting up. "It's called 'De Liryk.'" He repeated the words several times. "It's a pun. It means 'lyrics,' as in a story, or 'delirium.'"

He explained that he had started the new book before he was arrested, but that the police had seized his computer, which contained his only copy. (He was trying to get the files back.) The authorities told me that they had found in the computer evidence that Bala was collecting information on Stasia's new boyfriend, Harry. "Single, 34 years old, his mom died when he was 8," Bala had written. "Apparently works at the railway company, probably as a train driver but I'm not sure." Wroblewski and the authorities suspected that Harry might be Bala's next target. After Bala had learned that Harry visited an Internet chat room, he had posted a message at the site, under an assumed name, saying, "Sorry to bother you but I'm looking for Harry. Does anyone know him from Chojnow?"

Bala told me that he hoped to complete his second novel after the appeals court made its ruling. In fact, several weeks after we spoke, the court, to the disbelief of many, annulled the original verdict. Although the appeals panel found an "undoubted connection" between Bala and the murder, it concluded that there were still gaps in the "logical chain of evidence," such as the medical examiners' conflicting testimony, which needed to be resolved. The panel refused to release Bala from prison, but ordered a new trial.

Bala insisted that, no matter what happened, he would finish "De Liryk." He glanced at the guards, as if afraid they might hear him, then leaned forward and whispered, "This book is going to be even more shocking."

— *February, 2008*

In December of 2008, Bala received a new trial. Once more, he was found guilty. He is currently serving a twenty-five-year sentence.

Which Way Did He Run?

Firemen have a culture of death. There are rituals, constructed for the living, to process the dead. And so on September 11th, when members of Engine Company 40, Ladder Company 35, learned that every man from their house who responded to the World Trade Center attack—twelve, including a captain and a lieutenant—had disappeared, they rushed to the site, determined, at the very least, to perform the rite of carrying out their own. Eventually, they located their engine and ladder trucks, covered in soot, near Ground Zero, and tried to "visualize," as one of them later put it, what had happened: where the men had gone, what their last movements might have been. By the rigs, the searchers recognized some of the missing firefighters' extra shoes, a discarded shirt, and a pair of sunglasses. Slowly, in makeshift teams, the searchers fanned out into the rubble, trying to retrace their colleagues' steps, combing through the wreckage. There was nothing to be found. It was as if the fire had consumed not just the living but the rites of the dead as well.

Then that evening, as the number of missing grew into the thousands, word spread that rescue workers had discovered someone buried under the rubble. He was identified as Kevin Shea, and he was a member of Engine 40, Ladder 35. What's more, he was alive. He had been evacuated to a hospital in New Jersey, and his colleagues hurried there, believing that he could tell them where the rest of the men might still be trapped. "If there was one," Steve Kelly, a veteran member of the house, later recalled, "we were hopeful he could lead us to the others."

When the men entered the hospital room, Shea was lying in bed, awake. He had fractured his neck in three places and severed a thumb, but he seemed alert and happy to see them. After the men embraced Shea, they began to question him. Do you remember where you were? one of them asked.

"No," he said.

Do you know where the others were before the towers came down?

Shea looked at them, perplexed, and said, "The towers came down?"

The story of the survivor who was unable to remember what no one else could forget sounded like an urban legend. But two weeks after the attack I visited Shea, who had just been discharged from the hospital, at his firehouse on Amsterdam Avenue and Sixty-sixth Street, and he told me that he was indeed suffering from some kind of amnesia. "Technically, I'm not supposed to be working," he said. "But I can still answer phones, and I thought it might help to be near the guys."

Part Italian and part Irish, he is handsome, with intense brown eyes, but he wore a neck brace that pressed against his chin and the doctors had shaved his head, making his features seem disconcertingly stark. As he bent down to answer the phone, I could see curving along his scalp a long gash flecked with dried blood. "I fractured the fifth vertebra in my neck," he said.

Outside the firehouse, people were gathering to light candles in memory of the dead, and upon learning that Shea was inside they stopped by to see him. He had become, in a strange way, a shrine for the living—the one who made it out. A little girl walked in with her mother and handed him a donation for the company. "Thank you so much for what you did," she said. He smiled and extended his good hand to take the check, but as more people approached him he grew increasingly uncomfortable. "This isn't about me," he told a man who praised his courage. After the last person had departed, he turned to me and said, "Please don't make me out to be a hero."

He glanced around the room at the photos of the missing men and a notice for a memorial. He said, "Maybe I panicked and . . ." His thoughts trailed off, and he closed his eyes as if trying to conjure something out of the blankness. He seemed haunted not just by the gaps in his past but also by a single question that they prevented him from answering: What had he done in those crucial last moments that allowed him alone to survive? "I like to think I was the type of person who was trying to push someone out of the way to save them and not the type who ran in fear," he said. "But I can't remember anything, no matter how hard I try. It's like my memory collapsed with the building, and now I have to piece the whole thing back together again."

There are some things he does remember. He remembers Mike D'Auria, a twenty-five-year-old rookie with a Mayan tattoo on his leg. He remembers Frank Callahan, his captain, and Mike Lynch, another fire-fighter, who was about to get married. He remembers what they carried: a Halligan, a maul, an axe, a Rabbit Tool, eight-penny nails, utility ropes, wire cutters, chucks, and a screwdriver. He remembers waking on September 11th and the alarm sounding at the firehouse at 9:13 A.M. He remembers the men getting on the rigs. He remembers the rigs. He remembers asking the lieutenant if he thought it was a terrorist attack and the lieutenant saying yes and their riding in silence.

There are other things he remembers, too: his nickname, Ric-o-Shea; his age, thirty-four; and his favorite color, yellow. He remembers meeting his girlfriend, Stacy Hope Herman. He remembers growing up on Long Island and his parents fighting and his mother moving out when he was thirteen. He remembers some things even if he doesn't want to—things that refuse to dissolve, along with all the insignificant memories, with the passage of time.

Memory is a code to who we are, a collection not simply of dates and facts but also of emotional struggles, epiphanies, and transformations. And in the wake of tragedy it is vital to recovery. After a traumatic event, people tend to store a series of memories and arrange them into a meaningful narrative. They remember exactly where they were and to whom they were talking. But what does one do when the narrative is shattered, when some—or most—of the pieces of the puzzle are missing?

In the last week of September, I went with Shea to the St. Charles Hospital and Rehabilitation Center in Long Island. The doctors were uncertain if he was blocking out what had happened as a result of physical or psychological blows, or both. Mark Sandberg, a neuropsychologist, greeted Shea in the lobby and led him into a cramped office. After Sandberg closed the door, they sat down, facing each other. "I know very little about you," Sandberg said. "So what do you remember?"

"I can tell you what I remember and what I was told," Shea said. "I remember responding to the scene. I'm in Ladder 35, but they have an engine in there as well, and they had a free seat. I wasn't working that day, and I said, 'Can I jump on?' "

The doctor seemed surprised. "You were off duty that day?"

Shea explained that he was "buffing," or volunteering, which was "the right thing to do." He continued, "So the officer gave me permission, and I . . . went down the West Side Highway. . . . We noticed car fires and debris falling everywhere—like big falling carpets. There were pieces of metal and glass. And people were falling—"

"Do you recall that or did someone tell you that?"

Shea closed his eyes. "I recall that."

Sandberg made several notes on a pad, and then asked Shea to continue. On the way to the scene, Shea said, he pulled out the video camera that he sometimes used to document fire scenes for training. "I remember putting it in the plastic bag and putting it back in my coat," he said. "I knew I couldn't be filming that long." He then prepared to go into the chaos. "I don't remember anything after that, except waking up in the hospital."

"Are your memories back after that?"

"Yes, they started to come back. They were in and out. They were drugging me at the time, with morphine, I think. They said I was conscious, but I don't know."

"You can be conscious and have no memory. It's called post-traumatic amnesia."

"That's what this is?"

"That's what I'm trying to understand."

Shea fidgeted with his bandages. "Some say it's better not to remember. Maybe the fact that I don't know if I was trying to save someone, maybe that's helping me deal with the post-stress . . . or whatever you call it."

Sandberg asked how many men from his house who had gone down with him were lost. For the first time, Shea looked up from his bandages. "All of them," he said. "All of them but me."

He had never intended to become a fireman. Though he came from a long line of firefighters—which included his grandfather, his uncle, his father, and his older brother—he didn't fit the stereotype. He wasn't, as he put it, "a typical macho." He was smaller and more bookish than many of the other men; he disliked sports and didn't drink. Initially, he embarked on a career in computer software, at which he excelled, but by 1998 he felt compelled to follow in the family tradition.

When he was first assigned to Engine 40, Ladder 35, in the summer of 2001, he showed up at three in the morning. The men were going out on a call, and when they returned he greeted them with platters of eggs and French toast and chocolate-covered strawberries. "They were looking at me, like, 'Who is this freakin' guy?'" Shea recalled.

"A lot of the guys didn't know what to make of Kev," Steve Kelly says.

But he displayed an almost monkish devotion to the job, until he gradually found his place as the one who was always willing to lend a hand, speaking in frenetic bursts, saying, "Yes, sir," and "Negative K, sir," and answering the phone with the refrain "Firefighter Kevin Shea. How can I help you?" Although many in the house assumed that Shea would retire, given the severity of his injuries, he vowed that he would return to active duty by Christmas. "I have my family," he said, "but this is my family, too."

As he tried to heal, strengthening his muscles and maintaining a strict protein diet, he could not forget, as some amnesiacs can, that he had forgotten. He was reminded of the gaps in his memory when he flipped on the television or saw the relatives of the missing men.

One of the firefighters mentioned offhandedly to Shea that he had seen a news clip of a lone rescue worker who, instead of carrying out victims, was standing in front of the towers paralyzed with fear. "I hope I wasn't that kind of person," Shea said.

His brother Brian told me, "He needs to figure it out. I don't want him thirty years from now walking around angry at the world and not knowing why. I don't want him to be like one of these guys who comes back from Vietnam and loses his mind."

Shea agreed that he had to recover his past—"no matter what I discover." And so, still in bandages, he set out like a detective, sifting through clues.

He started with only a note from the hospital. It said, "Patient is a thirty-four-year-old white male firefighter . . . who was knocked unconscious by falling debris just outside the Trade Center."

Shea soon tracked down the neurosurgeon who treated him on September 11th and beseeched him for more details. The doctor said all he knew was that Shea was brought in on a stretcher and that the injuries to his neck were consistent with being hit by something from the front. "Is there anything else?" Shea asked. "Anything at all?"

The doctor thought for a moment. "Well, I remember one thing," he offered. "You said you crawled two hundred feet toward light."

Shea didn't remember crawling or even saying that he had done so. "How the hell could I have crawled two hundred feet with a broken neck?" Shea asked.

As he intensified his search, he tried to be methodical. He interviewed his family members and closest friends for any details that he might have mentioned in the hospital, and since forgotten. One of them told him that he had mentioned grabbing a Purple K extinguisher, which is used to put out airplane fires.

More people learned of his search, and he was inundated with tips. One morning, he flipped on his computer and showed me a list of dozens of individuals who claimed to have information. "People keep calling, saying, 'Yeah, I was there. I pulled you out.' It's hard to know what to believe."

Joe Patriciello, a lieutenant whom Shea had known for years, called and told him he had seen Shea moments before the first tower came down. "You embraced me in the command center," Patriciello said. "Don't you remember?"

"What command center?"

"In the south tower."

Shea saw an image in his mind: a room full of people. They were standing in the lobby of the south tower, which was soon decimated. "I remember that," Shea later told me. "I'm sure of it." He became excited. "It's possible other things could come back."

Not long after, Shea received a call from a doctor who had seen him at the scene. He informed Shea that he had been found amid the rubble on Albany Street. After their conversation, Shea pulled out a map of the city and spread it in front of him. He measured the distance from the lobby of the south tower, where he had hugged Patriciello, to Albany Street, trying to recall how he had got there. He made several notes: Saw Patriciello ten minutes before the first tower came down. Tower came down in nine seconds. Albany Street about one block distance.

Though he tried not to make suppositions, he began to construct fragments of his story. "I was found on Albany Street," he would tell people matter-of-factly. "I was in the lobby command center and hugged Lieutenant Patriciello."

On October 17th, more than a month after the attack, Shea visited his firehouse for the first time in a while. Pinned to the wall was a *Daily News* article about several firefighters who had rescued two men lying in the street after the first tower collapsed. One of the men was badly injured, his face blackened with ash. His name, the article said, was Kevin Shea. "I'm looking at it, going, 'What the hell, that's *me!*'" he recalls. He wrote down the name of each person in the article and asked other firefighters to help him find them.

A few days later, he parked his car outside a station on the Upper East Side, near his apartment. As he was walking home, a man on the street yelled out, "Oh, my goodness, Kevin Shea?" Shea looked at the man's face but didn't recognize him. "Don't tell me you don't remember," the man said.

"Remember what?"

"We went in the ambulance together."

Shea recalled that the *Daily News* said he had been rescued along with another bloodied firefighter. "You're the other guy?" Shea asked.

The stranger smiled. "That's me. Rich Boeri."

They shook hands, as if meeting for the first time. Shea took out a piece of paper and a pen, which he tried always to carry with him, and pressed Boeri for more information. Boeri said that they were transported in an ambulance to a police boat and taken across the Hudson River to New Jersey. "Did I say anything about the other guys from my company?" Shea asked.

Boeri shook his head. "You just kept saying, 'Did the towers collapse?' "

Days later, Shea was still overcome by the encounter. "I'm just walking down the street and out of nowhere he starts telling me what happened to me," he said. As Shea sensed more of the past emerging, he phoned one of the people who, according to the *Daily News* article, had saved him: Captain Hank Cerasoli. They agreed to meet at a diner on the Upper East Side, and Shea made his way there with his girlfriend, Stacy. "I hope I can handle it," he said.

When they arrived, Cerasoli was waiting inside with his wife. A modest man in his fifties with a bald head and a silver mustache, he wore his fireman's coat. Over eggs and French toast, Cerasoli described how he was struggling with his own memory loss. He had been hit on the head and initially could not recall the location of the firehouse he had worked at for seventeen years. His memories had gradually come back, and he recalled stumbling upon Shea in the middle of the street after the first tower collapsed. "I thought you were dead," he said. "You weren't moving at all."

Shea's face whitened, and Cerasoli asked Shea if he was sure that he wanted him to continue. When Shea nodded, Cerasoli explained how he and several others carried Shea on a backboard when they heard the second tower rumble. "We lifted you in the air and ran with you on the board, down an alleyway and into a garage. It suddenly got all black and dark." Cerasoli drew a map on a napkin, showing where the garage was, on the corner of West Street and Albany Street.

"Was I conscious?" Shea asked.

Cerasoli thought for a long moment. "I don't remember. There are some details I still can't remember."

Shea asked what happened next. Cerasoli said that the Fire Department doctor opened Shea's shirt and pants. "I was holding your hand. You kept asking me, 'Where are the others? Are they O.K.?' I said, 'Yeah, sure, they're O.K., they're out there laughing.' I didn't really have any idea, but I wanted you to feel O.K." Cerasoli paused, then asked, "So were they O.K.?"

Shea shook his head. "No, none of them made it," he said.

"I'm sorry," Cerasoli said. "I had no idea."

After they finished eating, Cerasoli's wife took a picture of them sitting together. "I know he doesn't want to forget this," she said.

Cerasoli reached over and put his arm around Shea. "God was with you that day," he said.

When he wasn't searching for his past, Shea went from memorial to memorial. One out of every ten people who died that day was a firefighter. Thirty-three died in Shea's battalion alone, and eleven in his house, including his captain, Frank Callahan, and Bruce Gary, a veteran whom Shea worshipped. "Gary was a senior man with over twenty years," Shea told me. "He was like Yoda in the house. He was very wise. I wanted to hang out with him all the time. I'm asking, 'Why you? You would have been a resource for everyone.' Me? I'm a positive guy, but when people have enough of positive they can't come to me."

Shea attended as many memorials as he could, but there were so many that he had to do what everyone in the department had to: choose between friends. In late October, as another service was taking place in the city, I accompanied Shea to a Mass in upstate New York for his lieutenant, John Ginley. Shea still couldn't drive, and Steve Kelly picked us up. Kelly and Shea wore their Class A uniforms: navy-blue suits and white gloves.

As they spoke in the car about the men who had died, Shea seemed detached, as if he were reading from a piece of paper. Several people close to him had noticed that he seemed increasingly numb. "I don't know what's wrong with me," Shea told me at one point. "I'm not sad enough I should be sadder."

While the other men spent more and more time together—searching at Ground Zero, eating their meals at the firehouse, drinking at P. D. O'Hurley's—Shea spent less and less time with his colleagues.

He now stared out the window at the changing leaves. "Look at them," he said. "They're all orange and purple."

"You sure you're O.K., Kev?" Kelly asked.

Shea lowered his window and let the wind wash over him. "Ten-four."

By the time we arrived at the church, scores of firemen were lined up.

There was still no body, and in place of a casket a helmet rested at the foot of the altar. "I will never forget those memories," one of Ginley's brothers said in his eulogy. "I believe in time this pain will become bearable, because all our memories will be alive in our mind."

I glanced at Shea. Unlike the other men, who had begun to weep, he was dry-eyed and his face was utterly blank.

By the end of October, Shea began losing interest in his search. "What's the point?" he asked me. "What am I going to figure out? They're all dead."

One day, he found, through the relatives of a deceased firefighter in his house, a news clip from September 11th that showed the men from Engine 40, his truck, going into the towers. At last the quest was over, he thought, as he prepared to watch the clip. On the grainy film he could see each of the men from his company going inside, but he wasn't there. "I don't know where the heck I was," Shea said. "I don't know what the hell happened to me."

Finally, he stopped looking for answers, and devoted himself to helping the families of lost firefighters. He was a featured speaker at fund-raisers, though he was suffering from pain in his hand and leg, where the contusions were, and in his groin, where the doctors had surgically removed large amounts of damaged tissue. At a fund-raiser in Buffalo in November, after having appeared only a few days earlier at another in California, he was wan and exhausted. "He's not letting himself heal," Stacy told me. "He's in so much pain, but he won't say anything."

As he stared off into space, a stranger asked for his autograph, and he walked away.

The next morning, Flight 587 crashed into the Rockaway Peninsula, near Kennedy Airport, and reporters, believing it was another terrorist attack, tried to track Shea down for comment. Rather than speak to them, he went to the hotel gym and got on the StairMaster in his neck brace, climbing to nowhere and watching the fire burn on TV. "How do you feel, Mr. Shea?" he said, parodying their questions. "How do you feel?"

"He's starting to have nightmares," Stacy said. "He's kicking and thrashing."

He told me, "I remember the dreams."

Emotions, once suppressed, overwhelmed him, and periodically he began to cry. "I don't know what's happening," he said.

He found an article about post-traumatic stress, and highlighted the words "It is O.K. to be in pain. That is the first principle of recovery."

By the beginning of December, many in the firehouse were showing their own symptoms of trauma. "You see signs," Kelly told me. "Marriages are starting to come under fire more than usual. I don't know if there is more drinking, but there is plenty of it."

While the rest of the men relied on the familial nature of the firehouse as a refuge, Shea, after drifting away, felt cut off. Many of the new recruits who had replaced the missing barely recognized him. In early December, Shea tried for the first time to reintegrate himself into the fabric of the force. "Being with the guys," he said. "That's the most important thing to me right now."

He went with them to Roosevelt Island for courses on antiterrorism. "He was so excited," Stacy said. "He got to wear his uniform again."

In mid-December, the doctors removed his brace. It was possible that, after the bone fused in a year, he could return to active duty. Yet in the kitchen, where the men gathered to eat and reminisce, he sensed that they were shying away from him. Sometimes when he showed up in the morning they barely acknowledged him, he said, and when he tried to engage them in conversation they seemed uninterested. "A lot of the guys are reluctant to even look at me," Shea told me one day, sitting in his car. "As odd as it may sound, I think I remind them of the others."

That month, at another wake, Shea stood off by himself. "I sometimes think it would've been easier if I had died with the rest of the guys," he said.

Kelly told me, "It's hard to watch. Every time I talk to him, he's not the same guy." Kelly went on, "First thing he needs to do is simply heal physically. Hopefully, then he can come back and be a full-duty fireman, because he lived for that, and he was going to move up in the department. He was brilliant in the books."

Shortly before the three-month anniversary of the attack, Shea showed up early for the Christmas party to help with preparation. Many of the relatives of the dead were there, and he served them hot dogs and sauerkraut. He worked alongside the other men, saying, "Yes, sir," and "Negative K, sir." "More of the guys are talking to me," he said. "Maybe in time it will get easier."

Hanging on the wall at the firehouse was the riding list from the morning of September 11th, a chalkboard that had the name of each member who had hopped on the rig and died. The men had put a piece of Plexiglas over it to preserve it as a memorial. At the bottom, scribbled almost as an afterthought, were the words "Kevin Shea."

"I need to go down," Shea said.

He had called me at home one night, his voice agitated, and it took me a moment to realize that he was referring to Ground Zero. He said someone in the Fire Department would pick us up the next afternoon in Chelsea.

It was a cold day, and Shea wore a sweatshirt and mountain-climbing boots. Stacy stood beside him, holding his hand. He had not returned to the area since that day and had consciously avoided pictures of it in the newspaper and on TV. Liam Flaherty, a member of Rescue 4, showed up in a Fire Department van. He had trained Shea at the academy and had been down at the site, searching for his men's remains, since September 11th, leaving only long enough to sleep. "I saw guys at their absolute best that day," he said as he drove. "Guys just kept running in. They went up as it came down."

We passed through several checkpoints, trying to follow the route Shea had taken with his own company. Shea pressed his face against the window, wiping away the steam from his breath. We could see the tops of the cranes rising out of the debris and, farther on, two huge metal beams, molded together in the shape of a cross.

"Look at that," Shea said, pointing out the opposite window. "That's Engine 40. That's the rig we drove in on." On the side of the road was a huge red truck, the number 40 painted on the side. "It must've been moved," Shea said. "We weren't parked there." He looked at me for reassurance. "Right?"

As we passed through the final checkpoint, Flaherty said, "This is it. You're in."

"There's the south tower," Stacy said.

"Where?"

"There. By the crane."

"Oh, my God," Shea said.

All we could see was a giant hole in the skyline. Flaherty parked the van and we climbed out. Flaherty got us hard hats and yelled at us to be careful as we approached the debris.

"Where's the lobby command post?" Shea asked.

"Ten stories underground," Flaherty said. "It's still burning."

Shea blinked his eyes. He began to recall, in a rush, all the pieces that he had strung together. "I grabbed a Purple K," he said. "I was going to look for my men in Ladder 35. There were bodies falling. I remember them hitting the ground. I remember the sound. I went to put out car fires. Then I went into the command post. I saw Patriciello." He closed his eyes. "I hugged him. I told him to be careful."

He stopped. How could he have got from the lobby command post to Albany Street? He couldn't run that fast. "Maybe you were blown out," Flaherty said. "A lot of guys were picked up and blown out from the concussion."

"Where's Albany?" Shea asked.

"It's over here," Flaherty said. We started to run, mud splattering our shoes. We turned down a small street. There were cars still covered in ash, their windows shattered. Shea recalled that the doctor had told him that he said he had crawled two hundred feet toward light. Shea walked several paces, then stopped and turned around. "This is where they found me," he said. "Right here." He looked back at the tower, surveying the distance. "Is there a garage around here?" There was one up the road, Liam said, and we ran again, past a burned-out building and several men in surgical masks. "This must be it," Shea said.

The garage was small and dank. We waited a moment, then were rushing out into the street again, down one alley and another, until we arrived at the edge of the Hudson River. "This is where they lowered me down on a stretcher."

As he finished his story, drawing new theories from Flaherty about being blown out, estimating the wind speed and the power of the concussion, we were cold and exhausted. By the time we got back to the site, it was dark, and the workers had turned on their spotlights. While the others wandered off, Shea walked toward what was left of the south tower.

He stood, listening to the cranes. I watched him for several minutes, then asked, "Are you O.K.?"

"Yeah."

He seemed aware that, after months of searching, he might never know everything—that there was no way to piece together a logical story for that day. "I'm so tired," he said. He wiped his eyes. No matter what happened, I offered, he'd done his job, and at some point he needed to let go of the rest.

Shea stepped closer to the hole, his feet balancing on the edge, and said, "I just wish I had learned one thing today—anything—that showed I was trying to save someone other than myself."

—January, 2002

Part
Two

"A strange enigma is man!"

SHERLOCK HOLMES, in "The Sign of the Four"

The Squid Hunter

On a moonless January night in 2003, Olivier de Kersauson, the French yachtsman, was racing across the Atlantic Ocean, trying to break the record for the fastest sailing voyage around the world, when his boat mysteriously came to a halt. There was no land for hundreds of miles, yet the mast rattled and the hull shuddered, as if the vessel had run aground. Kersauson turned the wheel one way, then the other; still, the gunwales shook inexplicably in the darkness. Kersauson ordered his crew, all of whom were now running up and down the deck, to investigate. Some of the crew took out spotlights and shone them on the water, as the massive trimaran—a three-hulled, hundred-and-ten-foot boat that was the largest racing machine of its kind, and was named Geronimo, for the Apache warrior—pitched in the waves.

Meanwhile, the first mate, Didier Ragot, descended from the deck into the cabin, opened a trapdoor in the floor, and peered through a porthole into the ocean, using a flashlight. He glimpsed something by the rudder. "It was bigger than a human leg," Ragot later told me. "It was a tentacle." He looked again. "It was starting to move," he recalled.

He beckoned Kersauson, who came down and crouched over the opening. "I think it's some sort of animal," Ragot said.

Kersauson took the flashlight, and inspected for himself. "I had never seen anything like it," he told me. "There were two giant tentacles right beneath us, lashing at the rudder."

The creature seemed to be wrapping itself around the boat, which rocked violently. The floorboards creaked, and the rudder started to bend. Then, just as the stern seemed ready to snap, everything went still. "As it unhooked itself from the boat, I could see its tentacles," Ragot recalled. "The whole animal must have been nearly thirty feet long."

The creature had glistening skin and long arms with suckers, which left impressions on the hull. "It was enormous," Kersauson recalled. "I've been sailing for forty years and I've always had an answer for everything—for hurricanes and icebergs. But I didn't have an answer for this. It was terrifying."

What they claimed they saw—a claim that many regarded as a tall tale—was a giant squid, an animal that has long occupied a central place in sea lore; it has been said to be larger than a whale and stronger than an elephant, with a beak that can sever steel cables. In a famous scene in "20,000 Leagues Under the Sea," Jules Verne depicts a battle between a submarine and a giant squid that is twenty-five feet long, with eight arms and blue-green eyes—"a terrible monster worthy of all the legends about such creatures." More recently, Peter Benchley, in his thriller "Beast," describes a giant squid that "killed without need, as if Nature, in a fit of perverse malevolence, had programmed it to that end."

Such fictional accounts, coupled with scores of unconfirmed sightings by sailors over the years, have elevated the giant squid into the fabled realm of the fire-breathing dragon and the Loch Ness monster. Though the giant squid is no myth, the species, designated in scientific literature as *Architeuthis,* is so little understood that it sometimes seems like one. A fully grown giant squid is classified as the largest invertebrate on Earth, with tentacles sometimes as long as a city bus and eyes about the size of human heads. Yet no scientist has ever examined a live specimen—or seen one swimming in the sea. Researchers have studied only carcasses, which have occasionally washed ashore or floated to the surface. (One corpse, found in 1887 in the South Pacific, was said to be nearly sixty feet long.) Other evidence of the giant squid is even more indirect: sucker marks have been spotted on the bodies of sperm whales, as if burned into them; presumably, the two creatures battle each other hundreds of feet beneath the ocean's surface.

The giant squid has consumed the imaginations of many oceanographers. How could something so big and powerful remain unseen for so long—or be less understood than dinosaurs, which died out millions of years ago? The search for a living specimen has inspired a fevered competition. For decades, teams of scientists have prowled the high seas in the hope of glimpsing one. These "squid squads" have in recent years invested millions of dollars and deployed scores of submarines and underwater cameras, in a struggle to be first.

Steve O'Shea, a marine biologist from New Zealand, is one of the hunters—but his approach is radically different. He is not trying to find a mature giant squid; rather, he is scouring the ocean for a baby, called a paralarva, which he can grow in captivity. A paralarva is often the size of a cricket.

"Squid, you see, hatch thousands of babies," O'Shea told me in early 2004, when I called him at his office at the Earth and Oceanic Sciences Research Institute, at the Auckland University of Technology. "Most of these will get eaten up by larger predators, but during periods of spawning the sea should be filled with an absolutely fantastic amount of these miniature organisms. And, unlike the adults, they shouldn't be able to dart away as easily."

Rival hunters once viewed his plan skeptically: if no one could find the animal when it was sixty feet long, how could anyone discover it when it was barely an eighth of an inch? Lately, though, many have come to see O'Shea's strategy as a potential breakthrough. "It offers several advantages," Clyde Roper, an American who is perhaps the world's foremost expert on squid, told me. Roper is a giant-squid hunter himself, who once descended underwater in a steel cage, in search of his quarry. "First, you could find the juvenile at shallower depths. That makes it a lot easier to catch. Furthermore, there are more of them around, because at that stage, even though mortality is high, the adult female will release up to four million eggs. That's a hell of a lot of baby giant squid running around." He added, "It's a matter of a numbers game, pure and simple."

In 1999, O'Shea studied what few had ever seen—the corpse of a baby *Architeuthis*, which was discovered off New Zealand. He described its curious morphology: two eyes spread disconcertingly far apart; a parrot-like mouth concealing a raspy, serrated tongue; eight arms extending outward from a torpedo-shaped head. Each elastic limb was lined with hundreds of suckers, ringed with sharp teeth. The skin was iridescent, and filled with chromatophores—groups of pigment cells—that allowed it to change colors. A funnel near its head could shoot out clouds of black ink. The specimen also had two extraordinary-looking clubbed tentacles. (When a giant squid is mature, it can stretch up to thirty feet.)

Armed with this rare expertise, O'Shea had spent the past five years mapping out where to find a baby giant squid and puzzling over how to catch one and grow it in a tank. This year, he told me, he would venture out during the summer nights of the Southern Hemisphere, when giant squid released their babies. "Come on down, mate," he said. "We'll see if we can't find the bloody thing and make history."

The bodies of dead giant squid have been found in nearly every ocean: in the Pacific, near California; in the Atlantic, off the coasts of Newfoundland and Norway; and in the Indian, south of South Africa. But no place is considered better for hunting giant squid than the waters around New Zealand. It is here that currents from the tropics and Antarctica converge, and the resulting diversity of marine life creates an abundance of plankton for squid to feed on. And it is here that, in recent years, more dead giant squid have been recovered than anywhere else.

I arrived in Auckland on a morning in late February, 2004, and O'Shea greeted me at the airport. He looked much younger than his age, thirty-eight. He wore khaki pants and a khaki-colored shirt, a uniform that evoked a safari ranger. He is small and trim, and has brown hair, which was sticking up as if he had just run his fingers through it. Peering through spectacles that made his eyes seem abnormally large, he confessed with some embarrassment that he had come for me the previous day. "I've been preoccupied with everything that's happening," he said.

He spoke in a soft yet intense murmur, and whenever I addressed him he would turn his head sideways, so that I was talking directly into his right ear. (Later, he told me that he had damaged his left ear in a diving accident.) He reached into his wallet and pulled out his business card; beside his name was a picture of an iridescent squid. While I was looking at it, he grabbed one of my bags and hurried to his truck, which, as soon as he opened the driver's door, exhaled a strange, pungent odor. "I do apologize," he said, as he rolled down the windows. "You'll find that everything around me smells of dead squid and ciggies." In the back seat was a metal pole that was three feet long, with a net on the end. I soon discovered that he carried it with him wherever he went, often slung over his shoulder, as if he were a butterfly hunter.

Over the next few days, we began making preparations for our maiden voyage. At one point, we were speeding down the highway, heading to the store for supplies, when he slammed on the brakes and reversed, in the middle of traffic. "I almost forgot," he said, parking in a lot that overlooked a harbor. He leaped out with the net and darted down a wharf, a lit cigarette dangling from his mouth. He leaned over the edge, the winds buffeting his face, and held the net high over his head. For a moment, he didn't move or breathe. "There," he said, and lunged with the net, slashing at the water. As he pulled the net in, his pant legs wet with spray, I glimpsed a dozen silvery sprat—a minnow-like fish—dancing in the mesh. "I know I look a bit like a bugger," he said. "But these things are rather important."

After he had flung the net into the water several more times ("Believe it or not, there is a technique to this," he said), he returned to his truck and tossed the sprat into a white bucket in the back seat. We travelled farther down the road, the sprat jostling behind us, and eventually stopped at an aquarium called Kelly Tarlton's Antarctic Encounter and Underwater World. (In its brochures, O'Shea was hailed as the "world-renowned squid man.")

He grabbed the bucket, and we headed inside. "This is where I keep them," he told me. He led me into a damp room with fluorescent lights, in which there was a round glass tank; inside, darting from side to side, were seventy baby squid, each an inch long. O'Shea explained that these squid, which are found in coastal areas, were a smaller species than *Architeuthis*. "Look at them," he said. "They're bloody marvellous, aren't they?"

O'Shea is one of the few people in the world who have succeeded in keeping not only coastal but also deep-sea squid alive in captivity. Unlike an octopus, which, as he put it, "you can't kill, no matter how hard you try," a squid is highly sensitive to its environment. Accustomed to living in a borderless realm, a squid reacts poorly when placed in a tank, and will often plunge, kamikaze-style, into the walls, or cannibalize other squid.

In 2001, during a monthlong expedition at sea, O'Shea caught a cluster of paralarval giant squid in his nets, but by the time he reached the docks all of them had died. He was so distraught that he climbed into the tank, in tears, and retrieved the corpses himself. "I had spent every day, every hour, trying to find the paralarvae, and then they died in my grasp," he told me. For two years, he was so stricken by his failure that he refused to mount another expedition. "I knew if I failed again I would be finished," he recalled. "Not just scientifically but physically and emotionally."

He couldn't stop wondering, though, about what had happened in the tank. His wife, Shoba, a computer scientist who was born in India, told me that sometimes in the middle of an unrelated conversation he would suddenly say, "What did I do wrong?" O'Shea became determined to correct what he called "my fatal mistake," and began a series of painstaking experiments on other species of juvenile deep-sea squid. He would subtly alter the conditions of captivity: tank size, intensity of light, oxygen levels, salinity. He discovered that the tank in which he had stored his paralarvae during the expedition had two lethal flaws: it had a rectangular shape, which, for some reason, caused the squid to sink to the bottom and die; and its walls were made of polyethylene, a plastic compound that, it turns out, is toxic to deep-sea squid. "Knowing what I know now, I feel like a fool," he said. "It was like walking them to their execution."

In the mid-nineteen-seventies, Clyde Roper managed to keep ocean-dwelling squid alive for fourteen days—then a record. O'Shea, using cylindrical tanks made of acrylic, had kept his latest coastal specimens alive for eighty days. Earlier, he had maintained a batch of deep-sea squid for more than seventy days, which he then returned to the wild, satisfied that his experiment was a success.

He held up his white bucket. "Watch this," he said, and dumped the sprat into the tank. Though the fish were bigger than the squid, the squid shot toward them, with their arms curved over their heads, hiding their tentacles; they looked metallic, except for their bulging green eyes. Then the squids' arms sprang open, and their tentacles exploded outward, lashing their prey. The fish squirmed to break free, but the squid engulfed them in a web of arms. They drew their frantic prey into their beaks, and the squids' stomachs turned bright red as they filled with the blood of the fish. Staring into the tank, I imagined what a full-grown giant squid might look like swallowing its prey.

When the squid finished eating, O'Shea said, "If I can keep *these* squid alive, there's no reason I can't keep the giant alive. I'll just need a bigger tank."

He was nervous about what would happen to his squid during our expedition—he had left the animals alone for only one day, on Christmas—and he anxiously arranged with an employee at the aquarium to care for them in his absence. "You need to treat them with reverence," he said.

We then headed to his university office, where he had to gather various things for the expedition. It was in an attic-like space, and seemed entirely devoted to what he described as his "lunatic obsession." Pasted to the walls and stacked on tables were pictures, many of which he had sketched himself, of giant squid, colossal squid, broad squid, warty squid, leopard squid. In addition, there were squid toys, squid key chains, squid journals, squid movies, and squid-related newspaper clippings ("WARNING! GIANT FLYING SQUID ATTACKING VESSELS OFF AUSTRALIA"). On the floor were dozens of glass jars filled with dead squid that had been preserved in alcohol, their eyes and tentacles pressing against the glass.

Many squid scientists wait for decades before getting their hands on the remains of an *Architeuthis*. O'Shea, however, has developed a large network of fishermen informants, and in the last seven years has collected a hundred and seventeen corpses. Together, these specimens offer a clearer picture of the giant squid. O'Shea has concluded that although the animals could be as heavy as a thousand pounds, most weigh between a hundred and four hundred pounds. (Females are typically heavier than males.) His squid collection also provided some of the first clues about the animal's diet. In an article recently published in the *New Zealand Journal of Zoology*, O'Shea documented the "gut contents" of his specimens, which included arrow squid and chunks of another *Architeuthis* ("proof of cannibalism").

In another recent experiment, O'Shea dissected a squid's statolith: a bonelike particle in the animal's ear that helps the animal balance itself. A statolith builds up rings of calcium deposits over time, he explained, and, like the rings on tree trunks, the layers of bone might help scientists determine a squid's age and growth rate.

Initially, O'Shea told me, he had thought that he would dissect his corpses in his office. But, after he made an incision in one, the specimen released a noxious odor, a mixture of rotting flesh and ammonium (which keeps the animal buoyant in the water). Students and faculty fled the building, and he was soon forbidden to make further dissections there. "I became quite unpopular after that," he said.

He began to pick up various jars. "Oh, here it is," he said, holding up what appeared to be a stem of tiny grapes.

"What is it?" I asked.

"The eggs from the ovary of a giant squid. I have a freezer full of 'em."

The phone rang. He stared at it without moving. "They'll only want something," he said.

He stuck a pair of tweezers inside the jar, pulled out a strand of eggs, and placed it under a microscope. "Go ahead, mate, take a look," he said. When I looked into the eyepiece, I could see at least a hundred eggs, each no more than two millimetres wide. O'Shea said that he planned to attach the eggs, which may produce pheromones, to an underwater camera, in the hope of luring a giant squid close enough to be captured on film.

He sat at his computer, typed for a few minutes, then stopped abruptly and ran out of the office. He returned moments later, carrying two hula hoops. "We're almost ready," he said.

The phone rang again. "Oh, bloody hell," he said, and let it ring. He picked up another jar, this one containing two black shells that appeared to lock together. "It's the beak of a giant squid," he said. I ran my finger along its sharp edge, which pricked my skin. He said he had found it inside the stomach of a sperm whale.

He began to race around again, and before long his arms were filled with a box of specimen jars, the hula hoops, a net, a hammer, a rope, a worn leather briefcase that was only half buckled, and several rolled-up maps. "O.K., I think we're about ready," he said. "I just need a smoke, and we'll be off."

For months, he had been carefully working out our destination, studying squid migration patterns as well as satellite readings of water currents and temperatures. His plan was to go south, where he had found the paralarvae before. At the last minute, however, he changed his mind. "We're going north," he said. As we got back in his truck, he added, "I should warn you, there's a bit of a cyclone coming our way."

For as long as sailors have been going out to sea, they have been returning with stories of monsters. The Bible speaks of "a dragon that is in the sea"; the Roman encyclopedia "Naturalis Historia" tells of an enormous "polyp" that was "smeared with brine and had a terrible smell." As the science writer Richard Ellis demonstrates in his 1998 book, "The Search for the Giant Squid," from these disparate accounts emerged a common portrait of a singular beast: a huge sea creature, with fearsome appendages—arms or horns or feet or legs or tails—that jutted out of its head. In the Odyssey, Homer describes a beast called the Scylla:

> She has twelve legs, all writhing, dangling down
> and six long swaying necks, a hideous head on each,
> each head barbed with a triple row of fangs . . .
> No mariners yet can boast they'd raced their ship
> past Scylla's lair without some mortal blow.

In Norway, sailors sometimes reported sightings of a tentacled predator, which they dubbed the Kraken. (The word is a colloquial term for a tree with the roots still attached.) In 1755, Bishop Erik Ludvigsen Pontoppidan included the animal in his "Natural History of Norway," claiming that the Kraken was the size of a "floating island," with horns as long as a ship's mast. He went on, "It seems these are the creature's arms, and, it is said, if they were to lay hold of the largest man-of-war, they would pull it down to the bottom."

Meanwhile, American whalers were exchanging their own stories of a "devilfish." In 1851, Herman Melville, who had worked for three years on a whaling ship, published "Moby Dick," in which he describes a sailor who is witness to "the most wondrous phenomenon": a "vast pulpy mass" with "innumerable long arms radiating from its centre, and curling and twisting like a nest of anacondas."

Around the same time, Johannes Japetus Smith Steenstrup, an eminent

Danish zoologist, decided to investigate the rumors himself. As Steenstrup sorted through the available evidence, he was drawn in particular to several accounts of a strange beast caught in the Øresund Strait in the fifteen-forties, and brought to the king of Denmark, at whose court it was preserved in a dried state as "a rarity and a wonder." Named a "sea monk," because its smooth-looking head evoked men of the cloister, it resembled, in an original sketch, a large squid. In an 1854 lecture, Steenstrup declared that the sea monk, like the Kraken, was "firstly a cephalopod"—a classification term which derives from the Greek words for "head" and "foot," and refers to animals whose tentacles sprout from their head. To the amazement of his audience, Steenstrup then held up a glass jar containing the jaws of a giant squid, which he said had been retrieved from a dead specimen off the coast of Iceland. He named the creature *Architeuthis* ("ruling squid")—marking, as Ellis has noted, "the official passage of the giant squid from the realm of fable into the scientific literature."

Just as seamen had previously exaggerated the evidence for the giant squid's existence, the scientific community now exaggerated the lack of it. Most scientists were still disputing Steenstrup's findings when, in November, 1861, the crew of the French steamship Alecton, in the middle of the Atlantic, saw a Kraken rise up before them. The captain decided that he had to capture it, and ordered his men to fire their muskets. The bullets seemed to have little effect, so they hurled harpoons, which appeared to glance off it. Finally, they wrapped a noose around its tail, but, as they began to haul the creature on board, its enormous weight caused the rope to slice through its boneless flesh. All that remained was a piece of the tail, which was soon dispatched, along with a detailed report, to the French Academy of Sciences. The report inspired Jules Verne's depiction of a menacing giant squid, but it did little to secure the organism a certified place in the animal kingdom. Arthur Mangin, a French zoologist, declared that the rotting tail was the remains of a sea plant, and urged "the wise, and especially the man of science, not to admit into the catalogue those stories which mention extraordinary creatures . . . the existence of which would be . . . a contradiction of the great laws of harmony and equilibrium which have sovereign rule over living nature."

Scientists continued to doubt Steenstrup's thesis until one day in 1873, when a fisherman off the coast of Newfoundland saw a creature floating on the ocean's surface and struck it with a hook. The animal was alive, and reached up and tried to seize him; the fisherman then grabbed an axe. Over the years, the story was embellished, but one fact was undeniable: the fisherman returned to shore with a tentacle from a giant squid, which was nineteen feet long. It was placed in a museum, in St. John's, Newfoundland, where the public could see it. At last, even the most ardent skeptic was forced to admit that the Kraken was real.

As the winds and rains from the cyclone began to descend on New Zealand, O'Shea stood in his back yard beside his boat, which rested on a trailer. The boat was not exactly what I had imagined it to be. It was barely twenty feet long and seven feet wide, with an outboard motor. There was no galley or head, and no place to sleep, except for a forward berth the size of a broom closet. "I suppose you were expecting one of those American yachts, weren't you?" O'Shea said with a smile.

Initially, he had planned to charter a vessel with a traditional squid squad—a professional crew and a team of scientists. Squid hunters from Japan, America, and Europe crisscrossed the sea in this manner, and O'Shea had been on such a voyage when he found his paralarvae. But such expeditions cost millions of dollars, and O'Shea is an academic who must cobble together funding for his research from private sources, like the Discovery Channel. He had already sunk a significant portion of his family's modest savings into his quest, and as a result he was unable to afford a hearing aid, among other necessities. "If I don't find a giant squid soon, I'll be ruined," he told me.

Yet, according to other hunters, part of the genius of O'Shea's scheme is that it can be executed relatively cheaply. Juvenile squid swim in shallower waters than adults, and he didn't need to descend, say, in a submarine. He also didn't require a ship that could accommodate a huge tank. By December, O'Shea had decided that he would go forward using his own fishing boat, and he whittled down his crew to three people: O'Shea, myself, and a graduate student in marine biology named Peter Conway, a gentle thirty-two-year-old vegetarian who rolled his own cigarettes and had never been on such an expedition. "The big swells make me a wee queasy," he confessed at one point.

O'Shea told me that he was not willing to wait for the cyclone to pass: there was only a short period each year during which adult squid migrated into the region to spawn and release their eggs. And so we set off in the truck, with the trailer in tow, and headed north, listening to Neil Diamond's slightly nasal tenor on the stereo. ("He's bloody brilliant, isn't he?" O'Shea said.)

Within a few hours, the exquisite landscape of New Zealand, with its long white shores and volcanic hills and sheep farms, was obscured in blackness as the storm intensified. The trailer rocked in the wind, which was approaching gale force. According to news reports, a nearby river had burst its banks, forcing local residents to evacuate. Civil-defense teams were being called up, and the power had gone out in several cities, including Auckland.

The police were warning motorists to stay off the roads, but we continued farther up the northern peninsula, past towns with Aboriginal names like Te Kao and Te Hapua, until we arrived at a wooden cabin, in the afternoon. We would stay here during the day, O'Shea explained, then launch the boat at night, when the squid rose upward in the water column to feed.

The cabin had no phone and no heat, and it was musty inside, as if it had been abandoned for years. "Not bloody much, is it?" O'Shea said, as he brushed some ants off the kitchen table. He didn't seem too dismayed, though, and while Conway and I unpacked our bags he spread his equipment across the floor and began to assemble a peculiar form. First, he took a round plywood board that was the size of a stop sign and drilled holes around its perimeter. He wove cable ties through the holes, then attached the board to a tube of fine-meshed netting that was large enough to accommodate him inside it. He was still working when Conway and I went to bed; when I got up the next morning, I found him in the same position. "It's coming along nicely," he said. A candle was burning beside him, and he held a sharp knife over the flame. Using the hot blade, he cut several holes into the sides of the net.

The slow, methodical work had put him in a reflective mood, and he told me how he first became interested in the giant squid. "It had never been my plan," he said. "When I was four or five, my parents got divorced, and I was sent to live with my grandmother. I didn't have many friends. I was one of these horribly geeky kids. I had glasses and a heart murmur and arthritis, and I spent all my time on the beach, looking for shells. I collected thousands of them. When I was thirteen or fourteen, I started to go out on commercial fishing boats in the summer to try to find the rarest kinds. I remember once, I was on this boat, and the fishermen pulled in this shell. I knew there were only one or two in all of New Zealand, and I let out this loud scream, and the captain came down and yelled at me for screaming, but I didn't mind. I was so excited to find it."

He burned another hole in the net, filling the room with an acrid smell. He said, "After I graduated from the university with a doctorate in marine biology, I went to work for the National Institute of Water and Atmospheric Research. In 1996, I got a phone call saying that a fisherman had found a giant squid down in Wellington, and did I want it. I'd never seen one, so I raced down to the jetty, and took one look at it, and it was the biggest bloody thing I'd ever seen. I knew it wouldn't fit in the car, and so I borrowed a trailer, and strapped it down with the tentacles draped over the car.

"Before long, the press got wind of it, and they started calling and asking me all these questions, and I didn't know anything about the giant squid. I spouted a bunch of nonsense, and I soon realized no one really knew *anything* about this blasted thing. It was this great unknown, this complete mystery. And I've been trying to solve it ever since."

He seemed slightly embarrassed by his candor. "What we need now are Coke bottles," he said. He had brought several empty one-litre containers with him; he sliced each bottle in half, so that the top part resembled a funnel. He inserted each funnel, the wide part facing out, into the holes that he had made in the mesh netting. He then sealed them in place with a glue gun. "We're ready for the final touches," he said. He slid a hula hoop inside the bottom end of the mesh sheath; the result looked like a Victorian skirt. Finally, he clamped the bottom of the net to a small glass container.

He climbed onto a chair and held the contraption up: it was roughly six feet long and cylindrical in shape, with a round hardwood top, a funnel-studded net draped along the sides, and a little glass jar dangling on the bottom. "Whaddaya think, chappies?" O'Shea asked Conway and me.

"What is it?" I asked.

"A giant-squid trap."

O'Shea pointed to the funnels excitedly, and explained that the paralarvae would swim through them and get trapped inside the net, eventually ending up in the glass jar. This rough-looking device had been carefully conceived: the net was made of extra-fine mesh, which would do less damage to the animals; the board was marine plywood, which would keep the net vertical in the water; and the Coke bottles were exactly the right size to trap the paralarvae. "It's ugly as sin, I admit, but it should do the job," he said, adding, "I'm a poor scientist, so it's a bit of Steve O'Shea invention."

He spent the rest of the day building a second trap, then announced that it was time to go hunting. The worst of the storm had blown out to sea, but the weather remained volatile, with gusting winds and dangerously high waves. Two surfers had drowned. "We'll have to do some reconnaissance," O'Shea said. Before sundown, we took a drive with the trailer, trying to find a safe place to launch the boat. We pulled into an inlet surrounded by volcanic cliffs. "This will have to do," O'Shea said.

He backed the trailer down the beach, and we put the boat in the water. I climbed on board, and O'Shea and Conway followed. It was cold, but O'Shea was barefoot, and he was wearing only cutoff jeans and a baggy T-shirt. "Righteo, then," he said, and gunned the engine.

O'Shea had no radar, but he had a navigational system with a small flickering display that signalled the location of the shore and the depth of the sea. It would be our only guide in the darkness.

"It'll probably be too rough out there for any fishing boats," O'Shea shouted over the noise of the engine. "But we're going to need to be careful of container ships. They can come up pretty fast." It was now twilight, and he squinted at one of the buoys that marked a safe route through the channel.

"What color is that?" he asked me.

"It's green," I said. "Can't you see it?"

"I'm not just deaf," he said. "I'm color-blind."

As we left the harbor, it began to rain, and the smooth channel gave way to swells. The boat leaped over the crests, its aluminum hull vibrating.

"A bit rough, ain't it?" Conway said.

"She's sturdier than she looks," O'Shea said of the vessel. He glanced at the forward berth. "Underneath those cushions are the life jackets. You don't need to wear them, but just so you know where they are."

The sun disappeared over the horizon, and for a while the sky released a flurry of bright colors, as if it had its own chromatophores. Then it grew dark, and the waves announced themselves not by sight but by sound, as they clapped against the bow. I slipped on my life jacket.

O'Shea said he knew just the spot for hunting, and he stared at the glowing dots on the navigational system. "Where are we going?" I asked.

"There," he said, pointing into the distance.

I peered over the windshield and saw something shadowy looming over the waves, as if it were the prow of a ship. As we got closer, I realized that it was a large, jagged rock. More rocks became visible, hundreds of them, all jutting skyward. A channel, forty feet wide, flowed between the rocks, and the water stormed through this opening as if it were racing down a chute. O'Shea sped straight ahead. As we approached the rocks, the boat began to tremble while the swells climbed from ten to seventeen feet; the bow plunged downward, the boat sliding wildly in the water. "Hold on, mate," O'Shea said. "Here comes a big one."

The boat soared upward, and I felt momentarily suspended in the air, as if I were a cartoon character who had just stepped off a cliff. Then the boat fell straight down, and another wave crashed into it, sending us hurtling backward. My notebook and pen slid to the deck. The peanut-butter-and-jelly sandwiches we had packed for supper tumbled out of their containers. "We just need to make sure they don't take us broadside," O'Shea said.

The currents were pulling us toward the rocks, and I could hear the massive waves crashing into them. I was holding a flashlight, and I shone it in front of us: there was a twenty-foot wall of water. I turned around, and discovered that another enormous wall was pressing down on us from behind.

"You won't find this in New York, will you, mate?" O'Shea said.

For a moment, I wondered if O'Shea was fully in command of his faculties. But we made it through the gap in the rocks, and he skillfully steered the boat into a protected inlet. It was indeed the perfect spot.

We dropped our anchor. O'Shea grabbed his homemade nets, and placed several glow sticks inside them. "The squid are drawn to the light," he said. He tied the nets to a lead weight, which he then dropped in the water. We watched the light grow dimmer as the traps sank. "Well, let's see what's down there," O'Shea said.

Though oceans cover three-quarters of the Earth—the Pacific alone is bigger than all the continents put together—the underwater realm has remained largely invisible to human beings. For centuries, there was no way for scientists to peer into the depths, no telescope that could gaze into the abyss. (A pearl diver can venture down no more than a hundred feet.) Until the nineteenth century, most scientists assumed that the deepest parts of the ocean—where the temperature was frigid, the pressure intense, and the light minimal—contained no life.

In 1872, the British government and the Royal Society launched the first major oceanic expedition, transforming a two-hundred-and-twenty-six-foot naval warship into a floating laboratory, equipped with microscopes and vats of pickling alcohol. Christened H.M.S. Challenger, the ship, with five scientists, roamed the globe for three and a half years. The crew was constantly dredging the ocean floor for specimens, and the work was repetitive, and brutal; two men went insane, two others drowned, and another committed suicide. The scientists, however, were enthralled with their discoveries. They catalogued more than forty-seven hundred new species—proving, as C. Wyville Thomson, the chief scientist, later noted, that living beings "exist over the whole floor of the ocean."

The voyage gave rise to the field of oceanography, but it also exposed the twin obstacles that would impede underwater exploration for generations: prohibitive costs and primitive technology. Even when scientists could finance expeditions, their equipment allowed them to study animals only after hauling them on deck—the equivalent of looking at a human corpse, then trying to imagine it alive.

In the nineteen-thirties, two wealthy Americans, Charles William Beebe and Otis Barton, used twelve thousand dollars of their own money to design a hollow steel ball with two quartz peepholes, which they called a "bathysphere," named after the Greek word for "deep." The vessel, which was four and a half feet in diameter, was tethered to a ship with a cable; if it snapped, the men inside would die at the bottom of the sea.

In 1934, near Bermuda, Beebe and Barton went down five hundred feet, then a thousand feet more, as greater and greater pressure pushed against the steel walls; they stopped at three thousand and twenty-eight feet. It was far deeper than anyone had ever gone. At one point, Beebe peered out, and spotted something that was at least twenty feet long. Later, in his autobiography, "Half Mile Down," he wrote, "Whatever it was, it appeared and vanished so unexpectedly and showed so dimly that it was quite unidentifiable except as a large, living creature."

In 1960, the United States Navy dispatched its own team of scientists to the bottom of the Mariana Trench, the deepest spot in the ocean floor, in the Western Pacific. (It is seven times as deep as the Grand Canyon.) The voyage was considered among oceanographers to be the equivalent of landing on the moon, but America was caught up in the Cold War, and, because such exploration had little military relevance, similar projects were soon abandoned.

According to one recent study, as much as ninety-five per cent of the oceans remains unexplored. It is believed that the seas contain as many as ten million species, of which fewer than half have been identified. By the nineteen-sixties, the giant squid had become, for oceanographers, an emblem of all that was still unknown about the seas.

In the mid-nineteen-sixties, Frederick Aldrich, a marine biologist from Canada, formed the first official squid squad. He distributed posters around Newfoundland that bore an illustration of a giant squid and the words "WANTED! DEAD OR ALIVE." On one hunting trip, he spent four days in a submersible that he had baited with raw tuna, but, like so many of his expeditions, this one was fruitless.

In the nineteen-nineties, as more squid hunters took up the chase, Clyde Roper decided to let the one animal that was known to prey on *Architeuthis* find it for him. For several years, in oceans ranging from the North Atlantic to the South Pacific, he and his squad paddled out to sea in inflatable kayaks and delicately attached "crittercams"—specially designed underwater cameras—to the bodies of sperm whales. To Roper's disappointment, the crittercams didn't spy a single giant squid. In 1999, Roper, who is sixty-six, underwent a quadruple-bypass operation; though he has promised his family to desist from all the fund-raising that such expeditions require, he told me, "I'm hoping to make one more voyage."

Meanwhile, the competition between rival squid squads has intensified. Xander Paumgarten, a publicist who helped to promote a 2000 expedition by Jacques Cousteau's son Jean-Michel, told me, "There's this all-out battle between these guys. Some of them totally hate each other." Roper told me that many of the hunters now work in secret. O'Shea shares his research with several colleagues, whom he calls "gentlemen," but there are some experts he calls "cannibals," with whom he refuses to speak. "A lot of these people are vicious," he said. "They want you to fail so they can be first."

Several weeks before I ventured out with O'Shea, I joined the squid squad of Bruce Robison, one of O'Shea's leading counterparts. Unlike other hunters, Robison has two underwater robots, which have superior imaging capabilities and speed through the water more quickly than divers or most submersibles. The robots belong to Robison's employer, the Monterey Bay Aquarium Research Institute, which was founded, in 1987, by David Packard, the billionaire technology guru. Situated a hundred miles south of San Francisco, the institute has an annual budget of thirty million dollars. On the expedition I was joining, Robison and his squad planned to sink a robot worth ten million dollars in Monterey Canyon, the deepest underwater chasm along the continental United States.

Robison and his squad are "opportunists," as he put it, meaning that they film more than just squid. ("If you only look for one animal," he said, "you'll always be disappointed.") Nonetheless, the squad had planned to spend six days in the same general area where, in 1980, Robison came closer than perhaps anyone to capturing an adult *Architeuthis*. That day, he had been trawling with a net nearly two thousand feet down; he decided to bring the net to the surface, and snapped its steel jaws shut. The bars clamped down on the tentacle of a live giant squid. Before the net reached the boat, the tentacle had torn off—leaving only twelve feet of it. "There was this big thing hanging off the front of the net," Robison recalled. "The suckers were still grasping." Robison's discovery offered the most accurate recording yet of a giant squid's depth in the water column. "Until then, most people thought they were only near the bottom," he said. Robison later dissected the tentacle and performed chemical analyses; the consistency of the tissue, and its high level of protein, led him to speculate that the giant squid was "a relatively strong swimmer." Robison told me that he had taken a bite of its raw, rubbery flesh. "How could I not?" he said, adding, "It was bitter."

When I arrived at the institute, Robison and his squad were already on board the ship. The vessel was named the Western Flyer, for a fishing vessel that John Steinbeck had sailed on during a 1940 expedition, a journey he later chronicled in "The Log from the Sea of Cortez." The Western Flyer was one of the most incredible ships I had ever seen. It was a hundred and seventeen feet long, with three layers of decks, and it had an unusual rectangular shape. Its boxlike frame rested on two pontoons, each running the length of the boat, allowing the Western Flyer to remain almost still in the roughest seas.

There were twenty-one people in Robison's squad, among them computer scientists, marine biologists, chemists, and engineers. To my surprise, there seemed to be no one on deck when I stepped on board. As I opened the main door, though, I was greeted by a clatter of men and machines. In the center of the cavernous room, surrounded by crewmen communicating through headsets, was the remotely operated vehicle, or R.O.V. It was hanging from a cable attached to a crane; it was the size of a Volkswagen and weighed some eight thousand pounds. At first glance, it appeared to be nothing more than a jumble of wires. The front of the machine, or at least what I presumed was the front, had two large spotlights, which could be rotated. On the top of the machine was an outer shell with a single word painted on it: "TIBURON," Spanish for "shark."

"Welcome aboard," Robison said.

Robison was standing near the R.O.V., coordinating much of the activity. He resembled an eighteenth-century whaling captain, with white hair and a white beard; even his eyebrows were inordinately thick and wild. He began to explain how the robot operated: a coated fibre-optic wire connected the ship to the R.O.V., sending signals back and forth. The machine was propelled by electric thrusters and had flotation devices that allowed it to hover with neutral buoyancy, much like a giant squid, despite weighing four tons. What's more, the R.O.V. was outfitted with eight cameras, providing, as Robison put it, "a complete portrait of a three-dimensional universe." He added, "Our mandate is to go and see what no one else can."

He led me around the rest of the ship, which had a dining room, a computer room, a laboratory, and a freezer for preserving specimens. On the upper deck, along with the bridge, were quarters equipped with televisions, which displayed the Tiburon's live feed. "The dirty secret is that you never have to get out of bed," he said. He left me to settle in my own private room. I soon realized that the boat had already set sail: it cut so smoothly through the water that I hadn't noticed it moving.

That afternoon, we drifted over the Monterey Canyon, and stopped to make our first probe. A team of half a dozen engineers and technicians prepared the Tiburon.

"How do we look on the starboard camera?" one asked.

"Good to go."

"Do you have thrust?"

"Roger that."

The crew stepped back and the lights on the Tiburon began to blink. A trapdoor slowly opened, revealing the ocean beneath, and the Tiburon hovered above it like a spaceship. The crane then lowered the R.O.V. into the turbulent water, its snubbed head pitching forward, its fibre-optic cable trailing behind it, like an endless tail.

I walked toward the stern and into the control room, where I expected to find Robison. It was dark, except for nearly two dozen glowing monitors, which broadcast color images from the Tiburon's myriad cameras, each one capturing a different angle. Robison sat beside the pilot, who steered the R.O.V. with a joystick.

Strange gelatinous creatures began to appear, which gave off dazzling displays of bioluminescence. There was a crustacean that walked through the water like a daddy-longlegs spider, and fish with jaws that were unhinged. There was a *Tiburonia granrojo,* a red balloon-like jellyfish that Robison and his squad had discovered and named for the R.O.V., and that was one of hundreds of new species that the squad had uncovered. There was a diaphanous animal, which they still hadn't identified, and called simply "the mystery mollusk." And there was, when the Tiburon reached the soft, craggy bottom of the ocean, a constant snowfall of decomposing skeletons and microscopic organisms.

Over the next several days, as the Tiburon descended as deep as two miles, we saw hundreds of squid: blue-eyed ones, translucent ones, polka-dotted ones. Observing these squid in their natural habitat, Robison said, provided clues to the behavior of their giant relative. When a camera zoomed in on an individual squid, we could see water entering the muscular sac, or mantle, that contains the squid's internal organs; it then inflated and contracted, shooting the water out through a funnel and propelling the squid like a bullet through the ocean. Watching the animals outrace the robot, I had a sense of why Clyde Roper once said of squid, "The only ones you catch are the slow, the sick, and the stupid."

Another reason for their elusiveness is their unusually large eyes, which enable them to discern predators in places where light is nearly absent. (The giant squid's eyes are thought to be the largest of any animal.) Squid also have highly developed brains for an invertebrate, and have nerve fibres that are hundreds of times thicker than those in human beings—allowing them to react in an instant. (For many decades, neuroscientists have relied on squid neurons for their research.) "By observing squid in their natural habitat, we have discovered that they are much more intelligent, much more complex than anything we suspected," Robison said.

As we watched, the squid seemed to be using light patterns, colors, and postures as a means of communication. They didn't just turn red or pink or yellow; ripples of color would wash across their bodies. And they would contort their arms into elaborate arrangements—sometimes balling them together, or holding them above their heads, like flamenco dancers. Robison explained that they use these movements and color changes to warn other squid of predators, to perform mating rituals, to attract prey, and to conceal themselves.

Several times, when the Tiburon got too close to them, the squid ejected streams of black ink. In the past, scientists assumed that it served solely as camouflage or a decoy. Robison told me that he and other scientists now believe the ink contains chemicals that disable predators; this would explain why he has seen deep-sea squid release black nimbuses in depths where there is no light. "As much as we know about squid, we still don't know that much," he said.

Robison noted that the behavior of giant squid, in particular, was poorly understood. No one knows just how aggressive giant squid are, whether they hunt alone or in packs, or whether, as legend has it, they will attack people as well as fish. After Robison caught the tentacle and descended in a submersible to the same spot, he said, "It occurred to me that there was a pissed-off squid out there with a grudge against me." (Other scientists suspect that the giant squid's violent reputation is undeserved; O'Shea, for one, contends that *Architeuthis* is probably a "gentle beast.")

The expedition ended without a glimpse of *Architeuthis,* but, at one point, several jumbo squid did appear on the ship's screens. They were only a fraction of the size of a giant squid—between five and eight feet in length and a hundred or so pounds—but they looked frighteningly strong. One night, several of the ship's scientists dropped a jig, a device specially designed to lure squid, over the side of the boat. They caught two jumbo squid. As they reeled each squid in, screaming, "Pump him up!," the weight and strength of the animals nearly pulled the men overboard. Several minutes later, Robison and I went to the ship's laboratory, where a scientist held up one of the jumbo squid. The creature was nearly as long as Robison is tall, and its tentacles were still lashing and writhing. "Now imagine a giant squid with a tentacle thirty feet long," he said.

After the squid was dissected, part of it was given to the cook. The next day, it appeared on a silver platter. "From beast to feast," the chef said, as we sat down for supper.

"Shall we take a peek?" O'Shea said, leaning over the stern of the boat. It was after midnight, several hours since we had dropped the traps in the water; the rain had stopped, but a cold wind swirled around us. As the boat rocked in the waves, O'Shea pulled in the line, hand over hand, because the boat didn't have winches. The traps weighed at least fifty pounds, and he climbed up on the side of the boat to get a better grip, his bare feet spread apart. As the first net emerged from the water, O'Shea shouted for Conway and me to haul it in, and we laid it on the deck, as icy water spilled around our feet. "Hurry, chappies," O'Shea said. "Get the torch."

Conway shined the flashlight into the net. There were no squid, but there were swarms of krill, and O'Shea seemed buoyed by the discovery. "We're definitely in squid eating country," he said.

He dropped the nets overboard again, anchoring them in place, and began the next phase of the hunt—towing a third, larger net behind the boat. "We'll trawl for fifteen minutes at about one and a half knots," O'Shea said. The maneuver was a delicate one, he explained: if he trawled too deep or not deep enough, the paralarvae would escape the net; if he trawled for too long, the net would suffocate what he caught. We drove the boat around for precisely fifteen minutes, then pulled in the net and dumped its contents—a thick, granular goop—into a cylindrical tank filled with seawater. The tank instantly lit up from all the bioluminescence. "There's plenty of life in there, that's for sure," O'Shea said.

He found no *Architeuthis* in the tank, but he was undaunted. "If it were easy, everyone would be doing it," he said.

By all accounts, O'Shea is tireless and single-minded: he works eighteen hours a day, seven days a week, and he no longer watches TV or reads newspapers. He never attends parties. "I'm not antisocial," he said. "I just don't socialize." His sister told me, "We'd love him even if he chased mushrooms, but we just wish he'd spend the same emotion on people as he did on squid." Shoba, his wife, who often calls him to remind him to eat lunch, said, "I don't want him to stop. I just wish he could temper it a little bit and see that there are other things out there."

People inevitably compare O'Shea's quest to that of Captain Ahab. But, unlike Melville's character, O'Shea does not think of the creature he pursues in grand symbolic terms. Indeed, he is constantly trying to strip the giant squid of its lore. He considers books like "20,000 Leagues Under the Sea" to be "rubbish"; his studies of dead specimens have led him to believe that the longest recorded measurement of a giant squid—fifty-seven feet—is apocryphal. "Now, if someone really wanted to prostitute the truth all they have to do is take the tentacle and walk and walk and walk," he once told me. "The bloody things are like rubber bands, and you can make a forty-foot squid suddenly look sixty feet." Unlike some other hunters, he thinks it is ridiculous to imagine that a giant squid could kill a sperm whale. He thinks of the giant squid as both majestic and mundane—

with a precise weight, diet, length, and life span. He wants it, in short, to be real. "We have to move beyond this mythical monster and see it as it is," O'Shea said. "Isn't that enough?"

After a while, he stood and dropped the trawling net back in the water. We worked until after sunrise. When we still hadn't found any squid, O'Shea said, "An expedition that begins badly usually ends well."

At the cabin, Conway and I took a brief nap while O'Shea plotted our next course. In the afternoon, we ventured into town for supplies. O'Shea warned us not to use his real name; he had recently campaigned to shut down a nearby fishery in order to protect the wildlife, and he said that he had received several death threats. "This is quite dangerous country for me," he said.

I wasn't sure how seriously to take his warning, but, when I accidentally used his name, he became tense. "Careful, mate," he said. "Careful."

Later that day, O'Shea was standing on the cabin porch, smoking a cigarette, when a villager approached. "Are you the guy chasing them monsters?" he asked.

O'Shea looked at him hesitantly. "I'm afraid that would be me," he said.

"I saw you on the telly, talking about them things," the man said. He reached out his hand. "After I saw you, I named my cat Architeuthis."

O'Shea brightened. "This mate here has a cat named Archie," he told Conway and me.

O'Shea invited the man in for "a cuppa," and soon he and the stranger were bent down over his maps. "They say you can find the big calamari out here," the man said, pointing to a reef.

Before long, another villager stopped by and was offering his own advice. "I'd try over here," he said. "Billy Tomlin said he once found a big dead one out in these parts." O'Shea took in the information. Fishermen sometimes embroider the truth, he said, but they also know the local waters better than anyone else.

That night, we went out again. Although we continued to haul up enormous quantities of shrimp and krill—sometimes there were so many that they could barely move inside the tank—we found not a single squid.

As the night lengthened, O'Shea seemed, for the first time, to grow dispirited. "The weather's causing havoc with the currents," he said.

After each haul, he'd study his charts and choose a new spot with renewed hope—"This could be it," he'd say—only to be disappointed again. When the sun rose, at six-thirty, casting its bright rays upon the sea, O'Shea raced the boat over to the two anchored traps. He said that he had often had the best luck at dawn; the creatures seemed to rear their heads before vanishing deep below. "Let's see what we got," he said, hauling the nets on board.

"Anything?" Conway asked.

O'Shea held one of the nets up to his eye, then dropped it in disgust. "Diddly," he said.

"We have to go farther out," O'Shea said the following night. We sped far into the Pacific, leaving the safety of the inlet behind. The hauls remained dismal; after each one, he aimed the boat farther out to sea, saying, "We have to go deeper, that's all."

Conway, who was looking increasingly pale, said, "Haven't we gone out enough?"

"I know the squid are out there," O'Shea said.

The less he found, the harder he seemed to work. He is not a big man, and his childhood illness had left his body somewhat brittle, yet he never slowed down as he pulled the net in with all its weight, then returned it to the water. His fingers were covered in blisters, his clothes were soaked through, and his glasses were stained with salt from the seawater.

"He's a bit of a fanatic, isn't he?" Conway said quietly.

As the cold nights wore on, we worked in a kind of fog. We were getting little sleep during the day, and it became harder to pay attention to the mounds of larval fish, shrimp, krill, and jellyfish; not even the sight of dolphins jumping in the waters nearby relieved the drudgery. At one point, I felt fatigued, and lay down in the forward berth. I could fit only if I bent my knees toward my chest. As I closed my eyes and listened to the waves smashing against the hull, I could hear O'Shea grunting as he pulled in another net and cursing when there was nothing inside.

On yet another night, at around four in the morning, as we pulled in the trawling gear and dropped the contents in the cylindrical tank, Conway shone a flashlight and asked, "What's that?"

O'Shea peered inside, and blinked several times, trying to keep himself awake. "Heaven help us!" he shouted. "It's a fucking squid!" He stared blearily into its eyeball. "It looks like Archie," he told us.

Although the creature was only the size of my thumbnail, I could see it, too—its tentacles, its fins, its eyes, its arms, its bullet-shaped mantle.

"This could be your dream squid," Conway said.

"Quick," O'Shea said. "Let's drain some of the krill before they crush it."

He held the cylindrical tank in the air, his arms shaking from exhaustion, as the waves pounded the side of the boat. "Steady!" he yelled. It was hard to see in the darkness—there was no moonlight—and as he poured some of the contents into a strainer, struggling to balance against the violent waves, something happened.

"Where did it go?" O'Shea asked.

"I don't know," Conway said. "I can't see it anymore."

"Jesus Christ," O'Shea said.

He grabbed a specially designed tank, which he had purchased expressly for transporting a baby giant squid, and poured the rest of the cylindrical tank's contents inside it. "Where is the bloody thing?" he said. "Where is it?"

He reached in with his hand, stirring the water frantically. "It has to be here," he said.

He pulled out one shrimp, then another, holding them under the light. "It's gone," Conway said.

But O'Shea didn't seem to hear. He sifted through the mounds of plankton, trying to find the baby squid's microscopic tentacles. At last, he stumbled backward, and put his arms over his head. "It's a fucking catastrophe," he said.

He fell back in the captain's chair, and sat motionless. I tried to think of something to say, but failed. "It was right there," O'Shea said to himself. "I had it."

After a while, he tried to drop the traps in the water again, but he no longer seemed able to muster his strength. "I can't take it anymore," he said, and disappeared into the forward berth.

That afternoon, O'Shea was sitting on the cabin porch, sipping a glass of whiskey. "Want a spot?" he asked.

"That's all right," I said.

He spoke in a whisper, and much more slowly than usual. He said he had pinpointed a new location to search, but I told him I thought I would stay behind and catch up on my work. He looked at me for a long moment. "That's what always happens," he said. "People get bored and give up. But I can't pay any attention to what's going on around me. I just have to stay focussed."

He took a sip of his whiskey. "I can already hear the critics saying, 'The great squid hunter lost his blasted squid again.' Do you know how it feels when everything goes to custard like this?" He fell silent again, then added, "I'm not going to stop. I'm not going to give up. I don't care if someone finds the squid first. I'll *still* go until I find it myself."

The next morning, when he pushed open the cabin door, he looked despairing. "Nothing," he said. "Nothing."

It was the end of the expedition; he had to go back to Auckland to lecture. We loaded up the gear and returned to the city. When we got there, O'Shea went to the aquarium to visit his specimens. In his absence, seventeen squid had died. The employee in whose care he had left them had posted a sign on the tank. It said, "They have a new trick . . . It's called 'jumping out of the tank and committing suicide!' "

O'Shea checked the temperature and salinity of the water in the tank, and offered the remaining squid some sprat. Then we drove to his house. As he got out of his car, he said, "You may want to take a look at this."

He led me into the garage, which was cluttered with tools and appliances. He started to clear off an enormous box. "You better put this on," he said, and handed me a gas mask.

I slipped it over my face, and he opened the top of the bin. Inside was a dead giant squid. "It's a twenty-seven-foot male," he said.

The carcass was ivory white and was floating in embalming fluids; its arms were so long that they were bunched together in folds, and its suckers were the size of a child's fist. "I'm preparing this one for a museum," he said.

He told me that he had buried one squid corpse in his garden, under a patch of watermelons. Leaning over the box, he picked up the dead animal's mantle, which was bigger than he was. "That's the head," he said.

He turned it over, and I could see a massive, lidless eye staring out at us.

"See here, this is the mouth," he said, speaking rapidly again. He stuck his fingers inside the white cusp of flesh, revealing a sharp black beak and a serrated tongue. "It'll cut right through your cartilage," he said.

Though O'Shea didn't have a mask on, he took a deep breath and, with great exertion, lifted half of the creature in his arms. He grabbed a tentacle and started to extend it. "Look at it. They're fantastic, aren't they?"

He ran his fingers up and down its limbs, opening and closing its suckers. For a moment, he shut his eyes, as if he were trying to imagine it underwater. Then he said, "The dead one is beautiful, but it's the live one I want."

— May, 2004

—⁓—

In December, 2006, near the Ogasawara Islands, south of Tokyo, a Japanese scientist and his squad finally captured a live giant squid. After spending years pinpointing a potential location, they attached a chunk of squid to a missile-shaped multipronged hook and dropped it more than two thousand feet down. Eventually, they caught a relatively small female giant squid, measuring eleven and a half feet long and weighing a hundred and ten pounds. As the men tried to reel it in, the giant squid spouted water from its funnel and struggled to escape. By the time the men pulled the elusive creature on board, it had died from injuries. O'Shea has not given up his quest.

City of Water

CAN AN
ANTIQUATED
MAZE OF TUNNELS
CONTINUE TO
SUSTAIN NEW YORK?

No one knows how many sandhogs are, at any given moment, working beneath the streets of New York City, but one winter morning half a dozen men could be spotted gathering around a hole on the northwest corner of Tenth Avenue and Thirtieth Street. The hole, surrounded by a tall aluminum fence, was thirty feet wide and reinforced with concrete. A priest had visited months before, to offer a brief prayer: "May God be with all ye who enter here, that the earth shall return ye safely." Now, as the sun rose, the men stepped from the snow-covered ground into a green metal cage, which was suspended over the chasm by an enormous winch. They wore yellow slickers and rubber boots with steel tips; they carried, among other things, flashlights, scissors, cigarettes, cough drops, knives, extra socks, and several twenty-pound crates marked "EXPLO-SIVES."

A worker who was to remain above ground pulled a lever, and the cage began to descend. As it accumulated speed, and the light from the surface grew thinner, James Ryan, one of the older men in the crew, peered over the edge into the void. He had a long, hard face flecked with scars. "We got nine cases of dynamite," he said. "That should be plenty."

His voice reverberated in the shaft as the men went down thirty, forty, fifty feet, then another fifty, then a hundred more. "Two hundred," one of them called out. By three hundred feet, they could no longer see anything above or below. Surrounded by darkness, and pressed closely together, the men exchanged sight for sound—the ping of dripping water, the echo of voices, the cable groaning overhead. At five hundred feet, the air became warmer, denser; one of the men put on a mask to keep out the dust that floated through the shaft. "All right," Ryan told me. "We're almost there."

A thin beam from a flashlight suddenly rose up from the bottom of the shaft, catching the men's faces. They were all part of the fraternity of sand-hogs, a rare breed of tunnel digger whose name comes from the workers who excavated the soft earth under the Brooklyn Bridge in the eighteen-seventies. The men in the cage with me were mostly middle-aged, with barrel chests and knotted fingers; dust had already begun to streak the skin around their eyes. A bell sounded, and the cage came to a halt, bouncing up and down on the cable. "This is it," Ryan said. "Brace yourself." He unsealed the cage door. We were nearly six hundred feet underground.

Until that moment, I had only heard tales of New York City's invisible empire, an elaborate maze of tunnels that goes as deep as the Chrysler Building is high. Under construction in one form or another for more than a century, the system of waterways and pipelines spans thousands of miles and comprises nineteen reservoirs and three lakes. Two main tunnels provide New York City with most of the 1.3 billion gallons of water it consumes each day, ninety per cent of which is pumped in from reservoirs upstate by the sheer force of gravity. Descending through aqueducts from as high as fourteen hundred feet above sea level, the water gathers speed, racing down to a thousand feet below sea level when it reaches the pipes beneath the city.

It is a third water tunnel, however, that is the most critical. Designed to meet expanding demand and to serve as a backup system in case something ever happens to City Tunnel No. 1 or City Tunnel No. 2, City Tunnel No. 3 has been under development since 1969, and was initially billed as "the greatest nondefense construction project in the history of Western Civilization." Already, twenty-four people have died building it—roughly a man a mile—and it is not expected to be completed until 2020.

As an engineering feat, the water-tunnel system rivals the Brooklyn Bridge and the Panama Canal. Yet it has the odd distinction that almost no one will ever see it, save for the sandhogs who are building it. Over the years, the men have constructed an entire city under the city, a subterranean world as cluttered as the Manhattan skyline: it includes four hundred and thirty-eight miles of subway lines, six thousand miles of sewers, and thousands of miles of gas mains. "If it's deeper than a grave," sandhogs often say, "then we built it." The water tunnels have become the sandhogs' greatest and most elusive achievement, an often deadly effort that has consumed generations. "I'll take you down there if you want," Jimmy Ryan had said when I asked him to show me the tunnel's newest section. "But, trust me, it ain't like Macy's down there."

A large, reticent man of fifty who prefers gestures—an upturned eyebrow or a curled lip—to words, he has spent nearly as many hours underneath the earth as above it. "I started working on the third water tunnel when I was a kid," he told me. "I'm still working on it, and I'll probably be buried in it." Ryan, who was elected president of the sandhogs' union, Local 147, in 1999, has trouble lifting his shoulders; his red hair has turned silver, and his broad chest is compressed, as if it were about to collapse.

After Ryan opened the cage, I stepped out with him and the other men into the bottom of the shaft. Water seeped down the sides of the opening and dripped on us. There was a pool at our feet, and as we moved forward the icy water spilled over the tops of our boots. I began to sink in the muck, and Ryan gave me his hand to pull me out.

"Don't stand under the shaft," he said. "If somethin' falls from the top, it'll go right through you." I looked up and could barely see the opening. Once, in Queens, a sixteen-ton winch fell down the shaft, crushing one worker and injuring seven others; another time, a man died after being impaled by a broken icicle.

As I followed Ryan into the tunnel's main artery, it was hard to orient myself. There were only a few scattered electric bulbs, suspended from wires clamped to rocks and shrouded in mist, and I blinked, trying to adjust to the watery light. Several of the men turned on flashlights; through the shadows I could see a hospital stretcher and emergency medical supplies propped against a wall. At last, the tunnel came into focus: a cramped, crumbling cavern that extended a hundred yards or so in either direction.

This stage of Tunnel No. 3 will eventually run nine miles, reaching down to the Manhattan Bridge and looping up to Central Park; its walls will be honed into a smooth cylinder, ten feet in diameter and lined with concrete. But at this early stage swords of black schist—formed more than four hundred million years ago—hung from the ceiling, which was buttressed with steel bolts to prevent collapse. Ventilation pipes ran along the sides of the tunnel, circulating the choked air, which, unlike the freezing air at the surface, was nearly seventy degrees, a humid mist of dust and fumes.

The men split into two groups and went to opposite ends of the tunnel, where they began painting detailed patterns on the rock face. Moving out from the center of the rock, they carefully dabbed white dots about three feet apart, forming an elaborate grid. Then the sandhogs mounted hydraulic drills and bored a ten-foot-deep hole into each mark, their arms and legs rattling up and down, the lamps on their hard hats shaking.

As the men prepared the rock face, listening to each echo for any sign of danger, they spoke in a private language: a jackhammer was known as a "jackleg"; a bucket, a "battleship"; the Nerf-like sponge used to clean a pipe was called a "rabbit." Sometimes, because of the noise, the men would simply draw images in the air, like mimes. After a while, they took out blowpipes, which blasted air and water into the holes, washing away the dirt. "Everything has to be done just right," Ryan told me.

With his knife, he opened one of the boxes of explosives. Inside were dozens of red sticks of dynamite. The men packed the sticks into the holes as if loading muskets. Each piece of dynamite was wired to the next, and soon dozens of cords crisscrossed the rock face. Then the men turned off the lights, one by one, until the tunnel was completely dark, except for a single flashlight that guided us back to the metal cage. "We need to be a thousand feet away," Ryan said, as we slowly rose to the surface. "It's not like the old days, when they'd blow the son of a bitch in your ear."

When we reached the street, the sun was fully in the sky, and Ryan squinted uncomfortably in the light. He leaned over a small detonator while the men cleared the intersection of pedestrians. A woman in a camel coat, who insisted that she was late for work, tried to force her way past. "One minute," Ryan said, cocking an eyebrow. Another sandhog put his hand on the T-shaped lever. "Now," Ryan said. The sandhog slammed the lever with both hands, yelling, "Fire in the hole! Fire in the hole!"

There was a great roar, a percussive rumble that grew louder and louder. The sidewalk and fences began to tremble, along with the ground beneath our feet. The crane that was suspended above the hole rattled from side to side. One bystander looked up at the sky, then down at the ground, not sure what was happening. "Is it a bomb?" another asked. A plume of dust rose out of the shaft. Then everything fell silent. The tunnel had advanced another nine feet. "All right, hogs!" the foreman yelled. And, before anyone noticed, Ryan and the other men vanished into the hole.

At the end of the day, the sandhogs congregated in the hog house, a small white shack with wooden benches, lockers, and a shower, inside the fenced area on Thirtieth Street. Yellow slickers, now black with mud, hung from hooks. A television set murmured in the corner, and several men stood around it in towels while another mopped the floor around their feet.

Ryan sat down at a table to talk with me. His elbow rested on his hard hat; a line of mud traced the side of his cheek. He had lost part of his hearing from the constant concussions, and he spoke louder than normal.

"No one wants to talk about it, but we're flirting with disaster," he said. The old tunnels, Ryan explained, were leaking "like a sieve"; some of the sections were built nearly a century ago and were in desperate need of repair. But until Tunnel No. 3 is virtually complete there will be no way to fix them. In part, this is because getting inside Tunnel No. 1 or No. 2 would require the city to shut the water off, and without a backup supply there would be serious water shortages. But it was more than that, and, as several sandhogs peered over his shoulder, Ryan started to draw a circle on the table with his muddy finger. "See this?" he asked me. "These are the valves that control the flow of water."

"They're hundreds of feet underground," another sandhog said.

The valves were designed, Ryan said, to open and close guillotine-like gates inside the cylindrical tunnels, stopping the flow of water. But they had become so brittle with age that they were no longer operable. "They're afraid if they try to shut the valves they won't be able to turn 'em back on," Ryan said.

He wiped some mud from his eyes. "Look," he said. "If one of those tunnels goes, this city will be completely shut down. In some places there won't be water for anything. Hospitals. Drinking. Fires. It would make September 11th look like nothing."

Ryan wasn't the only one who spoke of the tunnel system's frailties, even if the others did so in slightly less alarming terms. One day in the spring of 2003, I met Christopher Ward, the head of the city's Department of Environmental Protection, which is responsible for designing and operating the tunnel system. With a broad chest and a blunt, goateed chin, he looks more like a sandhog than like a politician, and has a tendency to lean forward when he speaks, as if about to leap to his feet. "People don't want to acknowledge it, but the useful life of a tunnel does exist, and at some point it does start to fail," he said. The metal valves, in particular, degrade until they can no longer withstand the pressure. Ward said that the original two tunnels were so dilapidated that it was too risky to try to shut off the water and repair them until City Tunnel No. 3 was operational. He added that there is still time before the aging tunnels collapse—"We're not talking about today or tomorrow"—though it is impossible to predict how much.

Others are more pessimistic. One D.E.P. scientist told me, "Some of the aqueducts are already hemorrhaging water badly," while a recent study by Riverkeeper, an environmental organization, concluded, "In some cases, this extraordinary infrastructure is literally crumbling." Upstate, in the industrial town of Newburgh, for example, water has begun to pour out of cracks in the underground aqueduct that feeds into the city tunnels—so much that the leaks have created a giant sinkhole.

Many experts worry that the old tunnel system could collapse all at once. "Engineers will tell you if it fails it will not fail incrementally," said Ward. "It will fail catastrophically." If City Tunnel No. 1, which is considered the most vulnerable, caved in, all of lower Manhattan and downtown Brooklyn, as well as parts of the Bronx, would lose its water supply. If the aqueducts gave out, the entire city would be cut off. "There would be no water," Ward told me. "These fixes aren't a day or two. You're talking about two to three years."

In the past, the city sometimes tried to assuage concerns about New York's water system, but Mayor Michael Bloomberg noted at a 2003 press conference that the aging pipelines were "very vulnerable" and that "this city could be brought to its knees if one of the aqueducts collapsed."

Anthony DelVescovo, the project manager who has been working on City Tunnel No. 3 for nearly fifteen years, echoed Bloomberg's warning. "What no one knows is that we're facing a potential apocalypse," he told me. "It's a race against the clock."

It is hard to imagine a city without water, its faucets empty, its hydrants dry, its plazas filled not with fountains but with citizens suffering from diseases spread by dirt and desiccation—to imagine, as Charles Einstein put it in the title of his 1964 futuristic novel, "The Day New York Went Dry."

For much of its history, however, New York was a parched city. Though surrounded by the sea, its principal supply of freshwater remained, as late as the eighteenth century, a single fetid pool in lower Manhattan called the Collect Pond. Human waste was dumped into it, along with the occasional dead body. Distribution of water was dominated by racketeers known as teamen, who roamed the streets with giant casks, gouging customers. In 1785, with the city's population reaching nearly thirty thousand, the New York *Journal* published an open letter to government officials complaining that the water supply had become a "common sewer." One daily newspaper declared that it was "sickly and nauseating," adding, "The larger the city grows, the worse this evil will be."

Even as the paper warned that a "plague will make a yearly slaughter until you furnish better water," pestilence spread through the squalid streets. In 1798, yellow fever wiped out two thousand New Yorkers, and venders wandered the streets yelling, "Coffins of all sizes!" The plague returned in 1805, 1819, and 1822. "New Yorkers are like the rich man told of in the Parable," one resident noted in the local paper. "They have no clean cool water to slack their thirst when the flames of the plague are devouring their vitals."

One summer morning in 1832, two children woke up in Manhattan with severe pain in their intestines. They stopped urinating and were overcome by thirst; they began to vomit and their skin turned blue. By the next day, they were dead, and two days later so was their mother.

Asiatic cholera, an excruciating disease that is spread, in large part, by water contaminated with feces, had struck. In barely a month, two thousand New Yorkers were dead, their bodies marked by a bluish tinge and puckered extremities; more than a hundred thousand residents—half the city's population—fled to outlying villages. By the time the scourge ended, the death toll had reached more than three thousand. A group of doctors who visited the city at the time reported a "constant and imploring" cry: "Cold water, cold water, give us cold water!"

Finally, in the winter of 1834, the Common Council vowed to locate new sources of water. But before plans got under way a fire broke out near Wall Street. Without enough water to extinguish it—the rivers were frozen solid—the flames leaped from roof to roof, carried by a gale-force wind. Within minutes, the fire had spread from Exchange Place to Water Street, then on to Front and South Streets, and still onward. (The smoke was visible as far away as Philadelphia.) The fire burned for twenty-four hours, and after it had consumed nearly seven hundred buildings and caused such mass looting that the military was called in, roughly a third of New York City lay in ruins. One witness, who called it "the most awful calamity which has ever visited these United States," wrote, "I am fatigued in body, disturbed in mind, and my fancy filled with images of horror which my own pen is inadequate to describe."

And so at last the city began to construct its first aqueduct.

By today's standards, the Croton Aqueduct is modest in scope, but at the time it was considered an architectural marvel. Begun in 1837 and completed in 1842, it extended more than thirty miles, running from the Croton Reservoir down the east bank of the Hudson River—an elegant, eight-by-seven-foot brick pipeline. When it was finished, church bells rang out across the city and thousands poured into the streets to parade past new fountains, whose water sparkled in the sun. Philip Hone, who eventually became mayor of New York, wrote in his diary, "Nothing is talked of or thought of in New York but Croton water. . . . Water! water! is the universal note which is sounded through every part of the city, and infuses joy and exultation into the masses."

Twelve years later, however, the city's demand for water again exceeded supply, and the pressure in the pipeline fell so low that the water could no longer reach the third story of a building. By 1882, with thousands of immigrants arriving each week, the *Times* pleaded, "More Water Wanted," adding, "The health of families . . . was jeopardized because sufficient water could not be secured." Yet, unlike the previous century, when the city had looked on impassively at civic problems, there was now an almost evangelical faith in human progress. In 1905, Mayor George McClellan, who had just inaugurated the city's first subway system, laid out a vision of "an additional supply of pure and wholesome water," a vision so bold that it struck many as evidence of hubris. At an estimated cost of a hundred and eighty-five million dollars—3.7 billion in today's dollars—it would be the largest municipal water system in the world. In 1907, at the groundbreaking, McClellan declared, "The course of human events is not permanently altered by the great deeds of history, nor by the great men but by the small daily doings of the little men."

Before long, thousands of laborers arrived in the Catskill Mountains and began clearing away vegetation. Under the expansive McClellan Act, which one judge complained gave "power that the Almighty would not delegate to an archangel," the city appropriated more than twenty-five thousand acres of land, including hundreds of homes around the area of Shokan, which is just south of Woodstock. Nine villages were torn down, some burned to the ground, and nearly three thousand residents driven out; even cemeteries were dug up. "The trees are all cut down and the village is fading as a dream," the Kingston *Freeman* reported.

Then dams were built, water was diverted from streams in the Catskills, and rain was collected. The entire elevated basin was flooded, creating one of several reservoirs that, together, are nearly as large as the island of Manhattan. In photographs of the Shokan area taken before the flooding, the land is green and expansive; months later, it is covered by a glasslike inland sea.

Meanwhile, sandhogs burrowed through mountains and under hillsides to construct the Catskill Aqueduct, a ninety-two-mile conduit that slopes gently downhill from Shokan to Storm King Mountain and then down to White Plains. At one point, it crosses below the Hudson River, at a depth of eleven hundred feet—an achievement that New York City's new mayor, William Gaynor, called "one of the greatest engineering feats in history." The hardest part of the project, however, was yet to come. According to the engineers' elaborate design, water would flow from the aqueduct into a reservoir in Yonkers. From there, it would be channelled into another tunnel—one dug deep beneath the city, and able to withstand the pressure of more than half a billion gallons coursing through it each day. This water would then begin flowing upward, into smaller and smaller pipes, ultimately discharging into the millions of faucets around the city. Construction on what became known as City Tunnel No. 1 began in 1911. Many men went down once and never went back. Those who stayed received about two dollars a day. Once, under the strain, a riot erupted twelve hundred feet underground, and workers attacked each other with picks and shovels.

The situation was equally difficult on the banks of the East River. According to "Liquid Assets," a history of the city's water system by Diane Galusha, natural groundwater made the rock so soft that the shafts which allowed sandhogs to descend into the tunnel became watery death traps. Engineers were forced to build on each bank a giant inverted box called a caisson—a risky device that was pioneered during the laying of the foundations of the Brooklyn Bridge. About fifteen feet on each side and weighing as much as two thousand tons, the steel-and-concrete boxes were sealed on all sides except the bottom. As they were lowered into the soft ground, compressed air was pumped into the caissons, pushing out the mud and water. To get into the caisson the sandhogs were lowered in a bucket down a steel shaft; from there they entered an air lock, much like a diving chamber. Air was pumped in, and the sandhogs could feel their eardrums strained to bursting, the blood rushing to the center of their bodies. Many assumed that they were dying.

Once the pressure in the air lock was equal to that inside the caisson, the sandhogs crawled through a trapdoor into the caisson, where, standing ankle-deep in mud, they began to dig from the bottom, removing the muck in a bucket through a hatch in the ceiling. As they dug, under pressure that was so great they could work for only two hours at a time, the caisson would slowly sink, allowing the sides of the box to carve the lining of a shaft. An engineer who had been in a caisson during the construction of the Brooklyn Bridge described the sensation this way: "The pulse was at first accelerated, then sometimes fell below the normal rate. The voice sounded faint, unnatural, and it became a great effort to speak. What with the flaming lights, the deep shadows, the confusing noise of hammers, drills, and chains, the half-naked forms flitting about, with here and there a Sisyphus rolling his stone, one might, if of a poetic temperament, get a realizing sense of Dante's Inferno."

More unnerving, though, was the threat of a "blowout"—a breach in the lining of the caisson wall, caused by a sudden imbalance of pressure, which created suction much like that of an airplane door opened in mid-flight, accompanied by a terrifying kettle-like screech. Men had a few seconds to climb inside the air lock; if they didn't make it, they could be sucked into the earth, as happened in 1916, during the construction of a tunnel under the East River, when three men were swallowed through a crevice; two died, while a third, Marshall Mabey, was propelled safely into the afternoon sky on a geyser said to be four stories high. "I felt myself being pushed into the hole," Mabey later explained to a reporter. "As I struck the mud it felt as though something was squeezing me tighter than I had ever been squeezed. I was almost smothered."

It's not known how many sandhogs died building the Catskill system, but in 1913 the Pine Hill *Sentinel* reported, "Approximately ten out of every 100 [workers] are killed or injured every year. More than 3,800 accidents, serious and otherwise, to workers on the great aqueduct have been recorded. . . . The men doing the rough work are virtually all foreigners or negroes. Owing to the laborers being so inconspicuous, the death by accident of one or more of them attracts no public attention."

In 1917, more than a decade after the work began, the last explosion was sounded. It was now possible to walk underground from Manhattan all the way to the Catskills. The city marked the accomplishment, but the event was more subdued than the Croton celebration. The moment a new fountain by the reservoir in Central Park was turned on, the skies opened up and rain poured down.

"Hey, can you smell it?" Jimmy Ryan asked.

"What is it?" I asked.

"Dynamite."

We were back inside City Tunnel No. 3, watching the sandhogs scoop out the blasted rock—"mucking it out," as Ryan called it. It had been only minutes since I watched the men detonate the explosives, and the misty air was laden with smoke and dust; soon, a thin yellow film covered everything. Rocks that had endured earthquakes had been smashed against the surrounding walls. Some were cracked in two, revealing bits of mica, beautiful white glimmers amid the dust; others were black and dull.

At this early stage, the method of digging through the rock was similar to that used on the first water tunnel. As Ryan put it, "You stick the dynamite in, blow the motherfucker up, then haul the shit out." It was a repetitive, driving ritual, one in which there was no day or night and the sound of concussions replaced the passage of time. The men now loaded crushed granite into enormous buckets that carried as much as twenty-eight tons in a single load and were hoisted out by a crane through the same shaft that the men had come down. Each sandhog had his own role in the operation. There were muckers and blasters and signalmen and nippers; these last remained above the hole, connecting materials to the hoist. One veteran nipper, Brian Thorne, told me, "Everyone has a skill. My best skill is rigging. The guys downstairs want to know they can trust the guy that's upstairs to put stuff over their head and not worry. If you hit someone, you can't say, 'Oops, I'm sorry.' That person is dead. So you always have to be on top of your game."

Over the years, Ryan had risen from mucker to foreman, or "walking boss," and now, as president of the sandhogs' union, he is largely responsible for the whole gang. One colleague paid him the highest compliment you can give a sandhog: "No job is too dirty for Jimmy." But as Ryan waded through the mud, his eyes peering out from under his hard hat, he seemed slightly removed. When younger sandhogs started to recall some near-death tale, he would arch an eyebrow and say, "You got some line," or "You're a real bullshit artist, aren't you?" Unlike the other men, who tell stories about the tunnel the same way fishermen spin tales about the sea, Ryan rarely speaks of his time underground. When his shift is over, he heads home to Queens, where he often changes from his digger uniform into bright golf pants and plays the links, trying to propel the ball with his sore arms as he breathes in the smell of freshly cut grass. His wife told me, "He never says a word about the tunnel. I don't know what he does down there."

Ryan is not, by the standards of the trade, a particularly superstitious man—he doesn't carry a lucky crescent wrench or refuse to go down on

Friday the thirteenth—but he maintains a constant watchfulness. And now, while the others told jokes, Ryan stood off by himself, quietly inspecting the walls to make sure there were no cracks that might cause chunks to shear off.

After a while, he trudged to the end of the tunnel, where there was a pile of smoldering rubble. At lesser depths, sandhogs had been known to uncover jewelry, murder weapons, false teeth, a chest of coins, a Colonial dungeon. "In the sewer tunnels, you sometimes find rats," Ryan said. "But this far down there are only sandhogs."

He reached into his pocket and pulled out a plastic bag, which he carefully unwrapped, revealing not his lunch but a pack of Marlboros. He was the only one who, in spite of the stinging dust, seemed always to work with a cigarette dangling from the corner of his mouth—like the detectives in the old dime novels he likes to read.

Some of the men propped a ten-foot ladder against the rubble and Ryan started to climb it, the embers of his cigarette leading the way. "Come on," he said. When I reached the top, he pointed down the tunnel, as if to say, Go on, take a look. And I saw a dozen figures moving through the dusty haze. There was a cacophony: men slamming picks into the jagged rocks, drills probing new holes, buckets moving back and forth amid sparks that flickered like fireflies. After five months of blasting and mucking, of two shifts working sixteen hours a day, of engineers and contractors measuring the quickest route, they had advanced only two city blocks, from Twenty-ninth Street to Thirty-first Street. But as I peered from one end to the other at the ceiling of rock, dripping with water and bathed in sulfurous light, I could sense the first hint of a design.

"So, what do you think of our cathedral?" Ryan asked.

Later, as he was taking off his boots in the hog house, Ryan told me, "You know, my grandfather did the same thing." He clapped his boots together. "He came to this country in 1922, from England. He started working first on the Holland Tunnel, but then they started the second water tunnel and he moved over to that. It was even bigger than Tunnel No. 1. It was pretty brutal. That much I can tell you."

In 1929, to keep pace with water consumption, which had increased by thirty-five million gallons per day since the first tunnel was built, the city began to construct Tunnel No. 2. Once again, another aqueduct was built, this one drawing water from the Delaware River. (It is still listed in the "Guinness Book of World Records" as the world's longest water-supply tunnel.) Once again, villages were flooded and cemeteries were dug up.

Nick Ryan, Jimmy's grandfather, was tall, with a muscular physique and red hair. Jimmy Ryan is said to resemble him, but Nick was more of "a wild man," as his grandson puts it, with a distinct hint of understatement. He was known for his penchant for whiskey, which in those days was often consumed in the tunnel. He had little, if any, formal education. Most of the sandhogs of his generation were recently arrived immigrants, typically from Ireland, Italy, and the West Indies, who would show up for work in their only set of clothes and wrap plastic bags around their shoes. The Board of Water Supply would sometimes put them in camps, and try to teach their children to read and write; the townspeople occasionally complained of "immigrant hordes." Black-and-white photographs taken at the time show Nick's gang standing in the tunnel, only a few beams of timber supporting the crumbling rock over their heads. Instead of a hard hat, Nick Ryan wore something more like a cowboy hat. In a 1936 log from one of the earliest meetings of Local 147, to which Nick belonged, there is a warning to the men not to pack pistols.

"Even during the Depression, most men wouldn't take these jobs," one miner who was in the union with Nick Ryan recalled in an oral history. "Nobody was going to go down and work with a shovel all day and then work in compressed air. We had some hard, hard people, and you had to be a rough commander. . . . They told you, Do it or get the hell out. So the only ones, as the insurance adjusters will tell you, that survived were the most fit."

Nick Ryan endured chest pains, broken limbs, bleeding sinuses, and caisson disease—the bends. Then, in 1937, with his family still in need of money, Nick Ryan took his eighteen-year-old son, Joe, down the shaft with him. "That's how my father learned how to survive underground," Jimmy Ryan recalled.

"Years ago, it started as a father-son business," a sandhog whose father worked side by side with Joe Ryan told me. "The fathers brought the sons in, then the brothers brought the brothers in, and the sons brought the cousins in. I don't know how you word this, but no one ever asked you your pedigree if you came here. They didn't care if you had a criminal record—as long as you worked you could stay in the hole."

Shorter and more compact than his father, Joe Ryan was known as Red. A ferociously driven and, to those who didn't know him well, intimidating man, he carried the burden—and perhaps the anger—of someone who had given up a football scholarship at Wake Forest University to work underground, helping to support a father who was sometimes out too late to make it to work on time. After Nick Ryan died, in 1958, his son briefly ran a gas station. But before long he returned underground—to the place that he knew best.

By the fifties, the city was already in frantic pursuit of more "pure and wholesome water." This time, it was not simply demand from an exploding population, or even droughts, that provoked alarm. This time, it was something that few, if any, had ever contemplated.

In 1954, unbeknownst to most residents of the city, several engineers went into a shaft to try to turn off the water supply in City Tunnel No. 1, to see if the tunnel needed repairs after being in operation for almost half a century. "Imagine your faucet after only ten years," Christopher Ward, the D.E.P. commissioner, said. "These things had been pounded away at for decades."

At the bottom of the shaft, sticking out of the tunnel, was a long bronze stem with a rotating wheel at the end. It was supposed to control the six-foot-diameter valve inside the pipeline. But when the engineers started to turn the handle, using all their might, it began to tremble and crack. "There was too much pressure on it," Ward said.

"They were afraid if they turned it any more the whole fucking thing would break," Richard Fitzsimmons, Jr., the business manager of the sandhogs' union, said.

After decades of building the world's greatest water system, the city had stumbled across its weak point, a single flaw that had rendered an otherwise invincible body mortal. "It scared the bejeezus out of people," Doug Greeley, an engineer in charge of the city's water distribution, said. There was no effective way to shut off the water, no way to get inside and weld a crack, no way to know if a tunnel was about to burst.

By the late sixties, officials had decided that something had to be done. "One of the original tunnels was seventy years old, and we were unable to repair any valves," Ed Koch, who was a congressman at the time, recalled. In some cases, he said, "we didn't even know where the valves were." Koch, who later served three terms as mayor, added, "You can exist without food, but you can't exist without water."

On a cold January day in 1970, the ground was officially broken for the third water tunnel, which would dwarf both of its predecessors. Designed to be constructed in four stages, it would extend sixty miles, from the reservoir in Yonkers through the Bronx and down to the southern tip of Manhattan, and then into Brooklyn and Queens. The project would include another underground aqueduct. More important, at the center of the entire system would be thirty-four specially designed valves that would be made not of bronze but of stainless steel, with shorter stems that could withstand greater force. (Most were manufactured in Japan, where city inspectors lived for two years to insure that they were made according to precise measurements.) All of the valves would be contained in a single centralized chamber, where they could be easily reached and turned off.

Construction on the chamber began in 1970 and was not finished until 1998. Though the tunnel sections that will feed into the chamber have not yet been completed, the D.E.P. gave me a glimpse inside the vault—which is in the Bronx, not far from the sandhogs' union hall. There is nothing above ground to indicate the vault's existence except a small guard tower and a sealed door that leads into a grassy hillside. "Ordinarily, we're not supposed to let anyone in," Greeley told me, standing outside the door.

Like many of "the pencils," as the sandhogs call the engineers, Greeley is a fastidious man: he has a neatly trimmed mustache and was wearing a blue blazer and a tie. The main door, which he unlocked as if it were a safe, was constructed out of solid steel. "They built this place during the Cold War," he said. "It's supposed to withstand a ten-megaton nuclear bomb."

As he pressed his weight against the door, it gradually gave way, emitting a loud sigh. It was damp and cool inside; the corridor was made of concrete. After descending a flight of metal steps, we rode an elevator twenty-five stories down. As Greeley opened another thick door, he said, "Prepare to have your perception of the water supply permanently altered."

The vault resembled an airplane hangar; it extended more than two hundred yards, with a domed ceiling that was forty-one feet high and walls that were cloaked in condensation and algae. Lights hung from the top like crescent moons. Suspended twenty feet off the ground, one after the other, were the valves, or, rather, the pipes that contained them: seventeen thirty-five-ton steel cylinders with studded bolts that reached horizontally from one side of the forty-two-foot-wide vault to the other. Each cylinder contained two valves. A metal gangplank ran alongside them, and Greeley walked excitedly to the first cylinder, running his hand along the torpedo-like shell. "This way, if a tunnel develops a crack, we can shut it off from here," he said. "Everything's right at your fingertips."

If a valve broke, the cylinder could be lowered down to the bottom of the vault, and carried out on tracks. One piece, Greeley explained, could be removed without disrupting the rest of the system. The old tunnels had run in a straight line from the reservoirs into the city, but City Tunnel No. 3 was designed with various redundant loops (upper Manhattan has a loop; Brooklyn and Queens have a loop) that would pass through the chamber, so that parts of the city can be taken off-line without cutting the water supply entirely.

Putting his hand on a small wheel that jutted out of the cylinder, Greeley said, "Here we can turn the valves on and off electronically or, if there's a power outage, even manually. Of course, if you did it manually, you'd have to turn it twenty-nine thousand times, but if you had to you could get a couple of guys down here and crank it away."

It was cold in the chamber, and Greeley shuddered as he held out his hand to demonstrate another innovation. "They're called butterfly valves," he said of the sluices inside the cylinder. Unlike the old guillotine-like sluices, these gates rotated slowly into position. "That takes off the pressure and makes it easier to close," he said, turning his hand clockwise. Though he had been in the vault dozens of times, he paused for a moment and looked out at the dozens of valves. Then he said, "Once the third water tunnel is finished, all the water in the city will flow like Zen."

In 1969, just before construction on the first stage of the third water tunnel began, Jimmy Ryan's father took him below the streets. "When I was eighteen, he said, 'Come with me,' " Jimmy Ryan recalled. "He was old school. You never asked what your father did. . . . Then they put us in this big bucket. I had no idea what to expect. It got darker and darker. My father told me to stay close and watch what he did. And that's how I became a sandhog. I was born into it."

Jimmy Ryan became known as the Red-Headed Hippie. "That was the style back then," Jimmy told me, somewhat defensively. "Even the old-timers had sideburns." If he was slightly rebellious, he had his father's unrelenting drive: he told me that he wanted to prove to his "old man" that he could do the job. Jimmy also had a forthrightness that made him popular among the men. "I can't say a bad word about Jimmy," Buddy Krausa, one of his old foremen, said, adding that Ryan was the type "who would never steal a crescent wrench."

After short stints on other jobs, the Ryans moved to the third water tunnel. On a summer day in 1982, Jimmy Ryan, Krausa, and a dozen or so other sandhogs went down a hole near Van Cortlandt Park, in the Bronx, where they were connecting a tunnel that would feed into the new valve chamber. The section had already been bored and they were in the final stages: building a steel form—it resembled the skeletal hull of a ship—around the contours of the carved-out earth, then pouring in concrete. To reach the cavern's ceiling, Ryan had climbed atop eighteen feet of scaffolding.

Around noon, some of the men stopped for lunch, but Ryan and a few others were still working when another sandhog, George Gluszak, who was a mile up the line, saw two twenty-ton agitator cars, which were used to mix concrete, racing down the tunnel. They had broken free from the brake car and were picking up speed along the steady decline. Some of the men tried to throw things on the tracks to slow them down, but it had no effect.

Jimmy Ryan was drilling when the cars slammed into the scaffolding, catapulting him twenty-five feet through the air. "Everything turned upside down," Ryan said. "I was knocked unconscious, and when I came to, all the lights had gone out. All I could hear were moans."

Krausa, who had not been injured, felt his way through the tangle of steel, rock, and machines. He could hear the other men calling out for help. Eventually, he found a flashlight and pointed the beam in front of him. "It was like nothing I'd ever seen," he said.

Sandwiched between two flatbed cars was Johnny Wademan, who had been drilling alongside Ryan. The two cars had collided under his shoulders and he was suspended in midair, his legs dangling, his arms outstretched. "He looked like Jesus Christ," said Gluszak, who, along with his team, had run through the darkened tunnel to the scene. One of the men shouted that Wademan was dead.

Ryan was bleeding profusely from his head. "Jimmy was hurt pretty bad," Krausa said. "God bless him, he was still looking for people, trying to help them. I don't know how he could walk."

In the corner, trapped between a concrete pipe and the wall, was a sandhog named Mike Butler. Most of his leg had been cut off, the crushed bone exposed; his foot, where the skin and tissue had been butterflied open, was pinned, so that he couldn't move. "He was bleeding to death," said Ryan.

Someone pulled out a penknife and, guided only by the unsteady beam of a flashlight, tried to pry him loose. His heel wouldn't budge. "I told him we were going to have to cut part of his foot off," Gluszak said. "He said, 'Do whatever you have to do.'"

While one sandhog held a cigarette to Butler's lips, another began to slice off his heel, severing what remained of the tendons and bone. "I took off my shirt, and wrapped his foot up in my undershirt and put a tourniquet around his leg," Gluszak said.

While Butler was being freed, the other men pulled Wademan down from where he had been suspended. As he hit the ground, they heard a groan. He was still alive.

It had been one of the worst accidents to date in the third water tunnel. Butler later had the rest of his leg amputated. Wademan's legs and hips were broken, six of his ribs were shattered, and he suffered severe head trauma. Ryan got a hundred and twenty stitches in his forehead and chin; he also had a broken knee, six fractured ribs, and two separated shoulders. It took him eight months to recuperate. When I asked him why he returned to work, he replied, "I'm a sandhog. That's all I know." He never went back to the scene of the accident, and he grew even quieter. "The accident took the life out of Jimmy," another sandhog said. "The exuberance."

"They ain't gonna do any psychological work on me," Ryan told me. "They ain't ever gonna penetrate this head."

Shortly after Ryan resumed working, he noticed that his father was having trouble breathing. "He'd walk thirty feet and have to stop," Ryan said. Then Joe Ryan started to cough up black phlegm. When Joe visited the doctor, X-rays showed spots on his lungs. He had contracted silicosis, a disease caused by years of breathing dust.

Jimmy Ryan said his father had always told him that sandhogs die unexpectedly. They die of cave-ins and blowouts. They die of explosions and electrocutions. They die of falling rocks and winches and icicles. They die of drowning. They die of decapitation and the bends. They die without legs, without arms. They die by plunging hundreds of feet or simply a few. They die quickly and, more often than not, painfully.

In May, 2003, on Ascension Thursday, Ryan put on a neatly pressed tweed jacket and a tie and drove from his home, in Queens, to St. Barnabas Church in the Bronx for a service in honor of all those who had died in the third water tunnel. The stone church had stained-glass windows that could be opened, admitting the unfiltered sunlight. Ryan sat toward the front, his jacket tight around his broad shoulders. Packed in the pews around him were Christopher Ward, the D.E.P. commissioner; Anthony Del-Vescovo, the contractor; and dozens of sandhogs and engineers. "Let us pray for all those who have been hurt or killed in construction of City Tunnel No. 3," the priest intoned.

"Lift them up," a sandhog responded. "Lift them up."

Ryan knelt against the front of his pew as the priest read the names of the twenty-four men who had died in the tunnel. "Lord have mercy on them," the priest said. When the service was over, Ryan and the others headed down the street to an Irish pub. "My father was one of the lucky ones," he said. "He held on until 1999. That's when the silicosis finally got him."

"I'm John Ryan. I think you met my father."

The young man was standing by a shaft for a tunnel on the corner of Thirty-sixth Street and First Avenue. Short, with compact arms, he looked more like his grandfather than like his father. He was twenty-eight, and his face had yet to develop the hard etchings of a sandhog. It was broad and frank, with bright-green eyes; red hair poked out of the front of his hard hat.

The other sandhogs called him "Jimmy's kid," but he had little of his dad's reticence. "You never know what's going on up there," he said of his father, with a smile. "I'm more of a bullshit artist." He looked up at the crane that was lowering materials down the hole. "I used to think my father was out of his mind. I was about eight years old when he got hurt. I still remember it. He didn't want to stay in the hospital and came home in a wheelchair. That's when I first realized what it meant to be a sandhog, and I said, 'Christ, I ain't ever gonna do that.' " He peered down the hole. "It's in your blood, I guess." Holding out his arms, he added, "We've probably got more muck in our veins than anything else."

"Nobody wants their kid to go into it," Jimmy Ryan told me later. "You'll always hope they'll find some kind of pencil job."

"I grew up wanting to be a baseball player," John Ryan said. "Then I dropped out of college, and one day my father came in the bar where I was working and said, 'All right, mister, you want to bartend? Come with me.' I'd never been in the hole before. I was scared. I won't lie to you."

"I can only imagine what he was thinking," Jimmy Ryan said. "We try to help each other."

John Ryan's great-grandfather brought home only a few dollars a week from his work on the water tunnel; today, sandhogs earn as much as a hundred and twenty thousand dollars a year. Though many are descended from tramp miners, they now often emerge from the hog house in tailored suits, their hair perfectly combed, as if they were bankers or accountants. Chick Donohue, the head of the hog house, has a degree from the Kennedy School at Harvard and is well known in city politics. He wears his Harvard ring on one hand and his sandhogs' union ring on the other. "That way, if I can't outsmart 'em with the left, I hit 'em with the right," he told me.

Just as sandhogs have gradually transformed the city, the city has gradually transformed the sandhogs. Some now arrive at the hole in a Cadillac or a BMW. John Ryan, who is engaged to be married, is buying a Colonial house in Nassau County. "A lot of guys are drawn to the money," he admitted. He paused. "And there's the camaraderie. That's a big part of it, too." He paused again, as if still searching for the deepest reason, then added, "Hell, I *like* it down there."

After five years on the third water tunnel, John Ryan had risen to foreman. His current mission was to build the city's newest "mole," a two-hundred-and-thirty-ton drill that would be placed at his father's site, on Tenth Avenue. Experimented with as early as the seventies, the mole was officially introduced in the water tunnels in 1992, and had become the sandhogs' most critical instrument—comparable, in the world of tunnelling, to the invention of the printing press. In February, 2003, the latest mole was transported from New Jersey to Manhattan, in pieces weighing sixty to a hundred and thirty tons, on a flatbed truck; the payload was the largest ever to cross the George Washington Bridge. The components were then lowered into the Thirtieth Street hole by a special crane that could withstand the enormous weight.

One day in February, after the mole had been assembled in the tight confines of the tunnel, John Ryan invited me to go down with him and see it. The pipeline was twelve and a half feet in diameter. The mole had already been driven nearly half a mile, and to reach the heading we had to ride a railroad car called a "man trip," which rattled from side to side. Groundwater seeped out of the surrounding rock, splattering against the walls as we sped past. After about five minutes, we came to a sudden stop. In the distance, I could see a monstrous machine that looked more like a space shuttle than a drill. The mole's hydraulic engines churned, and its blinking lights gleamed. "Come on," Ryan said excitedly, walking toward it. "That's only the trailing gear."

This gear—including a conveyor belt that carried out the crushed rock—took up most of the tunnel. A narrow gangplank had been built on the tunnel's side. Occasionally, to pass one of the fifteen or so sandhogs, we had to turn sideways, pressing our faces against the damp rock. As we went deeper, the mole began to resemble a colossal organism: its giant cylindrical arms gripped the walls and pushed the machine's mouth forward through the rock. In some compartments of the mole, engineers were peering at computer screens; the mole had lasers that registered the precise type of rock at the heading.

A siren sounded, and the men began to run up and down the plank. "What's happening?" I asked nervously.

"Nothing," Ryan said. "We're just starting it up."

The mole coughed and sputtered and shook. The temperature had been twenty degrees at the surface, but the mole heated the tunnel air to eighty degrees, and some of the men began to strip off their layers. After walking seventy-five yards, we reached the front of the mole: a round shield with twenty-seven cutters, each weighing three hundred and twenty pounds, pressed against the rock face, obscuring it completely. The cutters, driven forward by hydraulic propulsion, spun ferociously and noisily, chipping away at the granite, which was then carried out on the conveyor belt and loaded into muck cars. Ryan, who had grown up listening to tales of his forebears, said it was hard to believe that "my great-grandfather had only a goddam muck stick"—sandhog slang for shovel.

Indeed, until the mole was invented, tunnelling had changed only incrementally since the days of the Romans, who used fire and water to crack the rock and horses to carry it out. When a prototype of the mole was introduced in New York, in the seventies, many of the sandhogs feared it as much as they did caving rock.

"It's like that old story about John Henry," Chick Donohue explained, recalling the fabled contest between man and machine after the invention of the steam drill. "Well, when they introduced the first mole over in Brooklyn the cutters kept breaking, and the sandhogs would jump in with their shovels and picks. They knew they were competing for their jobs, and they were actually beating the mole! Of course, they then perfected the mole, and there was no contest."

The construction of the first water tunnel required no fewer than eighty men to drill and blast for at least a week in order to advance a hundred feet. The mole, with a fraction of the manpower, can tunnel that far in a day.

Yet, even with the mole, the third water tunnel has already taken six times as long as either City Tunnel No. 1 or No. 2; some people think it won't be completed, as scheduled, by 2020. "We should've been done with this thing twenty years ago," Jimmy Ryan said. "But the city keeps fucking around."

Conditions above ground have proved almost as difficult as those below. After the initial phase of a billion-dollar contract to build the tunnel was awarded to a consortium of companies, costs began to exceed estimates by the millions. When the city balked at the rising costs, the companies sued and the work stalled. Then, in 1974, when the city went bankrupt, construction was halted altogether. In all, nearly a decade was lost, and in 1981, with work proceeding only piecemeal and the ever-growing demand for water forcing the old tunnels to carry sixty per cent more capacity than intended, city officials were so desperate that they pleaded with the federal government to fund the project.

Meanwhile, charges began to surface that Tammany Hall–like machinations were contributing to the delays. The once vaunted Board of Water Supply, which oversaw the construction, had become a "Democratic patronage plum tree," as one critic put it. Stanley M. Friedman, the Bronx Democratic power broker who was later convicted of racketeering, was given a lifetime position on the board, with a salary of twenty thousand dollars, as well as an office, a secretary, a chauffeured car. "When I came in as mayor, it was a lifetime job given to retiring politicians," Koch told me. "They didn't do anything."

The board was dismantled. But in 1986 the man in charge of supervising purchasing for the water tunnel at the D.E.P., Edward Nicastro, warned that contracts were still not being properly monitored. "You'd be amazed at how easy it is to steal in the system," he told a reporter at the time.

In recent years, the greatest delays seem to be caused not by efforts to defraud the public but by attempts to placate it. Where the old water board once plowed over communities, the D.E.P. is now impeded by them. In 1993, when it tried to sink a shaft on East Sixty-eighth Street, Councilman Charles Millard protested that his office had received calls from parents whose children were "finding it difficult to concentrate." NUMBY, or "not under my back yard," movements sprang up. In 1994, after engineers had spent two years planning a new shaft site, residents in Jackson Heights held a protest, carrying signs that said, "DON'T GIVE US THE SHAFT." Engineers were forced to find a new location. "When we want to choose a shaft site, everyone says, 'Oh, the water system is a miracle, but please find another place,' " Ward told me. " 'We're building a co-op'—or hotel or park—'there.' " A D.E.P. engineer and geologist, Scott Chesman, added, "Instead of taking seven years to finish, we're on thirty years, and hardly any of it's been done. It's like the eighteen-hundreds again."

Indeed, for the first time the historic Delaware Aqueduct—the eighty-four-mile underground pipeline that carries the water from reservoirs upstate down to Yonkers, where it connects to City Tunnels No. 1 and No. 2—has begun to crack. According to some D.E.P. reports, in 1995 the aqueduct was losing about five hundred million gallons a month from leaks, which were creating massive sinkholes in Ulster and Orange Counties; in 2000, the monthly loss sometimes exceeded a billion gallons. An investigation by Riverkeeper warned of a potential "collapse" of the aqueduct, which would cut off as much as eighty per cent of the water flowing into the city.

In the spring of 2000, the D.E.P. decided to send a team of deep-sea divers down to do repairs on one of the original bronze valves in the Delaware Aqueduct, in the Dutchess County town of Chelsea, which had cracked, spewing a torrent of water through a hole the size of a quarter at eighty miles per hour. "For about two or three months, we built a mockup of the valve and a mockup of the bottom of the shaft," said John McCarthy, the engineer who oversaw the project. "We took the crew and experimented in a tank of about fifty feet of water, without any light, trying to simulate the conditions."

After practicing for days, the engineers transported a diving bell and a decompression chamber to the leak site. Four divers, who were hired from the same company that had helped to salvage the Russian nuclear submarine Kursk after it sank in the Barents Sea in August, 2000, had to remain inside the decompression chamber for twenty-four hours, in order to adjust to the intense water pressure underground. The chamber was about the size of a van, only round. On the outside were valves and hoses and an air-lock door to send in food (mostly fluids and peanut butter) and to remove human waste. The pressure in the chamber was gradually brought to the same pressure as that of the water seven hundred feet underground.

After breathing a mixture of ninety-eight per cent helium and two per cent oxygen for twenty-four hours, two of the divers crawled into a thirteen-foot diving bell that was attached to the top of the chamber. Once they had sealed themselves inside, the bell was lifted by a crane and lowered down the shaft that led into the aqueduct. There were only inches between the bell and the walls of the shaft. When the divers reached the bottom, one climbed out and swam toward the leak. (The other diver remained in the bell in case of an emergency.) He wore a wetsuit, a mask, and scuba equipment, and carried a small waterproof tool set. While struggling to stay in position against the pressure of the escaping water, he placed a brass plug in one of the holes, then sealed it with a clamp and an epoxy compound.

Each shift lasted at least four hours, then the bell was lifted up and two other divers went down. "It was not for the faint of heart," McCarthy said. The men spent ten days finishing the repairs, and fifteen more in the decompression chamber.

Still, far greater leaks are suspected somewhere between the Rondout Reservoir, in the Catskills, and a reservoir in Putnam County. In June, 2003, the D.E.P. sent a custom-made two-million-dollar submarine through forty-five miles of the Delaware Aqueduct. (The job was deemed too dangerous for a human.) The eight-hundred-pound craft, which was nicknamed Persephone, took three hundred and fifty thousand photographs. "The sub looks like a torpedo with catfish antennas," Commissioner Ward told me. "While a motor pushes it through, the antennas help it bounce back off the walls to stay within the middle of the tunnel." The Woods Hole Oceanographic Institution, on Cape Cod, and the D.E.P. are examining the pictures to evaluate the structural integrity of the pipeline.

But even if the locations of the leaks are determined, and if engineers can then concoct some way to plug them, most D.E.P. officials I spoke with do not consider this section of the aqueduct the most vulnerable. They are more worried about pipelines closer to the city—in particular, Tunnels No. 1 and No. 2, which, because of their greater depth and buried valves, are far less accessible, even to a self-piloted submarine. Some sandhogs believe that the only thing preventing these sections from collapsing is the pressure of the water pushing against their walls. A former chief engineer on the water system, Martin Hauptman, has noted, "We see headlines in the streets frequently where a 24-inch water main breaks and the street's flooded, basements are flooded, the subway is flooded, and people think *that* is a horrible situation. Failure of a tunnel is an entirely different situation. What bothers me most . . . is the element of time. You cannot buy time with a situation like that."

And there is now the additional threat of terrorism. Although the public's attention has focussed on the danger of someone's poisoning the water supply, officials believe that the system would likely dilute a toxin's effects. The greater danger, they say, is that a terrorist might blow up one of the pipelines before the third water tunnel is up and running. "That's the scary thing," Ward said. Fitzsimmons, the sandhogs' union leader, added, "If you attacked the right spots—I hate to say this, but it's true—you could take out all of the water going into New York City."

On the morning that I went down the hole with John Ryan, he told me, "My hope is that we can finish the third water tunnel, so my father will be able to see it completed."

The mole was boring into the rock. Several sandhogs had laid new tracks on the floor, pounding them into the rock with sledgehammers.

"All right!" Ryan yelled. "Let's check the cutter heads."

He looked up at me from under his hard hat. "You want to go?" he asked.

"Where?"

He pointed underneath the mole, where a small passageway led into the bowels of the machine. Two other sandhogs were already crawling in and, after a moment, I followed. First we had to crouch in a cavity no more than three feet by four feet. One of the sandhogs, who introduced himself as Peter, fumbled with the lamp on his hard hat. "Fucking thing's busted," he said.

The other worker turned his light on, and I could see that the passage led to a five-foot-long corridor that connected to the head of the mole.

"Whenever you're ready, John," Peter yelled to Ryan, who was outside the cavity, directing the operation. "You can roll the head."

We stayed in a crouch for several more minutes, watching the mole's cutters rotate several degrees one way, then the other, until at last they came to rest.

"This is the most dangerous part," Peter said. He then lay on his stomach and stuck his hands straight out in front of him and began to squirm, feet first, through the narrow passage leading to the mole's cutters. He slid through the mud and water, and I followed on my stomach. Soon, I was standing in mud and water up to my knees, staring at the giant metal blades. I tried to step away, but my back hit something hard: the head of the tunnel. We were sandwiched between the mole and the rock. "You just don't want anything to move," Peter said.

As groundwater seeped from the ceiling, hitting the machine, puffs of steam filled the cavity.

"Go ahead, touch it," Peter said, pointing to one of the blades.

I reached out and touched the edge: it was scalding hot, from friction. "You could fry an egg on it," Peter said.

The other sandhog squeezed into the crevice. Now the only wiggle room was above our heads. As the water crept up to our thighs, Peter craned his neck, inspecting the front of the tunnel to make sure the rock was sound. There was a series of grooved concentric circles where the blades had cut. "It looks like a dartboard, doesn't it?" Peter said.

"Like a tree," the other sandhog said.

They checked the blades to make sure they didn't require replacement. I told them I thought I needed to leave.

"Just a second more," Peter said.

The other sandhog exited first, followed by me, then Peter. When I saw John Ryan again, he looked at my muck-covered clothes, then clapped me cheerfully on the back. "Welcome to our fucking world," he said.

There was no man-trip car to take me back to the shaft, so I set out by myself, walking the length of the tunnel. "If you see a muck car coming," Ryan told me, "just hang on to the pipes on the side of the tunnel."

A few minutes later, the noise from the mole faded, and the tunnel was empty and still. Though it extended as far as the eye could see, this tunnel was not even one-sixtieth the projected length of the third water tunnel; it was a mere one-thousandth of all the miles of water tunnels and pipelines and aqueducts combined. For the first time during my underground excursion, I had some sense of this city under the city—of what many engineers refer to as "the eighth wonder of the world."

After a while, a light flickered in the distance and I thought it was a muck car. As Ryan had instructed, I hung on to the pipes on the side of the tunnel. But it was only a sandhog come to escort me out.

When I reached the top, I went into the hog house to change. On the bench beside me was a slender boy with a hard hat cocked to one side, as if it were a fedora. He looked astonishingly like Jimmy Ryan. It was Jimmy's younger son, Greg. "I started in 2000, over on the third water tunnel in Queens," he said. "They call us the millennial hogs."

Only twenty, he looked like a slightly ungainly teen-ager in his dirty white shirt and a slicker that seemed too loose for his narrow waist. He hung his Yankees cap in his locker and wrapped his supper, a veal cutlet sandwich, in a plastic bag. "It saves time to eat underground," he said.

Greg glanced at another sandhog who was dressing nearby. His left hand had been crushed under a beam in the hole, and his index finger was missing. "I still get scared sometimes," Greg said, lifting his hard hat and removing a pack of menthol cigarettes. He lit one and let it dangle between his teeth, the way he had often seen his father do. "My father told me not to think about it. It'll only make it worse."

Greg turned and headed outside, where his brother John was emerging from the cage, his face covered in mud. As John stepped onto solid ground, shielding his eyes from the blinding light, he clapped his hand on Greg's shoulder. "I'll see you, O.K.?" Greg nodded and, without a word, descended into the darkness.

— *September, 2003*

The Old Man and the Gun

Just before Forrest Tucker turned seventy-nine, he went to work for the last time. Although he was still a striking-looking man, with intense blue eyes and swept-back white hair, he had a growing list of ailments, including high blood pressure and burning ulcers. He had already had a quadruple bypass, and his wife encouraged him to settle into their home in Pompano Beach, Florida, a peach-colored house on the edge of a golf course which they'd purchased for their retirement. There was a place nearby where they could eat prime rib and dance on Saturday nights with other seniors for $15.50 a person, and even a lake where Tucker could sit by the shore and practice his saxophone.

But on this spring day in 1999, while his neighbors were on the fairway or tending to their grandchildren, he drove to the Republic Security Bank in Jupiter, about fifty miles from his home. Tucker, who took pride in his appearance, was dressed all in white: white pants with a sharp crease, a white sports shirt, white suède shoes, and a shimmering white ascot.

He paused briefly in front of the A.T.M. and pulled the ascot up around his face, bandit style. He then reached into a canvas bag, took out an old U.S. Army Colt .45, and burst into the bank. He went up to the first teller and said, "Put your money on the counter. All of it."

He flashed the gun so that everyone could see it. The teller laid several packets of fives and twenties on the counter, and Tucker inspected them for exploding dye packs. Checking his watch, he turned to the next teller and said, "Get over here. You, too."

Then he gathered up the thick packets—more than five thousand dollars—and hurried to the door. On his way out, he looked back at the two tellers. "Thank you," he said. "Thank you."

He drove to a nearby lot, where he had left a "safe" car, a red Grand Am that couldn't be traced to him. After wiping down the stolen "hot" car with a rag, he threw his belongings inside the Grand Am. They included a .357 Magnum, a sawed-off .30 carbine, two black nylon caps, a holster, a can of Mace, a pair of Smith & Wesson handcuffs, two rolls of black electrical tape, a police badge, five AAA batteries, a police scanner, a glass cutter, gloves, and a fishing cap. There was also a small bottle of medicine for his heart. No one seemed to notice him, and he went home, making what appeared to be a clean getaway.

After a brief stop to count the money, he got back in the car and headed out again. As he approached the golf course, the bills neatly stacked beside him, he noticed an unmarked car on his tail. He turned onto another street, just to make sure. There it was again. Then he spotted a police car pulling out behind him. He hit the gas as hard as he could, trying to outmaneuver them, turning left, then right, right, then left. He went past the North Pompano Baptist Church and the Kraeer Funeral Home, past a row of pink one-story houses with speedboats in the driveways, until he found himself on a dead-end street. As he spun around, he saw that a police car was barricading the road. One of the officers, Captain James Chinn, was reaching for his shotgun. There was a small gap between Chinn's car and a wooden fence, and Tucker, his body pitched forward in his seat, sped toward it. Chinn, who had spent almost two decades as a detective, later said he had never seen anything like it: the white-haired figure barrelling toward him seemed to be smiling, as if he were enjoying the showdown. Then, as the car skidded over the embankment, Tucker lost control and hit a palm tree. The air bags inflated, pinning him against the seat.

The police were stunned when they realized that the man they had apprehended was not only seventy-eight years old—he looked, according to Chinn, "as if he had just come from an Early Bird Special"—but one of the most notorious stickup men of the twentieth century. Over a career that spanned more than six decades, he had also become perhaps the greatest escape artist of his generation, a human contortionist who had broken out of nearly every prison he was confined in.

One day in 2002, I went to meet Tucker in Fort Worth, Texas, where he was being held in a prison medical center after pleading guilty to one count of robbery and receiving a thirteen-year sentence. The hospital, an old yellow brick building with a red tiled roof, was on top of a hill and set back off the main road, surrounded by armed guards and razor wire. I was handed a notice that said no "weapons," "ammunition," or "metal cutting tools" were allowed, and then escorted through a series of chambers—each door sealing behind us before the next one opened—until I arrived in an empty waiting room.

Before long, a man appeared in a wheelchair pushed by a guard. He wore brown prison fatigues and a green jacket with a turned-up collar. His figure was twisted forward, as if he had tried to contort it one last time and it had frozen in place. As he rose from the wheelchair, he said, "It's a pleasure to meet you. Forrest Tucker."

His voice was gentle, with a soft Southern lilt. After he extended his hand, he made his way slowly over to a wooden table with the help of a walker. "I'm sorry we have to meet here," he said, waiting for me to sit first.

Captain Chinn had told me that he had never met such a gracious criminal: "If you see him, tell him Captain Chinn says hi." Even a juror who helped convict him once remarked, "You got to hand it to the guy— he's got style."

"So what do you want to know?" Tucker said. "I've been in prison all my life, except for the times I've broken out. I was born in 1920, and I was in jail by the time I was fifteen. I'm eighty-one now and I'm still in jail, but I've broken out eighteen times successfully and twelve times unsuccessfully. There were plenty of other times I planned to escape, but there's no point in me telling you about them."

As we sat in a corner by a window overlooking the prison yard, it was hard to imagine that this man's career had featured wanted posters and midnight escapes. His fingers were knotted like bamboo, and he wore bifocals.

"What I mean by a successful escape is to elude custody," he continued, squinting out the window. "Maybe they'd eventually get me, but I got away at least for a few minutes."

He pointed to the places along his arm where he had been shot while trying to flee. "I still have part of a bullet in me," he said. "They all opened up on me and hit me three times—in both shoulders with M16 rifles, and with buckshot in the legs."

His voice sounded dry, and I offered to buy him a drink from the vending machine. He followed me and peered through the glass, without touching it. He chose a Dr Pepper. "That's kind of like cherry soda, isn't it?"

He seemed pleased. When I gave him the drink, he glanced at the candy bars, and I asked him if he wanted anything else. "If it's not too much trouble," he said, "I'd like a Mounds."

After he finished eating, he began to tell me what he called "the true story of Forrest Tucker." He spoke for hours, and when he grew tired he offered to continue the next morning. During our conversations, which went on for several days, we always sat in the corner by the window, and after a while he would cough slightly and I would offer to buy him a drink. Each time, he followed me to the machine, as the guard watched from a distance. It was only during the last trip to the machine, when I dropped some money, that I noticed his eyes were moving over everything—the walls, the windows, the guard, the fences, the razor wire. It occurred to me that Tucker, escape artist par excellence, had been using our meetings to case the joint.

"The first time I broke out of the can I was only fifteen," Tucker told me. "At fifteen, you're pretty fast."

It was the spring of 1936, and he had been incarcerated for stealing a car in Stuart, Florida, a small town along the St. Lucie River which had been devastated during the Depression. He told the police that he took it "just for a thrill," but as he sat in jail the thrill gave way to panic, and when a jailer removed his chains he darted out. Several days later, a deputy discovered him in an orange grove, eating a piece of fruit. "That was escape No. 1," Tucker says. "Such as it was."

The sheriff decided to transfer him to reform school. During his brief flight, however, Tucker had slipped a half-dozen hacksaw blades through the cell window to a group of boys he had met inside. "They hadn't broken out yet and still had the blades," he says. That night, after sawing a bar, he slithered out, helping two other boys squeeze through the tiny opening.

Unlike the others, Tucker knew the area. As a kid, he had spent a fair amount of time by the river, and it was in the river that the police found him and another boy, about an hour later, hiding with just their noses above water. The next day, the Stuart *Daily News* detailed his exploits under the headline "TRIO ESCAPE BY SAWING BARS OF CELL LAST NIGHT . . . SUPPLIED WITH HACK-SAWS, COLD CHISELS AND FILES BY BOY."

"That was escape No. 2," Tucker says. "A brief one."

Like the outlaws he read about in dime novels who were forced into banditry by some perceived injustice, Tucker says that "the legend of Forrest Tucker" began on the morning when he was unfairly sent away for only a minor theft. The story, which he repeated even as a boy, eventually spread throughout the town, and over time the details became more ornate, the theft more minor. Morris Walton, who used to play with Tucker as a child, says, "My sense is he spent his life in jail for stealing a bicycle and simply trying to escape. If he became bad, it was only because the system made him that way."

What Walton knew of Tucker's upbringing reinforced that impression. His father was a heavy-equipment operator who disappeared when Tucker was six. While his mother struggled in menial jobs in Miami, Tucker was sent to live with his grandmother, who was the tender of the bridge in Stuart. There he built canoes and sailboats out of scrap metal and wood, which he gathered along the riverbank, and taught himself to play the saxophone and the clarinet. "It wasn't like I needed a father to order me around," he says.

But as his reputation for cleverness grew, so did his rap sheet. By his sixteenth birthday, it included charges of "breaking and entering" and "simple larceny." After he escaped from reform school and fled to Georgia, he was sentenced to "be placed and confined at labor in the chain gang." Like all new inmates, he was taken to the blacksmith, where a chain was riveted around both of his ankles. The steel gradually ate into the skin, a condition known as shackle poisoning.

"The guards would give you the first three days to let you get your hands broken in with calluses," Tucker recalls. "But after that the walking boss would punish you, hit you with his cane or fist. And if you didn't work hard enough the guards would take you in the bathroom and tie your hands behind your back and put a pressure hose in your face and hold it there until you'd sputter and you couldn't breathe."

Although Tucker was released after only six months, he was soon convicted again, for stealing another car, and sentenced to ten years. By now, "we see a man who has been thoroughly cast out by society," Tucker's lawyer later wrote in a court motion. "Marked as a criminal at seventeen years old and constantly railroaded through judicial proceedings without the benefit of counsel, Forrest Tucker was becoming an angry young man." Tucker himself says, "The die was cast." In photographs taken after he was paroled at the age of twenty-four, his hair is cut short and he has on a white T-shirt; his once slender arms are coiled with muscles. His eyes are piercing. People who knew him say that he was extraordinarily charismatic—that girls flocked around him—but they also noted a growing reservoir of anger. "I think he had this desperate need to show the world that he was *somebody*," one of his relatives says.

At first, Tucker sought work playing the saxophone in big bands around Miami, and he seemed to have harbored ambitions of becoming another Glenn Miller. Nothing came of it, though, and, after a brief failed marriage, he put away his sax and got himself a gun.

The outlaw, in the American imagination, is a subject of romance—a "good" bad man, he is typically a master of escape, a crack shot, a ladies' man. In 1915, when the police asked the train robber Frank Ryan why he did it, he replied, "Bad companions and dime novels. Jesse James was my favorite hero."

When Tucker was growing up, during the Great Depression, the appeal of bank robbers, fuelled by widespread anger over defaults and foreclosures, was reaching its zenith. After the F.B.I. gunned down John Dillinger, in 1934, droves descended on the scene, mopping up his blood with their clothes. At least ten Hollywood films were devoted to Dillinger's life; one of them exclaimed, "His Story Is Written in Bullets, Blood and Blondes!"

Because the holdup demands a public performance, it tends to draw a certain personality: bold, vainglorious, reckless. At the same time, most bank robbers know that the society that revels in their exploits will ultimately demand their elimination, by incarceration or death. "They'll get me," Pretty Boy Floyd once said. "Sooner or later, I'll go down full of lead. That's how it will end."

Indeed, by the time Tucker set out to become an outlaw, in the late nineteen-forties, most of the legendary stickup men had already been gunned down. Still, he began to imitate their style, dressing in chalk-striped suits and two-tone shoes, and he would stand in front of a mirror, pointing a gun at his own reflection. Finally, on September 22, 1950, with a handkerchief tied over his face and a gun drawn in the style of Jesse James, he strode into a bank in Miami and made off with $1,278. A few days later, he went back to the same place, this time for the entire safe. He was apprehended as he was trying to crack it open with a blowtorch on the roadside.

His career seemed even more fleeting than that of most bank robbers, but in the county jail Tucker decided he was more than an ordinary stickup man. "It didn't matter to me if they gave me five years, ten years, or life," he says. "I was an escape artist."

He searched the prison for what he called "the weak spot." One day around Christmas, after weeks of looking, he began to moan in pain. The authorities rushed him to the hospital, where doctors removed his appendix. ("A small price to pay," Tucker says.) While convalescing, still chained to his bed, he started to work on the shackles. He had taught himself how to pick a lock using almost anything—a pen, a paper clip, a piece of wire, nail clippers, a watch spring—and after a few minutes he walked out, unnoticed.

He made his way to California, where he went on a spree of robberies, hurtling over counters, pointing his gun, and declaring, "I mean business!" He wore bright checkered suits and sped away in a flamboyant getaway car with tubes along the sides. He even talked like a character in pulp fiction. "This is a stickup, girls," he once said, according to witnesses. "I've got a gun. Be quiet and you won't get hurt."

Hoping to improve his take, Tucker began to cast about for a partner. "I didn't want any nuts or rats," he says, adding, "I'm from the old school." In the end, he found an ex-con named Richard Bellew, a tall, handsome thief with a high I.Q. and wavy black hair. Like Tucker, Bellew modelled himself on the stickup men of the nineteen-thirties, and he ran with a stage dancer named Jet Blanca. But Tucker chose him for another reason: "He always let me count the dough."

They began to hit one bank after another. After one heist, witnesses said the last thing they saw was a row of suits hanging in the back seat of the getaway car. The heists, which continued for two years, dominated the local headlines, often preempting coverage of the 1952 Presidential election and the McCarthy hearings. Tucker and Bellew were depicted as "armed men" who "terrorized" their "victims," but also as "dramatically attired" "hold-up artists" who "expertly stripped" the tellers of cash, leaving behind "only an impression of competent banditry . . . and one getaway car."

On March 20, 1953, more than two years after Tucker's escape from the hospital, F.B.I. agents surrounded him as he was retrieving loot from a safe-deposit box in San Francisco. Then they went to search the place Tucker had listed as his residence. There, in a spacious apartment in San Mateo, they found a young blond woman who said she had never heard of Forrest Tucker. She was married to a wealthy songwriter, she said, who commuted daily to the city, and they had just moved into a bigger apartment to make room for their five-month-old son. Her husband's name, she told the police, was Richard Bellew. Yet when the officers showed Shirley Bellew a photograph of the bank robber and longtime prison fugitive Forrest Tucker, she burst into tears. "I can't believe it," she said. "He was such a good man, such a good provider."

She recalled how her husband would come home every night and play with their baby, whom they had named Rick Bellew, Jr. "What's going to become of our little baby?" she asked. "What's his name going to be?"

"Let me tell you about Alcatraz," Tucker said one day as he sat in the corner of the visiting room, his walker resting against his leg. He had spread a napkin out in front of him and was eating a meatball hero I'd brought him and sipping a Dr Pepper. "There were only fifteen hundred and seventy-six people who ever went there. I was No. 1047."

Alcatraz, or "the Rock," had been converted from a military prison in 1934 as a way to confine the country's most notorious criminals, including George (Machine Gun) Kelly, Robert Stroud (the Birdman of Alcatraz), and Mickey Cohen. At least half of the inmates had previously attempted to break out of other prisons. Surrounded by the freezing San Francisco Bay and its deadly currents, it was built to be escapeproof. Al Capone, who was sent there in 1934, is said to have told the warden, "It looks like Alcatraz has got me licked."

Tucker arrived on September 3, 1953. He was thirty-three. He had been sentenced to thirty years. In his prison photo, he still has on a jacket and tie; his brown hair is brushed back with a touch of oil; he is slightly unshaved but still striking. Within moments, he was stripped naked, and a medical attendant probed his ears and nose and mouth and rectum, searching for any tools or weapons. He was given a blue chambray shirt with his number stamped on it and a pair of trousers, as well as a cap, a peacoat, a bathrobe, three pairs of socks, two handkerchiefs, a pair of shoes, and a raincoat. His cell was so narrow that he could reach out and touch both sides at the same time. "It was so cold in the cellblock you had to sleep with your coat and hat to stay warm," Tucker says.

As he lay in bed, he says, he thought about his wife and child. He remembered the first time he met Shirley Storz, at an event for singles in Oakland. He remembered how they skied at Lake Tahoe and were married in a small ceremony in September of 1951, how she sang in a choral group, and how he'd sit and listen for hours. And he remembered his son being born. "We loved each other," Tucker says of his wife. "I didn't know how to explain to her the truth—that this was my way of life."

Several weeks after he arrived, a guard roused him from his cell and led him into a tiny room that had a small window. Peering through it, he saw his wife sitting on the other side. He picked up the phone. "It was hard to talk," he recalls. "We had to look at each other through a piece of glass. She told me she had to make a life for herself. I said, 'The best thing you can do is make a life for you and our son.' I told her, 'I won't bother you no matter what, no matter how much I want to. I won't ring your phone.'" A few months later, he received notice that their marriage had been annulled.

By now, Tucker had developed several maxims, including "The more security, the more bizarre the method of escape must be." He began to concoct elaborate schemes with a fellow-inmate named Teddy Green, an escape artist and bank robber who had once dressed as a priest to elude the police and had broken out of the state penitentiary by shipping himself out in a box of rags.

Along with another inmate, they started smuggling tools from their prison jobs, hiding them in the laundry, and planting pieces of steel wool on other prisoners to set off the metal detectors, so that the guards assumed they were broken. They carved holes in their toilet bowls and tucked the tools inside, putting putty over them. At night, they used the tools to tunnel through the floor, planning to go out by means of the basement.

One day, according to internal prison records, a prisoner in solitary suggested that guards examine the cell toilets; soon a full-scale search was launched. A warden's report summed up the findings:

> The result of the shakedown of these toilets was the blow torch as I have mentioned, a bar spreader, a pair of side cutters, a brace and some bits . . . a screwdriver and one or two pieces of wire and a piece of carborundum stone.

All three prisoners were labelled "very dangerous escape risks" and locked in the Treatment Unit, better known as "the hole."

"I remember walking in with no clothes or shoes on," Tucker says. "The steel floor was so cold it hurt to touch it. The only way to stay warm was to keep walking." One night, he heard a haunting sound through the window. He couldn't see anyone outside, but he heard voices from below. They were the guards' children, singing carols. "It was the first children's voices I had heard in years," he says. "It was Christmas Eve."

As the time passed, Tucker began to teach himself the law, and before long he was deluging the court with appeals, which he wrote in a slanting methodical print. Although a prosecutor later dismissed one of his writs as pure "fantasy," he was granted a hearing in November of 1956. According to Tucker, as well as court records, the night before his court appearance, while being held in the county jail, he complained of pains in his kidneys and was rushed to the hospital. Guards were stationed at every door. When no one was looking, Tucker broke a pencil and stabbed his ankle. Because of the wound, the guards removed his leg irons, strapping him to the gurney with his hands cuffed. As he was being wheeled into the X-ray room, Tucker leaped up, overpowered two guards, and ran out the door. For several hours, he enjoyed the fresh air and the sight of ordinary people. He was apprehended, still in his hospital gown and handcuffs, in the middle of a cornfield.

The brief escape, for which he was tried and convicted, enhanced his reputation as an escape artist. Yet it was not for another twenty-three years, after Tucker had been released and arrested again for armed robbery, that he made his greatest escape. In the summer of 1979, while at San Quentin, a maximum-security facility that jutted out into the ocean and was known among cons as "the gladiator school," Tucker took a job in the prison industries and, with the help of two other inmates, John Waller and William McGirk, secretly gathered together scraps of wood and sheets of Formica, which they cut into strange shapes and hid under tarps. From the electrical shop, they spirited away two six-foot poles and several buckets. Then, in the furniture workshop, they found the final pieces: plastic dust-covers, paint, and tape, which they stored in boxes labelled "Office Supplies."

On August 9th, after months of preparation, Tucker exchanged nods with both of his confederates in the yard, signalling that everything was ready. While Waller and McGirk stood watch outside the lumber shop, Tucker drew on his childhood experience and began to fashion the pieces into a fourteen-foot kayak. "A hammer was too loud, so I had to use only tape and bolts," Tucker says. He had just enough paint for one side of the craft, the side that would face the guard towers, and as the others urged him to hurry he stencilled on it "Rub-a-Dub-Dub." Waller, who called the fifty-nine-year-old Tucker "the old man," later told a reporter from the Los Angeles *Times*, "The boat was beautiful; I wish my eyes were as blue as that boat."

They wore sailor hats and sweatshirts that Tucker had painted bright orange, with the logo of the Marin Yacht Club, which he had seen on the boats that sailed by. When the guard wasn't looking, they hurriedly put the kayak into the water. As they set out, the winds were blowing more than twenty miles an hour, and massive swells began to swamp the kayak. "The boat didn't leak a drop," Waller said. "We could have paddled to Australia. It was those damn waves over the side. When we finally reached the edge of the property at Q"—San Quentin—"the son of a bitch sank."

A guard in one of the towers spotted them clinging to the upside-down craft, kicking to shore, and asked if they needed help. They said they were fine, and, as if to prove it, McGirk held up his wrist and yelled, "We just lost a couple of oars, but my Timex is still running!" The guard, unaware that three prisoners were missing, laughed and went back to his lookout.

California soon unleashed a statewide manhunt. Meanwhile, police in Texas and Oklahoma began to report a strange series of holdups. They all had the same M.O.: three or four men would stroll into a grocery store or a bank, flash a gun, demand the money, and speed away in a stolen car. Witnesses invariably noted that they were all, by the standards of the trade, old men. One even wore what appeared to be a hearing aid. The authorities compared them to the elderly thieves in the film "Going in Style," and dubbed them "the Over-the-Hill Gang."

"That was when I was really a good robber," Tucker tells me. He is careful not to admit to any particular crime ("I don't know if they still have jurisdiction") or implicate any of his living partners ("Some of them are still out there"), but he says that by the age of sixty he had at last mastered the art of the holdup.

One day, while we were sitting in the prison visiting room, Tucker leaned forward in his chair and began to teach me how to rob a bank. "First of all, you want a place near the highway," he said, putting on his bifocals, his eyes blinking as if he were imagining a particular layout. "Then you need to case it—you can't just storm in. You need to size it up, know it like your own home."

"In the old days, the stickup men were like cowboys," he continued. "They would just go in shooting, yelling for everyone to lie down. But to me violence is the first sign of an amateur." The best holdup men, in his view, were like stage actors, able to hold a room by the sheer force of their personality. Some even wore makeup and practiced getting into character. "There is an art to robbing a bank if you do it right," Tucker said. Whereas he once cultivated a flamboyant image, he later developed, he said, a subtler, more "natural" style.

"O.K., the tools," he pressed on. Ideally, he said, you needed nail polish or superglue to cover your fingertips ("You can wear gloves, but in warmer climates they only draw attention"), a glass cutter, a holster, a canvas bag ("big enough for the dough"), and a gun ("a .38 or semi-automatic, or whatever you can get your hands on"). He said the gun was just "a prop," but essential to any operation.

There was one other thing, he said after a pause. It was the key to the success of the Over-the-Hill Gang and what he still called "the Forrest Tucker trademark": the hearing aid. It was actually a police scanner, he said, which he wired through his shirt; that way, he would know if any silent alarms had been triggered.

He removed a napkin from his pocket and wiped the sweat from his forehead. "Once you've got your cool car parked nearby, you've got your radio, your hands are covered with gloves or superglue, you walk in. Go right up to the manager. Say, 'Sit down.' Never pull the gun—just flash it. Tell him calmly you're here to rob the bank and it better go off without a hitch. Don't run from the bank unless you're being shot at, 'cause it only shows something is going on. Just walk to the hot car, real calm, then drive to the cool car. Rev it up, and you're gone."

After he finished, he seemed satisfied. "I've just given you a manual on how to rob a bank," he said. He reflected on this for a moment, then added, "No one can teach you the craft. You can only learn by doing."

A forty-year-old sergeant on the Austin police force, John Hunt, was assigned to investigate the mysterious holdups of the Over-the-Hill Gang. "They were the most professional, successful robbers that I ever encountered in all my years on the force," Hunt, who is now retired after a thirty-year career, told me. "They had more experience in robbery than we had catching them."

Then a chain-smoker with a drooping mustache and a slight paunch,

Hunt spent long days trying to catch the gang. With the advent of high-tech security, there were fewer and fewer traditional bank robbers; most were desperate drug addicts who made off with only a few thousand dollars before they were caught. The members of the Over-the-Hill Gang seemed to defy not just their age but their era. "They'd get up every day and be on the job," Hunt said. "Just as a welder gets good at welding, or a writer gets good over the years by writing, these guys learned from their mistakes."

In a one-year span, the Over-the-Hill Gang was suspected in at least sixty robberies in Oklahoma and Texas—twenty in the Dallas–Fort Worth area alone. The gang was also believed to be responsible for holdups in New Mexico, Arizona, and Louisiana. "SENIOR CITIZENS STRIKE AGAIN," one headline blared. "MIDDLE-AGED BANDITS PUZZLE DETECTIVES," another read.

In December of 1980, Hunt and forty other law-enforcement officers from at least three states held a conference in Dallas to figure out how to stop them. "You can't say how many lives they altered by sticking a gun in someone's face," a former F.B.I. agent told me.

Tucker seemed unable to stop, no matter how much money he accumulated. Although there are no official estimates, Tucker—relying on an array of aliases, including Robert Tuck MacDougall, Bob Stone, Russell Johns, Ralph Pruitt, Forrest Brown, J. C. Tucker, and Ricky Tucker—is believed over his career to have stolen millions of dollars, a fleet of sports cars, a bag of yen, and one Sambo's wooden nickel. In the spring of 1983, he embarked on his most audacious heist yet: robbing a high-security bank in Massachusetts in broad daylight by pretending that he and his men were guards making a routine pickup in an armored car. Tucker believed the plan was "a breakthrough in the art." On March 7th, moments before the armored car was scheduled to arrive, they put on makeup and mustaches; Tucker's wig had shrunk in a recent snowstorm, and rather than postpone the operation he decided to do without it.

The teller buzzed them in. Just as they were entering the vault, according to a police report, the manager noticed that "the dark mustache on one man and the white mustache on the other man were not real." One of the "guards" patted his gun and said, "This is a holdup."

Tucker locked the manager and two tellers inside the vault, and escaped with more than four hundred and thirty thousand dollars. But when the police showed the tellers a series of mug shots, they identified, for the first time, the leader of the Over-the-Hill Gang as the same man who had broken out of San Quentin in a homemade kayak three years earlier.

As the F.B.I., the local police, and the county sheriffs all tried to track him down, Tucker hid in Florida, checking in daily with Teddy Green, his old Alcatraz confidant. One June morning, Tucker pulled into Green's garage and waited while his friend walked toward the car. "I was looking at him," Tucker recalls, "thinking, My, what a sharp suit!"

A man jumped in front of Tucker's car and yelled, "F.B.I., don't move! You're under arrest."

Agents were everywhere, coming out of cars and bushes. Tucker glowered at Green, convinced that his friend had "ratted me out." Although Tucker insists that he never had a pistol—and none was ever found—several agents said they saw one in his hand. "He's got a gun!" one of them yelled, diving to the ground. The garage filled with the sound of gunfire. Bullets shattered the windshield and the radiator. Tucker, who had been hit in both arms and in the leg, ducked below the dashboard and pressed the accelerator, crashing outside the garage. He opened the car door and stumbled onto the street, his hands and face covered in blood. A woman with two children was driving toward him. "As I got closer," the woman later testified, "he started to look bloodier and bloodier—it was all over him—and I thought, This poor man has been hit by a car."

She offered him a ride, and he climbed into the passenger seat. Then, in her rearview mirror, she saw someone holding a rifle, and her six-year-old son cried out, "Criminal!" When she hesitated, Tucker grabbed the wheel and snapped, "I have a gun—now drive!" Her son began to sob. After a half-mile chase, they veered down a dead-end street. At a muttered "O.K." from Tucker, the woman scrambled out of the car and dragged her children to safety. Then Tucker himself stepped from the car and passed out.

A columnist for the Miami *Herald* summed up the capture of the longtime prison fugitive and leader of the Over-the-Hill Gang this way:

> There is something vaguely appealing about Tucker. . . . Old guys are not regularly associated with high crimes. . . . Tucker must also be admired,

in a twisted way I admit, for pulling off an incredible escape from San Quentin prison in San Francisco. . . . Tucker might have made a fortune selling the escape yarn to Hollywood and holing up somewhere. Instead he chose to resume the line of work to which he was dedicated. . . . The aging Robin Hood took from the rich, who were probably loaded with insurance.

Tucker's story had, at last, acquired the burnish of outlaw mythology. The battered Rub-a-Dub-Dub had been donated to the Marin Yacht Club and was later placed in a prison museum, and the Children's Hospital Medical Center in Oakland requested that Tucker be allowed to serve as grand marshal for its upcoming Bathtub Regatta. Amid the clamor, the F.B.I. showed up at a fancy retirement community in Lauderhill, Florida, where Tucker was believed to have been living. An elegant woman in her fifties answered the door. When they asked her about Forrest Tucker, she said she had never heard of the man. She was married to Bob Callahan, a successful stockbroker whom she had met shortly after her first husband died. When the agents explained that Bob Callahan was really Forrest Tucker, a man who had broken out of jail four years earlier, she looked at them in tears. "I told 'em, 'I don't believe a word you're saying,'" she recalled, nearly two decades later. "But they had him. They shot him three times."

An heiress to a modest moving-company fortune who looked, in her youth, a bit like Marilyn Monroe, she remembers meeting Tucker at the Whale and Porpoise, a private club on Oakland Park Boulevard. She had never encountered anyone so kind and gallant. "He came over and asked me to dance, and that was that," she told me.

She recalled how she went to see him in prison ("still in a daze"), not sure what to say or do. When she saw him lying there, pale and bloodied, she was overcome with love for this man who, she learned, had been in a chain gang at sixteen. As he begged her forgiveness, she told me, "All I wanted to do was hold him."

At first, awaiting trial in Miami, Tucker tried to break out of jail, removing a bar in his cell with a hacksaw and climbing onto the roof with a homemade grappling hook. But after his wife promised—to the consternation of her family and friends—to stay with him if he reformed, Tucker vowed to rehabilitate himself. "I told her that from then on I'd only look at ways to escape," he says, adding, "She is one in a million."

He returned to San Quentin, where he was nicknamed "the captain," and where, for the first time, his seemingly impervious constitution began to show its age. In 1986, he underwent a quadruple bypass. Although guards stood by the door in case he tried to escape, he now considered himself strictly a legal contortionist. Years earlier, at Alcatraz, he had written an appeal that went all the way to the Supreme Court in which he successfully argued that a judge could not, at sentencing, take into account prior convictions received when the defendant lacked counsel. ("It is time we become just a little realistic in the face of a record such as this one," Justice Harry A. Blackmun wrote in an angry dissent.) Now, with his failing health, Tucker unleashed another flurry of appeals, getting his sentence reduced by more than half. "This is to thank you," he wrote one judge. "It's the first break I ever got in my life. I won't ever need another."

He began to pour all his energy into what he saw as the culmination of his life as an outlaw: a Hollywood movie. Tucker had seen all sorts of films that echoed his life, among them "I Am a Fugitive from a Chain Gang," "Escape from Alcatraz," and "Bonnie and Clyde," and he wanted, at last, to see his story enshrined in the American imagination. He began to put his exploits down on paper, five pages at a time. "No one could have written this inside story of the Rock and what really happened there unless they had personally lived it," he wrote. He devoted two hundred and sixty-one pages to "Alcatraz: The True Story," while working on a second, more ambitious account, which he titled "The Can Opener." In it, he described himself as a throwback "to the highly intelligent, nonviolent type of criminal in the Willie Sutton mold," and, more grandly, as a kind of heroic underdog, pitted against a vast and oppressive system. "Tucker's obsession with freedom and escape has transformed itself into gamesmanship," he wrote. "This is his way of keeping his sanity in a lifetime of being the hunted. Each new 'joint' is a game, a game to outwit the authorities."

In 1993, he was released, at the age of seventy-three, and settled into the peach-colored house in Pompano Beach, which his wife had bought for them. He polished his manuscript and set up a music room in the den, where he gave saxophone and clarinet lessons for twenty-five dollars an hour. "We had a wonderful life," his wife said. Tucker recalls, "We used to go out dancing. She'd dress up real pretty, and I'd show her off." He composed music for her. "He has all these talents that had been wasted all these years," she told me. From time to time, he played in local jazz clubs. "I got used to being free," he says. But his manuscript failed to captivate people as he had hoped it would—"I called Clint Eastwood's secretary, but she said, 'Unless you have an agent, he won't read it' "—and the author of "The Can Opener" increasingly seemed trapped, an ordinary old man.

Then came the day in 1999 when, at the age of seventy-eight, he painted his fingertips with nail polish, pulled his white ascot up over his face, and burst into the Republic Security Bank with his gun. "He didn't do it for the money," his wife said. "We had a new car, nice home paid for, beautiful clothes. He had everything."

"I think he wanted to become a legend, like Bonnie and Clyde," said Captain Chinn, who apprehended him after what was believed to be his fourth recent robbery in the Florida area. A court psychologist who examined Tucker noted, "I have seen many individuals who are self-aggrandizing, and that would like to make their mark in history . . . but none, I must admit, that I heard that would want to, other than in the movies, go out in a blaze in a bank robbery. It is beyond the realm of psychological prediction."

After Tucker's arrest, the police put him in semi-isolation, fearing that even at seventy-eight he might somehow elude them. Despite his lawyer's pleas that his client could die under such conditions, he was denied bail. "Ordinarily, I would not consider a seventy-eight-year-old man a flight risk or a danger to the community," the magistrate said, "but Mr. Tucker has proved himself to be remarkably agile." On October 20, 2000, just before his case was scheduled to go to trial, and with his wife looking on, Tucker pleaded guilty. He was sentenced to thirteen years.

At one point, I found a report that the Department of Corrections had compiled, detailing Tucker's life. After pages listing his dramatic holdups and daredevil escapes, it concluded with a different kind of summary:

The defendant does not know the whereabouts of [his] daughter. He stated he did not have an active part in this child's upbringing. . . . The defendant has no knowledge of his son's whereabouts. The defendant did not partake in the rearing of this child.

"I thought he died in an automobile accident," his son, Rick Bellew, told me over the phone after I tracked him down in Nevada, where he was living and working as a printer. "That's what my mom told me to protect me." He didn't know the truth, he said, until he was in his early twenties, when Tucker was about to be paroled. "My mom was afraid he'd come up to me on the street and freak me out."

He said that after his father was taken away the authorities confiscated all their furniture and possessions, which had been paid for with stolen cash. They had to move in with his grandparents, while his mother worked in a factory to support them. "He left us with nothing," he said. "He turned our world inside out."

After Bellew read about Tucker's last arrest, he wrote him a letter for the first time. "I needed to know why he did it," he said. "Why he sacrificed everything."

Although Tucker could never give him a satisfactory answer, they struck up a correspondence, and in one of his letters Tucker told him something he had never expected: Bellew had an older half sister named Gaile Tucker, a nurse who lived in Florida. "I called her up and said, 'Are you sitting down?' I said, 'This is your long-lost brother.' She said, 'Oh, my God.' " Later, the two met, studying each other's features for similarities, trying to piece together a portrait of a man they barely knew.

"I don't have any ill feelings," his daughter told me. "I just don't have any feelings."

At one point, Bellew read me part of a letter that Tucker had recently sent him: "I'm sorry things turned out the way they did. . . . I never got to take you fishing, or to baseball games or to see you grow up. . . . I don't ask you to forgive me as there is too much lost but just so you know I wish you the best. Always. Your dad, Forrest."

Bellew said he didn't know if he would continue the correspondence, not because of what Tucker had done to him but because of what he had done to his mother. "He blew my mother's world apart," Bellew told me. "She never remarried. There was a song she used to sing to me called 'Me and My Shadow,' all about being alone and blue. And when she had cancer, and wasn't going to live much longer, I broke down and she sang that song, and I realized how bittersweet it was. It was her life."

In the spring of 2002, when I visited Tucker's third wife in Pompano Beach, she seemed to be still trying to cope. A small, delicate woman, now in her seventies, she had had several operations and lived alone in their house. "With Forrest gone, there's no one to fix things up," she said. She paused, scanning the den where he used to keep his musical instruments. "The silence is unbearable." She showed me a picture of the two of them, taken shortly after they met. They are standing side by side, their arms touching. He has on a red shirt and tie, and his wavy hair is neatly combed to one side. "God, he used to be so handsome," she said. "When I met him, he was a *doll*."

She turned the picture of him over several times in her hand. "I waited all those years," she said as she walked me outside, wiping her eyes. "I thought we had the rest of our lives together. What am I supposed to do now?"

One of the last times I met Tucker in prison, he looked alarmingly frail. His facial muscles seemed slack, and his hands trembled. Since his incarceration, he had had several strokes, and a cardiologist concluded that blood clots were gradually cutting off oxygen to his brain. His daughter told me bluntly, "He'll die in prison."

"Everyone says I'm smart," Tucker said to me. "But I'm not smart in the ways of life or I wouldn't have done the things I did." After a brief flurry of attention following his arrest, he had been all but forgotten. "When I die, no one will remember me," he said. His voice was almost a whisper. "I wish I had a real profession, something like the music business. I regret not being able to work steady and support my family. I have other regrets, too, but that's as much as one man can stand. Late at night, you lie in your bunk in prison and you think about what you lost, what you were, what you could've been, and you regret."

He said that his wife was thinking of selling their house and moving into a community where she could see more people. Although he and his wife still spoke regularly, Tucker said, she was too frail to visit.

"What hurts most . . . is that I know how much I disappointed my wife," he went on. "That hurts more than anything."

As he rose to go, he took a piece of paper from his back pocket. "I made this up for you last night," he said.

On it was a list of all his escapes, neatly printed. At the bottom, there was a No. 19—one more than he had actually made—left blank. As the guard fetched his wheelchair, he waved him away. "I don't need my chariot," he said. Then slowly, with his back hunched, he steadied himself against the wall and, with the guard standing behind him, inched down the corridor.

—January, 2003

Stealing Time

One summer night not long ago, Rickey Henderson, the greatest base stealer and lead-off hitter in baseball history, stood in a dugout, pinching the front of his jersey and plucking it several inches from his chest—"peacocking," as some players call it. He went through the same pregame rituals that he has performed since he was a rookie outfielder with the Oakland A's, in 1979. He sorted through a bunch of bats, asking, "Which one of you bad motherfuckers has got a hit in you?" Picking one up with resin on the handle, he cocked it back, waiting for an imaginary pitch, and talked to himself in the third person, the words running together so fast that they were nearly unintelligible: "Let's-burn-Rickey-come-on-let's-burn."

Henderson is accustomed not only to beating his opponents but also to lording his abilities over them. As a ten-time All Star for the A's, the New York Yankees, and seven other teams, he stole more than fourteen hundred bases—a record that is considered untouchable, like Joe DiMaggio's fifty-six-game hitting streak. He scored more runs than Ty Cobb, Babe Ruth, or Hank Aaron. Bill James, the oracle of baseball statistics, wrote, "Without exaggerating one inch, you could find fifty Hall of Famers who, all taken together, don't own as many records." Or, as Henderson puts it, "I'm a walking record."

As Henderson stepped onto the field, he stopped abruptly. A foul odor was seeping from under the dugout. "Where's it coming from?" one of his teammates asked. Several players bent down, trying to find the source of the smell; previously, the manager had found a dead rat in the stadium.

"I think it's coming from over here," one player said. "See that hole?"

Henderson tried to ignore the commotion and resume his routine. He walked toward the batter's box, moving casually, as if he were out for an evening stroll. An opposing player once noted that it took him longer to get to the batter's box than to drive to the stadium. Henderson has said that his slow approach is a way to get into a pitcher's head; opponents have said that it is simply another means for Henderson to let the world take stock of him. As he reached the batter's box, informing the world what Rickey was going to do to the ball, he again seemed disconcerted, and looked up at the crowd: there were only six hundred or so fans in the stadium, and many of the women had dressed up, as part of a promotional Eighties Night, in sequins and lace stockings, like Madonna in her "Like a Virgin" phase.

Earlier, Henderson had confessed to me, "Last night, I dropped down on my knees and I asked God, 'Why are you doing this to Rickey? Why did you put me here?'"

An announcer called his name on the scratchy P.A. system: "Now batting lead-off for the San Diego Surf Dawgs . . . RICKEY HENDERSON."

The man who once proclaimed "I am the greatest of all time!" was, at the age of forty-six, playing in the Golden Baseball League. It wasn't the majors. It wasn't even part of the minor-league farm system. It was an independent league, which consisted largely of players who had never made it to the minors, or had washed out of them. Created by two Stanford business-school graduates, the league—which began operating in 2005, with eight teams in Arizona and California—is widely considered to be the bottom of the bottom. Yet it is here that Henderson suited up for three thousand dollars a month, less than he could bring in selling a piece of memorabilia from his days in the majors.

"Come on, hot *dawwwg*, let's see what you can do!" a fan yelled.

Henderson tapped the dirt out of his cleats and got into his crouch, staring at the pitcher, a twenty-four-year-old right-hander for the Mesa Miners. Several nights earlier, Henderson had singled and stolen second base, sliding head first in a cloud of dust, to the delight of fans, but, this time, he hit a weak liner to the second baseman for an easy out. As he made his way to the dugout, one of the hecklers in the crowd yelled, "Hey, Rickey, where's your fucking wheelchair?"

Other baseball greats have insisted on playing past their prime: at forty, Babe Ruth, in his last major-league season, batted .181 for the Boston Braves. But Henderson's decision to go so far as to join the Surf Dawgs—which, the team's former publicist admitted, was frequently assumed to be a girls' softball team—has been a source of astonishment. His last stint in the majors was in 2003, when he played part of the season for the Los Angeles Dodgers. He hit a mere .208, with three stolen bases. (His last productive season was in 1999.) The Dodgers management, concluding that time had finally defeated "the man of steal," as he was often called, unceremoniously released him. He had played three thousand and eighty-one games, putting him fourth on the all-time list. He was forty-four years old, and most fans reasonably assumed that he would retire and wait for his induction into the Hall of Fame. Instead, he played the 2004 season with the Newark Bears, in the independent Atlantic League, before switching to the Golden Baseball League. Manny Ramirez, the Boston Red Sox slugger, who played alongside Henderson in 2002, has said that Henderson must be "crazy," and a sportswriter declared that it would take "a team of psychiatrists" to figure him out. Even one of his three daughters, Alexis, asked, "Dad, why are you doing this?"

A few hours before the game against the Miners, I found Henderson sitting on a metal chair in the Surf Dawgs' locker room, with his shirt off. He insisted that he was no different from anyone else in the league: he simply wanted to make it to the majors. But he also seemed shocked by his own predicament, by the riddle of age. As he put it, "There are pieces of this puzzle that Rickey is still working out."

He stood to put on his uniform. He is five feet ten, and, like a Rockette, most of his height seems to come from his legs, which he calls "the essence of my game"; they dwarf his torso, which always appears to be pressing forward, as if he were bursting out of a starting gate. His eyes betray frequent shifts in mood—they squint with displeasure, then widen with delight—and, during games, he often hides them behind wraparound sunglasses. He put on his jersey, which was white, with powder-blue sleeves, and pulled his pants above his hips; when he slipped on his cap, only the creases on his forehead and around his mouth confirmed that he was as old as many of his teammates' fathers. Extending his arms, he said, "Look at me. I ain't got no injuries. I got no problem with my eyes. My knees are good. The only problem I have is a little pain in my hip, and it ain't nothin' a little ice can't cure."

Henderson knew that he had only a few months to prove to a scout that he was able to play at the highest level—the major-league season ended in October. He told me that not long after he began playing for the Newark Bears he called Billy Beane, the general manager of the Oakland A's. Most of Henderson's greatest achievements in baseball, including his first World Series ring, in 1989, stemmed from his time on the A's, and he told Beane that he wanted to return to the team more than to any other. "Then I could go out the way I came in," he said. Beane responded that the A's, which were currently vying for a spot in the playoffs, had no room for him. Nevertheless, Henderson said, "I ain't giving up hope. I know if people would just come out to see me play they would realize that Rickey is still Rickey."

He arrived hours before a game, and would slash at balls as they shot out of a pitching machine at eighty-five miles an hour, while the Surf Dawgs' adopted theme song blared over the loudspeakers: "Who let the dogs out? Woof! Woof! Woof! Woof!" On some mornings, he could be seen running up and down the bleachers. Jose Canseco, who played with Henderson on the A's, and who helped to fuel the explosion of performance-enhancing drugs in the major leagues, has said of Henderson, "That's one of the guys who's not on steroids!"

"They kept that shit a secret from me," Henderson said. "I wish they *had* told me. My God, could you imagine Rickey on 'roids? Oh, baby, look out!" He laughed in an easygoing way. "Maybe if they weren't juicing there'd still be a spot on a ball club for me. People always ask me why I still want to play, but I want to know why no one will give me an opportunity.

It's like they put a stamp on me: 'Hall of Fame. You're done. That's it.' It's a goddam shame."

As Henderson was talking to me, one of his teammates, who had tousled hair and looked to be about eighteen, walked over. He was holding a baseball and a pen in his hand. He said to Henderson, "I feel funny asking, but could you sign this?"

Henderson smiled and signed the ball.

"Thank you, Rickey," the young man said, holding the ball along the seams, so as not to smudge the ink.

Henderson turned back to me, and said, "I'll tell you the truth. I'd give everything up—every record, the Hall of Fame, all of it—for just one more chance."

Base stealers are often considered their own breed: reckless, egocentric, sometimes even a touch mad. Ron LeFlore, who stole ninety-seven bases with the Montreal Expos, was a convicted armed robber; Ty Cobb, who was called "psychotic" by his authorized biographer, used to slide with his spikes in the air, in an effort to take out the second baseman; even Lou Brock, who was more gentlemanly, believed that one of his greatest assets was unbridled arrogance. Henderson, by all accounts, was a natural-born thief. Lloyd Moseby, a childhood friend of his who played for the Toronto Blue Jays, told *Sports Illustrated*, "Rickey hasn't changed since he was a little kid. He could strut before he could walk, and he always lived for the lights."

Henderson grew up with little outside the game: when he was two, his father disappeared, abandoning the family, and, after his mother moved to California to find work, he and his four brothers remained in Pine Bluff, Arkansas, for several years, in the care of a grandmother. In 1976, when Henderson was seventeen, the Oakland A's drafted him in the fourth round and assigned him to one of their minor-league teams, in Boise, Idaho. From the beginning, he was intense, moody, and flamboyant. If he hit what looked like an easy ground out, he sometimes refused to run it out, to the consternation of the manager. But, when he thought the opportunity was ripe, his speed was unparalleled. One night in Fresno, California, in 1977, he stole seven bases, tying the record for a single game. Two years later, in the middle of the season, the Oakland A's called him up to the majors.

With his new money, Henderson hired a group of detectives to find his father. "I didn't care if he was a bad guy or a good guy," Henderson told me. "I just wanted to know him." The private eyes reported back to his mother, who informed him, "Your father is dead. He died a few years ago in a car accident." In 1980, however, Henderson found an unlikely father figure in Billy Martin, the A's new manager. Martin was a pugnacious drinker who, on at least one occasion, slugged one of his own players. But he and Henderson shared an in-your-face approach to the game—Martin hung on his office wall a poster that said, "There can be no rainbow without a cloud and a storm"—and together they developed a manic style of play, known as Billy Ball, that was as terrifying as it was exhilarating. As Henderson has put it, "Billy was the publisher of Billy Ball, and I was the author."

Because the A's didn't have a lot of power, they couldn't rely on three-run homers and big innings; they had to manufacture runs, to create them out of the slightest opportunities. As the lead-off hitter, Henderson was the catalyst, or, as he likes to say, "the creator of chaos." He had remarkable strength (twice, he finished the season with a higher slugging percentage than Mark McGwire), but his principal role was to be a nuisance, a pest—to "get on base, any damn way I can," and begin wreaking havoc on the defense.

As part of his strategy, he had developed one of the most distinctive and infuriating batting stances ever seen. Each hitter has a strike zone that extends roughly from his chest to his knees. Henderson, by collapsing his shoulders to his knees—by practically doubling over—made his strike zone seem uncommonly small; one sportswriter quipped that it was "the size of Hitler's heart." With so little room for the pitcher to throw a strike, Henderson would frequently eke out a walk. (In 2001, he broke Babe Ruth's record for total walks, and is now second, behind Barry Bonds.) Or he would crush the ball—he is one of only twenty-five players in history with more than three thousand hits. Once he was on base, the chaos began: he would often steal second, then steal third; he stole home four times. In his first full year, he broke Ty Cobb's American League record of ninety-six stolen bases in a season, which had stood since 1915; two seasons later, he blew past Lou Brock's major-league mark of a hundred and eighteen. Thomas Boswell, of the Washington *Post*, wrote, "Not since Babe Ruth hit fifty-four home runs in 1920—thirty more than anyone else had hit in a season—has one of baseball's fundamental areas of offensive production been in such danger of major redefinition. . . . Now, perhaps for the first time, a player's skill is challenging the basic dimensions of the diamond."

His mere presence on the base paths was a force of psychic disruption. Distracted infielders made errors, and pitchers, finding themselves unable to concentrate, gave up easy hits to subsequent batters. As the former Yankee captain Don Mattingly has said, "Basically, he terrorizes a team." Henderson would score in ways that made his heroics nearly invisible: he would often get a walk, then steal second, then advance to third on a ground ball, and, finally, come home on a routine fly ball to the outfield. In other words, he regularly scored when neither he nor his teammates registered a single hit.

But there was also something out of control about Henderson. A base stealer takes his team's fortunes into his own hands; if he decides to run and gets thrown out, he can devastate a team's chances for a big inning. In 1982, Henderson didn't merely set a season record for steals; he also set one for being caught (forty-two times). The very traits that won him praise—bravado, guile, defiance—also made him despised. During a 1982 game against the Detroit Tigers, when he needed only one more base to tie Brock's record, he singled but had no chance to steal, because there was a slow base runner on second. Violating every norm of the game, Billy Martin ordered the man on second to take such a big lead that he would get picked off. Henderson's path was now clear, and he took off, sure that he was safe at second, but the umpire called him out, allegedly muttering, "You got to earn it."

Baseball has an unspoken etiquette about lopsided games, and Henderson's habit of stealing when his team was already trouncing an opponent was widely seen as unsportsmanlike. In 2001, while Henderson was playing with the San Diego Padres in a game against the Milwaukee Brewers, he took off in the seventh inning, when his team was leading by seven runs. The Brewers' manager, Davey Lopes, who had been one of the most aggressive base stealers of his day, was so incensed that he stormed onto the field, yelling that the next time Henderson came up to bat the pitcher was going to "drill" him. The threat was clearly in earnest, and

Henderson was removed from the game. "We're old school," Lopes said later.

And it wasn't just the way Henderson ran the bases that irked traditionalists. In 1985, after being traded to the Yankees, he was asked what it would be like to play on the same field that once knew Joe DiMaggio and Mickey Mantle, and he replied, "I don't care about them. . . . It's Rickey time." When he hit a home run, he would stop and watch it go over the fence, then arc ostentatiously around first base, one elbow outstretched like a bird's wing. Instead of simply catching a ball, he would make a show of snatching it out of the air. "I don't appreciate that hot-dog garbage in my ballpark," the former Orioles catcher Rick Dempsey, who once had to be restrained by an umpire from attacking Henderson, said.

Henderson earned a reputation for creating tumult off the field as well. He held general managers hostage with his contractual demands. "I've got to have my money guaranteed," he'd say. Or, in one of his more Yogi Berra-like phrases, "All I'm asking for is what I want." Once, when he couldn't find his limousine upon leaving a ballpark, he was heard saying, "Rickey don't like it when Rickey can't find Rickey's limo." In 1989, the A's signed him to a four-year contract worth twelve million dollars, which made him the highest-paid player in the game; but less than two years later, after several players surpassed that sum, he demanded a new contract. The pitcher Goose Gossage, who played with Henderson on the A's, once said, "Henderson set a new standard for selfishness. He made Jose Canseco look like a social worker." By the end of his career in the majors, Henderson was recognized as one of the best players of all time, but, in the view of many players and sportswriters, he was also "greedy," "egomaniacal," "Tropical Storm Rickey," "the classic baseball mercenary," and "the King of I." In other words, he was the last player anyone thought would join the Golden Baseball League.

"I can't be late," Henderson said.

He was at the Los Angeles airport, waiting for a morning flight to Yuma, Arizona, where, for a July game against the Scorpions, the Golden Baseball League was hosting Rickey Henderson Night. (The first thousand fans to arrive at the game would receive Rickey Henderson bobblehead dolls.) The league, realizing that Henderson helped give it legitimacy, had offered him various perks to sign on, and, unlike the rest of the players, he didn't have to endure long bus rides to away games—he flew by commercial airplane. And so, while the team was spending five hours on a bus to Yuma, Henderson picked up his bags and boarded the plane. He was wearing an elegant tan shirt and matching pants, and a gold Rolex studded with diamonds. During his career, he has earned more than forty million dollars in salary alone. He owns dozens of rental properties, as well as a hundred-and-fifty-acre ranch, near Yosemite National Park, where he spent time in the off-season with his wife and their daughters. He also has a Porsche, a Rolls-Royce, a Bentley, a BMW, a Mercedes, a Cadillac, a G.M. truck, a T-bird, and a Ferrari. "I've told major-league clubs, 'Don't worry about your bank account—I'll play for free,' " Henderson said. "This ain't about my portfolio."

As he waited for the plane to taxi to the runway, he checked his cell phone to see if his agent had called with any word from the majors. "Nothing," he said. After holding power over general managers for so long, Henderson seemed uncertain what to do now that they held power over him. He had even considered crashing a Colorado Rockies tryout for high-school and college players. He knew that his reputation had probably hurt his chances of being brought onto a team as an elder statesman and bench player. "There's always that concern: will Rickey be willing to come off the bench?" Henderson said. "I would. If you let me retire in a major-league uniform, you won't hear a peep out of me." Henderson regularly scoured the news reports for injuries and roster changes in the majors, to see if there might be an opening.

"Who's that new guy they got playing center field for the Yankees?" Henderson asked me.

"Tony Womack," I said.

"Womack, huh?" he said, then added in frustration, "My God, you mean to tell me I ain't better than him?"

He placed a call on his cell phone, and began talking over the roar of the engine. The stewardess, who seemed unusually tense, asked him sharply to turn the phone off. He said that he would, but requested that she ask him nicely. Within moments, security officers had boarded the plane to remove him.

"What the hell's going on?" he asked.

"Is that Rickey Henderson?" a passenger asked.

"Look how cut he is," another said. "I hear he never lifts weights—he only does pushups and situps."

"You'll have to come with us," an officer told Henderson.

I stood up to get off with Henderson, and the officer asked who I was.

"That's my biographer and lawyer," Henderson said.

The passengers began to shout, "You can't take Rickey!" But the stewardess wouldn't relent, although Henderson said that if he had done something to offend her he was happy to apologize. The plane took off without us.

"See, man?" Henderson said to me. "I cause controversy even when I don't do nothin'. That's the way it's always been."

The airline, seemingly embarrassed by his removal, tried to find us another flight, but the next one to Yuma didn't leave until the evening. "I gotta make my game," Henderson said. "It's Rickey Henderson Night."

Eventually, the airline found us a flight to Imperial, California, which was about an hour's drive from Yuma; from there, the airline said, it would provide a car to take us to the stadium. When we arrived at the Imperial airport, a middle-aged man standing in the baggage-claim area said, "Rickey, what brings you to Imperial?"

"Got a game tonight in Yuma."

"In *Yuma*?"

"Playing in a new independent league over there."

"You trying to make it back to the show?"

"That's the plan."

"Well, I sure wish they'd give you a shot. They never treat us old guys well."

We drove in a van across the desert to Yuma, which is known primarily for a prison that once housed outlaws from the Wild West. When we reached Desert Sun Stadium, Henderson seemed taken aback—it was little more than a field with bleachers and a water tank looming over it. "It ain't Yankee Stadium, is it?" he said.

The temperature was a hundred and nine degrees, and it was hard to breathe. Henderson signed autographs and posed for photographs with fans—"I'm, like, the Babe Ruth of the independent leagues," he said—and then went into the clubhouse to suit up. The bus for the rest of the team had already arrived, and the players were lounging in their underwear; a few were chewing sunflower seeds and discussing a rumor that a scout from a major-league organization had appeared at a recent game.

By now, Henderson knew most of his teammates' stories. There was Nick Guerra, a former college star who worked a construction job in the mornings to support his family. There was Scott Goodman, a slightly pear-shaped power hitter, who once hit eighteen home runs for a minor-league team affiliated with the Florida Marlins but was released anyway. And there was Adam Johnson, perhaps the most promising player on the team, a twenty-six-year-old starting pitcher who had lost only one game all season. The manager, Terry Kennedy, who had played fourteen years in the major leagues as a catcher, and whose father had played in the majors as well, told me, "I sometimes call this the Discovery League. Everybody here is trying to discover something about themselves—whether they should continue pursuing their dream or whether it's time to finally let it go."

Henderson and Goodman went out to the batting cage together. Goodman, who was among the league leaders in home runs and R.B.I.s, had been struggling with his swing in recent games.

"How you feeling?" Henderson asked him.

"Last night, I wasn't getting my bat out right."

"I don't mean last night. I'm not worried about last night. How do you feel now?"

"I don't know," Goodman said. "It's like I'm not getting my weight behind anything." He went into the cage and swung at several pitches.

"See your foot?" Henderson said. "You're stepping too far in, instead of toward the pitcher."

Goodman inspected the divot in the dirt where his front foot had landed. "You're right," he said. "I never noticed."

Kennedy told me that he had initially worried how Henderson would fit in with the team, especially considering his perks. "I was never into guys who chirp," he said. But, to his surprise, Henderson had gone out of his way to mentor other players. "I don't want to go too deep into his head," Kennedy said. "But something's clearly going on in there. I think maybe he's trying to show clubs that he's willing to be a different player."

After a while, Goodman and Henderson returned to the clubhouse.

They put on their road uniforms, which were gray and navy blue, and walked onto the field, their cleats leaving marks in the sticky grass. Despite the heat, more than four thousand people had come out for Rickey Henderson Night—the biggest crowd in Yuma since the opening night of the season. As Henderson took his position in center field, a yellow Volkswagen Beetle, with a pair of rodent-like ears attached to its roof and a curly tail sticking out of its trunk, circled the grass. "It's time to exterminate the competition," the stadium announcer said. "Truly Nolen Pest Control— We get the bugs out for you." After the first inning, Henderson sat on the bench, his uniform already soaked with sweat, while cheerleaders danced on the dugout roof over his head. The announcer said, "See if you can answer tonight's trivia question! The question is: What year was Rickey Henderson originally drafted by the Oakland A's?"

"Nineteen seventy-six," one of Henderson's teammates said.

"I wasn't even born then," another said.

At one point, with Henderson playing center field, a shot was hit over his head and he began to run, unleashing at least a memory of his speed. He looked back over his shoulder, trying to bring the ball into focus, and made a nice catch. "Thataway, Rickey!" his teammates yelled when he came back to the dugout.

Even though Henderson played well, with two singles and a walk, the Surf Dawgs lost, 5–0. His wife, who had come to see him play that weekend with two of their daughters, told the team's general manager, "Why won't he just quit and come home?" As he left the field, fireworks began to explode in the sky above him, the finale of Rickey Henderson Night.

One afternoon before a home game, Kennedy approached Henderson at the ballpark and asked if he would teach the other players the art of stealing. Kennedy knew that, in recent years, base stealing had been all but forgotten in the major leagues. Team owners, convinced that home runs brought people to the stadium, had built smaller and smaller ballparks; at the same time, players made their muscles bigger and bigger with steroids. Since 1982, when Henderson broke the single-season record for steals, home-run totals had risen by sixty-one per cent, while the number of stolen bases had fallen nearly twenty per cent. But Kennedy knew how devastating stealing could be: he had been with the San Francisco Giants in the 1989 World Series, when Henderson and the A's swept the Giants in four games and Henderson set a post-season record, with eleven stolen bases.

Henderson agreed to give a demonstration, and there was a buzz as Goodman, Johnson, and the other players gathered around first base. Henderson stepped off the bag, spread his legs, and bent forward, wiggling his fingers. "The most important thing to being a good base stealer is you got to be fearless," he said. "You know they're all coming for you; everyone in the stadium knows they're coming for you. And you got to say to yourself, 'I don't give a dang. I'm gone.'" He said that every pitcher has the equivalent of a poker player's "tell," something that tips the runner off when he's going to throw home. Before a runner gets on base, he needs to identify that tell, so he can take advantage of it. "Sometimes a pitcher lifts a heel, or wiggles a shoulder, or cocks an elbow, or lifts his cap," Henderson said, indicating each giveaway with a crisp gesture.

Once you were on base, Henderson said, the next step was taking a lead. Most players, he explained, mistakenly assume that you need a big lead. "That's one of Rickey's theories: Rickey takes only three steps from the bag," he said. "If you're taking a big lead, you're going to be all tense out there. Then everyone knows you're going. Just like you read the pitcher, the pitcher and catcher have read you."

He spread his legs again and pretended to stare at the pitcher. "O.K., you've taken your lead; now you're ready to find that one part of the pitcher's body that you already know tells you he's throwing home. The second you see the sign, then, *boom*, you're gone." He lifted his knees and dashed toward second base. After he stopped, he said, "I'll tell you another of Rickey's theories." Nearly all base stealers, he explained, begin their run by crossing their left foot in front of their right, as they turn their bodies toward second. That was also a mistake. "If you cross over, it forces you to stand straight up to get into your stride," he said. "That's the worst thing you can do as a runner. You want to start out low and explode."

As Henderson was conducting his demonstration, members of the opposing team arrived and began to look on. He said that the final touch was the slide. Before Henderson, the great base stealers typically went feet first. Henderson decided that it would be faster—not to mention more daring and stylish—to go in head first, the way Pete Rose, who was never a major base stealer, occasionally did. Yet each time Henderson tried the head-first slide he would bounce violently, brutally pounding his body. Then, one day, while he was flying to a game, he noticed that the pilot landed the plane in turbulence without a single bump. Henderson recalled, "I asked the pilot, I said, 'How the hell did you do that?' He said the key is coming in low to the ground, rather than dropping suddenly. I was, like, 'Dang. That's it!' " After that, Henderson said, he lowered his body gradually to the ground, like an airplane.

Henderson concluded by saying that if the base runner studied the pitcher, made a good jump, and slid well, he should beat the throw nearly every time. And, if for some reason he was caught, the moment he got back on base he should try to steal again. As Henderson put it to me, "To steal a base, you need to think you're invincible."

"Look at your head," the Surf Dawgs' hitting instructor said to Henderson one July afternoon. "You're dropping it down."

"I know it," Henderson said, stepping back in the batting cage. He took several more swings, but nothing seemed to be going right. "Come on, Rickey, you're better than this!" he yelled.

That month, his batting average had plunged from .311 to .247—one of the lowest on the team. In May, he hit only one home run; he had none in June. "He still sees the ball well," Kennedy, who was leaning against the cage, said of Henderson. "But he doesn't have the bat speed to get around."

After a dismal series against the Samurai Bears, an all-Japanese squad that had the worst record in the league, Henderson began staring at the ground in the outfield. Kennedy turned to his coaches and said, "I think we've lost him."

Kennedy, believing that Henderson was ready to quit, later called him into his office. "I understand if you're through," Kennedy said.

"No, man, it's not that. It's just my damn hitting. I can't get it straight."

As the weeks wore on, it became clearer that the defiant mind-set that had made him a great base stealer had, in many ways, trapped him in the Golden Baseball League. He was forever convinced that he could do the impossible. "When I went to play with the Newark Bears, I was sure I would be there for only a few weeks—that a major-league team would call me," he said. "But one week became two weeks, and now it's two years and I'm still waiting for that call."

Trying to improve his average, he started to experiment with his trademark crouch; he stood straighter at the plate, until he was an almost unrecognizable figure. "I remember at the end of my career I began to doubt my ability," Kennedy said. "I knew what I wanted to do, but my body wouldn't let me do it. And I called my father and said, 'Dad, did you ever start to think you weren't good enough to play this game?' And he said, 'I did, and once you do you can never get it back.' "

During the game against the Scorpions in late July, after Henderson had singled and was on first, he got into his three-step lead. I had been travelling with the team periodically throughout the season, waiting to see him steal. The crowd implored him to run, and several times the pitcher threw to first to keep him close. "Here he goes!" a fan yelled. "Watch out!" But, when the pitcher went into his motion, Henderson didn't move. He stood there, frozen. "What's wrong, Rickey?" another fan yelled. "Can't you steal anymore?" On the next pitch, Henderson took his lead again and wiggled his fingers. The pitcher seemed to dip his shoulder when he was about to throw home—his tell—but Henderson didn't break. After several more pitches, the batter hit a ground ball to short and Henderson was easily thrown out at second. As Henderson returned to the dugout, he shouted, "Goddam cocksucking sun was in my eyes. I couldn't see a goddam motherfucking bullshit thing." He sat in the dugout with his head bowed, and for the first time since I had seen him play he didn't say a word.

Two weeks later, in the middle of August, as the Surf Dawgs' season was nearing its end, word spread in the clubhouse that the Oakland A's had just phoned about a player. Kennedy came out and told the team the good news: a Surf Dawg was being called up to Oakland's AAA farm team. It was Adam Johnson, the pitcher. Afterward, Henderson told me, "I'm happy to see one of the guys get out of the league, to get a chance to move on." He seemed genuinely glad for him and refused to mention his own circumstances. On another night on the field, however, he pointed to the Surf Dawg logo on his jersey and said, "I never thought I might end my career in this uniform." I asked if he would retire at the end of the season. "I don't know if I can keep going," he said. "I'm tired, you know." As he picked up his glove, he stared at the field for a moment. Then he said, "I just don't know if Rickey can stop."

— September, 2005

—–∿–—

After the 2005 season, Henderson quit the Golden Baseball League, though he continued to hope that he would get a call to play again in the majors. In 2009, at the age of fifty, he was inducted into the Hall of Fame. He still insisted, "I can come back and play."

Part Three

"*A thick, black cloud swirled before my eyes, and my mind told me that in this cloud, unseen as yet, but about to spring out upon my appalled senses, lurked all that was vaguely horrible, all that was monstrous and inconceivably wicked in the universe.*"

DR. WATSON, in "The Adventure of the Devil's Foot"

The Brand

— ⟋⟍⟍ —

THE RISE
OF THE
MOST DANGEROUS
PRISON GANG
IN AMERICA

— ⟋⟍⟍ —

On a cold, damp December morning in 2002, after weeks of secret planning, the United States Marshals launched one of the most unusual dragnets in the organization's two-hundred-and-fifteen-year history. As the fog lifted on a small stretch of land in the northwesternmost corner of California—a sparsely populated area known primarily for its towering redwoods— nearly a dozen agents, draped in black fatigues and bulletproof vests, and armed with assault rifles and walkie-talkies, gathered in a fleet of cars. The agents sped past a town with a single post office and a mom-and-pop store, and headed deep into the forest until they arrived at a colossal compound, a maze of buildings surrounded by swirling razor wire and an electrified fence that was lethal to the touch. A gate opened and, as guards looked down with rifles from beneath watchtowers, the convoy rolled inside. The agents jumped out.

After entering one of the buildings and walking down a long corridor lined with surveillance cameras, the officers reached their destination: a fortified cellblock in the heart of Pelican Bay, California's most notorious prison. They could hear inmates moving in their ten-by-twelve, window-less cement cells. Pelican Bay housed more than three thousand inmates, men who were considered too violent for any other state prison and had, in the parlance of correctional officers, "earned their way in." But the men on the cellblock, which was known as the Hole, were considered so dangerous that they had been segregated from this already segregated population.

Four prisoners were ordered to remove their gold jumpsuits and slide them through a tray slot. While some officers searched their belongings, others, using flashlights, peered through holes in the steel doors to examine the inmates' ears, nostrils, and anal cavities. To make sure that the prisoners had no weapons "keistered" inside them, the guards instructed them to bend down three times; if they refused, the guards would know that they were afraid to puncture their intestines with a shank. Once the search was complete, the inmates were shackled and escorted to a nearby landing strip, where they were loaded onto an unmarked airplane.

All across the country, agents were fanning out to prisons. They seized a fifth inmate from a maximum-security prison in Concord, New Hampshire. They took another from a jail in Sacramento, California. Then they approached the Administrative Maximum Prison, in Florence, Colorado, a "supermax" encircled by snow-covered ravines and renowned as "the Alcatraz of the Rockies." There, in the most secure federal penitentiary in the country—a place that housed Ted Kaczynski, the Unabomber, and Ramzi Yousef, the man behind the bombing of the World Trade Center, in 1993—agents apprehended four inmates who were allegedly responsible for more than a dozen prison murders.

Before long, the marshals had rounded up twenty-nine inmates—all of whom were among the most feared men in the American prison system. One had strangled an inmate with his bare hands; another had poisoned a fellow-prisoner. A man nicknamed the Beast was thought to have ordered an attack on an inmate who had shoved him during a basketball game; the inmate was subsequently stabbed seventy-one times and his eye was gouged out.

Then there was Barry Mills, who was known as the Baron. Soft-spoken and intense, with a gleaming bald head, he was described by one of his former prosecutors as a "cunning, calculating killer." He liked to crochet in his cell and, according to authorities, compose lists of enemies to kill. In a previous court case, he testified that "we live . . . in a different society than you do. There is justified violence in our society. I'm here to tell you that. I'm here to tell all you that." He was not, he conceded, "a peaceful man," and "if you disrespect me or one of my friends, I will readily and to the very best of my ability engage you in a full combat mode. That's what I'm about." Once, at a maximum-security prison in Georgia, Mills was found guilty of luring an inmate into a bathroom stall and nearly decapitating him with a knife.

Along with the Baron and the other prisoners, five women on the outside were also seized, as well as three ex-cons and a former prison guard. Most of those apprehended—there were forty in total—were transported on a Boeing 727, with their legs and arms shackled to their seats, while guards patrolled the aisles, their rifles sealed in compartments out of arm's reach. Days later, the prisoners ended up in a Los Angeles courtroom, where they were accused of being members of an elaborate criminal conspiracy directed by the Aryan Brotherhood, or the Brand. Authorities had once dismissed the Aryan Brotherhood as a fringe white-supremacist gang; now, however, they concluded that what prisoners had claimed for decades was true—namely, that the gang's hundred or so members, all convicted felons, had gradually taken control of large parts of the nation's maximum-security prisons, ruling over thousands of inmates and transforming themselves into a powerful criminal organization.

The Brand, authorities say, established drug-trafficking, prostitution, and extortion rackets in prisons across the country. Its leaders, often working out of barren cells in solitary confinement, allegedly ordered scores of stabbings and murders. They killed rival gang members; they killed blacks and homosexuals and child molesters; they killed snitches; they killed people who stole their drugs, or owed them a few hundred dollars; they killed prison guards; they killed for hire and for free; they killed, most of all, in order to impose a culture of terror that would solidify their power. And, because the Brotherhood is far more cloistered than other gangs, it was able to operate largely with impunity for decades—and remain all but invisible to the outside world. "It is a true secret society," Mark Hamm, a prison sociologist, told me.

For the first time, on August 28, 2002, that world cracked open. After more than a decade of trying to infiltrate the Brand's operations, a relatively unknown Assistant United States Attorney from California named Gregory Jessner indicted virtually the entire suspected leadership of the gang. He had investigated hundreds of crimes linked to the gang; some were cold cases that reached back nearly forty years. In the indictment, which ran to a hundred and ten pages, Jessner charged Brand leaders with carrying out stabbings, strangulations, poisonings, contract hits, conspiracy to commit murder, extortion, robbery, and narcotics trafficking. The case, which was expected to go to trial in 2005, could lead to as many as twenty-three death-penalty convictions—more than any in American history.

One morning in 2003, I visited the United States Attorney's office in downtown Los Angeles, where the prosecution was preparing to arraign the last of the forty defendants. As I waited in the lobby, a slender young man appeared in a gray suit. He had short brown hair, and he carried a folder under his arm as if he were a paralegal. Unlike the attorneys around him, he spoke in a soft, almost reticent voice. He introduced himself as Gregory Jessner.

"I'm forty-two," he told me, as if he were often greeted with similar astonishment. "Believe it or not, I used to look much younger." He reached into his pocket and revealed an old office I.D. He looked seventeen.

He led me back into his office, which had almost nothing on the walls and appeared to be decorated solely with boxes from the case, one stacked upon the other. On his desk were several black-and-white photographs, including one of an inmate who had been strangled by the gang.

"An Aryan brother went in his cell and tied a garrote around his neck," Jessner said. He held out his hands, demonstrating, with tapered fingers, how an Aryan Brotherhood member had braided strips of a bedsheet into a noose. "This is a homicidal organization," he said. "That's what they do. They kill people."

He was accustomed, he explained, to murder cases, but he had been shocked by the gang's brutality. "I suspect they kill more than the Mafia," he said. "They kill more than any single drug trafficker. There are a lot of gang-related deaths on the streets, but they are usually more disorganized and random." He paused, as if calculating various numbers in his head. "I think they may be the most murderous criminal organization in the United States."

There are hundreds of gangs in this country: the Crips, the Bloods, the Latin Dragons, the Dark Side Nation, the Lynch Mob. But the Aryan Brotherhood is one of the few gangs that were born in prison. In 1964, as the nation's racial unrest spread into the penitentiaries, a clique of white inmates at San Quentin prison, in Marin County, California, began gathering in the yard. The men were mostly motorcycle bikers with long hair and handlebar mustaches; a few were neo-Nazis with tattoos of swastikas. Together, they decided to strike against the blacks, who were forming their own militant group, called the Black Guerrilla Family, under the influence of the celebrated prison leader George Jackson. Initially, the whites called themselves the Diamond Tooth Gang, and as they roamed the yard they were unmistakable: pieces of glass embedded in their teeth glinted in the sunlight.

Before long, they had merged with other whites at San Quentin to form a single band: the Aryan Brotherhood. While there had always been cliques in prison, known as "tips," these men were now aligned by race and resorted to a kind of violence that had never been seen at San Quentin, a place that prisoners likened to "gladiator school." All sides, including the Latino gangs La Nuestra Familia and the Mexican Mafia, attacked each other with homemade knives that were honed from light fixtures and radio parts, and hidden in mattresses, air vents, and drainpipes. "Everything was seen through the delusional lens of race—everything," Edward Bunker, an inmate at the time, told me. (He went on to become a novelist, and appeared as Mr. Blue in "Reservoir Dogs.")

Most prison gangs tried to recruit "fish," the new and most vulnerable inmates. But according to interviews with former gang members—as well as thousands of pages of once classified F.B.I. reports, internal prison records, and court documents—the Aryan Brotherhood chose a radically different approach, soliciting only the most capable and violent. They were given a pledge:

An Aryan brother is without a care,
He walks where the weak and heartless won't dare,
And if by chance he should stumble and lose control,
His brothers will be there, to help reach his goal,

For a worthy brother, no need is too great,
He need not but ask, fulfillment's his fate.
For an Aryan brother, death holds no fear,
Vengeance will be his, through his brothers still here.

By 1975, the gang had expanded into most of California's state prisons and was engaged in what authorities describe as a full-fledged race war. Dozens had already been slain when, that same year, a fish named Michael Thompson entered the system. A twenty-three-year-old white former high-school football star, he had been sentenced for helping to murder two drug dealers and burying their bodies in a lime-filled pit in a back yard. Six feet four and weighing nearly three hundred pounds, he was strong enough to break ordinary shackles. He had brown hair, which was parted in the middle, and hypnotic blue eyes. Despite the violent nature of his crime, he had no other convictions and, with a chance for parole in less than a decade, he initially kept to himself, barely aware of the different forces moving around him. "I was a fish with gills out to fucking here," he later said.

Unaligned with any of the emerging gangs, he was conspicuous prey for roaming Hispanic and black groups, and several of them soon assaulted him in the yard at a prison in Tracy, California; later, he was sent to Folsom, which, along with San Quentin, was exploding with gang wars. On his first day there, he says, no one spoke to him until a leader of the Black Guerrilla Family, a trim, angular man in shorts and a T-shirt, began to taunt him, telling him to come to the yard "ready" the next day. That night in his cell, Thompson recalled, he looked frantically for a weapon; he broke a piece of steel off his cell door and began to file its edges. It was at least ten inches long, and he sharpened both sides. Before the cell doors opened and the guards searched him, he said, he knew he needed to hide the weapon. He took off his clothes and tried to insert it in his rectum. "I couldn't," he recalled. "I was too ashamed." He tried again and again, until finally he succeeded.

The next morning in the yard, he could see the guards, the tips of their rifles glistening in the sun. The leader of the Black Guerrilla Family circled toward him, flashing a steel blade, and Thompson lay down, trying to extricate his weapon. Eventually, he got it and began to lunge violently at his foe; another gang member came at him and Thompson stabbed him, too. By the time the guards interceded, Thompson was covered in blood, and one of the members of the Black Guerrilla Family lay on the ground, near death.

Not long after this incident, several white convicts approached him in the yard. "They wanted me to join the Brand," Thompson said. Initially, he hesitated, in part because of the gang's racism, but he knew that the group offered more than protection. "It was like being let into a sanctuary," he said. "You were instantly the man—the shot caller."

To be accepted, according to Thompson and other gang members, each recruit had to "make his bones," which often meant killing another inmate. (One recruit told authorities in a sworn statement that the rite was intended to "create a lasting bond to the A.B. and also prove that he had what it takes.") Thompson also recited a "blood in, blood out" oath, in which he vowed not only that he would spill another's blood to get in but also that he would never leave the gang unless his own blood was fatally spilled. While many new members had a probationary period, which often lasted as long as a year, Thompson, because of his physical strength and his ability with a knife, was voted into the gang almost immediately. He was "branded" with a homemade tattoo gun (which inmates made out of a beard trimmer sold at the commissary, a guitar string, a pen, and a needle stolen from the infirmary). Sometimes members were tattooed with the letters "A.B." or the numerals 666, symbolizing the beast, a manifestation of evil in the Revelation of St. John. On Thompson's left hand, just above one of his knuckles, he received the most recognizable symbol: a green shamrock. "All I had to do was show that 'rock and I was in charge," he said.

He was moved from one state prison to the next, often for disciplinary reasons, but these transfers only helped him garner more influence, and he gradually rose through the Brotherhood's rarefied ranks. He met Barry Mills, a.k.a. the Baron, who had initially been incarcerated for stealing a car and became the gang's vanguard member, seemingly concentrating all his energies not on returning to the outside world but on remaining in the inside world, where he was, in the words of Thompson, "the hog with the biggest balls." And he met T. D. Bingham, a charismatic bank robber who was nearly as wide as he was tall and who could bench-press five hundred pounds. Nicknamed the Hulk and Super Honkey, he spoke in a folksy manner that concealed a burning intelligence, friends say. In photographs from the time, he has a black walrus mustache and a ski hat pulled down over his eyebrows. Part Jewish, he wore a Star of David tattooed on one arm and, without any apparent irony, a swastika on the other. Once, when he testified on behalf of another reputed Aryan Brotherhood inmate, he told the jury, "There's a code in every segment of society. . . . Well, we have a different kind of moral and ethical code." He later added, "It's a lot more primordial." One of his friends, referring to his propensity for violence, told me, "Sometimes he got the urge, you know what I mean? He got the urge."

Thompson soon became acquainted with the Brotherhood's inner sanctum. There was Thomas Silverstein, a talented artist with long flowing hair who, a counsellor noted in his prison file, "seems to be easily influenced by these men and is eager to please them." After shedding an enemy's blood with a handcrafted knife, he would often retire to his cell and draw elaborate portraits. One ink sketch showed a man in a cell with a claw reaching down toward him. Thompson also met Dallas Scott, a drug addict who once told the reporter Pete Earley, in the 1992 book "The Hot House: Life Inside Leavenworth Prison," "In your society I may not be anybody, but in here I am"; and Clifford Smith, who lost an eye after a black-widow spider bit him at San Quentin and who, when asked to carry out his first hit, said, "Yeah, bro, I'll do the bastard."

Thompson, who had only a high-school education, was being tailored for leadership. He was given many books, a curriculum that formed a kind of world view. He read Sun Tzu's "The Art of War" and Machiavelli's "The Prince." He read Nietzsche, memorizing his aphorisms. ("One should die proudly when it is no longer possible to live proudly.") And he read Louis L'Amour, whose pulp novels about romantic gunslingers who ride for "the brand" inspired the gang's nickname. "It was like you went to school," Thompson said. "You already hate the system, hate the establishment, because you're in jail, you're buried, and you start to think of yourself as this noble warrior—and that's what we called each other, warriors. It was like I was a soldier going out to battle."

Thompson said that, like other new members, he was trained to kill without blinking, without reservation. One A.B. instruction manual, which was seized by authorities, stated, "The smell of fresh human blood can be overpowering but killing is like having sex. The first time is not so rewarding, but it gets better and better with practice, especially when one remembers that it's a holy cause." During a confidential debriefing with prison officials, one Aryan brother described how members studied anatomy texts, so "that when they stab somebody it was a killshot."

In 1981, according to prison records, Thompson approached one of the gang's enemies "from behind and began stabbing him," and "continued" striking his victim "as he lay on the floor." Thompson once wrote in a letter, "Knife fighting, at its best, is like a dance. Under ideal conditions, the objective is to bleed your opponent—cutting hands, wrist, and arms and as the opponent weakens from blood loss, inflicting further damage to the face (eyes) and torso."

Inmates were frequently killing each other not because of any actual slight but because of the color of their skin. In one incident, Silverstein and an A.B. associate, Clayton Fountain, who, according to a friend, was eager to "make his bones," stabbed a leader of the rival gang D.C. Blacks sixty-seven times in the shower, then dragged his bloody corpse through the tiers while other white inmates chanted racial slurs. After Silverstein was charged with murdering another inmate, he boasted in court, "I have walked over dead bodies. I've had guts splattered all over my chest from race wars."

To try to rein the Brand in, prison officials, in desperation, had begun to place its members throughout the correctional system. (No inmate would publicly admit being in the gang, and, when asked under oath, would typically say, "Sir, I will not answer a question like that.") The dispersal measures, however, only spread the Brand's reach to penitentiaries in Texas and Illinois and Kansas, and still farther east, to Pennsylvania and Georgia. A once classified 1982 F.B.I. report warned that leaders were "recruiting for the A.B., only now they had the entire country to pick from." One letter from a gang member, which was obtained by Texas prison sociologists, said, "All members shipped from here last week have written back and it looks like the family is in the process of growing." Another stated, "We are growing like a cancer."

Upon entering a new prison, Brand members would often carry out a "demonstration" killing or stabbing, in order to terrorize the inmate population. The Baron reportedly ordered that one foe be "taken out in front of everyone, to let these motherfuckers know we mean business." Indeed, rather than conceal its murders, the gang flaunted them even in front of the guards, as if to show it had no fear of repercussions, of being shot or sentenced to life without parole. "We wanted people to think we were a little crazy," Thompson said. "It was a way, like Nietzsche said, of bending space and reality to our will."

On a Saturday morning in the fall of 1983, at Marion federal prison, in southern Illinois, Thomas Silverstein waited for guards to take him for a routine shower. Marion, which is about a hundred miles southeast of St. Louis, was opened in 1963, the year that Alcatraz closed, and was designed to cope with the profusion of violent gang members—in particular, men like Silverstein, who by then had been convicted of murdering three inmates and had earned the nickname Terrible Tom (as he often signed his letters, with looping strokes).

Before taking Silverstein to the bathroom, the guards frisked him, to make sure he hadn't fashioned any weapons. (He often had pens and other sketching tools for his artwork.) They also shackled his wrists. Three guards surrounded him, one of whom was a hard-nosed, nineteen-year veteran with military-style gray hair named Merle Clutts. Clutts, who was to retire in a few months, was perhaps the only guard in the unit who didn't fear Silverstein; he once reportedly told him, "Hey, *I'm* running this shit. You ain't running it."

As the guards escorted Silverstein through the prison, he paused outside the cell of another gang member—who, as planned, suddenly reached between the bars and, with a handcuff key, unlocked Silverstein's shackles. Silverstein pulled a nearly foot-long knife from his conspirator's waistband. "This is between me and Clutts," Silverstein hollered as he rushed toward him.

One of the other guards screamed, "He's got a shank!" But Clutts was already cornered, without a weapon. He raised his hands while Silverstein stabbed him in the stomach. "He was just sticking Officer Clutts with that knife," another guard later recalled. "He was just sticking and sticking and sticking." By the time Silverstein relinquished the knife—"The man disrespected me," he told the guards. "I *had* to get him"—Clutts had been stabbed forty times. He died shortly afterward.

A few hours later, Clayton Fountain, Silverstein's close friend, was being led through the prison when he paused by another inmate's cell. In an instant, he, too, was free. "You motherfuckers want a piece of this?" he yelled, waving a blade. He stabbed three more guards. One died in the arms of his son, who also worked in the prison. Fountain reportedly said that he didn't want Silverstein to have a higher body count.

It was the first time in the history of American federal prisons that two guards had been killed on the same day. "You got to understand," Thompson said. "Here were guys in restraints, locked in the Hole in the most secure prison, and they were still able to get to the guards. It sent a simple message: We can get to you anywhere, anytime."

As the gang's reputation for brutality was growing, so, too, were its ranks. Although the Brand continued to permit only a select few to become "made" members, it had thousands of followers, known as "pecker-woods," who sought out the perks of being associated with it: permanent protection, free contraband, better prison jobs (which were often dictated by trusty inmates who did whatever the gang demanded). As Thompson put it, "The guards controlled the perimeter of the prison and we controlled what happened inside it." But as the number of gang members, associates, and hangers-on swelled, managing the organization grew increasingly difficult.

When the Brotherhood was in its infancy, every member had an equal vote on critical matters; by the early eighties, this policy was creating chaos. In a previously undisclosed briefing, Clifford Smith told authorities, "We used to be one man one vote, included damn near everything. I mean, damn near everything. Somebody getting in, whacking somebody . . . You damn near had to have the whole state's okay. . . . You had to send some kites"—notes—"and runners and lawyers and this and that. It always got tipped off by the time we got back to you and said, 'Yeah, dump the guy.' . . . You can't have someone in the yard that you want to bump and let them be out there for two or three weeks." Smith said the gang members were becoming "like twelve horses teamed to one wagon, with each of them going in a different direction." An internal report at the time by the California Department of Corrections went so far as to predict that "the

A.B. will probably not propose a serious threat to law enforcement agencies in the future unless it gains a clear and well enforced chain of command."

Thompson started to push for just that. "I wanted to eliminate the irrationality and make it into a true organized-crime family," he said. "I wasn't interested in killing blacks. I was interested in only one thing: power."

He and other leaders hatched a plan with gang members who were incarcerated at a prison in Chino, in Southern California. These men, who were awaiting trials for the assaults or murders of fellow-inmates, were encouraged to represent themselves as attorneys, thereby allowing them to subpoena their colleagues around the country as witnesses. Each time a Brand member sent out a "writ," another member would have to be relocated to Chino. For several days, using what one member called "subpoena power unlimited" and exploiting the very legal system that was trying to stop them, most of the Brand was able to meet for hours in the yard, in what amounted to a private convention.

As Smith recalled, "We all get over in the corner one day and say, 'Damn, man, check this out, we got all the power right here. Let's take this one step further.'" The Brand's California leaders decided to establish a chain of command modelled loosely on the structure of the Italian Mafia. A council of about a dozen members would manage gang operations throughout the state prison system. Each council member would be elected by majority vote. He would be responsible for enforcing all of the gang's policies, which would now be codified; he also could authorize a hit at any moment, as long as it wasn't on a fellow A.B. member. The council's actions would be overseen by a three-man commission. Authorities say that Thompson and Smith served on the California council. In the federal prison system, where the gang set up a similar hierarchy in roughly a dozen maximum-security prisons, the Baron and T. D. Bingham allegedly became high commissioners.

The A.B.'s new structure strengthened its grip, but there remained one outstanding obstacle: snitches. Though other crime families had to worry about members "rolling over," in prison everyone had an incentive to "flip," and all an inmate had to do was whisper in a guard's ear. In the early nineteen-eighties, a former gang member, Steven Barnes, had testified in a

murder rap against one of the new commissioners and was housed in protective custody, where no one could get to him. In response, the Aryan
Brotherhood settled upon a new policy: If it couldn't get to you, it would
get to your family. "What we wanted to do was hit . . . Barnes's wife,"
Smith explained. "If we couldn't get to her, we'd move then to his
brother . . . or sister and from there we'd work our way down the list. . . .
That was policy that we'd established that we'd do from then on."

To carry out its new policy, Brand leaders needed to find a hit man,
someone who could, in the words of the gang, "step up." And so they
allegedly turned to Curtis Price, a forty-one-year-old made A.B. member
who was about to be paroled from Chino prison, and who would, according to a former gang member, "kill as to directions received from the A.B.
council." Described by his parole officer as "one of the most dangerous
state prisoners I've dealt with in my twenty-two years" of service, Price was
six feet tall, with short brown hair and vacant blue eyes. In photographs,
the bones around his pallid face protrude and give him a slightly ghostly
air. Price, who had once expressed hope of going into law enforcement, had
in more recent years stabbed another inmate and taken two guards
hostage, telling one, "I'll blow your partner's head off."

Court and prison records reveal that upon his release, on September
14, 1982, Price met a twenty-two-year-old mother of two children named
Elizabeth Hickey and stole several weapons from her stepfather's house,
including a twelve-gauge shotgun and a Mauser automatic. Price then
drove to the home of Steven Barnes's father, Richard, in Temple City, California, and shot him three times in the head, execution style. Barnes's
neighbors found him lying on his bed, face down, his cowboy hat resting
nearby.

Afterward, Price returned to Elizabeth Hickey's home and beat her to
death, crushing her skull in five places, in an apparent attempt to eliminate
her as a potential witness. He then bought a ticket to see the movie
"Gandhi." The gang soon received a postcard in prison. It said, "Business
has been taken care of."

At one point, I tried to find Michael Thompson. I had been told that
he had mysteriously dropped out of the Aryan Brotherhood shortly after

the Barnes killing, and had testified against Price, who, in 1986, was convicted of the two murders. Thompson became the highest-ranking defector in the gang's history. ("He's big, he's tough, he's mean, he's killed, and then all of a sudden he's gone, just rolled over," one A.B. associate said in disbelief.) Thompson was thought to have as many death threats made against him as anyone in prison; his family had been relocated, and he was being held in the correctional system's version of the witness-protection program. He was moved from prison to prison anonymously, and was often kept in a protective-custody unit, walled off from most inmates.

After weeks of searching, I called the prison where I had heard Thompson was incarcerated. The authorities insisted that there was no one there by that name. Moments later, I received a call from a law-enforcement official who knew I was trying to find Thompson. "They think you're trying to kill him," she said. "They're moving him out of the prison right now."

After explaining to officials why I wanted to speak with Thompson, I was able to get a letter to him, and, with his agreement, I headed to the maximum-security prison where he was being held under the name of "Occupant." To get inside the prison, I had to submit my car to a search, and I was given a checkered shirt to replace my blue oxford, which happened to match the color of some inmate uniforms and was therefore forbidden. There were several children with their mothers filing in alongside me; they wore white dresses or neatly pleated pants, as if they were attending church.

We passed through several steel gates, each door clanking loudly behind us, before reaching a brightly lit room filled with wooden chairs and tables. While the other visitors were allowed to sit freely with inmates, I was led to the back of the room, where a three-foot-by-three-foot bulletproof window was cut into the wall. A chair was placed in front of it, and I sat down and peered through the scuffed plastic. I could see a small cement cell, with a telephone and a chair. The room was sealed on all sides except for a steel door at the opposite end. A moment later, the door clicked open and Thompson, a giant of a man, appeared in a white prison jumpsuit with his hands shackled behind his back. As a guard removed his chains, Thompson bent forward and I could see his face. It was covered with a hermit-like beard. His hair reached to his shoulders and was parted down the middle, in the style that was fashionable in the seventies, when he was first convicted of murder. As he came closer to the glass, I could see, amid the thickets of graying hair, his bright-blue eyes. He sat down and reached for the phone, and I picked up mine.

"How was your trip?" he asked.

He spoke in a soft, courteous voice. I asked him why he had dropped out of the Brand, and he said he made his decision after the debate over whether to kill Steven Barnes's father and other family members. "I argued with them for days," he said. "I kept saying, 'We're warriors, aren't we? We don't kill children. We don't kill mothers and fathers.' But I lost. And they killed him, execution style, and then they killed Hickey, an innocent woman, just because she knew where Price had gotten the gun. And that's when I walked away. That's when I said, 'This thing is out of control.' " He leaned toward the window, his breath steaming the glass. "I am still willing to fight someone in here, head up, if I have to. That's the culture of where I live. But I was not for killing people on the outside, people in your world."

When I asked him what he initially found compelling about the gang, he paused for a long moment. "That's a very good question," he said. There was the protection, he suggested, ticking off the reasons. There was the sense of belonging. But that wasn't really it. For him, at least, he said, it was the rush of power. "I was naïve, because I saw us as these noble warriors," he said. In the eighties, he added, he had tried to change the nature of the gang. "I thought that by organizing we could make the gang less bloody. I thought we could strip away the irrational killings. But I was foolish, because at some level you could never remove that. And the structure only allowed the gang to be more deadly."

During our conversation, Thompson cited various philosophers, including Nietzsche, whose "true genius," he later wrote me in a letter, "the gang often misinterprets." It was hard to reconcile this cerebral figure with a man who said he had once helped to stab sixteen men in a single day. But, when I asked him about his training, he reached out with his hand and began, in almost clinical fashion, to show how to assassinate someone. "You can do it here on the right side of the heart, in the aorta, or here in the neck, or back here in the spine, which will paralyze someone," he said, moving his hand back and forth, as if slicing something. "I've been in jail thirty years now, and I know I am probably never going to get out. I am a dangerous person. I don't like violence, but I am good at it."

He had tried, he said, to isolate himself from other prisoners. "I don't go in the yard much," he said. "It's not safe." He said the only people he could really interact with were the guards, for fear of being recognized. "In here, I am lower than child killers and child molesters. Because I defected from the A.B., I am the lowest there is."

The gang had tried several times to get to him; after he was placed in the protective-custody unit, he said, the Brand sent in a "sleeper"—a secret collaborator—who had tried to stab him. "You need to understand one thing," Thompson said. "The Aryan Brotherhood is not about white supremacy. It is about supremacy. And it will do anything to get it. Anything."

A guard banged on the door. "I have to go now," he said.

As he stood, he pressed his hand against the glass, and I could see something green on his left hand. I looked closer: it was the faint outline of a shamrock. Armed with that tattoo, Thompson had told me, a man could take over an entire United States penitentiary.

In the fall of 1994, a bus filled with prisoners arrived at Leavenworth, Kansas, a maximum-security federal prison built almost a century ago. Out stepped a tall muscular man with a black mustache. His arms were covered with tattoos, and he soon appeared in the yard without a shirt, revealing a large shamrock in the middle of his chest. He was immediately surrounded by a group of white inmates. Many went to the commissary and paid to have their photograph taken with him, which they carried around like passports. "If you . . . were able to show that picture, it was just like standing next to your favorite pop star," one prisoner said.

The man's name was Michael McElhiney, but everyone called him Mac. A reputed A.B. member, he had just come from Marion, where he had been housed with Barry Mills, the notorious Baron. Mills, who later testified in court on McElhiney's behalf, said, "I look at him like a son."

McElhiney, a convicted methamphetamine dealer who had conspired to kill a witness, was so charismatic that, according to authorities, a juror once fell in love with him. However, in private letters, which were later confiscated by prison officials, Mac spoke openly of "the beast" inside him and referred to himself proudly as "an angry motherfucker." An F.B.I.

agent at Leavenworth described him as probably "a psychopath," while a close friend put it this way: "He likes to have everybody know that he's God."

An Aryan Brotherhood presence had long existed at Leavenworth, which was known as "the hothouse," because of its sweltering, catacomb-like cells. But McElhiney was determined to extend the gang's reach.

Although the Brand maintained remnants of its racist ideology, it had increasingly sought, according to a declassified F.B.I. report, "to launch a cooperative effort of death and fear against staff and other inmates . . . in order to take over the system." The Brand aimed, the F.B.I. warned, to control everything from drug trafficking to the sale of "punks"—inmates forced into prostitution—to extortion rackets to murder contracts behind bars. It sought, in short, to become a racketeering enterprise. The council member Clifford Smith had told authorities that the gang was no longer primarily "bent on destroying blacks and the Jews and the minorities of the world, white supremacy and all that shit. It's a criminal organization, first and foremost."

Using an array of white associates, who either coveted membership in the gang or needed protection, McElhiney set out to dominate Leavenworth's underground economy. His men went from tier to tier, demanding a tax from the sale of "pruno"—prison wine that could be brewed out of almost any cafeteria fruit (apples, strawberries, even ketchup). At the time, a man named Keith Segien was running a friendly poker game in the prison's B unit. One night on his way to his cell, Segien later testified in court, Mac was waiting for him. He told Segien to sit down.

Segien hesitated. "What's this about?" he asked.

"If I wanted you killed," Segien recalls him saying, "you'd have been dead by now." Then Mac added, "Someone told me you don't want me . . . to run the poker game, and I'm here to make money. I'm going to run the poker game." He asked if Segien had a problem with that.

"I said no," Segien testified. "That was the last day I ran the poker game."

Mac soon had gambling rackets operating in nearly every unit, on nearly every tier. As with the sale of pruno, inmates say, the guards often turned a blind eye, perhaps to mollify a seething population. Some guards, it seemed, had come to consider the Aryan Brotherhood presence as inevitable, and even used its leaders as surrogate power brokers. In one instance, a guard at Leavenworth went to McElhiney to get the O.K. before he released another prisoner in the yard. One longtime A.B. member compared the illicit operations in maximum-security prisons to bootlegging during Prohibition and to the high-roller tables in Las Vegas.

Currency is not allowed in prison, and inmates typically paid their smaller debts to the Brotherhood by offering free contraband or items from the commissary: cigarettes, candy, stamps, books. At the high-roller tables at Leavenworth, where imprisoned drug lords could place bets in the thousands of dollars, participants were allowed to play for a month on credit. The man in charge of the table kept a tally of wins and losses. At the end of the month, inmates say, Mac's men would collect the losses; usually, gamblers would pay up by having a relative or a friend send an untraceable money order to a designated A.B. person on the outside. If an indebted inmate didn't have the money mailed on time, internal prison records show, he was typically "piped"—beaten with a metal rod. McElhiney later acknowledged that he was funnelling the proceeds to his mentor Mills and to other reputed leaders of the Aryan Brotherhood, with whom he had "a pact" to take over the "gambling business."

McElhiney, who presided over the yard wearing sunglasses, his nails often stained yellow from chewing tobacco, then decided to focus on drug smuggling. In the past, the Brand had sought out almost anyone who could bring in its merchandise. In one instance, several inmates involved in a scheme told me, the gang offered to protect Charles Manson, and even conspired in a failed bid to help him escape; in return, Manson's cult of women on the outside helped to smuggle dope into prison for them.

According to authorities and court records, Mac now started to canvass the population for the most vulnerable inmates—those who were drug addicts or in debt to the gang or simply scared, and could therefore be forced to serve as "mules." One such person was Walter Moles, a drug user who was terrified of the gang. His father, who was terminally ill with emphysema, was planning to travel to Leavenworth to celebrate his son's birthday. According to Moles's later testimony, Mac instructed him to have his drug contact on the outside send Moles's father six balloons filled with heroin. Using coded language on the prison's tape-recorded pay phones, Moles then persuaded his father to transport the package.

Weeks later, when his father arrived, he sat beside Moles in the visiting room, under the guards' scrutiny. He carried the package in his underwear. Moles instructed his father to go into the bathroom, place two of the balloons in his mouth, then return and spit them into Moles's cup of coffee. His father said he couldn't do it. The heroin wasn't in six balloons. "It's in one big one," he said.

"How big?" Moles asked.

"A Ping-Pong ball."

Eventually, Moles's father managed to drop the balloon into his son's coffee cup. Moles tried to swallow it, but it got stuck in his throat.

His father started to panic. "Son, just give it back to me," he begged. "I'll send it back to where it came from."

"No, Dad, I can't," he said. He explained that the heroin wasn't for himself. "These guys I'm bringing it in for want their stuff."

His father didn't seem to understand: Who were these people?

Moles saw a guard's attention wander, and said that he had to say goodbye.

"Is it the end of the visit?" his father asked.

"If I'm going to do it, this is my only chance," Moles said. While his father distracted the guard, Moles untucked his shirt and forced the drugs into his rectum. After he got past the guards, he said, he gave "the stuff" to one of Mac's henchmen.

The next morning, Moles waited behind the bleachers in the yard for his cut. Suddenly, he felt something hard against the back of his head, and he collapsed to the ground. "I tried to get up," Moles later testified, "but I kept getting kicked."

Mac's men told Moles to stay down.

"What did I do wrong?" Moles asked. "What did I do wrong?"

Afterward, when an A.B. associate asked Mac why he had assaulted Moles and taken his share of the dope, Mac reportedly replied, "Fuck the little punk."

Heroin was now flooding into Leavenworth. According to authorities, inmates received more than twelve hundred positive tests for heroin during 1995. One prisoner estimated that forty per cent of the population was shooting up. "Heroin deadens everything," an inmate at Leavenworth said. "Speed, man, you're bebopping around and you're doing more time than you would normally because you ain't sleeping at night. . . . But the heroin, yeah . . . you're feeling no pain."

Because of the scarcity of supply and the unusually high demand in prison, authorities say, a gram of heroin that was bought on the street for sixty-five dollars was selling inside Leavenworth for as much as a thousand dollars. A former council member told me that the gang was bringing in anywhere from half a million to a million dollars a year from a single prison. As one F.B.I. agent put it, "You just do the math."

With his empire expanding by the day, Mac seemed more and more "out of control," as one former ally said. Although A.B. leaders were forbidden, under gang rules, to use heroin themselves, associates say that Mac would hole up in his cell with "a rig"—a homemade syringe typically constructed out of a needle stolen from the infirmary and a hollowed-out ballpoint pen. There, in what inmates describe as a heroin-induced haze, he would allegedly sit with A.B. henchmen and mete out his own form of justice, including murder.

McElhiney eventually became convinced that a snitch was trolling for evidence against him. Then one day, associates say, Mac sent word to his men that he had found the rat: Bubba Leger, a trusted associate who did most of the A.B.'s tattoo work and who only a few months earlier had posed proudly next to Mac for a photograph. In the rec cage one day, according to witnesses, one of Mac's associates nicknamed Ziggy, who was purportedly eager to make his bones, pulled out a knife and started stabbing Bubba. "Why you doing this?" Bubba pleaded. With blood flowing from his chest, Bubba stumbled over to the steel door of the cage and pounded on it, trying to get the guards' attention. In full view of the guards, Ziggy stabbed Bubba at least five more times. Bubba died moments later.

It was then, witnesses say, that they saw one of Mac's men take another weapon, a sharpened toothbrush, and plant it near Bubba to make it look as though he had used it first. Afterward, McElhiney was said to have enforced a long-standing Aryan Brotherhood policy, which required all witnesses to perjure themselves. " 'I'm going to give you a choice,' " an associate said that McElhiney told him. " 'You can either lie or die on this one.' " In a note, McElhiney, who shaved his head after the murder, instructed Ziggy what to do: "The defense you're going to have is self-defense." He went on, "Hang tough, Stud. As soon as you get a lawyer direct him to me without further ado. . . . Got it? Stress to him that it's a must he come see me 'fore you trust him—Our code word will be Mary Mary Quite Contrary."

Ziggy received a twenty-seven-year sentence and later appeared with a tattoo of a shamrock on his leg, but authorities were never able to prove that McElhiney had ordered the killing (though they did later convict him for smuggling drugs). During the investigation, one unexpected fact emerged: Bubba had not been a snitch after all.

"This isn't in the job description," Gregory Jessner said. The Assistant United States Attorney was standing on a loading dock outside the Los Angeles federal courthouse, stacking onto an old wooden dolly boxes of transcripts for his case against the Aryan Brotherhood. There were thirteen in all, and as he worked a small circle of sweat appeared on his starched white shirt. The son of a mathematician, he had a slightly cerebral air. "I don't really have a bulldog persona," he said. "I'm not like Marcia Clark." He had never read a John Grisham novel, and was known to pick up books by Cervantes and David Foster Wallace between trials.

After he had wheeled the boxes upstairs, occasionally bumping into walls and doors, he arranged them on a long wooden conference table, and caught his breath. Then he said, "These deal with just one murder in the indictment. It's nothing."

Jessner had started investigating the gang in 1992. A convicted murderer was found strangled in his cell at a federal prison in Lompoc, California, and Jessner was assigned the case. Law-enforcement officials often dismiss such crimes as N.H.I.s—"No humans involved"—because the victims are considered to be as unsympathetic as the perps. Trying to break through a web of perjury, Jessner located several witnesses who claimed that the A.B. had murdered a fellow gang member for, among other things, falling in love with a gay prisoner. Although the Brotherhood had a long history of trafficking in "punks," and although some of its members were known to receive sexual favors in return for protection, the gang considered open homosexuality a sign of weakness, a violation of the A.B. code. "The member made the mistake of kissing on the stairs," Jessner said.

Jessner was able to prove that an A.B. recruit had gone into his associate's cell, tied a bedsheet around his neck, and strangled him while an accomplice held his legs. Yet Jessner realized that he had done little to impede the gang; as with previous isolated prosecutions, he may have only strengthened it. The recruit was later said to have hung a photograph of his target on his cell wall, like an honorary plaque, and held a celebration with pruno on the anniversary of the murder.

As Jessner dug deeper into this violent subculture, he learned that there were no definitive statistics on A.B. crimes, because so few of them were prosecuted—and because so many associates from other gangs, including the Dirty White Boys and the Mexican Mafia, did its bidding. More general statistics on inmate violence provided a glimpse of what one sociologist once described as "the upsurge of rapacious and murderous groups" inside American prisons. According to the most recent Justice Department census, fifty-one inmates were murdered in prisons in 2000. Moreover, there were more than thirty-four thousand reported assaults by inmates on other inmates, and nearly eighteen thousand on staff. Rape is common; one study of prisons in four states estimated that at least one in five inmates has been sexually assaulted.

Jessner eventually started to dig into hundreds of violent crimes linked to the Aryan Brotherhood. Working with an officer from the Bureau of Alcohol, Tobacco and Firearms named Mike Halualani—a half-Japanese, half-Hawaiian agent who was as brash as Jessner was genteel—Jessner attempted to devise a strategy to break the gang's stranglehold. But the more he investigated the more it seemed that the gang defied any conventional notion of a prosecution. Jessner told me that he kept asking himself, "How do you stop people who see a murder rap as a badge of honor? How do you stop people who have already been stopped by the law and sentenced to life imprisonment?"

By the nineteen-nineties, authorities, hoping to create at least some deterrent, and to protect other inmates, had relocated nearly all the Aryan Brotherhood's top leaders, including the Baron, to what were then a new breed of prisons, called "supermaxes." These prisoners were held in single cells, locked down nearly the entire day, without, as one gang member put it, "seeing fresh earth, plant life, or unfiltered sunlight"; they exercised alone in an indoor cage, were fed meals through a tray slot, and had little, if any, human contact.

In the case of Silverstein, who was already serving multiple life sentences when he killed the guard Clutts, in 1983, the Bureau of Prisons had established a separate unit for him at Leavenworth, where he was held in a Hannibal Lecter–style cage. Though Silverstein continued to sketch, he was for years not permitted to have a comb or a hairbrush, and when the reporter Pete Earley visited him, in the late eighties, he had long wild hair and a beard. "They want me to go crazy," he told Earley. "They want to point their fingers at me and say, 'See, see, we told you he is a lunatic.' . . . I didn't come in here a killer, but in here you learn hate. The insanity in here is cultivated by the guards. They feed the beast that lingers within all of us. . . . I find myself smiling at the thought of me killing Clutts each time they deny me a phone call, a visit, or keep the lights on. I find it harder and harder to repent and ask for forgiveness, because deep inside I can feel that hatred and anger growing."

Jessner told me, "Within the gang's lore, Silverstein has become its Christ figure."

Even under these conditions, which some civil-rights groups considered a violation of human rights, the Aryan Brotherhood continued to flourish. Its members developed elaborate ways to communicate. They dropped notes through pipes that were connected to nearby cells; they tapped Morse code on prison bars; they forced orderlies to pass kites; they whispered through vents in "carnie," a convoluted, rhyming code language. ("Bottle stoppers" meant "coppers.") In addition, the leaders had developed a devoted coterie of women on the outside who had fallen in love with them through visits and correspondence and could serve as couriers, relaying messages back and forth between members. One woman who cooperated in the gang's illegal businesses later claimed she had Stockholm syndrome.

With the help of prison authorities, Jessner began to intercept a series of covert messages. Portions of the letters appeared to be blank, as if someone had been interrupted. After analysts applied heat with an iron and placed the paper under ultraviolet light, letters would appear, revealing "a secret message," as the F.B.I. wrote in an internal report. Cryptographers analyzed the "ink" of one such note, and discovered that the message was written with urine. The message itself was baffling; it had been scrambled into a code. "They have certain words that mean a certain thing," one former member said. "If they tell you that 'somebody's going to build a house in the country,' the prevalent word . . . is 'country,' because . . . that means 'murder.' "

Jessner and his team spent hours breaking sentences apart and reconstructing them. He started to see patterns in the messages: "baby boy" meant yes, and "baby girl" meant no. One day, prison authorities intercepted a note sent by T. D. Bingham, the A.B. commissioner, to the Baron. It said, "Well I am a grandfather, at last my boy's wife gave birth to a strapping eight pound seven ounce baby boy." Jessner feared that the reference to the baby's weight was code for 187, the California legal statute pertaining to murder; the fact that the baby was a boy suggested that a hit had been approved. Then analysts noticed that several of the letters had squiggly marks, almost like tails, on them. The words "eight pound," for instance, had curlicues on the letters "e," "g," "n," and "d." It appeared to be a code within a code.

After scrutinizing the letters, authorities determined that the note was in fact written in a biliteral cipher, a method invented by Sir Francis Bacon, the seventeenth-century philosopher. It involved using two distinct alphabets, depending on how the letters were drawn. An unadorned "c" referred to alphabet A, whereas a curlicued "c" represented alphabet B. Investigators went through the note, categorizing each letter by alphabet until they had a cluster of letters that all seemed to be a play on the initials of the Aryan Brotherhood:

bbbaaaaabbabaaababababbabaaababaaabaaabbbababbaabbaaabbaabbabb-baabb . . .

It still made no sense. But after analysts broke the letters into clusters of five, Jessner says, they started to realize that each cluster represented an individual letter. Thus "ababb" was an "A," "abbab" was a "B," and so on.

They had finally cracked the code; now they went through the letter again. It said:

Confirm message from Chris to move on DC.

Officials knew that "DC" meant the D.C. Blacks, a prison gang against whom the Aryan Brotherhood had recently declared war. But, by the time authorities decoded the letter, two black inmates had been found dead in their cells in Lewisburg, Pennsylvania: one was stabbed thirty-four times, the other thirty-five.

The Brotherhood began developing murder schemes that could succeed even in maximum-security environments. They started to befriend their foes, so they could one day "rock them to sleep." At Pelican Bay, where friends could apply to be cellmates, they sought to room with the very men they wanted to kill. "Deception was key," one member who strangled his cellmate acknowledged. Between 1996 and 1998, A.B. members at Pelican Bay murdered three inmates, and were suspected in at least three additional slayings.

In many cases, officials in the correctional system seemed powerless to stop the gang. At Folsom prison, after A.B. leaders were sequestered from the general population, the gang's associates protested by indiscriminately stabbing rapists and child molesters until the leaders were released. A few prison officials actually facilitated the Brotherhood's activities. At the supermax prison in Colorado, a guard was accused of becoming an Aryan Brotherhood disciple; at Pelican Bay, two guards were discovered encouraging the beatings of child molesters and sex offenders by gang members. A local prosecutor warned that officials at Pelican Bay were unable to stop a "reign of terror."

By the mid-nineties, Jessner says, the gang had evolved to the point that it had to appoint members to lead different branches of its operations—such as the "department of security" and the "department of narcotics." Though the Aryan Brotherhood's profits never rivalled those of the Italian Mafia or outside drug lords, its reputation for violence did. The gang had some of the most highly trained and ruthless hit men in the country. And inside the prison system the Baron had so grown in stature that he overshadowed the imprisoned head of the Italian Mafia, John

Gotti. According to authorities, in July, 1996, after a black inmate attacked Gotti at Marion prison, bloodying his face, the Mafia leader, who seemed ill prepared for the explosion of prison violence, sought the Baron's help in murdering his assailant. The Brotherhood seemed receptive to the idea—the Baron allegedly used sign language to communicate the price of the hit to an associate—but Gotti died before the hit could be executed.

It was around then that Jessner decided that the only way to take down the gang was the way authorities had taken down the Italian Mafia—by using the RICO statutes, which allowed the government to attack the entire hierarchy of a criminal organization rather than just one or two members. The goal, as Halualani put it, was to "cut off the head, not just the body."

In an audacious move, Jessner decided to pursue the death penalty for nearly all the gang's top leaders. "It's the only arrow left in our quiver," he told me. "I think even a lot of people who are against the death penalty in general would recognize that in this particular instance, where people are committing murder repeatedly from behind bars, there is little other option."

While Jessner was slowly trying to build a case, methodically flipping witnesses, decoding messages, and gathering forensic evidence, he had to be careful of "sleepers"—gang members pretending to cooperate with authorities in order to infiltrate the investigation. During a previous F.B.I. probe, agents reported that they were concerned that one snitch may "have in fact been a ploy by the A.B. to infiltrate the WITSEC program"—the witness-protection program—"and determine where all the government witnesses were housed."

As the Brotherhood grew stronger, it developed ambitions that extended beyond prison walls. Though many leaders were serving life sentences without parole, some members were being paroled—an outcome that authorities had long feared. "Most of the A.B. will be paroled or discharged at some future date and, in view of members' lifelong commitments, it would be naïve to think he would not remain in contact with his brothers," a declassified F.B.I. report stated. "The rule of thumb is that once on the streets, one must take care of his brothers that are still inside. The penalty for failure to do so is death upon the member's return to the prison system." Given the gang's ability to operate behind bars, the F.B.I. report warned of "what these gang members can do with little or no supervision." Silverstein himself has said, "Someday most of us finally get out of this hell and even a rational dog after getting kicked around year after year after year attacks when his cage door is finally opened."

On March 24, 1995, the door at Pelican Bay finally opened for Robert Scully, a reputed A.B. member and armed robber who had spent, with the exception of a few months, the previous thirteen years behind bars—many of them inside the Hole. For an Aryan brother, he was small: barely five feet four, and a hundred and forty-five pounds. But the thirty-six-year-old was known to work out obsessively in his cell, doing an endless routine of what the gang called "burpees"—standing one moment, then dropping to the floor to do a pushup, then hopping to one's feet again.

Brenda Moore, a lonely thirty-eight-year-old single mother who had long corresponded with inmates at Pelican Bay—and, in the process, had become one of the gang's female followers—picked Scully up at the prison gate in her truck. Scully wore powder-blue sweatpants, a sweatshirt, and a watch cap. He had two hundred dollars in his pocket. Scully had previously sent Moore a series of seductive letters. In one, written on pink paper, he said, "All extraneous subversion manifests itself when we connect." In another, he wrote, "I will always be with you as you are one of me now. Our synergy is infinite."

After leaving the prison, the couple drove to the beach, where Scully walked along the shore, collecting seashells. The following day, though, he found a sawed-off shotgun, and he and Moore set out for Santa Rosa, driving south along Highway 101. Six days after Scully's release, they stopped near a saloon in the middle of the night. A police car pulled up behind their pickup truck. As a fifty-eight-year-old deputy sheriff approached with his flashlight, Scully leaped out with his shotgun. The deputy raised his hands over his head, but Scully shot him between the eyes.

The Aryan Brotherhood was now killing on the outside with as little hesitation as it had on the inside. Similarly, the gang was expanding its racketeering operation onto the streets. In letters written in 1999 to one recent parolee, the Baron said, "We especially need for some to step-up," and, referring to the gang's shamrock symbol, he urged, "START POLISHING THE ROCK out there!!!" The gang allegedly enlisted paroled A.B. members and associates to become drug dealers, gunrunners, stickup men, and hit men. Some Pelican Bay inmates were discovered mapping out establishments to rob.

That same year, a reputed Brand member on the streets walked into the Palm Springs home of a drug dealer who wasn't sharing enough of his profits with the gang. Witnesses told police that the A.B. member pulled out a .38 and unloaded five bullets into the man's chest and head, telling everyone in the room that this was for "the fellows"—the Aryan Brotherhood—up north at Pelican Bay, and warning that new brothers were being released every day.

A year later, in a letter disguised as privileged legal mail, the gang spoke of plans to "buy a warehouse with offices on some large acreage." The letter's author, a member who was about to be released, added, "I'll outfit it with a well-stocked law library, computer research desk, copy machine, iron pile, pool table, big screen TV, car and bike garage with tools, handball courts, etc. This will be the Brand Ranch. . . . This will be home base for us out there."

Around the same time, a longtime reputed A.B. member confided to authorities that he had been approached at the supermax in Colorado by the gang and asked for technical help in making bombs. The gang, he was informed, was planning terrorist attacks on federal facilities across the United States. "It's become irrational," he told authorities after declining to help. "They're talking about car bombs, truck bombs, and mail bombs."

Just when the Brotherhood seemed poised to take a particularly violent turn, Jessner unleashed the United States Marshals. Nearly four decades after the gang was born, it found itself under siege.

The courthouse where one of the first trials against the Brand would take place was in the middle of a verdant forest in Benton, Illinois, about thirty miles from Marion prison. It had been built on the edges of a circular clearing, and stood not far from a dozen or so dilapidated brick storefronts. Some of the stores had been shut down; others had signs offering discounts, as if they would soon join them.

A single alleged A.B. murder, which was included in Jessner's sprawling indictment, also fell under the jurisdiction of the United States Attorney in the Southern District of Illinois. The trial, which began in September,

2003, centered on David Sahakian, McElhiney's most feared cohort, the man who had once reputedly had an inmate stabbed for bumping him during a basketball game. He was charged with ordering two alleged associates to murder a thirty-seven-year-old bank robber named Terry Walker during a 1999 race war at Marion. Sahakian, along with his two associates, faced the death penalty. The trial offered a glimpse of what would happen in Los Angeles, where Jessner planned to prosecute forty people, including McElhiney and the Baron.

Even though the Benton trial involved only one A.B. member and two associates, the United States Marshals walled off the entire building. For the first time in the court's history, cement barricades had been placed around the exterior. To get inside, I had to pass through two metal detectors.

Nearly a dozen marshals, dressed in black suits and black shoes, led the defendants, whose wrists and ankles were shackled, into the courtroom. Sahakian wore gray slacks and a gray short-sleeved shirt. Everything about him was big: his hands; his stomach; his long, sloping forehead. Whereas in old photographs he had an unruly beard—it apparently had inspired his nickname, the Beast—now he had only a goatee, which made his face look even larger.

His wife was in the gallery, and he winked at her as he sat down. She told me that they had met twenty-five years ago, and that for twenty-three of those years he had been behind bars. Petite, with blond hair and a blue miniskirt that exposed well-toned legs, she gave off a strong scent of perfume. She sat right behind him, taking notes throughout the trial. At one point, she told me, "They keep saying he's a boss of the Aryan Brotherhood and that he ordered everyone around. But I don't believe it. He can't even order *me* around."

When a pathologist took the stand, the prosecution projected on a large screen a photograph of Walker's body. It was stretched out on a metal table. There were bloodstains on his chest, his eyes were open, and his mouth appeared to be frozen midspeech. The pathologist described each stab wound. Then he pointed to a hole in the heart—it was the one that killed him, he said.

None of the defendants looked up at the screen, and, apart from the marshals and Sahakian's wife, the gallery was empty. Nobody from the victim's family was there. Jessner had told me that most of these victims had already been cast out by society, and, when they were killed, few people, if any, cared. "I feel a certain obligation to defend those who have no one to defend them," he had said.

After a break in the trial, the defendant who had purportedly held the victim down during the attack refused to come out of a holding room. The judge ordered the marshals to forcibly carry him out. Sahakian leaped to his feet and said that that wasn't necessary. "If I go back there," he said in a commanding voice, "he'll come out." At last, a marshal went out to the holding room and escorted the defendant into the courtroom. He walked with pointed slowness and stared at the prosecutor. "What the fuck you looking at!" he yelled.

Six marshals quickly hovered around him. As he sat down, he slammed his chair into the groin of one of the agents. Eventually, order was restored, and, when an inmate who had helped stab several black inmates took the stand as a government witness, Sahakian rubbed his fingers along the arm of his chair. Each time the witness made allegations against Sahakian, he seemed to grip the chair more tightly. His knuckles turned white. Finally, he glanced toward me in the gallery and said, "Don't believe a word he's saying. He's nothin' better than a shit-house rat."

"Don't use that language, honey," his wife said.

"Metaphorically speaking," he said.

Several inmates who had told authorities that they were prepared to come forward had also said that they were frightened to do so. One said that since he had turned on the A.B. his family had been threatened. Another, who had provided evidence, was staying in his cell, clutching his rosary beads. He said, "I'll say my prayers that I don't get about seventy-five holes in me."

Jessner was sitting at his desk at his headquarters in Los Angeles, preparing pretrial motions. While he was awaiting a verdict in the Benton trial, he needed to get ready not just for one trial but for potentially five or six—since not all forty defendants could be held safely in one courtroom. Security was already a challenge; most of the inmates, including the Baron and McElhiney, were being held in single cells at the West Valley Detention

Center, outside Los Angeles. Some defendants had been found with drugs and concealed razor blades.

Fearing that the gang might turn on its own, Jessner had placed a few A.B. members in other prisons. In a letter, the Baron had told another gang member, "It's likely necessary for us to step-up and conduct a thorough evaluation of every brother's personal character and level of commitment, as we currently possess some serious rot that is in fact potentially a cancer!" He added that it should be "a top priority to wipe them off the face of this earth!"

Jessner said he knew that the gang was trying to hold on to its operations, but he was optimistic about the upcoming trials. "I can't say for sure if another gang will take the Brotherhood's place, or if new leaders will replace the old ones," he said. "But I know that if we succeed it will send a message that the Aryan Brotherhood can no longer kill with impunity."

Jessner got up and started heading toward the courtroom, to attend a pretrial hearing. He was wearing a charcoal suit that seemed too loose for his small frame. I asked him if, as some feared, he had been "put in the hat"—marked for assassination.

He blanched. "I don't know," he said. He later added, "It's a pretty big hat."

The United States Attorney had arranged extra security for him, including a secure parking space nearby. One of his colleagues had declined to work on the case after his wife objected. "I worry," Jessner admitted. "You can't help but worry."

He paused and looked at me. He wouldn't feel right if he stopped, he said. "I don't believe that because you rob a convenience store you should receive a death sentence. I don't believe that our prisons should be divided into predators and prey." As he headed into the courtroom, he added, "I don't believe that that is what our system intended by justice."

— February, 2004

—⟋m⟋—

The case against the Aryan Brotherhood produced nearly thirty convictions. The gang's two most feared and powerful leaders, Barry Mills and T. D. Bing-

ham, were found guilty of murder, conspiracy, and racketeering. The jury, how-ever, deadlocked on whether they should receive the death penalty, and they were sentenced to life without parole. David Sahakian, whose initial trial in Benton led to a hung jury on the count of ordering the murder of Terry Walker, was later retried and found guilty. He was sentenced to twenty years. After failing to obtain the death penalty against other leaders of the gang, the prosecution dropped charges against Michael McElhiney; he is not expected to be released from prison until 2035, when he will be seventy-eight years old.

Crimetown, U.S.A.

There was a certain tidiness to the killings in Youngstown, Ohio. Usually they happened late at night when there were no witnesses and only the lights from the steel furnaces still burned. Everyone suspected who the killers were—they lived in the neighborhood, often just down the street—but no one could ever prove anything. Sometimes their methods were simple: a bullet to the back of the head or a bomb strapped under the hood of a car. Or sometimes, as when they got John Magda, they went for something more dramatic, tranquillizing their victim with a stun gun and wrapping his head in tape until he could no longer breathe.

Then there were those who just disappeared. Police found their cars on the side of the road, empty, or food still warm on dinner tables where they had been eating. The victims had, in the most classic sense, been "rubbed out." The only sign of the killers was an artistic flourish: a dozen long-stemmed white roses that the victims typically received before they vanished.

So, when Lenny Strollo ordered the hit that summer night in 1996, there was no reason to believe it would go down any differently. Strollo was the Mafia don in Mahoning County—a stretch of land in a valley in northeastern Ohio that encompasses Youngstown and smaller cities like Canfield and Campbell, and that is home to more than two hundred and fifty thousand people. From his farm in Canfield, where he tended his gardens, Strollo ran a criminal network that comprised extortion rackets, illegal gambling, and money laundering. He also oversaw many of the killings in the region. Only weeks earlier, Strollo had had his main Mob rival gunned down in broad daylight. This time, Strollo's choice of target was more brazen: the newly elected county prosecutor, Paul Gains.

The Mafia didn't ordinarily "take out" public officials, but the prosecutor, who was forty-five years old, had resisted the customary bribes and campaign contributions. What's more, Strollo had heard that Gains intended to hire as his chief investigator the man the don most loathed, an F.B.I. agent named Bob Kroner, who had spent two decades pursuing organized crime in the region.

As usual, Strollo employed layers of authority, so that nothing could be traced back to him. First, he gave the order to Bernie the Jew, on whom he relied for muscle. Bernie, in turn, hired Jeffrey Riddle, a black drug dealer turned assassin who boasted that he would become "the first nigger ever inducted into the family." Riddle then brought in his own two-man team: Mark Batcho, a fastidious criminal who ran one of the most sophisticated burglary crews in the country, and Antwan "Mo Man" Harris, a crack dealer and murderer who still lived with his mother.

That Christmas Eve, as Batcho and Harris later recounted, the three men packed up everything they needed: walkie-talkies, ski masks, gloves, a police scanner, a .38 revolver, and a bag of cocaine to plant at the scene in order to make it look like a drug-related killing. After sundown, the men drove out to the prosecutor's house, in a Youngstown suburb. Gains was not yet home—his house was dark inside—and Batcho got out of the car and waited behind a lamppost near the garage. He attached a speed loader to the revolver to enable him to shoot faster. Then he tested the voice-activated walkie-talkie, but there was no response. He tried again—nothing. Incredulous, he ran back to the car and said he couldn't kill anyone without "communication."

The three men drove to a nearby parking lot, where they programmed their cell phones so that they could dial one another at the touch of a button. When they returned to Gains's home, they noticed that a car was in the driveway, and the lights in the house were on. "O.K.," Riddle said. "Get out and go do this."

Batcho exited the car, carrying the gun and the bag of cocaine. He crept up to the house, his heart racing. The garage door was open, and he said, "Hey, mister," but no one answered, and he kept walking. A door leading into the house was also ajar, and he decided to go in. As he made his way down a corridor, he could hear Gains talking on the phone in the kitchen, only a few feet away. Batcho hesitated, as if contemplating what he was about to do. Then he rushed forward, bursting into the kitchen, pointing the gun at the prosecutor's midsection. He pulled the trigger, then fired again. Gains collapsed to the floor, blood seeping from his forearm and side. Batcho stepped closer, and Gains put up his hands to ward him off. Batcho aimed near Gains's heart and pulled the trigger, but the gun kicked back, jamming.

Batcho ran out of the house, stumbling into the darkness. He fell and, getting back up, hit the button on the cell phone, screaming, *It's done! Come pick me up*. He saw the car approaching from down the street and darted toward it. As the car slowed, he jumped into the back seat, crouching down.

"Did you kill him?" Riddle asked.

"I think so," Batcho said uncertainly.

"You don't know?" Riddle said.

"The gun jammed."

Harris looked at him coolly. "Why didn't you go in the drawer and get a steak knife and stab him to death?" he asked.

Riddle said that they had to go back and finish the job, but just then the police scanner crackled with news of the shooting. Riddle hit the gas and sped along the back roads. Fearing that the police might pull them over, Harris tossed the gun out the window. The men realized that the speed loader was missing, and started screaming at each other. Then from the scanner came the news that Gains was still alive.

It was a remarkably inept professional hit. Police found the speed loader outside Gains's house, along with a clean footprint. Within days, a sketch of the shooter appeared in the local newspaper, the *Vindicator*. Yet the crime scene was so messy that investigators concluded that Strollo's men could not have been behind it. Gains told friends that if the Mob had done it he'd be dead. Batcho, who had taken to wearing disguises, gradually emerged from hiding. Once more, it looked as if the murderers would escape punishment.

Then several months later, in the spring of 1997, the prosecutor received a telephone call at his home. "Are you Paul Gains?" a woman asked.

"Yes," he said. "Who's this?"

"I know who shot you," she said.

When the woman disclosed details about the crime that few could have known, Gains summoned Kroner and other F.B.I. agents, who were in the midst of a three-year sting operation against organized crime in the Mahoning Valley. The next day, Kroner and his men visited the woman, who was an ex-girlfriend of an associate of the hit men. "I know everything," she said. "I know other people they shot."

Her information would lead authorities to the three assassins and help solve a Mob hit for the first time in the county's history. Meanwhile, Kroner and the F.B.I. had begun to break apart what was believed to be the most crooked county in America—a place where the Mafia had ruled with impunity for nearly a hundred years and where it still controlled virtually every element of society. The don's influence extended to a chief of police, the outgoing prosecutor, the sheriff, the county engineer, policemen, a city law director, defense attorneys, politicians, judges, and a former assistant U.S. attorney. By July of 2000, the F.B.I. probe had produced more than seventy convictions. Now Kroner and his colleagues were closing in on the most powerful politician in the region, a man whom they'd caught on tape scheming with the Mob nearly twenty years earlier but who had eluded them ever since: United States Congressman James Traficant.

The Mahoning Valley is today one of the most depressed areas of America, but it was an economic boom that first gave rise to the local Mob. During the first half of the twentieth century, the valley was at the center of the burgeoning steel industry. Mills churned around the clock, blackening the sky. Thousands of immigrants—Poles and Greeks and Italians and Slovaks—descended on the area, believing they had found the Ruhr Valley of America; meanwhile, racketeers thought they had discovered their own Little Chicago. The streets were lined with after-hours joints, where steel-workers drank and played *barbut,* a Turkish dice game, and where capos, dressed in white-brimmed hats and armed with stilettos, ran the numbers, or "bug," as the locals called it. Like Chicago, Buffalo, and Detroit, Youngstown had all the elements the Mob needed to flourish: a teeming immigrant population accustomed to arbitrary and violent authority, a prosperous economy, and pliable local politicians and police.

Yet Youngstown was too small to have a Mob family of its own, and by 1950, as the rackets grew into a multimillion-dollar industry, the Pitts-burgh and Cleveland Mafia families began fighting for control of the region. Cars and stores were bombed—warnings to anyone who allied himself with the wrong side. A local radio station ran public-service ads featuring an earsplitting *bang* and the slogan "Stop the bomb!" In 1963, the *Saturday Evening Post* reported that local "officials hobnob openly with criminals. Arrests of racketeers are rare, convictions rarer still, and tough sentences almost unheard of." The newspaper dubbed the area Crime-town, U.S.A.

By 1977, the Mob war had become even more violent. On one side was Joey Naples and Lenny Strollo's faction, which was controlled by the Pittsburgh Mafia; on the other were the Carabbia brothers—known as Charlie the Crab and Orlie the Crab—who were aligned with Cleveland. "It seemed like you'd get up every morning and get in your car and hear someone else had been murdered," the F.B.I. agent Bob Kroner told me.

First, there were Spider and Peeps—two petty cons hit within a few weeks of each other. Then came one of Naples's drivers, shot as he changed a tire in his driveway, and a crony of Peeps's, who was gunned down outside his apartment. Then John Magda, who was discovered, his head wrapped in tape, at the dump in Struthers, and, next, a small-time bookie who refused to go easily—he was first bombed and later shot through his living-room window as he watched television with his wife. Then Joey DeRose, Sr., killed by accident when he was mistaken for his son, Joey DeRose, Jr., a Carabbia assassin; and, finally, a few months later, the son, too. "Oh my God, they got Joey," his girlfriend screamed when police told her they had found the car he was driving burning on a country road between Cleveland and Akron.

In 1976, Kroner arrived in Youngstown and descended into this violent underworld. He was a former high-school math teacher who turned in his books for a badge in 1971, and who could be seen around town, in his neatly pressed suit and tie, trailing reputed hit men and banging on the doors of the All-American Club and other Mafia hangouts. Though he came from a family of cops, which included his father, Kroner didn't look like one: he was too tall and slender, almost delicate, and he lacked the easy manner of the police who played craps in the shadow of the courthouse. He wore penny loafers in a city where most people wore boots, and spoke with a certain formality.

His F.B.I. predecessor, according to the agency's own affidavit and informants, had allegedly consorted with gangsters, and was later appointed Youngstown's chief of police at the Mafia's behest. But Kroner was hostile to the local dons. Prickly and shy, he spent hours alone in his small office, smoking cigarettes and listening to intercepted conversations between the different factions. Like a cartographer filling in the blanks on a map, he made little diagrams of each family, to which he added further details whenever he received a tip from an informant. He did everything he could to bring down the Mafia's enterprise: tapping its members' phones, tailing their spotless Cadillacs, subpoenaing their friends. Before long, Strollo and his cronies gave him the ultimate epithet: "motherfucker."

In December of 1980, Charlie the Crab, the head of the Cleveland faction, disappeared without a trace, and, soon after, Kroner searched the apartment of one of the city's most notorious assassins. The apartment was cluttered with knickknacks, and Kroner and his partner went through each room carefully. In a cabinet, Kroner noticed a breadbox and opened it. Inside, tucked amid the stale bread, was an audiotape. When he played it, he heard male voices, saying, "He's a scared motherfucker" and "You either play our fucking game or you['re] going to be put in a fucking box." Two of the voices, Kroner was sure, belonged to Charlie and his brother, Orlie the Crab. There was also another voice, one Kroner thought he recognized from television and radio. Then it dawned on him: it was James Traficant, a former college football star, who had recently been elected sheriff of Youngstown.

Later, Kroner and his partner, acting on a tip, drilled open the Carabbias' sister's safe-deposit box, where they found a similar tape with a handwritten note. It said, "If I die these tapes go to the F.B.I. in Washington. I feel I have more people after me because of these tapes and . . . I pray and ask God to guide and protect my family."

Back at headquarters, Kroner and his colleagues listened to a jumble of voices on the tape arguing about which public officials they thought were allegedly being paid off by the rival Pittsburgh Mob.

"You believe they got all them fuckin' people?" Orlie said.

"I know they got" him, Traficant said, referring to one prominent politician.

"Oh, they definitely got" him, Charlie said.

Traficant paused, as if running through other names in his mind. "I don't know all of them," he finally said. "But I know it's a fuckin' fistful."

With its Pittsburgh rival controlling many of the valley's politicians, the Cleveland faction knew it needed some powerful representatives of its own. And the tapes, apparently made by Charlie the Crab at two meetings during the 1980 sheriff's campaign, appeared to show them buying Traficant. "I am a loyal fucker," Traficant informed the Carabbia brothers, "and my loyalty is here, and now we've gotta set up the business that they've run for all these fuckin' years and swing that business over to you, and that's what your concern is. That's why you financed me, and I understand that."

The arrangement appeared to be an old-fashioned one: Traficant acknowledged receiving more than a hundred thousand dollars from the Cleveland faction for his campaign; in exchange, he indicated that he would use the sheriff's office to protect the Carabbias' rackets while shutting down their rivals.

Charlie told Traficant, "Your uncle Tony was my goombah . . . and we feel that you're like a brother to us. We don't want you to make any fuckin' mistakes." Traficant assured his benefactors that he was solid, and that if any of his deputies betrayed them "they'll fuckin' come up swimming in [the] Mahoning River."

But, according to the tapes, Traficant was not worried primarily about his deputies; he was worried about the Pittsburgh Mob. As Charlie knew, Traficant had accepted money from Pittsburgh, too—some sixty thousand dollars. (The first installment had come with the message "I want you to be my friend.") The young candidate for sheriff was now double-crossing the Pittsburgh family: he had just given over at least some of its money to Charlie the Crab in order to prove his loyalty, and he knew that when the Pittsburgh family found out it would retaliate. "Look, I don't wanna fuckin' die in six months, Charlie," Traficant said.

Kroner and his colleagues could hear Traficant hatching a plan to protect himself from the Pittsburgh Mafia and the officials they controlled. "Let's look at it this way, O.K.?" he said. "They can get to the judges and get what they need done. . . . What they don't have is the sheriff, and . . . I'm one step ahead." On the day he was sworn into office, Traficant said he'd take some of the money the Pittsburgh family had given him and use it as evidence to arrest them for bribery. What's more, Traficant rehearsed what he and the Crabs would say if their secret dealings were ever uncovered by the authorities: "I was so fucking pissed off at this crooked government, I came to you and asked you guys if you would assist me to break it up, and you said, 'Fuck it . . . we'll do it.' O.K.? That's gonna be what you're gonna say in court."

"Orlie, too?" Charlie asked. "He's got a bad heart—"

"Look . . . I'm not talking fucking daydreams," Traficant said. "If they're gonna fuck with me, I'm gonna nail them." Traficant was taken with the audacity of his plan. "If you think about it," he mused, "if I fuckin' did that—"

"You can run for governor," Charlie said.

They all broke into laughter.

After Kroner and his superiors reviewed the tapes, they called Traficant down to headquarters. Kroner had never met the sheriff before, and he watched as he settled into the chair across from him. Traficant, who was forty-one years old and had once worked in the mills, was an imposing figure, with wide shoulders and a flamboyant, brown toupee that stuck up on top. Kroner told Traficant that he had watched him play quarterback at the University of Pittsburgh. (An N.F.L. scout once said that Traficant, "at the most critical point in a game," would "keep the ball himself and run with it," bowling over anyone in his path.)

What happened next at the F.B.I. meeting with Traficant is in dispute. According to sworn court testimony from Kroner and other agents present, Kroner asked the sheriff if he was conducting an investigation into organized crime in the valley. Traficant said he wasn't. Kroner then asked him if he knew Charlie the Crab or Orlie the Crab. Traficant said he'd only heard of them.

You never met them? Kroner asked.

No, Traficant said.

You never received money from them?

No, he said again.

Then Kroner popped in the tape:

TRAFICANT: "They have given sixty thousand dollars."

ORLIE THE CRAB: "They gave sixty. What'd we give?"

TRAFICANT: "O.K., a hundred and three."

After a few seconds, Traficant slumped in his seat. "I don't want to hear any more," he said, according to Kroner. "I've heard enough."

In the F.B.I.'s version of events, Traficant acknowledged that he'd taken the money, and he agreed to cooperate in exchange for immunity. In front of two witnesses, he signed a confession that read: "During the period of time that I campaigned for sheriff of Mahoning County, Ohio, I accepted money . . . with the understanding that certain illegal activities would be allowed to take place in Mahoning County after my election and that as sheriff I would not interfere with those activities." But several weeks later, the F.B.I. says, when Traficant realized that he would have to resign as sheriff and that the reason for his resignation would become public, he recanted his confession. "Do what you have to do," he told Kroner, "and I'll do what I have to do." Or, as Traficant later told a local television reporter, "All those people trying to put me in jail should go fuck themselves."

Kroner and the F.B.I. arrested Traficant for allegedly taking a hundred and sixty-three thousand dollars in bribes from the Mob. The indictment charged that he "did knowingly and willfully combine, conspire, confederate, and agree" with racketeers to commit crimes against the United States. He faced up to twenty-three years in jail. To everyone's astonishment, Traficant decided to represent himself in court, even though he wasn't a lawyer and even though the judge warned him that "almost no one in his right mind" would do so.

On the day of the trial, in the spring of 1983, Traficant paced the courtroom, wearing a short-sleeved shirt and slacks. He told the jury what he vowed on the Carabbia tapes he would say: that he was conducting "the most unorthodox sting in the history of Ohio politics." In a role that he said deserved an "Academy Award," Traficant told the rapt jury and gallery that he had been acting all along as an undercover agent, trying to convince the Carabbia brothers he was on their side so that he could then use them to shut down the more powerful Pittsburgh faction. "What I did, and what I set out to do very carefully," he said, "was to design a plan whereby I would destroy and disrupt the political influence and the Mob control over in Mahoning County."

He admitted taking money from the Mob, but said he did so only because he wanted to prevent his opponent in the campaign from getting it. Though he agreed that he had signed "a statement" in front of the F.B.I., he said it was different from the "confession" introduced into evidence. He insisted that he lied to the F.B.I. about the sting because he couldn't trust its agents, and that if Kroner and the F.B.I. hadn't intervened he would have cleansed the most corrupt county in the country. "The point of the matter I want to make is this," he said. "I got inside of the Mob." He added, "I fucked the Mob."

When Kroner took the stand, testifying that he had seen Traficant sign the confession, the sheriff leaped to his feet and yelled, "That's a God-damned lie!" During cross-examination, he taunted his F.B.I. adversary, saying, "Oh, I see" and "No, Bob." Traficant referred to himself as "my client" and asked reporters, "How am I doin'?" In a region embedded with corruption and wary of federal authorities, he became, by the end of his defense, an emblem of the valley, a folk hero. There were parties held in his honor, and residents wore T-shirts championing his legal struggle. It didn't matter that the I.R.S. would later find Traficant liable for taking bribes and evading taxes, in a civil trial in which he invoked the Fifth Amendment. Or that the money he had allegedly taken as evidence for the sting was never turned over. Or that one of his deputies claimed on the stand that Traficant had repeatedly asked him to shoot Traficant in order to make it look like an attempted Mob hit and delay the trial. ("He wanted me to wound him, but not to maim him," the deputy said.)

Traficant understood his community better than anyone else. It took a jury four days to decide to acquit him of all charges. Charlie the Crab was wrong about one thing: Traficant wouldn't become governor—he would become a United States congressman.

By the time Traficant went to Washington, D.C., in 1985, the economy in the Mahoning Valley was already disintegrating. The worldwide demand for steel had plummeted, leaving the area in a near-permanent recession. Mills were shuttered; department stores were boarded up. By the end of the decade, the population in Youngstown had fallen by more than twenty-eight thousand, while the sky, leaden for half a century, turned almost blue.

Traficant, who would be repeatedly reelected to Congress by overwhelming margins, railed against the closings. When one of the last steel mills in the region filed for bankruptcy, in the late nineteen-eighties, Traficant sounded like Charlie the Crab. "I think this is beyond all this talking phase," he warned, adding that if the owner ripped off a local industrial facility then someone should "grab him by the throat and stretch him a couple of inches."

Though prosperity had once brought the Mob to the valley, depression now cemented its rule. The professional classes that did so much to break the culture of the Mafia in Chicago and Buffalo and New York in the nineteen-seventies and eighties practically ceased to exist in Youngstown. Much of the valley's middle class either left or stopped being middle class. And so Youngstown experienced a version of what sociologists have described in the inner city. The city lost its civic backbone—its doctors and lawyers and accountants. The few upstanding civic leaders who remained were marginalized or cowed. Hierarchies of status and success and moral value became inverted. The result was a generation of Batchos, who worshipped the dons the way other children worshipped Mickey Mantle or Joe DiMaggio. (Batcho had a tattoo of a Mob boss on his left arm, and told people proudly that he'd "take a bullet for him.")

Meanwhile, Lenny Strollo and his partners, in need of players for their cash-strapped casinos, began catering to the local drug dealers and criminals, who were the only people left with money to spend. The Mob, which had once competed with the valley's civil society, now all but displaced it. As late as 1997, in the small city of Campbell, Strollo controlled at least ninety per cent of the appointments to the police department. He fixed the civil-service exam so that he could pick the chief of police and nearly all the patrolmen. The city law director brought the list of candidates for promotion to Strollo's house, and the don would pore over it, making his choices. An attorney familiar with the city told me that Strollo could "determine which murderers went to jail and which ones went free."

In 1996, three Mob hit men, including Mo Man Harris, were on their way to kill their latest target when the Campbell police pulled them over for speeding, according to people in the car. In the vehicle, the cops found an AK-47 rifle, a .357 Magnum revolver, and a 9-mm. pistol. One of the assassins used his cell phone to call Jeff Riddle, who rushed to the scene and told the police that the men were running an errand for Bernie the Jew. The cops let them go.

In the rare instances when the police arrested a reputed mobster, Strollo and his associates paid off the judges. Once, a judge refused to fix an assault case, and so Strollo dispatched Batcho with a walkie-talkie and a silencer to wound the defense attorney, Gary Van Brocklin, in order to force a mistrial. As Batcho later recalled, "I said, 'Are you attorney Gary Van Brocklin?' And he said, 'Yes, I am.' . . . And I shot him right in the knee." Andy Arena, who was Kroner's boss at the F.B.I., told me, "I don't know how an honest defense attorney could make a living in this town."

Strollo's influence extended to the valley's representative in Congress as well. Traficant's top aide in the district, Charles O'Nesti, served as the "bagman" between Strollo and the city's corrupt public officials, as O'Nesti himself later admitted. (Traficant had hired O'Nesti in 1984, despite his claims on the infamous tapes that O'Nesti was a Mob crony whom he would arrest as part of his so-called sting to clean up the valley.) While working for Traficant, O'Nesti would meet Strollo at the don's farm or scheme with him on the phone. The two even conspired to steal a stretch of city pavement as it was being laid down.

The F.B.I. sting that would start unravelling this web of corruption began in 1994. By then, Kroner was married and had two daughters; and he had given up smoking through hypnotism and put several pounds on his slender frame. One morning, as he met with other agents in their cramped local office, he was despairing. He had recently witnessed the disintegration of one of his few triumphs: fourteen months after he had secured a conviction against Strollo for gambling, his nemesis had reemerged from prison and reasserted his power. Even when we bust them, Kroner thought, they just come back.

So Kroner and his colleagues opted for a new approach. Rather than attack the Mob from the top, as they had in the past, they'd start at the bottom, with the numbers runners and the stick handlers at the *barbut* games. The investigation was based on the theory of carpenter ants—if you don't eliminate all of them, they simply multiply again. Kroner says, "We set forth right in the beginning that we were not going to stop until we got to the nest, and if it meant having to work deals with people we had lots of evidence against, that's what we were going to do."

One of the first people they persuaded to cooperate was a local bookie named Michael Sabella, whose clothes always smelled of fish. After being questioned by the feds on a separate matter, he agreed to wear a wire around to the county's gambling dens. Eventually, he provided enough evidence that investigators were able to wiretap several low-level members of Strollo's sprawling enterprise, who, in turn, gave them enough evidence to tap more phones, and so on. As the number of intercepted conversations grew into the thousands, Kroner and his partners, John Stoll and Gordon Klau, spent days and nights sifting through transcripts. "We really put a strain on our families," Kroner once told a reporter. "It was a difficult period."

Still, after more than a year they hadn't penetrated Strollo's inner circle. Hoping to "shake the tree," as Kroner put it, the agents raided several gambling joints. Afterward, they had established enough links to Strollo that a judge granted them the authority to install listening devices in the don's kitchen and to tap his telephones. Kroner and his colleagues soon began picking up snippets of incriminating conversations. They heard what sounded like a plot to shake down a priest and what some "asshole did before . . . he got whacked."

At one point, Kroner received a tip from an informant that Strollo was planning to kill one of his rivals, Ernie Biondillo. Feeling a moral obligation to warn Biondillo, Kroner picked up the phone and called him. "This is Bob Kroner," he said. "You know who I am?"

"Yeah, I know who you are."

"Well, I need to sit down and talk to you alone."

They met that night in a dark parking lot. Biondillo was in his Cadillac, and pulled alongside Kroner's car. The men spoke through their open windows. Kroner hoped the warning would encourage Biondillo to cooperate with the investigation. But Biondillo just kept saying, *Who the fuck wants to kill me?*

Kroner looked at him warily. "I can't tell you that. I'm not out here to start a war."

Unable to get an answer, Biondillo drove off in his Cadillac. Several months later, he was riding in his car and turned down a deserted street, when two vehicles boxed him in. A pair of men wearing rubber masks and holding guns opened fire, killing him.

Though Kroner was sure that the hit was ordered by Strollo, the F.B.I. still didn't have the evidence to arrest him. But, by the summer of 1996, the authorities were closing in, and Strollo, sensing it, became increasingly paranoid. On the phone, he spoke almost exclusively in code. Once, Strollo had a premonition that a longtime confidant was wearing a wire, even though he wasn't. Another time, Strollo became convinced that an airplane flying overhead was tailing one of his bookies. When someone tried to calm him down, he snapped, "This is my life you're talking about. . . . I got to fight for survival."

Strollo was consumed with his nemesis, Kroner. On the telephone, he would say, "Bob, can you hear me? Can you hear me?" Strollo sent one of his men to find out if Kroner's father could be paid off to control his renegade son, but word came back that the father was honest, too. Knowing his phones were tapped, Strollo tried to plant evidence to suggest that Kroner was somehow on the take. He told associates that Kroner had received bribes from Little Joey and was running drugs through the valley.

One day, Strollo sounded threatening toward Kroner and other F.B.I. agents. "I don't know what I'm going to have to do about these guys," he said. Not long afterward, unbeknownst to the F.B.I., Strollo ordered the assassination of Gains. The bungled hit—and the phone call from the "scorned woman," as Kroner referred to the Mob associate's former girlfriend who contacted Gains—broke open the F.B.I.'s investigation. In 1997, Bernie the Jew, Riddle, and Harris were all charged with attempted murder. As Batcho was walking near his house, an unmarked car pulled up behind him and two men jumped out. "Are you Mark Batcho?" one of them said.

"No, I'm not Mark Batcho. I don't know him."

Despite his denials, Batcho was taken into custody, where he became what he called "the lowest form of life"—a Mob rat. Kroner and his men had finally infiltrated the Mafia's "nest." On a cold morning shortly before Christmas in 1997, F.B.I. agents fanned out through the valley, arresting more than twenty-eight Mob associates. Kroner showed up at Strollo's door with an arrest warrant. As Strollo was being handcuffed, he said to Kroner, "Are you happy now, Bob?"

In the end, nearly all of Strollo's underlings pleaded guilty and turned evidence against one another, except for Bernie the Jew and Riddle, the two men who had adopted the old Sicilian code, even though they could never be officially inducted into the Mafia. "The only ones who had any balls were a schwartze and a sheeny," said one of the lawyers involved in the case.

Just before Bernie was about to go on trial, he insisted that Strollo would never turn on them and break his oath of silence. But even as Bernie was speaking Strollo was cutting a deal with the prosecution. Strollo told Kroner, "You win."

"I will probably be under indictment" in the next few months, Traficant said on C-SPAN, staring into the camera. It was March, 2000, almost two decades since he was first arrested by Kroner and the F.B.I. The Congressman, who was now running for his ninth term in the House of Representatives, wore a sombre black coat and tie; his pompadour was sticking up more than usual, and his long sideburns gave him the look of an aging biker. In his sixteen years in Congress, Traficant had earned a reputation as an eccentric populist. He often appeared on the House floor, in polyester suits, speaking about the plight of the working class and railing against the I.R.S.; he closed his speeches with the signature line "Beam me up, Mr. Speaker." In a political city seemingly without memory, he had become known as simply "the honorable gentleman from Ohio."

Now he looked as if he hadn't slept for days. "Hawks are circling, buzzards circling, sharks circling . . . trying to kill the Traficant election," he stammered. He paused, his cheeks reddening. "Let me tell you what: Twenty years ago—not quite—I was the only American in the history of the United States to defeat the Justice Department. . . . They have targeted me ever since." Pointing his finger into the camera, he continued, "I'm targeting them. They better not make a damn mistake. . . . I am mad and . . . I'm going to fight like a junkyard dog in the face of a hurricane, and . . . if I beat them you're now watching one of the richest men in America, because I'm going to sue their assets all apart."

Even stranger than his warnings to the Justice Department and the F.B.I.—and his admonition that he would shoot any unexpected late-night visitors to his house—were Traficant's threats to his own party. He warned that if Democratic leaders didn't stand by him he would switch parties. And, as further compensation for his loyalty, Traficant demanded a list of favors for his district: "I want an empowerment zone from the President of the United States—and I expect it this year—and I want additional appropriations." On national television, he seemed to be extorting not only members of Congress but also the United States President.

His threats came after authorities had already convicted several people connected to him. Among them were O'Nesti, his top aide and Strollo's bagman; a disbarred attorney who had once advised Traficant, and who was implicated in the scheme to murder the prosecutor Paul Gains; and two former deputy sheriffs who had served in Traficant's sheriff's office, and who were convicted of taking bribes from the Mob. According to accounts first detailed in the *Vindicator* and the Cleveland *Plain Dealer*, investigators were looking into, among other things, whether the Congressman received illegal contributions—including the use of a Corvette—from associates in the valley. Authorities had homed in on two brothers, Robert T. and Anthony R. Bucci, who owned a paving company in Traficant's district and allegedly delivered materials and did construction work on the Congressman's seventy-six-acre farm. Both brothers appeared to be enmeshed in the city's network of corruption. On one of the F.B.I.'s wiretaps, O'Nesti could be heard conspiring with Strollo to steer a million-dollar contract to the Buccis' company. Robert Bucci had since fled the country after allegedly transferring millions of dollars to an offshore account in the Cayman Islands.

Throughout the investigation, Traficant had steadfastly maintained his innocence, and the valley was bracing for a second epic trial. "Here's what I'm saying now," he insisted on c-span, "and I'm saying this to the

Justice Department. . . . If you are to indict me, indict me in June so I can be tried over the August recess. I don't want to miss any votes."

Not long after, I travelled to Youngstown, hoping to learn more about the case against the Congressman and the Mafia's hold on the region. Though it was the middle of the day, the downtown area was eerily empty. Rows of stores were boarded up, and the ornate façades of buildings were crumbling. Finally, I saw a light in a clothing store, where an old man was folding Italian suits. When I went in and asked him about the Congressman, he said, "Ain't no one gonna get rid of Traficant. Traficant's too sharp." He recalled fondly the "henchmen," including Strollo, who bought hand-tailored clothes from him. "They didn't wear red or pink suits like they're coming out with now," he said. When I pressed him about the local corruption, he shrugged. "Who cares? If you're working and making a living and nobody is bothering you, why are you going to butt in?"

That night at the restaurant in my hotel, several Youngstown natives who were in their seventies and eighties were sitting around a table arguing about the Congressman. "Traficant produces," one of the men said. "That's what counts."

"Damn right!" another said.

A frail man with white hair said, "When I was eight years old I delivered newspapers downtown, and I would always go by this speakeasy on Sunday afternoon. Well, one day the owner says, 'I want you to meet someone.' So I went over and it was Al Capone." He paused, then repeated, "Al Capone."

Another man at the table, who had remained silent, suddenly said, "You see this? This is typical Youngstown. Here's an educated man, an attorney, and Traficant is a god of his, and he's still raving about meeting Al Capone."

Later, Mark Shutes, an anthropologist at Youngstown State University who had studied the region, told me, "We have socialized ourselves and our offspring that this is the way the world is. . . . There is no sense in this community in which gangsters are people who have imposed their will on our community. Their values are our values."

During the latest Democratic primary for Congress, Traficant faced two opponents who railed against his alleged Mob ties and noted that he would soon be indicted. Still, Traficant won the primary with more votes than his two main competitors combined. Traficant seemed invulnerable; some congressional Republicans had even begun to defend him, apparently hoping he'd follow through on his threat to switch parties. "Jimmy Traficant is not being done right by," Representative Steve LaTourette, Republican of Ohio, told the Cleveland *Plain Dealer*. "There isn't a finer man, there isn't a finer member of Congress, there isn't a finer human being."

Emboldened by his popular support, Traficant attempted to do what he always did: rally the valley against the outsiders he claimed were trying to besmirch its name. Over the last year, he has defiantly called his convicted former top aide, O'Nesti, a "good friend" and championed a local sheriff convicted of racketeering, arguing that he should be moved to a prison closer to Youngstown to be near his ill mother. Traficant said of members of the F.B.I., "These sons of bachelors will not intimidate me, and they won't jack me around."

Though he refused to talk to me or to other reporters ("I'll only make an official statement when I'm actually killed," he said), he and his staff released a torrent of press releases attacking those pursuing him. "TRAFICANT BILL WOULD CREATE NEW AGENCY TO INVESTIGATE JUSTICE DEPARTMENT," one release said. Another said, "TRAFICANT WANTS PRESIDENT TO INVESTIGATE FEDERAL AGENTS IN YOUNGSTOWN." On the House floor, where his speech was protected against suits for libel, he was even bolder. "Mr. Speaker, I have evidence that certain F.B.I. agents in Youngstown, Ohio, have violated the RICO statute and . . . stole large sums of cash," he claimed. "What is even worse, they 'suggested' to one of their field operative informants that he should commit murder. Mr. Speaker, *murder*."

Before I left Youngstown, I stopped by the F.B.I. office in Boardman, Ohio, where Kroner and his boss, Andy Arena, were trying to fend off Traficant's allegations. They were careful not to say anything about the pending investigation of the Congressman, but it was clear they were under siege. On talk radio, Traficant supporters denounced Kroner as a thief, a con man, a crook, a creep, a liar, and a dope dealer. "The thing that most depressed me," Kroner told me, "was when I became the subject on talk radio one day and they were discussing my integrity." He folded his arms. "I just have to block out [those] things." Rather than a hero, he had become almost a pariah. "Everything is turned upside down here," Arena said.

As Kroner sat in his neatly pressed jacket and loafers, with his twenty-year-anniversary F.B.I. medallion mounted prominently on a thick gold ring, he seemed slightly defensive. "Every time we charge another public official, the [media] presents it as another black eye for the community," he said. "I'd prefer if they'd portray it to the community as another step in cleansing ourselves. We've got to take a look at what's being done here as a positive thing."

After a while, Kroner offered to show me around the valley. As the sun was setting, we drove in his car past the old steel mills, past the Greek Coffee House and the Doll House and other gambling dens, past the place where Bernie the Jew met with his team of hit men and where Strollo had Ernie Biondillo killed. "We're a part of this community like everyone else," Kroner said. "We suffer the same problems if we live in a corrupt town." He paused for a moment, perhaps because he couldn't think of anything to add or perhaps because he realized that, after a lifetime of fighting the Mafia, there was little more that he could do. Finally, he said, "As long as they choose to put people in office who are corrupt, nothing will ever change."

—July, 2000

—᜶—

In November, 2000, Traficant was elected to a ninth term in Congress. Six months later, he was indicted on ten counts of bribery, racketeering, tax evasion, and obstruction of justice. Among the charges were that he did political favors for the Buccis in exchange for free construction services on his farm, and assisted others in return for thousands of dollars in kickbacks. Traficant was also accused of asking an aide to lie to a federal grand jury and to destroy incriminating evidence. (The aide told authorities that Traficant watched while he took a blow-torch to envelopes that had once contained cash payoffs to the Congressman.)

The trial began in a federal district court in Cleveland in February of 2002, and, as Traficant had done nearly two decades earlier, he decided to represent himself. He accused the prosecution of having "the testicles of an ant," and at one point stormed out of the courtroom. Yet this time a jury found him guilty on every count.

Saying he was "full of deceit and corruption and greed," the judge sentenced Traficant to eight years in prison. In addition, the judge ordered that he pay more than a hundred and fifty thousand dollars in fines and nearly twenty thousand dollars in unpaid taxes, and return ninety-six thousand dollars in illegal proceeds.

As Kroner looked on, Traficant was led away in handcuffs. Kroner soon retired from the F.B.I. On July 24, 2002, the House of Representatives voted 420 to 1 to expel Traficant—making him only the second congressman since the Civil War to be expelled from the institution. While he was in prison, Traficant was put in solitary confinement for trying to foment a riot. In September of 2009, after serving seven years, he was released on probation. He was greeted in Youngstown by more than a thousand cheering supporters, many of them wearing T-shirts that said "Welcome Home Jimbo." Traficant announced that it was "fifty-fifty" that he would run for Congress again.

Giving "The Devil" His Due

THE DEATH SQUAD
REAL-ESTATE
AGENT

No one remembers who first saw him in the neighborhood, but Emile Maceus was nearly certain that Emmanuel "Toto" Constant—the man everyone called "the devil"—was now standing on his front stoop. The man was six foot three, maybe more; he wore a coat and tie, and his tightly curled Afro was neatly combed. He had come, he said, to show a client Maceus's house, a three-bedroom in Queens Village, New York. He was a real-estate agent, he said, and had seen the pink "For Sale" sign on the front lawn.

Maceus stared at him. The man's face was pudgier than Maceus remembered from Haiti, during the military regime of the early nineteen-nineties. Back then he had been bone-thin and ghostlike, sometimes appearing with an Uzi or with a .357 Magnum tucked under his shirt. To help keep the junta in control, he had terrorized the population with his paramilitary squad—a legendary outfit of armed civilians who, together with the Haitian military, allegedly tortured, raped, and murdered thousands of people. "Can we look around?" the man asked.

Maceus wasn't sure what to do. Maybe it wasn't Constant. He was bigger than Maceus recalled, more genial, and before Maceus knew it the man was walking through his house, poking his head into each room, looking at the floorboards and the toilets, taking note of the overhead space in the kitchen, and commenting in Creole. In the living room, the man passed a poster on the wall of Jean-Bertrand Aristide—the once and future Haitian President, and the paramilitaries' archenemy—but didn't give it a second look. Maybe he was just a real-estate agent after all, just another Haitian immigrant trying to survive in New York.

But, as the real-estate agent was leaving, Maceus kept thinking, What if he *is* Toto Constant? Maceus knew that in 1994, after the United States overthrew the military regime, Constant, a fugitive from Haitian justice, had been allowed, inexplicably, to slip into the country. Maceus had heard that, after Constant had finally been arrested and ordered deported, he had in 1996 mysteriously been released under a secret agreement with the U.S. government—even though the Haitian government had requested his extradition and U.S. authorities had found photos of his group's victims, their bodies mutilated, pasted to the walls of his Port-au-Prince headquarters like trophies. As the man was opening the front door, Maceus's curiosity overcame him. He asked in Creole, "What's your family name?"

The man hesitated. "Constant."

It *was* Toto Constant. For an instant, the two Haitians stood there, staring at each other. Then Constant and his client sped off in a car. Maceus went inside and found his wife. She was trembling. "How could you bring that devil in my house?" she shouted. *"How could you?"*

News of the encounter, in the summer of 2000, spread through the city's sprawling Haitian community, from Flatbush to Laurelton to Cambria Heights to Brooklyn, as it would have in Haiti—by *teledjòl,* word of mouth. Constant had ventured out into the community several times since the U.S. government had set him free, but never with such audacity—selling houses to the same people he had driven into exile. When he first arrived in Queens, he seemed to emerge only periodically. He was spotted, someone said, at a disco, clad in black, dancing on the day of Baron Samedi, the voodoo lord of death who guards cemetery gates in his top hat and tails. He was seen at a butcher shop and at a Blockbuster. Haitian-community radio and local newspapers reported the sightings—"HAITI's GRIM REAPER PARTYING IN U.S.," one headline announced—but he always managed to vanish before anyone could locate him. Finally, in 1997, the rumors led to a quiet street in Laurelton, near the heart of the Haitian community, where for years exiles had hoped to shed the weight of their history—a history of never-ending coups and countercoups—and where Constant could be seen sitting on the porch of the white-stucco house he shared with his aunt and his mother. "The whole idea of Toto Constant living free in New York, the bastion of the Haitian diaspora, is an insult to all the Haitian people," Ricot Dupuy, the manager of Radio Soleil d'Haiti, in Flatbush, told his listeners.

It was not long before residents draped the street's trees and lampposts with pictures of Constant's alleged victims, their hands and feet bound with white cord or their limbs severed by machetes. Neighbors shoved one of the most horrifying pictures—a photo of a young boy lying in a pool of blood—under Constant's door. Yet a few days later Constant was back on his porch. Locals came by and spat at his bushes; they stoned his door. Then, after Constant's appearance at the Maceus house, an angry crowd surrounded his home, yelling "Murderer!" and "Assassin!" Someone spotted a figure down the road—a well-known ally of Constant's, "a spy," as a protester cried out—and the crowd chased after him. When he disappeared and there was still no sign of Constant, the crowd marched to the real-estate office, four miles away, where it threatened to drive the Haitian owner out of business unless he fired his new employee.

By November of 2000, Haitians had created permanent Toto Watches—networks that tracked Constant's every whereabouts. At about this time, Ray Laforest, one of the Toto Watchers, agreed to show me where "the devil" could be found. He told me to meet him near the real-estate office, in front of which Constant had been seen smoking on his lunch break. Laforest was a large man, with a beard and sunglasses. He carried with him several posters, and when I asked him what they were he unfurled one, revealing an old black-and-white photograph of Constant. A mustache curled down around the corners of the reputed death squad leader's mouth, and several crooked teeth showed between his lips. In bold letters, the poster said, "WANTED: EMMANUEL 'TOTO' CONSTANT FOR CRIMES AGAINST THE HAITIAN PEOPLE."

Laforest told me that Constant had disappeared since the protest. "He's gone into hiding again," he said. After Laforest taped one of the

"WANTED" posters to a lamppost, we got into his car and drove through the neighborhood, past a series of elegant Tudor houses, until we arrived at the house where Constant had last been seen. "Why are you stopping?" I asked.

"I'm numb," he said. "If I saw him right now, I'd tie him up myself." He told me that Constant's men and other paramilitaries had dragged one of his friends from a church and shot him in broad daylight, and that earlier his own brother had been tortured by the Haitian military. We waited for several minutes, parked behind a bush. *"Bay kou bliye, pote mak sonje,"* Laforest said.

"What does that mean?" I asked.

"It's an old Creole proverb," he said. "Those who give the blows forget, those who bear the scars remember."

LETTING TOTO SPEAK FOR TOTO

I had been looking for Constant ever since I heard that a man facing charges in Haiti for crimes against humanity was living among the very people against whom the crimes were said to have been committed. Unlike Cain, who was cast out of his community, Constant had become an exile in a community of exiles, banished among those whom he had banished. Though he had fled justice, he could not escape his past. He had to face it nearly every day—in a glance from a neighbor, or a poster on the street.

More important, he was, for the first time, confronted with the prospect of real justice. In the fall of 2000, the Haitian government put him on trial in absentia for the 1994 murders of at least six people in the town of Raboteau. Dozens of others were also on trial. It was a historic case—the first major attempt by the Haitian government to prosecute anyone for the brutal crimes committed by the military regime and to test its judicial system, which had been corrupt for so long that it was essentially nonexistent. And there was mounting pressure on the U.S. government, at home and abroad, to extradite Constant.

When I reached his lawyer, J. D. Larosiliere, he told me that things were at their most critical juncture. A barrel-chested Haitian-American who speaks a combination of formal English and street slang and has a penchant for finely tailored suits, Larosiliere told me that he was often referred to as "the Haitian version of Johnnie Cochran." Denying that there had even been a massacre at Raboteau, he said that if Constant was sent back to Haiti he would likely be assassinated. Because of the desperateness of the situation, Larosiliere agreed to let Constant, whom many thought had disappeared, meet with me.

So, one afternoon several days later, I headed to Larosiliere's office, in Newark, New Jersey. When I arrived, Larosiliere was in a closed-door meeting, and as I waited outside in the foyer I could hear the sound of Creole punctured by occasional bursts of English. Suddenly, the office door swung open and a tall man in a double-breasted suit hurried out. It took me a moment to recognize Constant—he looked at least thirty pounds heavier than in the pictures I'd seen of him taken during the military regime. He still had the same mustache, but on his heavier face it no longer appeared so menacing. He wore a turtleneck under his jacket and a gold earring in his left ear. "Hey, how you doing?" he said, speaking with only a slight accent.

To my surprise, he looked like an average American. We sat down in a small conference room lined with books. He paused, rocking back in his chair. Finally, he said, "It's time for Toto to speak for Toto."

It was the first of more than a dozen interviews. As he told me his story over the next several months, he often spoke for hours on end. He turned over his voluminous notes and private papers, his correspondence and journals. During that time, I also interviewed his alleged victims, along with human-rights workers, United Nations observers, Haitian authorities, and former and current U.S. officials within the White House, the State Department, the Immigration and Naturalization Service, and the intelligence community, many of whom had never before spoken publicly about Constant. I also gained access to intelligence reports, some of which had previously been classified, and State Department cables. With these and other sources, I was able to piece together not only the story of Emmanuel "Toto" Constant but also much of the story of how the U.S. government secretly aided him and later shielded him from justice.

Voodoo Paramilitary

In October of 1993, the U.S.S. Harlan County, loaded with military personnel, was sent steaming toward Haiti's capital, Port-au-Prince.

President Bill Clinton had dispatched the ship and its crew as the first major contingent of an international peacekeeping mission to restore to power Haiti's first democratically elected President, Jean-Bertrand Aristide. Aristide was a political priest, a wiry, passionate, bug-eyed orator who had risen to power in late 1990 on a mixture of socialism and liberation theology. The downtrodden of Haiti, which is nearly everyone, called him Titid and revered him; the military and the economic élite reviled him as an unstable radical. He was deposed in a coup less than a year after taking office and ultimately fled to the United States. Since then the military, along with roaming bands of paramilitaries, had murdered scores of people. The bloodshed had galvanized the international community, and the ship's arrival was hailed as a turning point in the effort to reestablish some semblance of public safety and the island's democracy.

On October 11th, as the Harlan County neared port, a group of U.N. and U.S. officials, headed by the chargé d'affaires, Vicki Huddleston, and accompanied by a large press corps, came to formally welcome the ship and its troops. The assembly waited at the entrance to the port for a guard to open the gate, but nothing happened. Documentary footage shows Huddleston sitting in the back of her car with the C.I.A. station chief. Speaking to another embassy official, she says into her walkie-talkie, "Tell the captain [of the port] I am here to speak with him."

"Roger, ma'am. We have passed that repeatedly to him, and we are getting nowhere."

"Well, tell him I'm here at the gate and I'm waiting for the authorities to open it."

"He doesn't want to talk right now. . . . He ran away."

"Open the gate."

"We're having some problem with hostile staff. We may have a situation."

At that moment, a band of armed men, under the direction of the then little-known thirty-six-year-old paramilitary leader Toto Constant, stormed the area. The men, who had already blocked the dock where the Harlan County was supposed to tie up, surrounded Huddleston's car, banging on the hood and yelling in English, "Kill whites! Kill whites!"

There were only about a hundred in all, many of them potbellied and armed with little more than pitchforks. But the show of force, only a few days after U.S. soldiers had been killed in Somalia, proved terrifying. Constant put on a savvy performance for the press cameras: his ragtag troops banged on sheepskin drums and shouted "Somalia" as if it were a battle cry. They drank and caroused through the night, turning their vehicles' lights toward the open sea where the Harlan County was still waiting. Finally, President Clinton ordered the ship to leave. It was one of the most humiliating retreats in U.S. naval history, and a surprising one even to those who forced it. "My people kept wanting to run away," Constant told reporters afterward. "But I took the gamble and urged them to stay. Then the Americans pulled out! We were astonished."

That day was the coming-out for Constant and his Front for the Advancement and Progress of Haiti, better known as FRAPH, which in Creole evokes the word *"frapper,"* meaning "to hit." (Constant said the name had come to him in a dream.) Organized by Constant several months earlier, FRAPH was described by its leader as a grass-roots political organization—"a mysterious event"—that would rise from the masses and replace the remnants of Aristide's populist movement. The party literature, which Constant composed on an old manual typewriter and handed out to the press, explained that "FRAPH is a popular movement of unity, where all the social sectors are firmly intertwined to bring perfect harmony."

But FRAPH was a peculiar sort of political party: although it offered free food and liquor to lure supporters, most of its thousands of followers were drawn from the armed bands that operated at the military's behest and from former members of the now defunct Tonton Macoutes, the infamous paramilitary organization named for a child-snatching bogeyman in Haitian fairy tales. At rallies, FRAPH members would slam their right fist into their left palm in mass salutes. And although FRAPH's literature spoke of unity, Constant declared publicly, "If Aristide were to return, he would die. Aristide and his supporters are the enemies of this country."

Despite such warnings, Constant tried to cultivate an image as the only gentleman in a band of thugs. At the official launching of FRAPH, as his men flanked him with guns, he released a handful of doves. Rather than don a soft hat and sunglasses, or camouflage pants, like other paramilitaries, he often appeared in a sharp blue suit and tie and carried a bamboo cane, which he leaned on as he walked. He had been raised within Haiti's tiny aristocracy, and had studied at Canadian universities and worked briefly in New York as a Haitian diplomat. He spoke English with only a slight accent, and translated for the press in Spanish and French. "Never forget that I am from the establishment," he liked to say. "I am not just any Joe out there. I'm *Constant.*"

Still, there was something frightening about him. His eyes, set deep in his head, were glassy and jittery. U.S. officials and reporters said that he was wired on cocaine (Constant has always denied this), and he was known to stay up all night, driving wildly through the streets, his body-guards hanging out the back of the car with their machine guns. In public, he usually appeared with a man named Jojo, a fierce former Macoute who claimed that his pregnant wife had been murdered by Aristide's supporters and who was regarded as a merciless killer. "He is not afraid of anything," Constant still says of Jojo respectfully.

With Jojo as his partner, Constant began to set up FRAPH offices in every town and village. Members received special I.D. cards and machine guns. Like the old Macoutes, they operated as part local bosses, part spies, part extortionists, part militia, and part political cadre. But at their core they were an extension of the military's might, a brutal "force multiplier," as one U.S. intelligence report put it, which would allow the regime the deniability that a prudent government always looks for in the use of mur-der. "FRAPH's will is an order," Constant declared shortly after the storm-ing of the port. "When we ask for something, the entire country has to accept it."

"FACIAL SCALPING"

More and more packs of armed men began to roam at night, looking for Aristide supporters. They were believed to be FRAPH, the police, or the military, or a combination of the three, but they were usually careful to dis-guise themselves with hoods or women's clothing (a trademark of the old Macoutes). They carried tire irons, M16s, Uzis, pistols, machetes, axes, and "voodoo powders," which were widely believed to be lethal. They broke into homes and seized their political enemies. "I realized that I was among animals," an Aristide supporter who was taken prisoner by one of these armed packs told human-rights monitors. "At first they played with me, taking out their guns and saying I would die. Then they took me to a little torture chamber where there was a small bed. . . . They started beating me about the buttocks with their truncheons, one after the other. At that moment, I thought I would die. I passed out. When I came to, I was in a cell with another man. There were rivers of blood on the floor. Some of it was mine."

In 1994, after an extensive investigation, the O.A.S./U.N. International Civilian Mission reported, "The scenario is always substantially the same. Armed men, often military or FRAPH members, burst into the house of a political activist they [sought] to capture." If he wasn't there, the intruders attacked his wife or sister or daughter. "One guy took me by the hands and led me to the front porch," a woman told Human Rights Watch. "He said lie down. He said, 'If you don't, I'll split your head open.' . . . He pulled his pants down to his knees, lifted up my nightgown, pulled down my underpants, and raped me."

Faceless bodies began to appear in the streets. The assailants had developed a kind of art known as "facial scalping," a bloody ritual in which a person's face was peeled from ear to ear with a machete. It was a way to torture people even in the afterlife, because, many believed, such mutilation would prevent a proper burial—trapping the spirit eternally in purgatory.

As the bodies piled up, Constant held forth. He would often sit in a rattan chair in the courtyard of the house that had been his father's, a sprawling Art Deco mansion with a swimming pool and fountains, and speak to the press. Unlike other paramilitary leaders, who purposely remained in the shadows, Constant craved attention. He let reporters sleep in his garden. He cut back the hedges to make more space for them and handed out T-shirts emblazoned with FRAPH's name. "At one point, I was the most interviewed person in the world," he recalls. "It was incredible." Constant enjoyed playing the role of statesman. He warned the United States not to intervene and threatened to shut down the country in protest of the world embargo put into place after the coup. He called for the dissolution of Haiti's parliament, echoing Jojo, who had earlier warned that, if it didn't disband, FRAPH would call on the people to "tie up the deputies." As Constant put it, "A leader has to know how to play with the army, the power, and the people."

As he cultivated the press, Constant also courted Haiti's *houngans,* or voodoo priests, a potent psychological force. He portrayed himself as an embodiment of the most ferocious spirits. He held public ceremonies in front of the markets or at temples, where his men laid out small skulls. At a typical ceremony, he would lie on the ground, surrounded by skulls and fire. Then, as he rose from the flames, the crowd would chant in Creole, "Toto for President! Without Toto, Haiti can't have a life." Though he still carried a .357 Magnum, he insisted that he no longer needed it. "I have the power of voodoo with me," he said.

GENERAL CONSTANT'S BOY

In Haiti, nearly every leader has a hidden history, a family closet usually filled with the bones of enemies. Constant inherited the secrets, and to some degree the power, of his father. Gerard Emmanuel Constant had been the Army chief of staff under Haiti's dictator François "Papa Doc" Duvalier during the nineteen-sixties. A loyal soldier, he once famously rose from his bed in the middle of the night to execute, along with other officers, more than a dozen of his friends at the dictator's command. He remained a symbol of the old ruling order after it had collapsed.

But shortly after the military coup, in September of 1991, as his disciples emerged from the barracks to restore the Duvalier system, the seventy-two-year-old general slipped into a coma and died. All the military leaders and former Duvalier supporters turned out for his funeral. "It was a real phenomenon," Constant says. "I was inheriting all my father's protection and power and people. It was a symbolic transference." In his private papers, Constant went further: "My prominence, some might argue, is destiny. . . . To be the first son of General Gerard Emmanuel Constant is the call to arms for Emmanuel Gerard Constant, myself."

It was not long before people feared the younger Constant even more than they had feared his father. By the middle of 1994, thousands of Haitians had been slaughtered or had disappeared, and although no one knew for sure how many had been killed by FRAPH itself (most human-rights observers had by then been driven out of the country), the group was universally considered the most brutal of all the right-wing paramilitary outfits. Witnesses, many of them found floating on rafts as they tried to escape to the United States, told international authorities that Constant's men, in an effort to wipe out opposition, were annihilating the population. Even FRAPH members started to flee in disgust. "When they kill and rape people, we [new members] are forced to sit and watch," a former recruit told U.S. authorities, according to a declassified document obtained by the Center for Constitutional Rights for use in a lawsuit against FRAPH. Later, as part of their initiation, this same man said, the recruits were made to join the assaults.

Though Constant continued to deny the allegations, by 1994 the U.N. had concluded that Constant's organization was "the only political movement [in Haiti] whose members have been linked to assassinations and rapes." In the spring of 1994, a secret cable from the office of the American military attaché in Port-au-Prince warned, "All over the country, FRAPH is evolving into a sort of Mafia." Its members were "gun-carrying crazies," one cable stated, eager to "use violence against all who oppose it."

According to witnesses, when a FRAPH member turned up dead in Cité Soleil, a sprawling slum in Port-au-Prince, in December of 1993, Constant's men descended within hours. Carrying machine guns and machetes, they torched a thousand houses in revenge, killing more than a dozen people. The Human Rights Watch/Americas-N.C.H.R. described how "they entered the neighborhood, looked for specific persons and shot them on sight, doused the precarious one-room shacks with gasoline, set them alight. . . . Firefighters were turned back by armed men . . . [who] nailed doors shut, imprisoning people in their homes."

Constant, who some witnesses claimed was at the scene, denied FRAPH's involvement. "If I was going to really react, there would be no more Cité," he later said. But by the autumn of 1994 he was no longer merely the head of FRAPH; he had become, in the eyes of most Haitians, the embodiment of the regime: the voodoo lord of death, Baron Samedi, himself.

A Mysterious Escape

In July of 1992, Brian Latell, the leading C.I.A. analyst for Latin America, visited Haiti to gather intelligence as policymakers in Washington tried to assess military rule in Haiti. Afterward, in a report later obtained by the press, he wrote, "I do not wish to minimize the role the military plays in intimidating and occasionally terrorizing real and suspected opponents, but my experiences confirm the [intelligence] community's view that there is no systematic or frequent lethal violence aimed at civilians."

Playing down the bloodshed (Latell called the head of the junta, Lieutenant General Raoul Cedras, "a conscientious military leader"), the report conflicted with those coming from human-rights organizations, the press, and even the State Department. But, along with subsequent C.I.A. reports, it had a profound impact on U.S. foreign policy and on the decision of whether to launch a military invasion to restore the exiled Aristide to power. Whereas President Bill Clinton was pushing for such a move, many in the C.I.A., along with elements in the Pentagon, feared that Aristide was a dangerous populist. In fact, Aristide was a problematic figure. (He had once suggested necklacing his enemies with burning tires.) But a crucial C.I.A. report, which was circulated on Capitol Hill just after the Harlan County incident, seemed to exaggerate his instability, claiming that he was so unbalanced psychologically that he had once had to be hospitalized. The charge later proved to be false, but at the time it fuelled American opposition to an invasion and contributed to the ongoing vacillation in Washington. "There were factions in the process who didn't want to get involved in Haiti and could use these intelligence reports to strengthen their position," a former Clinton Administration official says.

The evidence of "systemic" and "frequent lethal violence aimed at civilians," however, was overwhelming. And in September of 1994, three years after the coup and almost a year after the Harlan County's retreat, President Clinton finally ordered a full-scale invasion to end what he called the "reign of terror." "We now know that there have been . . . over three thousand political murders," he said. In preparation for battle, Constant changed FRAPH's name to the Armed Revolutionary Front of the Haitian People and, according to news accounts, stockpiled weapons and "secret" powders that, he declared, would be able to "contaminate water so that the GIs will die." He claimed that one of these powders had been ground from the bones of AIDS victims. Appearing in camouflage pants and a black T-shirt, a machine gun at his side, he no longer gave any hint of the diplomat. "Each FRAPH man," Constant said, "must put down one American soldier."

But before war broke out the junta, faced with the might of the United States, agreed to relinquish power. Thousands of U.S. soldiers easily seized the island. Surprisingly, FRAPH was allowed to remain an active force. When asked why, U.S. soldiers said they had been told by their superior officers that FRAPH was a legitimate opposition party, like Republicans and Democrats. U.S. soldiers even stood by, insisting they were not a local police force, while FRAPH members beat back civilians who had spilled onto the streets expecting liberation. It was only after random bands of FRAPH members mowed down a crowd of Haitians and shot and wounded an American photographer, and a radio conversation was intercepted in which Constant and his men threatened to "break out weapons" and "begin an all-out war against the foreigners," that U.S. forces reversed their stance. On October 3rd, they stormed FRAPH headquarters. A jubilant crowd gathered outside, cheering them on. Inside, amid piles of nail-embedded sticks, Molotov cocktails, and trophy photos of mutilated corpses, soldiers surrounded more than two dozen FRAPH members. They bound their hands and gagged them, while the crowd shouted, "Let them die! Let them die!" As the soldiers departed with their FRAPH prisoners, the crowd rushed inside, smashing the headquarters.

Back at his father's mansion, Constant listened to a police scanner, waiting for the soldiers to seize him. His wife and four children had already fled. At one point, he yelled at a journalist, "Everybody who is reporting the situation bad . . . by the grace of God, they will wind up in the ground!" But though other FRAPH members were taken into custody Constant remained free. The U.S. Embassy spokesman, Stanley Schrager, whose assassination Constant had called for only two days before, even arranged a press conference for him outside the Presidential Palace. News footage shows Constant standing under the glaring sun, sweating in a jacket and tie. "The only solution for Haiti now is the reality of the return of Aristide," he said. "Put down your stones, put down your tires, no more violence." As he spoke, hundreds of angry Haitians pushed against a barricade of U.S. soldiers, shouting, "Assassin!" "Dog!" "Murderer!"

"If I find myself in disagreement with President Aristide," Constant pressed on, his voice now cracking, "I pledge to work as a member of loyal opposition within the framework of a legal democracy."

"Handcuff him!" people yelled from the crowd. "Tie him up! Cut his balls off!"

As the barricade of troops gave way, U.S. soldiers rushed Constant into a car, while hundreds of jeering Haitians chased after it, spitting and beating on the windows. At the time, U.S. authorities insisted to reporters that the speech was meant to foster "reconciliation," but a senior official told me later that it had been a disaster: "Here we were protecting him from the Haitians when we were supposed to be protecting the Haitians from him."

Throughout the occupation, ensconced in his house, where, he says, U.S. soldiers routinely came by to check on his safety, Constant tried to reinvent his past. "We're the ones who kept this country secure for a year," he told reporters, adding, "Aristide needs an opposition, and . . . I am the only organization right now that . . . can allow us to say there is a democracy." But the incoming government took a different view—and within a few months Constant was ordered to appear before a magistrate investigating charges of torture and attempted murder against him. On the day of the hearing, people saying they were victims waited for Constant outside the courtroom. He never appeared. Later, he told me that on Christmas Eve of 1994, with a small suitcase and what money he could stuff into his pockets, he had crossed the border on foot into the Dominican Republic, made his way to the airport, and then, using a valid visitor's visa that he had obtained before the coup, caught a plane to Puerto Rico. From there, he flew to the mainland United States without incident, ending up days later on the streets of New York City.

He managed to transmit a radio broadcast to his followers back home. "As for you FRAPH members," he said, "close ranks, remain mobilized." He went on, "FRAPH people, where are you? FRAPH is you. FRAPH is me." The Haitian government demanded that the United States do something. Finally, in March, 1995, Secretary of State Warren Christopher wrote a letter to Attorney General Janet Reno, saying, "Nothing short of Mr. Constant's removal from the United States can protect our foreign policy interests in Haiti."

Two months later, saying that Constant had been allowed to enter the country owing to a "bureaucratic error," I.N.S. officials surrounded him in Queens as he went to buy a pack of cigarettes. They forced him to the ground and frisked him. He was taken to Wicomico County Detention Center, on the Eastern Shore of Maryland; in September, a judge ordered his deportation to Haiti. As he waited for the outcome of his appeal, he wrote letters to world leaders, including Nelson Mandela. ("I could not hope to fill one of your footprints, yet here am I writing to one of the few men in all the world that could understand my situation, being in a white man's jail.") He grew a beard, and read Malcolm X and Che Guevara. "I am . . . a political prisoner," he wrote in a letter to Warren Christopher. At one point, he was placed on a suicide watch.

Then, in December of 1995, as the I.N.S. inched closer to deporting him, Constant decided to play the only card he had left. He threatened to divulge details of U.S. covert operations in Haiti, which he said he had learned about while secretly working for the Central Intelligence Agency.

The Perfect Recruit

The story Constant tells begins around Christmastime, 1991. It was shortly after the coup, and he was working at Haiti's military headquarters when Colonel Pat Collins, the U.S. military attaché at the Embassy, phoned and asked him to lunch. "Let's meet at the Holiday Inn," Collins said.

Collins, who, a government spokesman confirmed, was working for the U.S. Defense Intelligence Agency at the time, could not be reached for comment. But an associate says he was known to show up often at Haitian military headquarters. Constant says Collins was there on the night of the coup. And Lynn Garrison, a Canadian who served as a strategist and an adviser to the junta, told me that Collins was present in the days that followed, conferring with the new regime.

At the Holiday Inn, Constant says, he and Collins sat by a window overlooking the pool. Many people, Collins said, were impressed by Constant's background and suggested that Constant might play an important role in the power vacuum left by Aristide's ouster.

Constant was a tempting choice for recruitment by U.S. intelligence. He spoke impeccable English, knew his way around the military, and, as one of the new regime's top advisers, occupied an office right next to that of the junta's head, Raoul Cedras. Since the coup, Constant had taught a course on the dangers of Aristide's liberation theology at the training site for the National Intelligence Service (S.I.N.). The service, according to the New York *Times,* had been created, funded, trained, and equipped by the C.I.A., starting in 1986, to combat drug trafficking, but it had quickly become an instrument of terror (and even, according to some U.S. officials, a source of drugs).

Constant says that Collins told him, in this first meeting, that he wanted him to meet someone else at Collins's home. "I'm not going alone," Constant remembers saying, only half joking. "I'm going to come with a witness." He says that he and an associate drove to Collins's residence that night. Although the streets were pitch-black, owing to a fuel shortage, Collins's house was completely lit up. Constant says they went upstairs, into a small antechamber next to the master bedroom, where a man with dark hair was waiting. He had on a short-sleeved shirt, and Constant noted his muscles. "I'm Donald Terry," the man said.

Constant says that, as they sat drinking cocktails, Terry began to pepper him with questions about the stability of the current military regime, and pulled out a booklet—"a roster"—containing the names and backgrounds of officers in the Haitian armed forces. He and Collins asked Constant who were the most effective.

A few days later, Constant says, Terry asked to meet again, this time alone at the Kinam Hotel. "Why don't you join the team?" Terry asked.

"What's the team?"

"A group of people working for the benefit of Haiti."

It was then, Constant says, that Terry divulged that he was an agent of the C.I.A.

The U.S. government will not comment on any questions regarding Donald Terry, and Terry himself could not be reached. But the C.I.A. had been deeply involved with the Haitian military and the country's politics for decades. Constant remembers that, in the nineteen-sixties, his father served as an informal adviser to an agent who used to stop by for conferences on their porch. According to press reports, the agency, after starting S.I.N., had planned to finance various political candidates in the 1987 Presidential elections, until the Senate Intelligence Committee vetoed the plan.

Constant says that eventually he agreed to serve as a conduit between the Haitian military regime and U.S. intelligence. He says he was then given the code name Gamal, after Egypt's former nationalist leader, Gamal Abdel Nasser, whom he admired, and a two-way radio, with which he checked in regularly.

It is impossible to confirm all the details in Constant's account. A C.I.A. spokesman stated that it was "not our policy" to confirm or deny relationships with any individuals. But there is little doubt that Constant was a paid informant. After Allan Nairn first reported Constant's connection to the intelligence community, in *The Nation* in October of 1994, several officials acknowledged it to reporters, and many have confirmed it to me. What has been a mystery is the nature of the relationship: just how big an asset was Constant? U.S. authorities have maintained that he was nothing more than a two-bit snitch. But interviews with several people connected to the intelligence community, coupled with Constant's own version of events, suggest that from the beginning he was a generous font of information, and later, according to at least some, a full-fledged operative. After the coup, he helped run a little-known operation called the Bureau of Information and Coordination (BIC), which collected various kinds of data: the number of deaths and arrests in Haiti, the number of adherents of liberation theology, and so forth. Constant says the data collection was for the purposes of economic development, but it clearly had another purpose: military intelligence.

According to Constant, and to a non-Haitian connected to the intelligence community, Constant and another BIC member were the first to enter one of Aristide's private quarters, where they found a hoard of secret documents. Some of these ended up in the hands of U.S. intelligence officers, who in turn provided the documentation for controversial reports claiming that Aristide was mentally unbalanced, contributing to the voices against him in the United States.

A former senior C.I.A. official justified using an informant who was as potentially problematic as Constant thus: "You can't help these bad guys accomplish stuff, but you got to give 'em money to find out what's happening in groups like that. And if you're going to recruit in a terrorist group like FRAPH, you're not going to get any functional equivalent . . . [of] a Western democrat. . . . To find out what's going on, you rather rapidly end up in the same position as the F.B.I. with the Mafia—recruiting and paying money and even granting freedom to lower-level folks, even some high-level folks."

Another former high-ranking government intelligence official put it more bluntly: "Look, we could have gone to the nuns [in Haiti] and asked them [to give us information]. But I'm sorry—the nuns are nice people, but what they know about terrorism is nothing." This same official observed that Constant was "one of a whole range of people we had relationships with, all with the knowledge of the Administration." He said he believed that Constant stood somewhere "on the spectrum of the relationship, from someone who talked to you occasionally to tell you things he wanted you to know to someone who was a wholly owned, salaried subsidiary, who provided information even to the detriment of his cause."

Constant says that by the time he officially created FRAPH, in 1993, he had been assigned another handler, John Kambourian, who would drive with him through the mountains of Petionville, exchanging information. When I reached Kambourian by telephone and asked him about Constant, he told me to speak to Public Affairs at the State Department and hung up. It remains unclear how involved U.S. intelligence officers were, if at all, in the actual formation and evolution of FRAPH. A C.I.A. spokesman stated for the record that the "C.I.A. had no role in creating, funding, or guiding the FRAPH organization."

But Lynn Garrison recalls that when Constant was trying to start a secret police force, even before FRAPH, Collins told Garrison directly, "Let's let it play out and see where it takes us." A U.S. government official involved with Haiti during the military regime goes even further, saying it was common knowledge in intelligence circles that Collins was involved with FRAPH long before it became an official organization (by which time Collins had left the country). "If he didn't found FRAPH, he was at least very, very close to it," this official told me. Trying to explain why the C.I.A. or the Defense Intelligence Agency (D.I.A.) might form such an alliance, this official added, "People are always looking for counterbalance, and at that point Aristide was not in power. I'm not excusing it, but they didn't quite know what FRAPH was going to become."

Despite the existence, at the time, of internal State Department documents portraying the organization's members as thugs and assassins, Constant says that his handlers never asked him about FRAPH's alleged rapes and murders. What's more, he says, the C.I.A. and the D.I.A. encouraged him to help derail Aristide's return and even knew beforehand about his demonstrations against the Harlan County, which helped to delay the invasion for nearly a year. A C.I.A. spokesman denied to me that the

agency pushed its own foreign-policy goals in Haiti, but Lawrence Pez-
zullo, the U.S. envoy to Haiti at the time, along with other U.S. officials,
publicly accused the C.I.A. of exaggerating the threat of the Harlan
County, thereby derailing Aristide's return and, in essence, pursuing its
own agenda. Constant told me, "If I'm guilty of all these things they say,
then they are guilty of them, too."

The Breakup

Toto Constant's relationship with U.S. intelligence, according to both
Constant and several C.I.A. officials, continued undisturbed until the
spring of 1994. It was then, Constant says, that Kambourian called and
said they had to meet. He told Constant to bring the radio. "I'm sorry,"
Constant remembers Kambourian saying, "but we can't see you anymore."

"Why?" Constant asked.

Kambourian said that, in the wake of the Harlan County incident and
Constant's rhetoric against the President, Washington wanted to sever its
ties.

U.S. officials say that intelligence contacts with Constant were more or
less cut at this point. Cooperation between FRAPH and the U.S. military
was eventually curbed as well, and in October of 1994 American forces
stormed FRAPH headquarters. Afraid for his life, Constant went to meet
Lieutenant General Henry Shelton, who was in charge of the occupation.
Constant recalls, "I told Shelton straight out, 'I'm a son of a general, and I
inherited his honor and dignity, and that's why I'm here to ask what the
rules of engagement are, because I don't understand them.' "

According to a transcript of an oral history that General Shelton
recorded during the invasion, Shelton had no desire to meet with Constant. But Shelton and Major General David Meade decided to see if they
could get from him what they wanted: first, that he provide a complete list
of FRAPH members and the location of their weapons caches; second, that
he call each one of his key thugs and tell them to surrender their arms; and,
third, that he publicly accept Aristide's return and transform FRAPH into a
peaceful political party.

"We were using a little bit of psychological warfare on Constant,"
Shelton, in his oral history, disclosed. "I sent Meade in first. Meade was to

go in and tell [Constant] that he was getting ready to meet the big guy. . . . I gave Meade about twenty or thirty minutes to set the conditions, and then I arrived and my security guy, the SEAL, entered the room . . . rattling the doors and kicking on doors to make sure the place was secure before I came in, as they always did. But Constant saw all this, and it was kind of like seeing a meeting with the Godfather being set up . . . and so he got very nervous at that time, and his eyes got very big." It was then, Shelton said, that Meade walked out and he walked in. "[Constant] immediately stood up and smiled and stuck out his hand, at which time I just said to myself, 'Remember two things—force and death they understand.' So I looked at him and I said, 'Sit down!' and he immediately sat down, and the smile left his face . . . and I said to him, 'I understand that you have agreed to all the conditions that we have set for you to keep us from hunting you down and members of your organization.' And he said, 'Oh, yes, yes, I have no problem with any of that.' And then he started, 'But Haiti is . . . ' And he started into his role about the history of Haiti and how important the FRAPH is. I let him get about ten seconds into that, and I cut him off and told him very curtly that I was not interested in hearing any of that right now."

The next day, Constant gave the speech accepting Aristide's return and casting himself as the new leader of the democratic opposition. According to a highly placed U.S. official, the speech was outlined by Constant's old C.I.A. contact, Kambourian, and handed over to the U.S. Embassy, which in turn dictated it to Constant, who apparently accepted it without his usual bravado. "He could have been imprisoned," the official told me, "but the judgment was made that as long as we could get out of him what we wanted it would be O.K. for him to walk around."

General Shelton may have wanted little to do with Constant, but other elements of the U.S. government seem to have done more than just keep an eye on him. Immigration authorities told me it was "impossible to believe," as one put it, and "totally bogus," as another said, that Constant could have entered the United States at that time on a valid visa without help from either someone in the U.S. government or forged documents. "Everyone knew he was a killer," a former I.N.S. official says. "His picture was everywhere." Constant told me that he did alert certain U.S. officials before he left, and "it's possible they did something." A high-ranking intelligence-community source, although not commenting directly on Constant's case, said, "On the high end of the spectrum, the director of the C.I.A. can bring in fifty to a hundred people in the top spy category. These are people to whom we owe a lot, because they have risked their lives doing things of great value to our nation, so it is [if] you want to get out, we will get you out; you want to get in, we will get you in, get you a house, whatever. . . . Lower down, you can do everything from a little help around the edges to supplying visas."

How Toto Got Sprung

Sitting in Wicomico County Detention Center, on the verge of being deported with the full support of the State Department and the I.N.S., Constant leveraged the potential exposure of his old connections to save himself. Threatening to divulge the details of his relationship with the C.I.A., he filed a fifty-million-dollar lawsuit against Warren Christopher and Janet Reno for wrongful imprisonment. "C.I.A. operatives collaborated with the Plaintiff," his lawyer maintained in the suit. To underscore his warning, Constant appeared on "60 Minutes" in December of 1995 in his prison jumpsuit. "I feel like that beautiful woman that everybody wants to go to bed with at night, but not during the daytime," he told Ed Bradley. "I want everybody to know that we are dating."

It was at this point that Benedict Ferro, who was the district director of the I.N.S. in Baltimore at the time of Constant's incarceration, began to see things that he had never seen before—things that were, as he puts it now, "off the scale." Ferro had worked for the I.N.S. for more than thirty years, and he was used to working on cases that involved sensitive government issues. After Constant made his threats, Ferro says, highly placed officials throughout the government began to get involved, even though the Administration had already publicly and privately indicated that Constant would be returned.

A cover page from a May 24, 1996, Justice Department memorandum titled "Emmanuel Constant Options" indicates that those consulted in the process included Samuel Berger, the Deputy National-Security Adviser; Strobe Talbott, the Deputy Secretary of State; Jamie Gorelick, the Deputy Attorney General; and David Cohen, the Deputy Director of Operations for the C.I.A. "Look, they came out of the woodwork when [Constant] started singing," says Ferro, who is now the president of INSGreencard.com.

It was then—"at the eleventh hour," as Ferro recalls—that government officials received information regarding a plot to assassinate Constant when he was returned to Haiti. Many at the I.N.S. maintained that, even if true, the report merely meant that Constant should remain in a U.S. prison until a later date. "We have Cubans from the Mariel boatlift who remain in jail," Ferro says. "We have people from the Middle East who are in jail who can't be sent back. This is not a new process." But, according to several officials involved in the deliberations, the information swayed the senior decision-makers. "I didn't want to send someone, even a killer like Constant, to his summary execution," one person involved in the case told me. When I asked a senior official who it was that had uncovered the plot on Constant's life and prepared the classified report, he answered simply, "Reliable U.S. intelligence sources."

Ferro and several of his colleagues at the I.N.S. made one last attempt to press their views, insisting that they could not in good conscience send a suspected terrorist into a community where he might harm U.S. citizens or where, just as likely, U.S. citizens might harm him. But it didn't matter. The final decision was hammered out over several days, and senior officials from the Justice Department, the State Department, and the National Security Council participated. "To this day, I can't understand why he's not rotting in a U.S. jail," Ferro says. "We were not reinventing the process. He was just treated differently than any other murderer or terrorist."

Ferro himself gave Constant the good news.

"They called me at the prison and said I could get my things and go," Constant says today, still surprised.

"I basically just read from the script," Ferro says. "This guy was believed to have murdered and assassinated all these people, and we released him into our society. It was outrageous."

A copy of the legal settlement that set the terms for Constant's release, which I obtained from Constant, reveals certain conditions: Constant must live in his mother's home in Queens and must remain within the confines of the borough except for visits to the I.N.S. office in Manhattan; he must check in with the Immigration and Naturalization Service every Tuesday; and he must not talk about, among other things, Haitian politics or the details of the legal agreement. "I like exposure," he says, "so this is the worst thing they can do to me, this gag order." (As may by now be apparent, Constant takes an expansive view of the restrictions.) Constant's formal legal status is this: he is under an outstanding order of deportation whose execution has been withheld on the advice of the State Department.

When I asked Warren Christopher about the deal with Constant, he said he could not recollect the details of what had happened and would try to call me back. Later, his assistant called and said that he still didn't have "sufficient recollection of the matter that you discussed to comment." Constant's lawyer, J. D. Larosiliere, who has continued to cite the threat to his client's life, says, "I knew that he wasn't going to be deported, but I needed a hook in the legal system to allow them to have a way out. Plausible deniability. That's all this game is about. Plausible deniability."

A "Tell-All Autobiography"

One day, after our initial meeting in Larosiliere's office, Constant invited me to his house in Laurelton, where he was living, as he put it, "like a hostage." Part of a long row of nearly identical English Tudors, the house had fallen into disrepair: the façade, once white, was weather-stained, the front steps needed paint, and the storm window overlooking the porch was shattered. Haitians had told me, among other things, that Constant kept the bones of his victims in his room, practiced late-night voodoo rituals, stored C.I.A. arms in the basement, and shot trespassers.

As I hesitated on the stoop, the front door suddenly opened and Constant appeared, holding a cigarette. "Come on in," he said. I followed him into the living room, which was musty and dimly lit; the walls were covered with Haitian art, and the couches and chairs were draped in plastic. Constant sat across from me in a rocker, swaying back and forth as he smoked. During our initial encounter, I had pressed him about FRAPH murders and rapes. He said that there was no evidence implicating him and that he could not be held accountable for every member of such a sprawling operation. "If somebody the day of the vote killed another individual in the street of New York, and they found he just voted Democrat, they're not going to make Clinton responsible," he said. He insisted, "My conscience is clear."

Now, as I started to ask him more questions, he took a tape recorder from his pocket and said that he was working on a book about his life. "I went to take a class about self-publishing your book, and one of the things the guy told me was if you're talking about your past, then record yourself," he said. I thought he wanted to make sure I quoted him correctly, but a moment later he handed me a book proposal: "This proposal offers a 'hot' new 'tell all' exposé on Emmanuel 'TOTO' Constant code name 'GAMAL,' and FRAPH. . . . The market analysis suggests that with at least 2 million Haitians in the U.S. and at least 50,000 others in the U.S. who have interest in Haiti . . . this book could easily sell over 1 million copies." The book was tentatively titled "Echoes of Silence." He had drawn up a dummy book jacket that said:

> Emmanuel "Toto" Constant, notorious leader of FRAPH . . . and alleged murderer, rapist, and terrorist thug, breaks the yoke of silence. Speaking from his heart, he exposes the real man behind the villainous images. Interesting, provocative, informative and sensitive, "Echoes of Silence" candidly portrays the complexities of life in Haiti, where nothing is simple. It might lead one to conclude: The political frenzy in Haiti, as addictive and dangerous as any narcotic, keeps the masses alive mentally and emotionally even while it kills.

This was Constant's latest attempt to earn a living. Since his release from prison, he had tried all sorts of ways to set himself up. He had taken computer classes. He had sold used cars. But, each time he had found employment, the other Haitian immigrants in the community had risen up and driven him from his job. "The worst time is when they came in front of the real-estate office . . . because I really had a good situation," he said.

Since that day, he had become what he called an "investment consultant," which seemed to mean selling and renting properties as covertly as possible. Whenever I was with him, his cell phone would ring with a prospective client. Once, I listened to him raise and lower his voice like an auctioneer: "*Hello. Oui. Oui* . . . I saw the apartment. . . . They were asking one thousand one hundred dollars, and I'll bring it down to *a thousand*. . . . Everything is included. . . . O.K.? . . . It's Cambria Heights, very nice neighborhood, very quiet, very, very safe. . . . I'm working very hard for you."

His wife had moved to Canada with their four children out of fear for their safety. "My wife is leaving me," he told me at one point. "We're having discussions about the kids. I wanted them to come the way they used to, and she doesn't want them to. So we're having an argument, but everything will be O.K."

After a while, his phone rang, and I asked if I could look around the place. "No problem," he said.

I headed upstairs, past several cracked walls and closed doors. Constant's room was on the third floor. It was small and cluttered with videos and men's fashion magazines. By his bed was a framed picture of him from his appearance on "60 Minutes." In one corner was a small shrine. Candles and figurines of Catholic saints, which often play a role in voodoo, were arranged in a neat circle.

As I bent down to inspect them, Constant called out my name. One of the statues was the patron saint of justice; on its base was inscribed, "Be ever mindful of this great favor and I will never cease to honor thee as my special and powerful patron."

Constant called my name again, and I hurried downstairs. "Let's go out," he said, putting on a leather jacket.

As we walked through Laurelton, the sound of *compas,* Haitian dance music, blared from grocery stores. We passed several men smoking in the cold, chatting in Creole. "I need some meat," Constant said, heading toward a butcher shop.

The store was packed, and we could barely fit inside. A small circle of Haitians were playing cards in the back. As Constant pressed up against the counter, I realized that everyone was staring at him. "I need some goat," he said, breaking the sudden silence. He pointed at some enormous hind legs hanging from a meat hook. He glanced at the back, where several people seemed to be saying something about him, but he appeared unfazed. The butcher began to cut through the bone and gristle of a goat leg. His thick arm pushed down, slicing in clean strokes. "Everybody here knows who I am," Constant said on the way out. "Everybody. They've all read about me or seen my picture."

He darted across the street to a barbershop. A "Closed" sign hung on the door, but we could see the barber inside, and Constant banged on the window, pleading with him to take one more customer. "There's another barbershop down the street," he told me, "but if I went there they'd slit my . . ." His voice trailed off as he drew his fingers across his throat and let out a strange laugh.

A Courthouse in Haiti

The trial was more than a thousand miles away from New York. On September 29, 2000, a Haitian court began trying Constant on charges of murder, attempted murder, and being an accomplice to murder and torture—charging him, in effect, with the Raboteau massacre. I went there with J. D. Larosiliere a few weeks later, as the trial was reaching its climax. Twenty-two people—mostly soldiers and FRAPII paramilitaries—were being prosecuted in person. Constant and the leaders of the junta were being tried in absentia.

Although the U.S. invasion had stemmed the bloodshed, the country remained in shambles. Eighty per cent of the people were unemployed, and two-thirds were malnourished. Gangs roamed the streets. Drug-running planes took off and landed with impunity. Even the heralded new democratic system was believed to be rife with fraud. Aristide, after having put a protégé in power, was running for the Presidency again amid allegations that he was trying to pack the parliament with his supporters. Political thuggery and assassination, this time from both the right and the left, were beginning to occur again. "Now everyone knows I was right," Constant told me later. "Everyone has seen what has happened under Aristide."

The trial itself was a potential flash point for violence. The U.S. Embassy warned Americans to stay away from the area for fear of "large scale demonstrations, tire burnings, rock throwing and worse." As our plane landed, Larosiliere told me that he had been warned about potential assassination attempts. "If they attack me, it will only help me prove my case," he said. "If I'm not safe, then how can my client be safe?"

At the airport, we met a muscular man with mirrored sunglasses and a military bearing, who would serve as Larosiliere's "attaché." "You cannot depend on the police to have security," the attaché told me. "So you need to be armed to protect yourself." The attaché pushed our way through a crowd of taxi-drivers, bag handlers, beggars, and pickpockets. I smelled flesh and sweat and food, and as we rushed to the car I tried to deflect the arms outstretched to help me with my things. "Welcome to Haiti," Larosiliere said.

The city of Gonaïves, where the courthouse was situated, is only seventy miles from Port-au-Prince, but, because nearly all the roads in Haiti are unpaved, it took us half a day to get there. The courthouse was in the center of the city, surrounded by tractor-trailers—a makeshift barricade to prevent mobs from rushing in. We entered a small, squat building, where armed guards searched us for weapons; the attaché told me he had left his gun behind, but he stayed close to Larosiliere's side. We passed through one room and then another; finally, to my surprise, we headed into an open courtyard, where the trial was being held under a billowing white canopy. The judge sat at a table, wearing a black robe and a tall hat with a white band. He had a bell in place of a gavel. The twenty-two accused sat nearby, behind a cordon of armed guards. Larosiliere joined the other defense lawyers, and the attaché and I found a place in the back with the scores of observers and alleged victims.

I had barely sat down when a lawyer for the prosecution began to scream at Larosiliere, jabbing his hand in the air and demanding that Larosiliere tell the court who he was and why he was there. The attaché, who had been at my side, was on his feet before Larosiliere answered. The crowd filled with murmurs: *Toto Constant! Toto Constant!* People looked around as if Constant might be under the canopy. The lawyer began to bark again at Larosiliere; the attaché now stood by Larosiliere's side, his arms crossed on his chest.

Most of the alleged victims had already testified that on April 22, 1994, soldiers and FRAPH members had descended on the village of Raboteau, known for its staunch support of Aristide. They described being driven from their homes, forced into open sewers, robbed, and tortured. In past attacks, the villagers had fled to the sea, where their fishing boats were tied up. But when they did so this time, they said, the attackers were waiting for them in boats and opened fire. "I climbed aboard my boat," one of the villagers, Henri-Claude Elisme, said in a sworn deposition. "I saw Claude Jean . . . fall under the soldiers' bullets." Abdel Saint Louis, a thirty-two-year-old sailor, said, "I fled . . . into a boat. . . . I then saw Youfou, a FRAPH member, piloting a group of soldiers. They fired in my direction. I called for help. They arrested me, beat me, and forced me to guide the boat. Seeing other people in a boat, the soldiers fired in their direction and hit two girls: Rosiane and Deborah."

By the end of the assault, according to the prosecution witnesses, dozens of people were wounded and at least six were dead; the prosecution estimated that the actual toll was much higher. Most of the bodies had allegedly been buried in shallow graves along the sea and washed away. "When I went down to the shore, I saw [my brother's] boat covered in blood," Celony Seraphin testified. "I only found him on April 28 . . . tied up with Charité Cadet; both had been murdered. I was not authorized to remove the body. . . . I demand justice for my brother."

The testimony occasionally elicited angry shouts from the spectators, and the judge would ring his bell, trying to quiet the courtyard. That afternoon, Karen Burns, a forensic anthropologist from the United States, was sworn in. A Canadian expert on DNA was scheduled to follow her. It would be the first time that forensic evidence and genetic evidence were introduced in a Haitian court, and the courtyard fell silent. Burns stood in the center of the gathering, surrounded by the skeletal remains of three people, excavated from the edge of the sea in Raboteau in 1995. As she spoke, spectators and jurors craned their necks to look at the bones. Burns held up one and said, "This is the pelvis right here." She put it down and picked up another bone. "This individual was found with a rope tied around his neck, and this is the rope that was retrieved." As she held up the rope, there were several gasps.

Larosiliere—who, like his client, maintains that the massacre was fabricated as propaganda to discredit FRAPH and the military regime—remained unimpressed. "I live for testimony like this," he told me that night, drinking a glass of rum, as we sat with the attaché at the hotel restaurant. "She did a scientific study on a site with no integrity. Everyone and everybody walked around it. Come on. You know I can go to grave-yards and pick up skeletons from anybody and put them down."

Refilling his glass, Larosiliere said that if there had been any organized military involvement at all no evidence would have been left on the beach. "Those bodies would be put on a truck, and they'd be taken out on the Rue Nationale—"

"You got it," the attaché agreed.

"—or the highway—"

"At night," the attaché added.

"—and dumped into—"

"The Source Puante," the attaché said.

"Sulfur ditches," Larosiliere explained. "The best place, because the sulfur eats the body."

As he spoke, several international human-rights observers sat down next to us, and soon one of them began to argue with Larosiliere about Constant. Larosiliere said, "If for one instant, sir, I believed that Haiti could sustain a true trial for my client, I'd be the first one to throw him on the plane."

Later, Brian Concannon, an American human-rights lawyer who had spent most of the previous five years in Haiti spearheading the trial, told me that the trial was extraordinarily fair by any standard. Indeed, he said, it had become a kind of prototype for the judicial system in Haiti. Perhaps most important, despite Constant's fears that he would be killed, not a sin-gle defendant so far had been harmed in prison or in a courtroom. "The defendants were given the benefit of all their rights under Haitian law and under international treaties to which Haiti is a party," Concannon said. "They were allowed to present witnesses, alibis, and exculpatory evidence."

As for Constant, Concannon said, the case was based on the same legal precedent used to prosecute Nazi leaders after the Second World War and, more recently, war criminals in Yugoslavia and Rwanda. "Constant started an organization that was specifically designed to [carry out]—and in fact carried out—massive violations of human rights," he said. "He was in charge of a criminal organization and is responsible for the crimes of that organization."

On the second day of our visit, Larosiliere decided to stage a protest.

In the middle of the proceedings, he rose from his chair and stood stiffly in the courtroom. The trial came to a halt, and everyone stared at him. Then he marched out the door, the attaché a few feet behind him. There was an angry chorus of murmurs. A prosecution lawyer denounced the move as merely a ruse, a sign that Constant's lawyer had intended from the outset not to use the tribunal for justice but only to discredit it. ("My understanding of an adequate murder defense is that you spend more than a few hours at the trial," Concannon told me. "We've worked on this case full time for four and a half years.")

After Larosiliere left, I sat for a while and stared at the dozens of alleged victims sitting on the back benches. Many of them had bought suits for the trial. The young women, some of whom had been shot, wore white dresses that somehow stayed pristine in the dusty heat; they sat with their backs perfectly straight. On several occasions, these people had walked miles to the capital to pressure their government for justice. They had written songs about what had happened. And they sat there now, as rain began to fall, and as a clerk collected the bones strewn on the table, and as rumors filled the country that another coup attempt had been thwarted in the capital.

As I finally rose to go, a young man who had seen me arrive with Constant's lawyer stopped me. Before I could say anything, he spat at my shoe and walked away.

The Verdict

"They tried to get me to come out to beat me up," Constant told me shortly after I returned. He was eating a piece of chocolate cake in a Queens diner. Tensions in the community had intensified since the beginning of the trial. Larosiliere had instructed him to leave the house during such demonstrations, to avoid confrontations. But Constant always remained nearby. "I have to protect my mother and aunt in case one of them go crazy," he told me.

Ricot Dupuy, of Radio Soleil d'Haiti, told me candidly, "There are Haitian groups who have toyed with the idea of taking the law into their own hands and killing him."

Constant claims that he has a small coterie of supporters who keep an eye out for him. "I can tell you, when they come in front of my place, fifty per cent of the people out there are my people," he said. "They pass by in case there is any trouble."

Though it is hard to know the precise numbers, Constant maintains some hold over a small following of former FRAPH members, Tonton Macoutes, soldiers, and Duvalierists who also live in exile. Demonstrators say that in at least one instance a car showed up outside his house to monitor them. "They came by taking pictures of us, and we took pictures of them," Ray Laforest told me.

"I don't want to play a deadly game," Constant said of Laforest, "but I have stuff on him, and . . ." He let his thought trail off.

One day, I was sitting with Constant in his house, reading a chapter of his book, when his phone rang. After he took the call and hung up, he said, "You're here for a part of history. The verdict came out. I've been sentenced to life imprisonment and to hard labor, and they're taking over all my property in Haiti."

He dropped into his rocking chair, lighting a cigarette and looking around the room. The jury had deliberated for four hours and had found sixteen of the twenty-two defendants in custody guilty, twelve of them for premeditated murder or for being accomplices to murder. Those who had been tried in absentia were convicted of murder and ordered to pay the victims millions of dollars in damages. "I hate to lose my things back home," Constant said, "because eventually my mother has to go back there."

He lit another cigarette and drew on it deeply. "I better call J.D.," he said, referring to Larosiliere. He picked up his cell phone, trying to concentrate. "They have a verdict against me," he said into the phone, leaving a message for his lawyer. "I need to speak to him. O.K.? They have sentenced me to life and hard labor!"

A few minutes later, the phone rang, and Constant picked it up in a hurry. But it was a reporter asking him for a comment. He managed a few words and hung up. The phone rang again. It was Larosiliere. "What do you think's going to happen here?" Constant asked nervously. "O.K. . . . yes . . . *O.K.*"

He handed me the phone. I could hear Larosiliere's voice crackling through the receiver before I put it to my ear. "I have one word to say about all this: bullshit." Larosiliere said that the Haitian government would now try to extradite Constant, claiming that a legitimate tribunal had convicted him with the blessing of international observers. But, he said, they still had to show that the verdict was fair and prove in a U.S. court that Constant deserved to be sent back.

Constant called me a few days later. His voice was agitated. "There are all these rumors out there that they're about to arrest me," he said. "That they're coming for me." He said that he had to check in with the I.N.S. the following day, as he did every Tuesday, but he was afraid the authorities might be planning to seize him this time. "Can you meet me there?"

By the time I arrived at the I.N.S. office in Manhattan the next morning, he was already standing by the entrance. It was cold, and his trench coat was wrapped around him. He told me that his mother, who was in Florida, had called to tell him that other Haitian exiles had been arrested. I could see circles under his eyes. Pacing back and forth, he said that he had stayed at a friend's house the night before, in case the authorities showed up at his house to arrest him.

I followed him into the elevator and up to an office on the twelfth floor. Constant tried to check in at the front desk, where a poster of the Statue of Liberty hung, but an I.N.S. official said they weren't ready for him yet. He sat down and started to ponder why he had been kept free for so long: "A friend of mine told me one day—he works for intelligence here—and he said there is somebody, somewhere, that is following everything about me."

A few minutes later, a clerk yelled out his name, and Constant leaped to his feet. He approached the desk with his I.N.S. form and checked in. The official took the sheet of paper and walked into a back room, where she consulted with somebody. Then she returned and, just like that, Constant was smiling, leading me to the elevator, calling his mother to say that he was O.K., and rushing across the street to buy a new suit in celebration of his freedom.

The next week, two dozen Toto Watchers gathered outside the I.N.S. carrying signs that showed alleged FRAPH victims: a murdered boy with a shirt pulled over his head; two men lying in a pool of blood. "We are here to demand that Toto Constant be sent back to Haiti," Kim Ives, a writer for the Brooklyn-based newspaper *Haïti Progrès*, yelled through a bullhorn. "If you're opposed to war criminals and to death-squad leaders living as your neighbors in New York City, please join us." There was a sense that this was the last chance to persuade the U.S. government to deport Constant—that if it wouldn't do so now, after the conviction, it never would. A U.N. expert on Haiti, Adama Dieng, who had served as an impartial observer at the trial, had already called the verdict "a landmark in [the] fight against impunity."

Outside the I.N.S. office, several in the crowd were bent over, trying to light candles in the freezing wind. "How can they not send him back?" a Haitian man asked me. "He has been found guilty by a Haitian court. Why is the C.I.A. protecting him?" Suddenly, there was a loud, unified chant from the crowd: "Toto Constant, you can't hide! We charge you with genocide!"

Au Revoir?

At one of our last meetings in 2001, after Jean-Bertrand Aristide and George W. Bush had each been sworn in to their respective offices, Constant called and said that he had to see me. His legal status remained unchanged. He had been talking to his "advisers," he said, and he needed to tell me something. The political terrain had shifted in both countries, he said. There was more and more resistance to Aristide, even in Queens. Bombs had recently exploded in Port-au-Prince, and the regime had blamed Constant. He denied any role, but he said that Haitians from all over were calling, waiting for him to act, to step up.

At the Haitian restaurant where we met, he told me that people had "been publishing articles, and they say, 'Look at this guy who has been convicted for murder in Haiti and he's getting stronger and stronger every day.'" He sipped a glass of rum. "A lot of people in Haiti are watching me. They haven't heard from me. They don't know what's going to happen, but everyone has their eyes on me, and people are sending me their phone numbers from Haiti. People here try to reach me. Political leaders are trying to reach me. There is a perception that if . . . Aristide is on the go, *I'm* the only one that can step in. I can't let that thing get to my head. I have to be very careful and analyze it and make it work for me."

As people entered the restaurant, Constant looked over his shoulder to check them out. He waited for two Haitian men to sit down, and then he turned back to me and said that he had to do something dramatic or he would be a hostage in Queens for the rest of his life. "If I stand up and make a press conference, and even if I don't say anything but I just attack Aristide, that's going to give strength to the opposition down there, that's going to give strength to the former military, that's going to give strength to the former FRAPH members, that's going to give strength to everyone who didn't have the guts because they didn't see who would take the lead."

He had recently received a new spate of death threats, he said. Someone had gotten hold of his cell-phone number and had warned, "I'm going to get you no matter what you do."

I asked if he was afraid of what might happen if he so brazenly broke his gag order and called a press conference. He said that he wasn't sure what would happen, but it was his destiny. "I've been prepared since young for a mission, and that's why I've stayed alive," he said. He glanced over his shoulder again, and then he leaned toward me. "I'm either going to be President of Haiti," he said, "or I'm going to be killed."

—June, 2001

———ண்———

In July, 2006, Constant met a more mundane and unexpected fate: he was arrested in New York for defrauding lenders of more than a million dollars in an elaborate real-estate scam. This time, none of Constant's connections could protect him from the law. Tried in New York, he was found guilty and sentenced to up to thirty-seven years in prison. The state's attorney general, Andrew Cuomo, said, "Constant will no longer be a menace to our society."

Author's Note

Nine of these stories first appeared in *The New Yorker*. Three were published elsewhere: "Giving 'The Devil' His Due" in *The Atlantic*; "Which Way Did He Run?" in the New York *Times Magazine*; and "Crimetown, U.S.A." in *The New Republic*. Some of the pieces have been updated and revised.

Acknowledgments

As always, I am indebted to David Remnick and *The New Yorker*, where nine of the twelve stories first appeared. Without Remnick's fierce commitment to narrative journalism, his keen editorial judgment, and his unwavering support, these pieces would not have been possible. At every turn, I have benefitted not only from his help, but also from that of the magazine's other extraordinary editors. Daniel Zalewski, whose invisible fingerprints are on nearly all of these pieces, has infinitely improved my work, and made me a better journalist. I am equally lucky to have in my corner Dorothy Wickenden, Henry Finder, Susan Morrison, Pam McCarthy, Elizabeth Pearson-Griffiths, Ann Goldstein, Mary Norris, Carol Anderson, Virginia Cannon, and Amy Davidson. The *New Yorker* fact-checking department, led by Peter Canby, is a writer's secret blessing.

I am also grateful to the New York *Times Magazine*, *The New Republic*, and *The Atlantic*. Many editors with whom I worked have had a profound and lasting influence on me: Peter Beinart, Jonathan Chait, Jonathan Cohn, Albert Eisele, Joel Lovell, Adam Moss, Cullen Murphy, Christopher Orr, Martin Tolchin, and Jason Zengerle. Perhaps no one has had a deeper impact on me as a writer than the late Michael Kelly, whom every day I miss as a mentor and a friend.

Acknowledgments

My agents Kathy Robbins and David Halpern at the Robbins Office continue to be my best and most devoted allies, always managing to steer me in the right direction. The same is true of the irreplaceable Matthew Snyder at CAA. I am also grateful to Katie Hut, Ian King, and the rest of the Robbins Office, as well as to Susan Lee, who has helped me with research and fact-checking.

It was Bill Thomas at Knopf Doubleday who first read these stories in disparate form and thought they would work as a collection. His editorial vision and immaculate editing made this book a reality. Sonny Mehta championed this project and helped bring it to fruition. And the entire team at Knopf Doubleday once again proved to be an author's greatest asset. In particular, I want to thank Bette Alexander, Maria Carella, Janet Cooke, Melissa Danaczko, Todd Doughty, John Fontana, Suzanne Herz, Rebecca Holland, Coralie Hunter, James Kimball, Lauren Lavelle, Beth Koehler, Lynn Kovach, Beth Meister, John Pitts, Anh Schluep, Steve Shodin, Suzanne Smith, and Anke Steinecke.

My deepest debt is to my children, Zachary and Ella, and to my wife, Kyra, who is not only one of the best journalists in the business but also the wisest and the most decent. There are no acknowledgments that could ever express to them my gratitude and love.

Condition noted
Water damage.
6/11/13
JC